# The English Teacher's Handbook

**edited by Roy Blatchford**

**Hutchinson**

London  Melbourne  Sydney  Auckland  Johannesburg

Hutchinson and Co. (Publishers) Ltd
An imprint of the Hutchinson Publishing Group
62–65 Chandos Place, London WC2N 4NW

Hutchinson Publishing Group (Australia) Pty Ltd
16–22 Church Street, Hawthorn, Melbourne, Victoria 3122

Hutchinson Group (NZ) Ltd
32–34 View Road, PO Box 40–086, Glenfield, Auckland 10

Hutchinson Group (SA) (Pty) Ltd
PO Box 337, Bergvlei 2012, South Africa


First published 1986

Set in Palatino by Folio Photosetting, Bristol

Printed and bound by Anchor Brendon Ltd., Tiptree, Essex

**British Library Cataloguing in Publication Data**
The English teacher's handbook.
1. English language — Study and teaching
I. Blatchford, Roy
420'.7'1    LB1576

ISBN 0 09 161230 6

# Contents

# Introduction

It is through language that each of us makes sense of experience and categorizes the world in which we live. Language defines the social fabric and carries with it certain values and assumptions. Above all, it works as a communication system. If we can persuade young people growing up in our multi-cultural society to view language as a living, shifting force which shapes lives and atitudes, they will hasten to arm themselves — to become more competent language users. Our central task as teachers of English will have been achieved.

It is an intriguing fact that if we examine much of the content of English lessons, one feature is particularly striking: namely, that a large proportion of the subject matter comes into the classroom with the *students* rather than with the teacher. As I. A. Gordon once observed:

'What after all is English? As a result of its varied origins it has been many things in the past. English has been figures of speech and parsing and general analysis, the correction of sentences and rules for the use of 'which' and 'that'. English has been the qualities of prose style. English has been the periods of literature, gush about Shelley and chit-chat about Charles Lamb, the enjoyment of literature and be hanged to the external examination. English, cries one group, should contain a solid grammatical preparation for the learning of Latin. English, cries another, should be the core subject. English, cry yet other voices, should never have been allowed into the syllabus; English is what my typists should have larned at school. English, laments many a floundering novice teacher, is the most difficult subject of all to teach. English? responds a treble voice, I speak English don't I? My cobbers understand me. Why the heck should you have to teach me English at all?'

This *Handbook* is *not* about the theory of English teaching. It is about its *practice* in classrooms. It is a collection of tried and tested material; a book to dip into for ideas and suggestions, for advice and stimulus, for resources and guidance. It opens with the broad issues of managing and leading a department before moving into the key aspects of Writing, Talking, Reading and Listening. Other chapters focus on the teaching of literature, comprehension, assessment, GCSE or CPVE and the use of micros. For every teacher of English this *Handbook* is a comprehensive compendium and valuable source of reference.

Roy Blatchford

# The contributors

**David Allen** is Inspector for English with Nottingham Local Education Authority. He has been Head of English at various schools, and is the author of *English Teaching since 1965* and articles on the teaching of English. He is a member of the committee of the National Association of Advisers in English.

**Roy Blatchford** is deputy headteacher at the William Ellis School, London. He is the series editor for the Hutchinson *Checkbook* series and has edited a variety of plays and short story series. He is also a freelance contributor for *The Times Educational Supplement* and ILEA's *Contact*.

**Chris Bridge** is the Coordinator, Languages Faculty, at Glossop School. He has written for *English in Education* and is a member of the National Association for the Teaching of English.

**Paul Cheetham** is Head of English at Lord Williams' School at Thame. He has taught English in several schools and was Head of English at St Edward's School, Oxford. He has edited editions of *Emma* and *Romeo and Juliet* and is the chairman of the Southern Examining Group.

**Bill Deller** is General Adviser (English) in Lancashire. He has taught English in several schools.

**Dr Melvyn Elphee** is Head of English B at Atlantic College, and was formerly Head of English at the City of Portsmouth Boys' School. He has a PhD in eighteenth century theatre studies, has contributed several articles to *The Times Educational Supplement* and is co-author of *Oral* in the *Checkbook* series. He is also a tutor on the Shakespeare course with the Open University.

**Richard Exton** is currently District Inspector for English with the Inner London Education Authority. He has written articles in ILEA's *The English Magazine* and is on the editorial board for the magazine.

**Terry Gifford** is Senior Lecturer in English at Bretton Hall College of

Higher Education and is a former Head of English at Yewlands Comprehensive School, Sheffield. He is co-author of *Ted Hughes: A Critical Study* (Faber 1981), and is review editor for *English in Education*. In 1984 he won a Yorkshire Arts New Writer's Award for his poetry and mountaineering literature.

**Sue Horner** is Head of English at High Green School, Sheffield and has taught English at several other schools in the Sheffield area. She has written articles for *English in Education* and is currently Assistant Secretary of the National Association for the Teaching of English.

**Jim Payne** is an Interactive Video Programme Designer with Sony UK. He was previously Head of English at Vauxhall Manor School, and is the author of the South London CSE Mode 3 in English.

**Gervase Phinn** is General Adviser for Language Development in Rotherham. He has previously been Head of English in several schools and is a regular contributor to *The Use of English* and *Remedial Education*. He is a writer of short stories and plays.

**Patrick Scott** is Director of Durham Sixth Form Centre College. He is the editor of *Coursework in English: Seven Case Studies* and author of *Case Study Comprehension*. He is the Chair of the National Association for the Teaching of English.

**Don Shiach** has been Head of English in two schools, and has written a wide range of books on English including *Framework English Books 1, 2, 3; The Critical Eye; Framework Examination English A and B; Steps to Spelling* and *Punctuation in its Place*. He is an Assistant Chief Examiner for 'O' Level English Literature.

**Brigid Smith** is Director of Studies in the Communications Faculty at Stewards School in Harlow. Previously she was Head of Remedial Education there. She is currently doing research for a MPhil/PhD on the use of language experience approach with poor readers in secondary schools.

**Nigel Toye** is Second in English and Head of Drama at The Meridian School, Royston, Herts. He is a member of the committee of the London and East Anglia 16+ Drama Syllabuses, a member of the East Anglian Examinations Board Drama Panel and a member of Herts Drama Teachers' Association Committee.

**Malcolm Watts** has now left teaching to become a sales executive. Previously he was Head of English and Drama at the Howard of Effingham School, Surrey. He is a contributor to the journal *School Organisation*.

# Acknowledgements

The authors and publishers would like to thank the copyright holders below for their kind permission to reproduce the following material:

The Controller of Her Majesty's Stationery Office for the diagram on p. 106 from *A Language for Life* (Crown copyright 1983); Faber & Faber Ltd for 'Afternoons' on p. 272 from *The Whitsun Weddings* by Philip Larkin; Patrick Scott and Nelson–Harrap for pp. 356–8 from *Case Study Comprehension*; the estate of R. S. Thomas and Grafton Books for 'Cynddylan on a tractor' on p. 255 from *Song at the Year's Turning*; the Virginia Woolf estate and the Hogarth Press for p. 262 from *To the Lighthouse*.

# 1 Leading the English Department

Malcolm Watts

It has been said that if you aim at nothing in particular, you generally succeed. Nothing is truer in teaching, and certainly not in leadership. A group of people such as teachers in a school, in a department, need leading. The very fact of limited time and resources and increasing public expectations suggest this; the nature of human potential confirms it.

What is the meaning of leadership in a school department? It is not, perhaps, the heroic charismatic image of the charming autocrat — indeed not. It is much more about leading a team. A leading colleague rather than a commanding leader. Certain qualities are necessary in the leader of any department, not least the English department. You must first *believe in the task*. The semi-committed, half-believing English teacher does not convey, either to pupils or to colleagues, the necessary conviction. The task of the English teacher is no small one. His or her work is obviously exposed to the other subject areas. There must be a clear sense of the assignment and a strong but modest belief in its centrality to the educational process.

Secondly, you must be capable of *leading by example*. Words are cheaper than actions. People mostly respond to what people do rather than what they merely say. The real energy of leadership in school is found in the day-to-day exercise of exemplary teaching. The department head is a leader of teachers. It is their own sense of professionalism that must be nourished. Administrative ability, whilst important, is insufficient.

# The department

The key to consistent success in leadership is relationships. Management is about people. They are the primary resource of any school and need the most careful management. A damaged book is sometimes quickly reparable; a damaged relationship is not; it needs time and care. You do not have to like everybody evenly and fully. But you do need to respect and regard everyone genuinely. There is no contradiction between recognizing one's colleagues' shortcomings, and encouraging, praising or complimenting them. Faults are more easily admitted, more readily remedied, in a secure context of genuine regard than in one of criticism. Of course, rules and regulations are necessary. Department policy must be implemented. But most people respond better to suggestions or reminders than to outright demands or negative criticism. Schools can be insecure places for teachers. Departments therefore should do their best to ensure as secure a working environment as possible. The Head of Department (HOD) must make 'thank you', 'well done', and 'I understand' regularly used parts of his or her vocabulary. It must be honest, of course, and not at the price of condoning clearly poor work. Build up an atmosphere in which people feel trusted and appreciated.

The relationships of individuals within a department large or small, are not the responsibility of the HOD; the management of them and their interaction *is*. You need to be tactful and thoughtful in handling people who are hostile to each other. You might find, for example, that giving teachers a shared responsibility or task will reduce the dislike between them. Always speak positively of your colleagues. Offer necessary criticism constructively and privately. Never make more than two or three criticisms at any one time. More than that is demoralizing rather than constructive. Every member of a department should feel that their reputation is safe with the HOD. You must be trustworthy; gossiping about colleagues is one of the most serious faults of a team leader. In a climate where people speak only positively and, wherever possible, praisingly of department colleagues, even fragile relationships can gain strength.

# Relationships with pupils

The individual teacher's relationship with pupils should also take a lead from the HOD. Be fair, firm, understanding and interested. Different people have, of course, different strengths in relating to pupils, but the tone, the general characteristics of the English Department's relationship to pupils can be guided.

# Relationships with the rest of the school

A department head has a responsibility to relate to the people and the tasks of other departments. The English Department always, as we know, receives more scrutiny than any department. English, the service subject! Keep the Head, deputies and other colleagues informed about your department's work. Most Heads *want* to be informed. They often quickly know when things go wrong; they are not so quickly aware of daily achievements, or the regular progress of the department. Take initiatives in keeping the Head informed of plans, policy development and needs of personnel. Clear memos, succinctly written, should be used. Give the Head plenty of 'mental space' in which to consider and digest the material. Adopt whichever practice of communicating that best suits the Head rather than yourself. Keep the Head fully aware of your thinking where its implementation might properly benefit from his or her comment or advice. Your annual report highlighting the reasons for the department's success, its plans for improvement in areas of failure, the seeking of advice — this is a major way of building up a professionally supportive Head/HOD relationship. Whatever the personal relationship, the responsibility for a sound professional relationship is as much with the HOD as with the head teacher. Heads are human too. The department is a part of a larger whole. It serves many of the pupils' best interests but by no means all of them. Nor is it always (it sometimes is thought) the only department with the superior insights and exemplary pupil–teacher relationships. Indeed, one of the dangers of isolation is the belief that other departments are less good, less effective than in fact they are. You must ensure you have a good picture of the whole school's ethos, its central policies and its broader objectives. And you must articulate that to your colleagues.

You must represent the department's philosophy to the school at large. Certainly to your fellow department heads and to the senior management as well. Misunderstandings and misconceptions can so quickly harm a department's image and therefore its morale. The HOD is an ambassador, he or she is to interpret, to give life to, the intentions, concerns, and aspirations of colleagues. When, for example, a 'Language Across the Curriculum' policy is developed, he or she will need to be tactful, inventive and patient. He or she will also be wise to avoid any central part in such a policy. Nevertheless, in this as in other matters, he or she will need to invite not reactionary stances, but support and interest.

Sometimes the English department (where it is responsible for drama as well) is expected to produce the school play. Some departments are happy to do this, some are not. It is, however, an opportunity to bring the English department into closer cooperation with the rest of the school. Forming an Arts Committee is a way of inviting colleagues from all other departments to join the group to act as a think-tank, clearing house, organizing body, for all the arts activities in the school, including the school play. You, as Head of English, should perhaps decline any invitation to lead the committee. Instead, encourage a corporate interest and support for the musical, dramatic, painting, sculpture, and other arts presentations.

All easier said than done, but worth the time it takes. You must endeavour to encourage your colleagues, when necessary, to be positively supportive and involved in the school's broader activities. Colleagues may feel, quite properly, that their time belongs mainly to the department. There is, however, the department role and the wider school role and the latter has its legitimate demands. Extra-curricular activities, working parties, inter-disciplinary work — these have their own value and serve the purpose of widening the experience and perspective of the department member. Just as the department benefits immensely from a team spirit so does a school. A team of department heads, of year heads, of house heads — whatever the category is, it is the mode of operation that is important. The head of school has the challenging task of creating a corporate spirit amongst his or her staff; a ponderous assignment and one not to be made more difficult than it need be by the English department falling down on its responsibility to be a part of the school as a whole. Any head teacher will regard and respond to an HOD who shows they want to make their department the best in the school.

## Establishing a philosophy

A HOD should know three things clearly and have conviction about them.

1  What the English teacher is to do
2  In what ways the task can be done
3  Why he or she is doing it

English teaching, traditionally, is an area of philosophical difference across the spectrum from the traditional to ultra progressive. The position taken is not our concern here but the *need* for one is. The tussles of the years as to what English is and how it should be taught are evidence not so much of mistaken ideas but rather of the intrinsically broad nature of the 'subject'. Even so, you must achieve a basic philosophical consensus. Only by doing so can a 'team spirit' be developed. The department will benefit from embracing different personalities and classroom approaches but unity over main objectives is crucial. They must be a matter of department policy. They cannot be left to individual preference or whim. As HOD you must direct your thinking and that of your colleagues to the pupils. Keep personal hobby-horses on a tight rein!

Employ particular enthusiasms for their value in improving the English of the pupils. Ask every member of the department to write down their ten main objectives in English teaching. You can then direct the department towards a clear starting point. From there you should move on to the 'what' and the 'how' of the department's work.

# Philosophy into practice

Every department should have an instrument of policy: a guide for and encouragement of good practice. Producing an instrument of policy gives you an ideal opportunity to discuss both policy and practice and can lead to the clarification of policy and revitalization of practice. You must be clear about your thinking and that of your colleagues. Consider every area of the department's work.

- Content of English under the headings **Listening, Talking, Reading, Writing** with aims and objectives of each
- Methods of assessment and marking policy
- Profiling of pupils' work and progress
- Resources and their use
- Parental involvement and contact
- Responsibilities of individual department members
- Pattern of departmental meetings
- An anthology of ideas and approaches for the classroom
- An index to out-of-school resources, agencies, suppliers of audio–visual aids etc.

Your essential concern as the HOD in your leadership of such a review is to produce a *practical* and professional document. Use an agreed schedule which might look something like this:

**First month** (of, say, two year schedule)
1 Initial meeting to present the project with a proposed outline of content and schedule for discussion

2 Meeting to decide responsibilities for sub-committee work (e.g. preparing a paper on **Listening** with ideas for classroom approaches)

**Each month** (of the first eighteen months)

1 Full department meetings to review progress and validate sub-group proposals
2 Sub-group meetings on specific areas of policy and practice

**End of year one**

1 Full review of year's work with any necessary adjustments to remainder of schedule.

**At eighteen months**

1 Arrange details of typing/printing of the document, artwork, deadlines, revision etc.

**End of two years**

1 Presentation of the documents to head teacher, county inspector, governors.

(It is, of course, important to invite the advice and expertise of the Head, the English inspector and others in the process of producing the document.)

Ensure that in all stages of the work there is praise and encouragement for all that is being done and the effort expended. Your starting point will always be 'each of my colleagues wants to do a better job, even better than they are presently doing —they are professionals'. English teachers are especially vulnerable. Accountability, high public profiles for language performance of children, and the traditional commitment of the English teachers to pupils as people rather than mere recipients of academic information, all make this so. The psychological environment, therefore is the HOD's initial and persistent reponsibility. It has been said that there is no growth without pain — true enough — but keep pain to a minimum! Be tolerant and tactful and, by careful insertion of useful questions and approaches to the task, keep it alive.

# Harnessing personnel

A wise head teacher once said of his mixed-ability school population: 'everyone of them is gifted — the challenge is finding the gift'. Most English departments are mixed-ability too. How, then, with teachers of varying quality, can the full potential of the group be harnessed? First, you need to recognize that you are not and need not be the full revelation of excellence! None of us possesses all the necessary qualities of leadership, management, and classroom inspiration. Other colleagues will have areas of insight, competence and sensitivity you do not have and these you must recognize wherever evident. Do not feel threatened by excellence in others.

If you see the department in this way you will provide the chance for a genuine team to develop. Just as pupils need to succeed and be allowed to enjoy the confidence that follows so too do your colleagues. You need to identify clearly and regularly the strengths and potential strengths of those whose teaching environment you significantly influence. Is someone especially good at achieving successful class discussion and group work? Is someone else particularly able in encouraging less motivated pupils? Is there another colleague with an approach to marking whose experience and ideas will be useful for the rest of the department? Everyone has some expertise, some natural talent. Identify it or them and integrate them into the corporate expertise of the department. That is the HOD's task.

There is a good psychological reason for this. It means that colleagues will feel they have a stake in the department. And they will believe, rightly, that they as individuals are highly valued. The consequence of this is a real nourishment of individual and, thereby, corporate confidence. Psychologists make it clear that self-image is important. It is the most influential determinant in our relating to others. In a team where people are valued, energies are spent positively. Trust builds up. Effectiveness increases. Pupils are very perceptive in measuring the relationships between teachers. A cohesive department, one with a belief in itself and a commitment to its task, is attractive to those it teaches. And the learning improves.

Attend to detail. Note or note down on paper the extra time a teacher spends with some pupils at break or lunch-time; note who handles those theatre trip arrangements, who shows initiative, who quietly gets on with things someone else was due to be doing — the normal day-to-day quality of classroom teaching. Then, thank, praise and thereby encourage your colleagues. If at first you feel you sound insincere, try to put yourself in your colleagues' positions. The more you remember what it is like to be one of a team from whom much is expected, the more likely is it that your encouragement will be genuine.

But what happens if the encouragement seems to fail? There will be instances — perhaps only one in an HOD's experience — when the encouragement to a colleague should be to consider seriously another area of work. Given that there is good reason for the HOD's own teaching and management to be respected there are times when, what is privately believed by other colleagues and known by the HOD to be true, must be said. Some teachers are in teaching because they drifted into it. Most of them find that the drifting resulted in their finding their gifts and they look back on a wise move. They are good teachers. Others, however, battle on against increasing odds. They simply cannot be successful in the classroom. There is a point at which the HOD (together with the Head or another suitable colleague) should encourage moving out of teaching into something more appropriate. There may be pain but if there is honesty and warmth there will also be a sense of release. Pride often prevents one from admitting what one knows to be true. When the truth is spoken there is often gratitude; it may not be immediate but sooner or later it will come, directly or indirectly expressed.

# Department members' rights

1 **The right to gain increased professional expertise.** You must plan the tasks of your department and vary the teaching and organizational assignments of colleagues. Make a three-year plan of your proposals for the staff. Fix a meeting with each of them which is private but relaxed and find out what their own aspirations and wishes are. Discuss any ideas you have about them. Then make a chart with the name of the teacher, their present responsibilities, and what you would like to see them doing by the end of each of the next three years. Make the teachers concerned aware of what you have in mind. Refer to your chart at the beginning of each term when you are planning the activities of the department for the term.

2 **The right to be challenged.** New opportunities in a department's work present challenges to a teacher. He or she does not have to be an ambitious high-flyer to be able and ready to respond to such challenges. In developing an Instrument of Policy, individual strengths and interests can be utilized to the advantage of the whole department.

3 **The right to a proper role in decision making**. Some departments work on a totally democratic approach. Others have a more consultative approach whereby the HOD takes account of his or her colleagues' views. Whatever the pattern of management, every team member should feel a significant part of it.

4 **The right to be kept in the picture**. Team membership means team interest. Numerous matters are handled by the HOD or the department second; it is important to keep the department fully informed of department business.

5 **The right to know the HOD's view of individual performance**. This one sounds difficult but it should not be. Great discretion, trust and mutual regard are obviously necessary. Nor should it be a one-way traffic. It is a good HOD who is ready and able to take constructive criticism and it serves only to make him or her more able to lead their team. An annual relaxed interview with each department member seeking their views on how the department can further develop is valuable. In it you should offer an assessment of that colleague's performance offering both praise and constructive criticism.

# Listening

The HOD is the departmental problem-solver. The difficult class or individual, the seemingly endless marking load, the periods of frustration or moments of apparent failure — at times like these the HOD has to enable a colleague to understand the problem clearly, to see that there are ways through it (rather than around it!) and that he or she is ready and as able as possible to help. When colleagues are facing a difficulty, the HOD's first responsibility is to listen. Listening is now regarded, is it not, as one of the four areas of the subject English? It is also the least taught and the least well taught, probably because we as adults like more to speak than to listen. Listening involves more than hearing facts. It involves hearing feelings. When a teacher complains of the poor performance of such and such a class he or she might be stating a fact but really meaning that he or she is feeling a failure. When you are being attacked in some way by a colleague, the first thing to do is to listen — not react. Communication requires a listening mind (and heart!). Somebody believes that they are in some way being neglected, misunderstood, undervalued or exploited. You may become a dartboard. Do not allow yourself to be walked over or abused but be a good listener. Do not feel personally attacked. Do not be defensive. Read what is underneath the surface statement of facts (or assertions). Keep the lines open. Enable the relationship to withstand heat by enabling the other person (or people — it may be the whole department!) to be honest and remain respected, regarded and important. When we fail to do this our defensive response is to try to dominate, to control — 'I am the Head of this department'.

17

Relationships are, in the end, more important than the authoritarian exercise of authority!

To solve problems effectively is to care about what you are doing together as a team. It means finding ways of helping people get things done. The task is by no means easy and will often require help from some more experienced colleague or friend outside the school. But you should be prepared to seek such advice so as to be the better able to help those whose work you have some responsibility for.

## Expectations

It is often said that we get what we expect from our pupils. Generally that is true too of our colleagues. But to expect too much too soon or to fail to recognize the overall demands of the school upon a teacher is unfair and unhelpful. Nor is it sensible or realistic always to expect the same of everybody.

Few English departments are staffed by career teachers, all specialist trained, all eager to develop their expertise and, perhaps, their promotion prospects! Most departments enjoy and are positively enriched by the services of mixed commitment. Some teachers, because of commitments to family and other interests outside school, are just unable to give more than a satisfactory level of time. Still others are teachers of many years standing who have, perhaps understandably, arrived at the 'ticking-over' point. Their teaching career has sown its earlier enthusiastic seed; younger teachers should now bear the responsibility for enterprise and enlightened development.

Happily, the profession retains an attraction for those whose interest is full, whose capabilities are considerable. English departments frequently are their destinations. The balance of a department's corporate commitment is the HOD's best guide-line as to what his or her expectations should be. We can, however, list some of the expectations that apply to every teacher.

1 **Commitment to policy** — a readiness to put into practice what the department has established as its philosophy, methodologies, procedures. The HOD may not only expect this, he or she must ensure it. The department's own self-respect and resolution can be weakened by a failure to 'encourage' colleagues who themselves weaken the department's overall performance.

2 **Commitment to progress** — a belief in the view that the best interests of pupils entail a readiness to improve our teaching and

their learning. This should not be in a pious, merely idealistic way, but in a practical, realistic way. This may mean more thoughtful planning of lessons, more effective assessment of pupils' work more readiness to question how things are done, how they are taught.

3 **Commitment to principle** — a readiness to stand by the fundamental aims and objectives of the department. In times of cut-backs, of reduced curriculum time, of reduced staffing, there must be firmness in stating and retaining the necessary conditions and provisions whereby to achieve the department's goals. This will not be easy. Nor will it always be successful. But the principle must be honoured.

Expectations of this nature, when properly explained and consistently expected can only benefit a department and, therefore, the pupils. That must be good.

# Monitoring department performance

The great majority of teachers want very much to do a good job well, and to know that they are being effective. English teachers are traditionally committed to the individual pupil as a person, a human being potentially imaginative, creative, and capable of using language resourcefully. It is essential, therefore, to monitor a department's performance. It simply means ensuring that what the department needs and wants to do, it actually succeeds in doing. Schools are busy places, increasingly so. The pressure upon teaching staff often results in a lack of 'mental space' wherein to review the work being done. Whilst the individual teacher will seek to be thorough and effective it is your task as HOD to monitor supportively the progress you and your department are making.

Monitoring is not 'checking up on'. Nor is it an attempt to detect slackness for the sake of it. Monitoring is noting the extent to which aims and objectives are being realized. The focus is upon processes rather than people. The emphasis should, in fact, be upon the department monitoring itself. The approach is mutual rather than hierarchical. There are several practical methods. Contact time between the HOD and the whole team and individual members of it is important. Hold regular department meetings and plan a range of content for them across each term. Ordinary administration will occupy some of the department's time but do not let it dominate and limit consideration of more educational concerns. Make sure you review with individual colleagues their own areas of teaching and organizational responsibility. New courses, probationary teachers, problem classes or individuals — these and other matters will need particular attention.

Here is a pattern of department meetings which you can adapt to your own needs and priorities:

**1 Autumn term**
- A look at longer term objectives (for example, a reading programme to cover three years)
- A discussion of short-term experiments
- Assessment of resources and future needs
- Suggestions for curriculum development
- Department in-service training (linking with nearby schools, for example, and inviting appropriate speakers)

**2 Spring term**
- A term of workshops directed at very practical teaching matters: sharing ideas, modes of assessment, considering problems, encouraging one another (most departments have off-days!) — less formal get-togethers with which to lubricate the day-to-day classroom processes

**3 Summer term**
- Planning, as a team, dates and ways of appraising the coming academic year's curriculum
- Plans for innovation
- Assessing the nature of, and solutions to, the past year's problems

**4 Annual**
- Planning the various department dates, target and deadline dates
- Determining capitation expenditure
- Considering and agreeing staff responsibilities and timetable commitments

Make sure that everyone is informed well in advance of the date of a meeting, reminded nearer the time, and provided with an agenda to think about. At the meeting itself, provide tea and something to eat; make a prompt start; follow a clear agenda. The department will appreciate this and will be more willing to give up the time to attend.

# Setting an example

As HOD you will be constantly looked to for the highest standards — and rightly so. Colleagues should never be able to say with any foundation that their leader is not working as hard as they are; you should be working harder than they are; you are being paid to do so! You must, of course, delegate but only to allow you to do other things which should aim at improving the overall performance of the department. In doing so you must ensure you support the colleagues taking on your work. They must not be overloaded. Do not ask them to undertake tasks which give an imbalance to their overall work. Delegate creatively so as to develop colleagues' experience and expertise. Above all, think. Good managers are thinkers. They set an example in thinking through the implications of the department's policies. The force and clarity of the HOD's thinking will be evident in the quality of his or her ideas, teaching and recognition of colleagues' needs for professional development.

Be reliable. Maintain good time-keeping. Keep agreements made with colleagues. Do not make commitments to your team members (over timetables, for example) which future developments might make quite impractical. However, where commitments or agreements have been made, you must adhere to them wherever humanly possible. Every individual teacher of English on your staff must be able to trust you. In meetings with the Head you must represent the best interests of each department member. If teachers cannot trust you, morale in the department will suffer seriously. Equally, do not misrepresent colleagues' failings; both achievements and difficulties of teachers should be passed on to the Head. The honesty, tact and reliable judgment of the HOD must gain reputation. People trust those who try to say what is true.

# Managing resources

Resources are a priority. Money may be tight but the department needs adequate resourcing. Make sure you have an overall view of your colleagues' needs. Certain items put themselves at the top of a buying list: set texts, basic language texts, stationery etc. Plan for the likely needs of a year, two or three years ahead. Resources are frequently not employed to their maximum usefulness; they have to be understood, considered and their potential examined. Often a considered appraisal of one or more resources twice a year will cover the existing facilities and highlight gaps.

Departmental workshops, too, might expose needs for resources: 'I really want to do this with my third year group but we don't have the right resources.' So why not produce something? Encourage a mentality of looking ahead and calculating future needs. Give the department 'mental space' in which to think about what a future course, exam change, policy change, will imply for resources — and plan to produce or buy.

So much good method and approach, so many ideas and inspirations begin and end in the classroom and never find their way into a central resource system for others to employ. Some teachers, otherwise creative and effective, teach year in, year out from commercially-produced resources or just contrive with 'chalk and talk'. Had they brought their minds to bear upon what they themselves could produce, the department that most values the creativity of the human mind would itself have been more creative. As HOD you must encourage the building up of colleagues' own resources for the benefit of everyone.

Time of course is the problem. The rushed worksheet is so often all that seems possible. However, the HOD should gently but steadily develop the view that a good department is as much a resourceful department as it is anything else. Planning ahead is necessary. Standards should be high and expertise employed. Enable colleagues to put into the form of accessible resources what they know and do best. Spread the expertise!

## To lead or not to lead

If one were presented at one go, in a few minutes, with the nature of department leadership in all its aspects, the inclination might be to run! It is not an easy task. You never get on top of it, you merely become better at it. The determination required, the self-discipline, the patience, the attention to detail, these and the other skills and qualities also needed are considerable. But the rewards are significant too. The most notable reward for any leader is response to that leadership. That one should be in a position of influence amongst pupils is often a privilege; no less so is it to be a leader amongst colleagues.

*Recommended reading for this chapter appears at the end of Chapter 2, page 37.*

# 2 Organising the English Department team

Richard Exton

## The problems of human beings and children

There are two basic problems which all Heads of English have to face and which make their task of organizing the English Department extremely difficult: first, they are working with other human beings; and secondly, they all have full-time jobs to do teaching children. Were it not for these two facts, all would be well; and indeed books have been written to show how easy it is, with perfect colleagues and no time or energy constraints, to organize the perfect English Department. This chapter is written with full awareness of the limitations — both individual and institutional — of any school situation, but is incorrigibly optimistic about what is possible. It is precisely because constraints exist that teachers should be willing to work together, if the conditions are created by a Head of English, in order to allow the best possible teaching to take place. Satisfaction for teachers and benefit for children are closely related and both depend to a great extent on a happy and well organized department.

## Getting the work done

Relationships form within specific frameworks and are affected by particular systems and their administration. Inevitably they are intimately bound up with the nature of the department and its aims, and ultimately will derive from the decision taken by the HOD about how to get done all the work which is necessary if pupils are to develop to their full potential. Clearly, whatever the size of the school, there is too much work for the Head of English to do alone, and probably too much to be done by teachers with scales for responsibility. It seems, then, that the bulk, if not all, of the department will be involved in the department's work; in which case, how might it be organized? Making sure that jobs get done and everyone is involved is best arranged at the first department meeting of each year. Produce a list of jobs to be done, with the responsibilities of the HOD and others with specified scales of responsibility already marked. The department members then agree about who should accept responsibility for the remaining jobs. The following is a list produced by one department:

## English Department: Responsibilities Tasks Chores

Bookshop
Publications
Film and narrative
Media studies
VCR (arranging for)
Theatre visits
City & Guilds (i/c)
Timetabling: Pupils
            Staff
            Rooms
Discipline/support
Cover
Cover lessons
Students
New teacher induction (in depth)
Help/support for part-time
    members of Dept
Dept meetings
Dissemination of information
Attending outside meetings
Dealing with inspectorate
Annual report
Sending for inspection copies
Checking through catalogues
Ordering books (i.e. SBNs etc.)
Stock checking
        unpacking/stamping
        assignment to years
        storing away
Stock ordering
Topping up in eng. room

Examination entries: public
                    mocks
Exam setting coordination
Administration internal exams
Setting e.g. 3rd year exam
            4th year exam
GCSE:
'A' Level
Checking/supervision of stock
        Room G
            E
        Eng Rm
        118
Retrieving 'lost' stock
Resources, building up of
Filing cabinets
Visitors
Greek literature
Classical studies
Myths/legends
Displays/environment
Guidelines
Syllabus
Assessment: (hounding!)
            (doing!!!)
Curriculum
Responding to outside demands
    (e.g. questionnaires)
Attending HOD meetings
Consulting with Head/D. Head
    on Dept matters

Book-boxes
Emergency books (buying, etc.)
Assignment/reassignment of texts
   (which books go to which year)

Staff welfare
Liaison (administrative) with ESL
Drama
Remedial

Clearly there is more work to be done than the teachers with scale posts can accomplish. If left to struggle alone they will fail, the department will decline and the pupils will suffer, react and make life more difficult for *all* teachers.

There are a number of consequences which follow from a decision to create a department which acts collectively and assumes a particular framework of relationships. As a Head of English, you are likely to have more energy and/or commitment to the job than most people in the department. Make sure that this does not lead you to make unreasonable demands of them, especially when other members of the department are part-time in the school (and only paid as such) or when they have other jobs within the school. The HOD must find some way of involving them so that they make a real contribution to the work of the department, but a way which does not make unreasonable demands or force them into a role which it is impossible for them to fulfil. It would seem reasonable not to expect such people, for instance, to undertake the routine administrative work of the department, beyond that, of course, which involves them in using and maintaining department systems. On the other hand, if they are not involved in the shared responsibility of developing policy and resources, they might be seen by the full-time members of the department as parasites, and an atmosphere could develop which might prevent the department as a whole working effectively.

The question of what any teacher might be expected to do is difficult to determine in the absence of any specified contractual obligations, and a HOD must be sensitive to a range of pressures on individuals. Teachers must prepare lessons and mark work for their own classes, but beond this it will be a matter for the HOD to show that contributing to the English team will make life easier for its individual members, thus clearing space for family and other commitments and allowing a positive answer to the question, 'Is there a life after school?'

Probably the most effective way of involving the 'part-timers', and indeed all members of the department, apart from encouraging regular attendance at department meetings, is to involve them in a standard department practice of giving them a concrete task relating directly to the particular classes which they teach, and which can be accomplished over a period of time. This might be the production of a dossier of materials around a particular class reader, which would feed the particular lessons of the individual producing them, as well as building up the resources of the department as a whole. Alternatively, ask a pair or small group of part-timers, perhaps including a full-time English specialist, to produce materials and teaching strategies for a book they will all be using in the course of the year. This will give the department a richer vein of ideas, materials and approaches tested and moderated in real classroom use.

## Theory and practice

Implicit in this way of working is the belief that each member of the department can contribute at the level of theory and practice to the department's working. Tasks to be worked on can be set at the regular department meeting organized well in advance and with full emphasis on the importance of everyone's attendance. The HOD should offer a provisional list, but make sure that everyone is involved in drawing up the year's agenda of tasks, arguing for priorities, making new suggestions and challenging current practices. Every task should be given a realistic, agreed end-date, at which the teacher responsible will report back to the full department. This gives another opportunity for thinking about teaching strategies, the relationship between materials and objectives, and what the objective should be. It also makes both the teacher and the rest of the department aware of the contribution every member is making.

It is crucial that the theoretical preoccupations of the department — how to develop comprehension skills, how to teach an understanding of the nature of narrative, for example — are never separated from practical considerations. But equally, the department should never forget that all practice derives from theoretical positions, often unstated and assuming the status of 'common sense', which should constantly be reviewed. In other words, theory, without which a department can become stale and its members cease to develop professionally, must always be grounded in the concrete. The suggestions above achieve just that and help, at the same time, to set up relationships within the department which lead to effective teaching and fruitful learning for the pupils.

Junior members of the department, totally committed to notions of equality, may also feel unable to contribute because they do not *feel* equal. It is no good HODs thinking of themselves as open, approachable and 'equal', if members of the department do not perceive them that way. It is not always easy for someone at the bottom of a hierarchy of experience to contribute fully. The system of working in pairs with reports back to the full department is probably the best way of overcoming such problems, particularly if the more reticent teacher is placed with a sensitive, more experienced colleague.

To summarize: a good English Department will be one in which every member is part of a team and has a concrete role to play and which, despite natural hierarchies inherent in the current salary structures, is organized so that decisions are reached collectively and policy and materials developed by the whole team.

Its HOD will not be taking all the initiatives, directly delegating work or making all the decisions, but will have to be sensitive to the needs of individuals within the department. He or she will need to chair formal meetings, and to work hard at informal links. The HOD must never be too busy to spend breaks and lunch-times in the staff-room with the other members of the department. It is often here that the vital work is done: the HOD can monitor the day-to-day moods of the department so that adjustments can be made in the routine of work; he or she can make sure that less experienced teachers are supported at times of crisis with 'difficult' classes; he or she can feed developing ideas or worries into the formal structure of meetings.

### Checklist
The HOD should

- take initiatives
- encourage others to take initiatives
- delegate
- encourage volunteers
- take decisions
- encourage collective decisions

In an effective English Department

- decisions are reached collectively
- policy is formed by the team
- materials are developed by the team
- everyone (specialist and nonspecialist) feels part of the team
- teachers with scale points for English do more than those without

# Running meetings

If the department is to operate as a team it must meet on a regular, formal basis. (*See also* Monitoring department performance pages 19 to 20.) Ideally one period a week is timetabled, preferably at the end of the day so that it can continue after school if necessary. A number of schools arrange their time-tables to make departmental meeting time one of their major priorities. If it is not possible, then meetings will have to be after school in order to allow time for proper discussion, and, of course, such meetings cannot be made compulsory. But for a department to work successfully, regular attendance by the bulk of the department at such meetings is crucial. Full department meetings could be once a fortnight with the intervening week used for smaller groups within the department to meet and work on their particular tasks.

It is at the regular, full English Department meeting that the work of the department is drawn together. These meetings must be properly structured and not bogged down with routine administration. Set a fixed time at the beginning of the meeting to deal with such matters as the collection of information such as examination entries, or the fixing of dates. This time should also be used for the dissemination of information from outside agencies and the school hierarchy. The HOD must recognize that what seems unimportant to her or him may be of great interest and relevance to someone in the department. (A department notice-board helps in this sharing of information, providing that it is kept up to date and interesting.) The rest of the meeting should deal with the main areas of the department's work.

# Writing the syllabus

An English department must have a syllabus. But it is less clear what form that should take. (*See also* Philosophy into practice pages 13 to 14.) In my view it should be a series of documents with different audiences and uses, and it should be a regular item on the department's agenda. One part of the syllabus — written for parents and governors — is a clearly written statement, free from jargon, of the department's overall aims. It should not be bland, but genuinely express the department's positions on matters central to English as a school subject. For example, it might be a matter of debate within the department whether the document talked about the department's priority in the teaching of literature in terms of 'enjoyment', 'appreciation' or 'understanding'; or whether issues of gender and race in language and representation are given a central place. A draft of such a 'syllabus' written by the HOD for presentation to parents, governors and non-English teaching colleagues in the school, could form the basis for several department meetings, before being rewritten, in the light of discussion, for publication. The syllabus of a department which works collectively as a team must be the product of that team if it is to have any meaning. And in any event, a syllabus simply issued by a HOD and filed is likely to be a worthless thing.

The 'public' syllabus, which might better be described as a manifesto, will be of little use as a guide to action, because it will not be detailed enough. So the second part of the syllabus is a general guide to thought and practice, while the third part will describe administrative systems, list sets of available books, state the location of materials and so forth, and can easily be written by the HOD.

I suggest that the whole department should regularly discuss an aspect of English teaching — comprehension, poetry, narrative, or whatever — basing the discussion on a general paper presented by a pair of teachers from the department, and grounding it in the concrete situation of the school. The paper would then be rewritten, in the light of discussion, by the HOD, and duplicated as part of the department's syllabus. In this way the syllabus changes and develops as the department changes and evolves. It is both theoretical and practical and a detailed guide to current thought and practice for teachers joining the department.

English syllabuses will be different from those of many other subjects because language — the basic subject of English — does not develop in a linear way. Pupils will 'do' the whole of English each year, though at different levels of sophistication. Summary, for example, is not something which suddenly has to be taught at 16+, but is being developed in the first year (as indeed it was in the junior and infant school) through such tasks as pupils telling a friend about a book they have read. Consequently, the syllabus documents will necessarily be general statements. But these general discussions and documents interlock with the production of units of work for specific year groups on specific texts or specific areas. The production of materials should be described and documented in the department syllabus, and will be in a constant relationship with the more general theoretical aspect of the syllabus which has itself emerged from discussion anchored in a specific institutional framework.

# Deciding on methodology and teaching strategies

The second major item which should be a regular concern of the full department meeting is the question of how the syllabus is to be executed, that is to say, with methodology and teaching strategies. Individual teachers have their own 'style', and pupils benefit by meeting a range of styles during their school career. Equally, particular aspects of English demand particular styles and teachers need constantly to develop their professional skills by learning teaching strategies appropriate to the differing aspects of the subject. It might, for example, be the case that a teaching style which involves the teacher standing at a blackboard and talking a great deal is not totally appropriate for a class which is meant to be learning how to develop the language of persuasion. Teaching strategy and style is a matter for the whole department, not just the individual within it. Consequently, discussion of methodology in relation to syllabus and particular institution is essential to the English Department.

Issues of methodology will arise when the department discusses its approach to language development. If it is agreed that pupils develop language skills by listening to a teacher, reading examples of good English and practising correct forms through a variety of exercises, then a particular style of teaching will follow. If, on the other hand, the department believes that language develops in use in concrete situations and from a base of already existing competence, then quite different strategies of small group discussion preceding written tasks will be appropriate. It is not a question of 'either will do': each method is integral to the theoretical position adopted. However, it is likely that a department committed to collective work and policies is likely to wish to see such methods replicated in some form in the classroom. Regular discussion of method and approach is essential.

# Keeping up with new developments

English has developed fast in the past dozen or so years. The changes in the subject have derived from academic work in the field of linguistics and subsequent developments in learning theory and in literary studies. A department should be aware of such changes and should work out a position in relation to them. But teaching children is a full-time activity and one which is particularly wearing. How, then, can discussion of new theoretical positions become part of the department's framework of action?

1 Make sure that the department is represented at all in-service courses organized locally and that a report is made at subsequent full department meetings.
2 Use the new blood which enters the department in the form of students or teachers fresh from the departments of education.
3 Ideally individuals within the department should keep up to date by reading key theoretical texts. It might be the HOD's responsibility, but there may be someone with a particular theoretical interest who can be delegated to be watch-dog and 'expert' in that field.

It is crucial that teachers in an English department do not adopt a cynical anti-theoretical stance which results from experiencing the worst kind of academicism sometimes found in education departments where theory is totally divorced from practice. It is easy to slip into a rejection of theory as a kind of excuse for the tiredness which follows a day's teaching, marking and preparation. But without a serious attempt to develop a theoretical base from which to work, the department will fall prey to existing orthodoxies which deny their own theoretical status and attempt to pass themselves off as 'common sense' and 'sound practice', or to passing fashions which offer to solve all the world's problems! There is no alternative but to make a commitment to engage in the effort and to be aware of the key theoretical debates.

# Departmental systems

No department can operate satisfactorily without a set of fully worked out and supervised administrative systems. Conditions for English departments vary enormously from school to school. There are those fortunate enough to have a department room with telephone and attached stockrooms alongside a suite of rooms used only for the teaching of English. What is more typical, perhaps, is for the teaching to be spread around the school in non-specialist rooms with the HOD establishing squatters' rights in a corner of the general staffroom. There is usually a stockroom, or at least, a series of stock cupboards. The suggestions for administrative systems which follow assume the worst!

## Organizing the books

English teachers must have access to books. However, some check will be necessary to avoid the loss of books, and to avoid the 'best' books being grabbed by a few teachers who then hide them away for the rest of the year. The following system which is used in a number of schools is effective in achieving these objectives.

Books are organized and stored under two broad categories: 'Class Readers' and 'Others'. Class Readers are assigned to particular year groups; they are reviewed annually by the whole department and teachers within a particular year group decide among themselves which books they wish to read with their classes and, roughly, when. A card index for each book is kept centrally. Each card lists the book title and number of books held by the department. It is divided into columns for the number of books being used, the class, the date taken, date returned and teacher's name. The person responsible for ordering stock can thus see, at a glance, which sets need 'topping up' and by how many. For the period that a set of books is signed out, the particular teacher is responsible for their safekeeping and storage, be it in a cupboard in a classroom or a shelf in the staffroom.

'Other' books are organized differently. Because of expense, it makes sense to have single sets of a range of books used flexibly throughout the year, rather than multiple sets of few books issued out for lengths of time to individual teachers. Thus, a set of books, for example one of the dozen poetry anthologies available on the poetry shelves in the department stockroom or in the poetry cupboard, is booked for a single or double lesson a week in advance. It is taken just before the appropriate lesson and returned immediately after it, thus freeing that book to the rest of the department for the rest of the year. The booking system could be operated by the member of department responsible for stock supervision, or it could be simply a signature in an exercise book kept in the cupboard, or the insertion of a booking 'slip' in the appropriate pile of books. This system is especially effective if a 'nagger' is appointed to encourage the speedy return of sets to the stockroom or cupboard.

Course books may fit into either the class reader system or the 'once only' use system according to whether teachers prefer to use a course book for a whole year or to collect it for occasional lessons.

A third category of books is central to many English departments — the 'book-box book'. Although all English departments encourage, and indeed train, pupils to use both public and school libraries, many departments see private reading as a central activity for English classes in school. To encourage the activity of reading in a systematic way, supply each English class with a selection of paperback books, stored in a cardboard box or on a shelf, to act as a class library and to be a source of books for private reading in regular English lessons.

Many departments also insist that teachers demonstrate the worth and enjoyment of private reading by reading themselves rather than using the time for catching up on marking! Pupils keep a personal record of books read in a section of their English folder or, better still, offer an account of the book with comments on a card index which accompanies the book-box. In this way, pupils who know each other and each other's tastes can see at a glance what they might enjoy. In some schools the 'box' is added to by pupils; sometimes the box is topped up after department discussion and feedback; or a notional sum of money from the year's allowance might be allocated for individual teachers to spend in adding to the book-box. The system is initially expensive to set up, but head teachers have often been known to find some extra money to help out, for after all, reading is recognized as important by the whole school.

(One way to make a limited start on book-boxes is to break up sets of readers, short stories and poems which are no longer needed as full sets, or which cannot be 'topped-up' because they are out of print. The decisions about what to keep as class readers, what to introduce, what to phase out, will all be made at the regular department meeting and administered by the person responsible.)

## Exercise books or folders?

The major problem with exercise books is their lack of flexibility (not to mention their heaviness for those who take their marking home or who do not have a fixed base in school). Pupils are likely to need access to writing paper in most lessons — be it to make notes or to do more formal written work — and equally they are likely to be doing written homework at least once each week. If homework often develops out of classwork, then there is a false division between 'homework book' and 'classwork book'.

Equally, if we are to encourage the notion of drafting and the idea of writing as a developing, provisional activity, the division between 'roughbook' and 'best book' falls down. The only really effective way which I have found to solve the problem is for each pupil to have two folders: one contains 'work in progress' — relevant to a current topic, or awaiting marking — and another for completed, marked, 'finished' work, which is kept centrally by the teacher and added to and indexed regularly by the pupil. This system has the advantage of avoiding the tragedy of lost books; it ensures that there are no empty pages at the end of the year; and it acts as a developing record of a pupil's work. It also means that work done around a novel, for example, can be kept together, rather than be scattered through a book interspersed with other work. There is a real sense of pride apparent in the indexing and sorting out sessions: the pupils can see, appraise and organize their work, developing the editorial skills which are essential to communication and to progress.

## Storing materials and work

It is essential that every English department has at its disposal a number of filing cabinets for storage of resources, information and pupils' work. The whole system is based upon the sharing of materials, and thus the worksheets, dossiers, resource banks have to be accessible, secure, and easy to retrieve. A large lateral filing cabinet, placed near the staffroom or the main English teaching rooms works well. The cabinet is organized into year sections where materials are stored in multiples and the original stencils stored in a stencil file. The key to the cabinet is kept centrally, and each member of the department is responsible for ensuring that worksheets are replaced or new ones run off. When new sheets or materials are produced, they are reported on at the full department meeting and added to the system. A list of what is available in each section is kept inside the door of the cabinets as an aide memoire, and an up-to-date list of materials and where they are located, adjusted annually, forms part of the department syllabus which all members of the department have.

The kind of material kept in this central system will only include tested items which the department knows to be of lasting value. But there are other worksheets which individual teachers produce — often on Banda sheets —for specific purposes but which may be a source of ideas for others. The Banda masters are placed in a separate drawer, according to year group, and kept in the department room or general staffroom for others to raid for ideas or direct use. Those which prove successful can then be reported at the department meeting and transferred to the more permanent system.

The pupils' folders of completed work need to be placed in the classroom used for teaching so that pupils will have access to their folders when necessary. In a sense, these folders act as a record of progress but many schools demand a more formal system and the one I am going to propose will be kept alongside the folders of work and in the same filing/storage system.

## Keeping records

It is crucial to have an assessment system which is there for a good reason and is useful to pupils, teacher or parents, and preferably to all three groups. Parents need to know how their children are progressing as do the children themselves. And teachers need to know how effective their teaching is so that they can adjust it as necessary. Any system of assessment, then, must give such information. A generalized mark or grade is useful only to categorize children and to make broad comparisons between them. Sixteen-plus examinations will do just that at the end of the Fifth Form, but as someone has said, the act of weighing yourself does not automatically make you thinner. What English teachers need is some way of analysing progress and competence in a whole range of different facets of English, all of which are interrelated and interdependent. The system must be flexible and must not be time-consuming or it will not be maintained. Finally, the system must integrate into the teacher's normal pattern of work otherwise it will become a burden. The system I suggest is this:

For each class which a teacher has for English, there is a loose-leaf folder. The name of each pupil heads a sheet of paper together with details such as 'house', relevant medical information, whether English is the pupil's first language etc. This part of the system could be completed at the same time as the mark book or attendance register is filled in at the beginning of the year. Inside the folder is a check-list of skills/activities/aspects of English, which the department has agreed are appropriate for that year. The check-list can be as detailed as the department determines but is intended to help the teacher — 'Have I done any work on first person narrative this year?' for example. Using the items on the check-list as paragraph headings, the teacher in the course of marking work, and certainly once a term, will jot down statements for each pupil about progress/attainment/problems in the various areas of English. This assessment folder is an aide memoire for the teacher in planning work and is a valuable reference point when writing reports or on parents' evenings. This system is far more thorough and helpful than a mark out of one hundred resulting from the hurried marking, late nights, of scores of stories and comprehensions done in two hours once or twice a year! Practice in examination technique is obviously necessary for pupils, but has little to do with assessment.

So, each teacher will have detailed comments on a child's work, a folder of the work itself, and, I would suggest, a brief record, kept in the day-to-day mark-book, of the classwork and homework set during the year. All of these could be made available to inspectors, head teachers and, perhaps more importantly, to a new teacher taking over a class. The folder system also allows for records to accompany a pupil if moved between classes for any reason.

All this assumes that the department will have a common policy for 'intervening in children's writing'. By this I mean teacher comments, conventions for indicating slips or errors, and, if necessary, a marking or grading system. Any policy in use needs to be made explicit to pupils and their parents.

## Dealing with absences

Every department needs a system to deal with the classes of teachers who are absent. A system that involves everyone in a minor way is more effective than one which relies upon the stamina and/or goodwill of a noble individual. If an absence is known about in advance, the problem is straightforward: the teacher in question leaves clear instructions with the member of staff responsible for cover. The lesson left must be easy enough to be administered by even a reluctant non-specialist who is losing precious free time. For unexpected absences a dual system is useful. First, the department should create a 'bank' of easily administered cover-lessons. Secondly, many departments have found it useful to 'pair' teachers who are teaching similar classes. They make sure that they have a general idea of what kind of work is going on in each other's classrooms. Cover teachers are then referred to the 'pair' of the absent member of department who can suggest work appropriate for that class. Or the 'pair' can leave the cover teacher to supervise ongoing work in her or his own class and go to teach the absent colleague's class: this is often easier to do and more satisfactory for the class than to explain to a non-specialist what he or she might do.

## Endpiece – a realistic conclusion

I began this chapter by pointing to the failings of a number of books which offer advice about leading and organizing a department. I suggested that they underestimated the human and material constraints involved, and promised that I would be very much aware of such constraints. I need now, I think, to take a short detour into literary theory in order to justify my claim.

Recent work developed from a structuralist and post-structuralist perspective has shown that all language and literary productions — of which this chapter is one — are rule-governed, that they are the product of a particular set of material determinants, but because they are part of a semiotic system, meanings will only be produced in specific acts of reading. Which is all a fancy way of saying, I am writing this chapter from a particular perspective drawing upon concrete experience, but you, the reader, are consuming it within a totally different set of circumstances at a much later period in time. The suggestions I have made, when they appear as a straightforward narrative of some eight thousand words and are read in twenty minutes in the full knowledge of a particular school, with a particular Head and particular members of department, may appear utopian. Indeed this chapter may seem no different from the ones I criticize.

Let me attempt, then to try to limit the inevitable plural text I have set free by insisting that the frameworks, systems and relationships I have proposed cannot be set up overnight and all at once; but they can emerge over a period of time, with different rates of development, in response to the pressures which institutions and people exert on us all; and that, in any event, an English department that operates as a team will be in a constant state of movement as conditions and people shift. Even if the teachers appear to remain the same, the pupils certainly change, and time continues. The underlying structure of chapters like this create a sense of tidiness and order which can mislead.

What I have produced is not a blueprint but an argument and it is an argument based on the need (a) to solve particular problems, (b) to do a reasonable job teaching and (c) still have a life outside school. The solutions to these problems are in many senses the real authors of this text. You must now become the author of the text as you insert it into your own framework, systems and sets of relationships.

(With acknowledgments to members of the ILEA English Advisory Team and Mulberry School (formerly Tower Hamlets School) English Department, particularly Geraldine Purcell.)

# Recommended reading

*The Teaching of English*, AMA, CUP, 1962

*The Preachers of Culture: A Study of English and Its Teachers*, Margaret Mathieson, Allen & Unwin, 1975

*Language and Education*, F D Flower, Longman, 1966

*Thought and Language*, L S Vgotsky, MIT Press, 1962

(All four titles are important background reading for teachers of English.)

*Language in Education*, Open University Course Team, Routledge & Kegan Paul, 1972

*Thinking and Language*, Judith Greene, Methuen, 1975

*Developments in English Teaching*, Michael Saunders, Open Books, 1976

*Language Across the Curriculum*, edited Michael Marland, Heinemann, 1977

*Thinking About English*, Michael Paffard, Ward Lock, 1978

*English Teaching Since 1965: How Much Growth?*, David Allen, Heinemann, 1980

*English at School: The Wood and the Trees*, Darrick Sharp, Pergamon, 1980

*Teaching English*, Tricia Evans, Croom Helm, 1982

*The English Department Book*, ILEA English Centre, 1982

*New Directions in English Teaching*, edited Anthony Adams, The Falmer Press, 1982

*English In Schools: What teachers really try to do*, 1983, Institute of Education, London University

*English from 5 to 16; Curriculum Matters*, an HMI Series, HMSO, 1985

*See also* the three landmarks on any survey of the subject's development during this century:

*The Newbolt Report*, 1921
*English for the English*, George Sampson, 1921
*A Language for Life*, HMSO, 1975 (The Bullock Report)

# 3 Providing for the ability range

Sue Horner

## English for all

Such is the range of activities, skills and understanding which is required of pupils in English lessons that it is quite unrealistic for teachers to assume a generalized level of ability across them all, and if they are not to aim at the minority in the middle and miss the rest, teachers must find strategies for dealing with this.

## Step One: What to teach

The first task in establishing a syllabus which will be appropriate for the range of ability is to decide on the elements of English that should be common to all. Such a list might include:

1  Listening, writing, reading and sharing poems
2  Discussing our own and others' experiences and ideas
3  Reading fiction individually
4  Reading fiction all together
5  Improving technical accuracy in writing
6  Improving effectiveness in oral communication, listening and speaking
7  Drama, mime, role play
8  Developing critical facilities and discrimination
9  Creating new meanings for self and others
10  Expressing opinions clearly and persuasively

Make sure that the list contains only the most important elements, so that when teachers begin working on materials and methods for one of the items, they are directing their efforts to a major contribution to the

English syllabus. Concentrate on what should be the *core* experience of English for all pupils, a balance of all the richness available, so that you can agree a common core on which to base a syllabus which everyone can and will implement.

## Step Two: Draw up guidelines

When this is decided, you can produce guidelines for practice for all classes. For example, a department may agree that each class will:

- Read a novel together each term
- Do a unit of work on a theme each term
- Have a silent reading lesson each week
- Keep a journal of comments and reactions to English lessons each week

These guidelines are embodiments of the principles you have previously established, rather than ends in themselves and should be regularly reviewed to assess whether they are achieving the aims for which they were established. English must not be reduced to a dull list of knowledge, skills and areas of experience — we are trying to create space for children to think, grow, and shift their ground, but teachers do need help with structuring a term's work or a week's lessons. An enabling, overall scheme can provide a supportive framework so that pupils and staff know what is demanded of them

There are spin-off advantages of guidelines, too. The department can explain its policies to people outside the department and can defend itself much more cogently if attacked. Work for classes whose teachers are absent is easier to find and likely to be more fruitful within the guidelines. Within the overall policy, individual teachers can develop their own differences of emphasis and strengths. Those who are keen and able to tackle poetry, for example, can encourage those who are less confident in that area and share resources with them. Cooperation between small groups of teachers is the most effective way of producing useful materials of a high standard.

## Step Three: How to teach what you want to teach

Next, you need to outline the types of activities and topics that should be covered with each year group and identify the resources for that work. These might include:

- class novels
- poetry books

- a filing cabinet drawer of printed materials
- short story collections
- a teachers' library of relevant books
- class library collections
- course books (with the best sections picked out)
- 'one-offs'
- drama cards
- photographs
- a catalogue of reviewed and indexed audio and video tapes
- a 'good ideas' file
- a 'work in progress' file

Then you are ready to begin in the classroom.

# Teaching styles

Getting the best out of everyone means giving everyone a wide range of tasks, experience and stimulus for all kinds of reading, writing, speaking and listening. Different teaching styles are appropriate for different types of learning. Within the framework of your authority in the classroom, you can negotiate different roles appropriate to your aims in a particular lesson. When this is clear, you can negotiate different relationships with the class.

Teachers need an array of techniques which are used for different occasion and to encourage different responses:

1 Director, producer, authority
2 Provider of materials and resources
3 Chairperson of a discussion
4 Adviser and arbiter
5 Friendly adult
6 Marker and examiner
7 Encourager and enabler
8 Entertainer
9 Source of knowledge and expertise
10 Listener

Your own mix of these will depend on the type of work in hand, but also on your personality, the school, the class, the time of year and numerous other variables. Be conscious of your selection of style for particular activities. For example:

1 If, after reading 'In the Middle of the Night' by Philippa Pearce, you want pupils to share their fears and nocturnal imaginings, you will need to be a confidential *listener*, an encourager.

2 To persuade a class that a novel is worth reading become an *entertainer* with a colourful rendering of a particularly exciting or moving passage, with different voices and dramatic pauses.

3 In a heated debate about experiments on animals, the group will contribute more if you become a dispassionate *chairperson* and *listener* rather than a source of authority and knowledge.

A detailed self assessment of a teacher's performance in just one lesson is a sobering experience. Ask yourself:

- Exactly how did I encourage learning?
- How many doors did I shut?
- What specifically did Joe/Chris learn today?
- What did I do to promote this learning?
- What could I have done better?

When using small working groups, decide what would be the most effective form of grouping for the lesson you propose — by friendship, sex, interest, attitude, ability. The groups that form most readily are self-chosen. If you have decided on some other grouping, explain to the class why it is more appropriate, either in terms of the nature of the work to be done or in terms of the attitudes of the pupils.

## Flexible groupings

Where groups of classes are 'blocked on', the timetable allows for flexibility of grouping. A choice of activity may be offered for a limited period to cater for varying needs and interests. The choice may be organized around types of work, themes or authors, and makes use of the different expertises of staff. 'Circuses' may last for, say two weeks, and offered to pupils to help them with areas they feel they need to develop, or want to concentrate on. For example:

| | |
|---|---|
| Different types of activities: | poetry |
| | media studies |
| | story writing |
| | drama |
| | researching a topic |
| On an author, e.g. Shakespeare: | looking at the language |
| | dramatizing a scene |
| | introducing his theatre and background |
| | introducing his plays |
| | reading some of his poems |

On a theme, e.g. Peace and War: The film *Threads*
                                         *Protest and Survive?* (booklets)
                                         poems of World War I
                                         extracts from *The Siege of*
                                         *Krishnapur*

Pupils may do one or some of these, and with guidance, make good choices.

English is usually taught in full-sized classes, with little technician support and a very heavy preparation and marking load. It is also a 'cheap' subject in the capitation figures in terms of pupil contact time, particularly when compared with Science or Craft, Design and Technology. Therefore, argue to have, say, six teachers with five classes. But rather than just distributing pupils evenly among teachers, on a random or a selected basis, consider that it is possible to satisfy more demands more flexibly by using one teacher as 'float'. This teacher may be called upon to cater for specifically identified needs of groups of pupils. This might include:

1 setting up a piece of discursive writing with a group of average ability pupils.
2 a small group dramatizing an episode of a novel for the rest of the class to discuss.
3 withdrawing pupils to help them with technical matters, such as paragraphing.
4 in-class team-teaching when different roles are needed.
5 working on high-level literary critical skills with the most able pupils.
6 detailed discussion with one pupil of a piece of work.

When planning work, the class teacher may identify particular pupils or resources that may profitably be handled differently —the 'float' teacher can then be booked to do this while work for the rest is organized according to their needs.

# Marking

Vital information for differentiating achievements must be noted and recorded for future reference. The traditional system of giving a mark out of ten or a grade for a piece of work is simple but does not give pupils enough appropriate feedback on their progress or on individual pieces of work. It is much more helpful to offer comments.

Respond to the intentions of the writing, find something to praise and something for the pupil to work on in the next piece. If a pupil has been adventurous in what has been attempted and yet has failed to spell many words accurately, consider leaving the spelling uncorrected this time, and acknowledge its originality. On the other hand, to mark every punctuation error of a fluent writer may have a salutary effect — if there is a pattern of error which can be learned and corrected.

This need not make record-keeping an impossibility. At the beginning of the year, prepare a card or book system with space for each child for:

1 comments from the previous teacher or record card
2 recording books read and borrowed
3 noting any actions suggested and whether these were carried out
4 notes on discussions at parents' evenings
5 particular successes and contributions in lessons and home-works
6 records of when books, homework, folders were forgotten
7 a copy of what was said on the report

Carefully kept records help you to identify patterns of behaviour, difficulties and achievements effectively, to write authoritative reports quickly and easily, and to build up departmental records of pupils as they move from one teacher to the next.


# Class reading

The attention and interest generated by an animated reading of a story or novel should be familiar to all English teachers. Pupils who would have difficulty reading a story to themselves are able to follow it in a copy as it is read to them, and are freed to reflect on the characters and their actions, and to comment on how the story relates to their world. Here are three examples of how class novels may be used with pupils of a range of ability. They show varied approaches whch may be used as models with other texts.

1 *Grinny* by Nicholas Fisk
   (a) Three or four lessons of reading from the book is sufficient to establish that Grinny is an alien who has come to earth for some probably nefarious purpose. Pupils are then given an 'Identification Document' which they fill in to help them make up their own alien, its environment and intentions.

(b) Two possible story plans are offered outlining six chapters or stages of a plot which pupils may use when planning their own stories.

(c) In drama lessons pupils role play a situation where they are immigrants to another planet and have to conform to the way of life there. This relates to Grinny's difficulties in coping with the conventions of being human.

(d) As the book continues in class, pupils begin their long stories, possibly in diary form.

(e) When the first chapter has been written, these are read aloud among groups of friends who may comment, ask questions and make suggestions before the story has progressed too far. This process is likely to be repeated more than once.

(f) In another drama lesson, the immigrants demand certain rights from the inhabitants of the alien planet.

(g) All pupils write their complete stories as rough drafts before copying them up, complete with illustrations, into a booklet they make, with a cover, title and contents pages. Writing alongside the reading allows ideas to be used as they are generated, and hints offered on how plots may be structured, leading up to the final dénouement and uncovering the aliens' true identity. The more imaginative and fluent writers in the class use the ideas as springboards for their own; the less confident draw directly on the material, but nevertheless make their own use of it. The subsequent display of stories is impressive and attracts attention from other pupils.

## Official Identification Document

This document is highly confidential. If it falls into human hands it will reveal everything there is to know about us.

Name:

Age:

Planet of origin:

Physical description:

Able to transform into human shape?    Yes    No

Description of type of education:

Description of building lived in:

Description of vehicle driven:

Description of job:

Other planets visited:

Reason for visiting Earth:

The rest of this form should be completed during your stay on Earth.

Description of disguise on Earth:

    Name:

    Age:

    Appearance:

Description of arrival on Earth:

    Date:

    Time:

    Place

Description of humans met:

Translation of important words into our language:

| | |
|---|---|
| Car | Office |
| School | House |
| Public house | Teacher |
| Factory | Man |
| Woman | |

Problems during mission:

Mission accomplished?    Yes    No

## Alien on Earth

**Cover**
Design a cover for your project. Choose a title e.g.

> Diary of an Alien
> Alien on Earth
> Mission Earth

Now you have to choose a way to tell your story.

1 You could *be* the Alien.
2 You could *be* a human who has met the Alien — and perhaps you didn't know it was an Alien at first.
3 You could decide to be a writer with a good story to tell.

WHATEVER YOU DECIDE, YOU MUST NOW PLAN YOUR STORY IN CHAPTERS OR SECTIONS, SOMETHING LIKE THIS:

1 Arrival on Earth — first impressions
     first conversation
2 Everything seems strange — problems with the language
     making mistakes
3 Alien starts to put plan into action
4 Humans are suspicious — why?
5 Alien protects his identity and plans
6 What happens next?

## Another world

**Cover**
Design a front cover for your project. Use a title e.g.

> My Space Diary

Travel into Space
Space Objective

1 What is the date — present day or in the future?
What is the space craft like?
What is the name of the planet and what does it look like
from outer space?
Describe landing and what planet looks like from the
ground.
What colours are there?
Inhabitants — what they look like, how they speak, their
habits.
How they react to the landing.
Mental and physical reactions of the visitor.

2 What food is eaten on this planet?
Describe the inside of a home and the daily routine.
What is done in leisure time — and at work?

3 A tour — describe what the town looks like.
Are there schools, shops etc.?
What forms of transport are there?

4 A trip out of the town.
What is the landscape like
Are there mountains, rivers etc.?
What sort of plants and animals?

5 Return home.
Departure from the planet.
Souvenirs to take home.
Reactions back home.

**2** *Joby* by Stan Barstow

This book lends itself to dramatization — scenes like the ones with Gus and his gang on the bridge; Joby being thrown out of the cinema; Gus and Joby caught shoplifting. Third year groups read the relevant sections very carefully for clues as to how to play the scenes, and arguments arise over interpretation of character — all good comprehension work. The reading and drama are accompanied by a sheet of activities to do after most chapters, and once interest in the story has been established, pupils can work through these. Some are easier than others (*see* Chapter 1 and Chapter 8) and it may be unwise to insist that every pupil tackles all tasks, but a quiet word with the bright or rapid workers should ensure that they push ahead while others work more steadily. It is important to keep the story going, and setting a minimum of written work for all, with more demands made privately to some, is a feasible method of keeping written work going as well. A sheet of tasks to be done after the book has been completed should also be available. Here again, whilst stipulating a minimum amount, different expectations can be made clear to individuals — 'I'd like you to try number —'; 'Before you write yours up, show me your notes'; I think you'll find more to say if you look again at chapter —', for example.

---

## Joby

**Chapter 1**
Joby's family and friends are introduced in this chapter — Mum, Dad, Daisy, Mona, Snap.

Choose 3 of these and write down what we know about them from this chapter.

**Chapter 2**
On page 40 Snap and Joby agree to meet the next day. Write a play-script of what happens when they meet. You should introduce Gus and Elsa into the scene.

**Chapter 3**
While at the barber's, Joby goes off into a daydream. Imagine you are waiting for something (e.g. at the dentist or the hairdressers) and write your own daydream.

---

### Chapter 4

Imagine you are the cinema attendant who is explaining what happened in the cinema to Joby's father *or* to his wife *or* the cinema manager. Describe the events from the attendant's point of view, using the words he says in the book (pp. 58–65 and 73–76), and showing clearly his attitude to what happened.

### Chapter 5

Read pp. 81–82. "so now he looked through the tear at his world and though it seemed in almost every way the same it was in fact different". What has caused Joby's world to look so different? Write a paragraph about each cause (e.g. his mother's illness), explaining what worries and puzzles Joby.

### Chapter 6

At the end of the chapter (p. 103) Joby's mother writes to him from hospital, telling him off. Write the letter that Joby sends back to his mum, explaining about his problems and why he is getting into trouble.

### Chapter 7

In this chapter Joby becomes very friendly with Gus, and leaves Snap on his own. For *both* Gus and Snap, draw the following columns and fill in at least 5 things in each column.

| What Joby likes about (Gus or Snap) | What Joby dislikes about (Gus or Snap) |
| --- | --- |
| | |

Then say which you would prefer as your friend, and say why.

### Chapter 8

(a) Tell the story of the incident in which Gus and Joby are caught shoplifting from the point of view of either Joby *or* Gus *or* the Shopkeeper, as they might tell a friend.

(b) Do you think the Shopkeeper did the right thing?
What would you have done if you had been the
Shopkeeper?

**Chapters 9 and 10**
At the end of chapter 9 (p. 141) Joby's mother sat for a long
time in a darkened room. In chapter 10 Joby finds his father
deep in thought by the riverbank (p. 148). Write two long
paragraphs decribing what each of them is thinking. Look at
these chapters for hints to help you.

## Joby

1 Give each chapter a title.

2

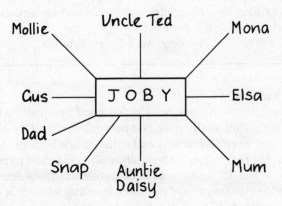

List all these people that Joby knows in the order of their
importance to Joby. Do this for
(a) the beginning of the book (you might use the work
you did on chapter 1)

(b) the middle (the end of chapter 5)

(c) the end

For each list, explain the reasons why you have put the first three.

3 What sort of person is Aunt Daisy? Re-read pp. 55–57, 87–89, and p. 93. Write down as many things as you can about her, thinking out why she says things and what they show about her.

What does Aunt Daisy think of Joby?

Do you think you would like Aunt Daisy if you met her?

4 Choose Joby *or* Gus. In what ways do you think you are like him? Are there any ways you are definitely different?

5 (a) Make a list of the things about Gus Wilson that Joby does not like.

(b) Re-read p. 74. Why does Joby pick a fight with Gus at this point? (think about Joby's state of mind and about how it is difficult to back down after a while).

(c) Does Joby realize the trouble he is getting into? How do you know? (see pp. 106, 109–110, 115–118)

(d) p. 124. Why does Joby now want to get as far away from Gus as possible?

6 Joby changes during the book. Choose 4 of the following and explain how his feelings, attitudes and understandings develop during the book.

Elsa, Mum, Sex, Honesty, Aunt Daisy, Friends.

### 3 *Kes* by Barry Hines

The approach to this popular book makes good use of all the talents in a fourth year mixed-ability class, and particularly the 'Billy' characters who, like him, 'have a job to read and write'. As the book progresses — read in class by the teacher, with pupils reading the characters' lines — pupils are asked to work in pairs to construct charts for different characters to show the sorts of expressions and opinions that character habitually exhibits. Those for Billy and Jud tend to have some unprintable elements, but as they search through, pupils find that, for instance, the head teacher uses phrases like 'What is this generation coming to?'; the English teacher probes, 'What does that mean? How do you spell that?' while the PE teacher has a different style 'Caspar — Wake up, lad. Get in that shower.'

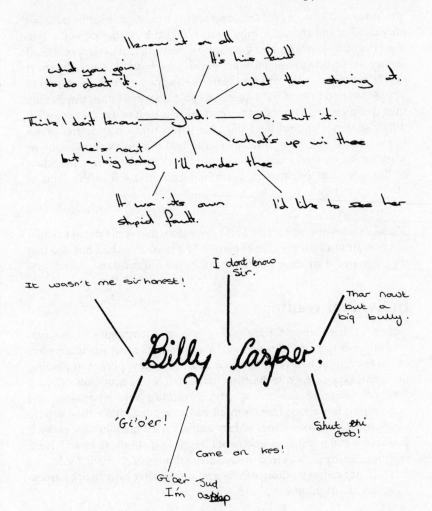

From the charts pupils are asked to draw conclusions about the sort of character that is revealed. These are drawn together at the end when the class is asked to imagine that after he leaves school Billy gets into trouble again and is brought to court. Someone in the class will know about court proceedings and it can be elicited that social reports are called for before sentences are passed. The class is to enact a court scene when all the people who know Billy give some opinion of his character and circumstances. All the possible witnesses are listed, including family, teachers, local tradesmen and friends, and in pairs pupils opt for one of these characters, and write out a script of questions and answers for the court scene. Attention must be paid not only to what the character might say, but also how that person might react in court — would Mrs Caspar be defensive and defiant or would she try to play the loving mother? Pupils who have chosen to be court officials determine the order of witnesses' appearances as each pair of pupils is called to read their questions and answers. Other pupils may then question the witness. At the end there is heated debate as to what Billy's sentence should be: would his father turn up and offer him a home? Should he go to Borstal? Could he become a gamekeeper, or work for the farmer? In all this each pupil's accumulated understanding of the story has been used, examined and adjusted in the light of others' comments.

These examples are described and exemplified in some detail to show not only how all-ability classes can study a book together, but also that they can profit by each other's experiences and understanding.

# Individual reading

Unless schools devote time and effort to encouraging individual reading of fiction, conclusive evidence shows that this reading peters out at the age of twelve or thirteen and only a few persist in reading beyond this age. The role of fiction in feeding the imagination, offering ways of ordering the world, giving models for expression and demanding the active involvement of the reader, make this activity worthwhile. A good school library and a varied class library make it possible for all pupils, regardless of interest and ability, to benefit from reading silently for a period of say, forty minutes each week. Of course this will not happen automatically and the teacher must work hard to establish the right atmosphere.

These are guidelines for organizing individual reading:

1  The teacher must read as well as the pupils.
2  At the beginning of the year (and at other times) the teachers should read extracts from the books available to the pupils with varied interest and reading levels. The demand for these books is likely to be high.
3  Suggest that no pupil should return a book unfinished without consulting the teacher, and a rule of thumb should be that to give the book a chance, the first fifty pages must be read.
4  Stand firm — no comics, motorbike books etc.
5  Make personal recommendations to pupils — once they trust the

teacher's judgement, they will read almost anything suggested.

6 Ask pupils to keep a 'reading record' with their comments on the books read, so that others may use this as a guide.

7 Always refer to these 'reading records' when writing reports. They may be a simple form, but pupils are then encouraged to keep them accurately.

| Date started & finished | Title | Author | Comment |
|---|---|---|---|
| | | | |
| | | | |

8 Liaise with the remedial specialist about the reading ability of the least able, but do not be afraid to stretch these pupils — if they have seen the story on television they will often cope with a book which might otherwise be beyond them.

9 Organize lessons where pupils talk about and read from books they have enjoyed. If the class library is stocked with small numbers of some titles, pupils will enjoy reading the same book simultaneously.

10 Use published journals which review new books, order a copy of the ones recommended, then ask staff and pupils to read them before ordering more copies. In this way unnecessary expenditure on books that just stay in the cupboard should be avoided, and word goes round about 'the good reads'.

11 There is no substitute for a regular time each week, for all first to fifth years, devoted to reading silently together.

12 Some other ground rules for the lesson may be necessary: changing books and filling in 'reading records' may be done only in the first or last five minutes of a lesson, for example. But once a quiet concentrated atmosphere has been established this may be relaxed a little.

13 It is worthwhile trying to establish, for the most and least able, individual reading programmes. Offer a list of five books to read before they are next faced with the problem of choosing a book. For the most able this advice could be in the form of 'try several works by D H Lawrence, or Ernest Hemingway or Susan Hill'.

14 Check the 'reading record' at least once every half term to see if there are any discernible trends — reading too easy or too difficult books, often not finishing books, always reading science fiction, always choosing collections of short stories, etc. Then

make sure these pupils know that they should see the teacher before they choose their next book.

15 Observe pupils when they are reading; much can be learned about their reading habits from this.

When other teachers have to substitute for an absent English teacher they think silent reading must be the easiest lesson in the whole school. Make sure they are disabused of this idea and understand exactly how much work is required to encourage a successful reading habit.

# Writing stories and poems

Whatever their ability, pupils have common interests and enthusiasms and they write most effectively when their interest has been aroused. For mixed-ability classes the following reminders will be helpful:

1 What pupils are trying to say is more important than how accurately it is expressed. This priority must rule the teacher's reaction to this type of work.

2 Pupils tend to be appreciative of each other's work rather than critical, and less able pupils find unexpected approbation in an atmosphere of general sharing of ideas and work.

3 Less able pupils find *structures* very helpful — story lines in cartoon form, headings, sections in which to plan work. These may be offered to anyone in the class, not just given to certain individuals.

4 If writing is done in class then the teacher should expect to be going round offering advice and encouragement to work in progress. This is an opportunity to remind some of what has been agreed about their work and to ensure others are not floundering.

5 Make sure all stimulus material (stories or poems) is available to all — do not underestimate the difficulty of reading for some. Read all materials aloud or have them available on tape.

6 Be flexible.

# Resources

A wide range of resources is necessary for teaching mixed-ability classes, but these can be built up over time, rather than being essential immediately.

1 Cassette tape recorders should be readily available. They enable oral work to proceed and be monitored. A mixed-ability group

reading a play on to tape may rehearse a weak reader before each contribution to the recording, but when the tape is played back this contribution is seen to be as valuable as anyone else's, and boosts the confidence of the less able reader. A pupil who becomes frustrated with the speed at which he or she writes may find it helpful to record the story and transcribe it subsequently when all the thoughts have been saved on tape. Cheap recorders are suitable for pupils to use, but better quality ones with good reproduction are needed for playback to the whole class.

2 Class libraries which contain a wide range of fiction are invaluable in giving the teacher access to appropriate reading material.

3 It is not necessary to buy class sets of all book resources; often small numbers of several titles will enable greater flexibility.

4 Stories read on tape can be another means of resourcing small group work, and can be used as a standby if some pupils find the work set either too easy or too hard.

5 Teacher-devised materials must be centrally stored and well labelled. If it is well presented pupils are more likely to respect it and fewer sheets are likely to end up as paper aeroplanes.

6 Share out the recorded audio and video programmes for review and record your comments in a card index.

| Title: | Tape No | Prog No |
|---|---|---|
| Series: | Length of programme: | |
| Age group: | Rating: | |
| Content/Comments: | | |

7 Keep a shelf of staff reference books — including recent books relating to the teaching of English, single copies of story collections, course books, relevant journals and anything else that could be useful as source material.

## More and less able pupils

Throughout this chapter there are suggestions for how both more and less able pupils in the same class may be fully occupied and stretched. One further useful strategy is to have ongoing work available so that if a piece of work set is inappropriate or finished quickly then pupils have something else to turn to, rather than the teacher conjuring something up at that moment. For more able pupils this work may be related to a topic they are interested in such as play writing or extended story writing or reading. These tasks should be different from ordinary English lessons and since they will be largely pursued independently pupils must have the motivation and ability to do this. For the less able pupil there may be a programme of work arranged to supplement English work, concentrating on the particular needs of that pupil. In both cases this work needs to have been negotiated with the teacher, but once established it is an extremely useful back-up.

It is, of course, vital to make specific contact with the 'Remedial' or 'Learning Support' specialists in the school. They can:

1 diagnose particular difficulties and construct a learning support programme related to them.
2 advise on reading levels of books and materials.
3 help with the selection and manufacture of materials on particular skills, which may be at a higher level than commonly called 'remedial'. This work may be seen as remedying skill deficiencies in more able pupils, such as speech marks, paragraphing, handwriting and apostrophes.
4 advise teachers on whether their lesson plans and resources are approachable by less able pupils — involvement at the planning stage is essential.
5 attend English department meetings to share deliberations and influence plans.
6 offer in-class support so that less able pupils are helped to cope with the normal demands of the English lesson, rather than exempted from them.
7 offer intensive help when a pupil encounters a particular difficulty so that a conclusion is reached quickly rather than prolonged.

In these ways the Learning Support specialist can work hand in hand with the English teacher to promote coherent provision for all pupils. In turn, the English teacher may learn much from this cooperation.

# Units of work

## A range of work

Teachers of mixed-ability classes must structure work so that, at times, rather than all pupils tackling one task, a range of tasks is provided which will allow pupils of different interests and abilities to tackle assignments which develop their own work individually. The elements of variety and choice are essential, and a unit of work — story writing, opinion writing, library work, making tapes of reading, plays, discussions, poetry writing, interviews, grammatical work, collecting or editing writing, comprehension, illustrating, sequencing, dramatic presentations — may offer all these activities.

The aim here is to encourage pupils to be more responsible for their own work and to choose activities which not only interest them but which they perceive as useful. Whilst this is happening, the teacher is concentrating on providing the resources which allow this choice to be available and on helping individual pupils to make good choices. Introductory lessons are necessary not only to start off the theme (if that is appropriate), but also to explain the intentions behind the way of working and how pupils should proceed. Tasks may be set out on:

1 individual sheets
2 grouped on a particular topic (e.g. under a general theme of Animals, subgroups such as Hunting, Pets etc.)
3 grouped by the nature of the work (e.g. library work, storysriting, plays)
4 grouped round resources (e.g. work from one source book, or a poetry anthology, or a collection of children's writing)

This will vary according to the topic, the resources and the teacher's predelictions. All teachers can compile lists of good things to do, but quake at the organizational horror of keeping tabs on each pupil, the resources, the hardware and the work. The following section sets out some basic strategies:

## Strategies

1 **Use a trolley** Collect together worksheets, paper, books, cassette tape recorders, glue, scissors, and all the other paraphernalia on a trolley, which can be wheeled out of the stockroom, rather than the teacher having to stagger under a vast load and set it out each lesson. This trolley is then also available for other teachers to use, with the same materials.
2 **Preparing worksheets** The teacher needs to be sure that all pupils in the class can tackle at least some of the tasks. Within the unit of work it is possible to design assignments for less able pupils which fit into the overall scheme and yet offer a structure which they can follow. Perhaps more important than grading the work is the necessity to phrase worksheets and instructions clearly enough for pupils to be able to follow them without constantly having to ask for clarificaion. Careful layout and organization is required so that

pupils can find their way round the unit.

(a) Have a 'master sheet' to which pupils may refer to see the range of work available.

(b) On a large sheet draw up a matrix of tasks and pupils so that they can tick off when a particular task is finished.

(c) Ensure all cross referencing is clear, e.g. titles of worksheets.

(d) Lay out worksheets so that all instructions which require action are in one typeface, or within a box, or in a particular position on the page.

(e) Make worksheets look interesting by the use of drawings, different typefaces, boxes etc.

(f) There may be occasions when it is desirable to have to hand instructions which explain more fully what is required in a particular task, and which may structure the work more fully for a less able pupil. This foresight may save the teacher several explanations and allows pupils to proceed without having to demand personal attention. If several more able pupils have opted to do a particular task then the teacher may wish to call them together briefly to give them one or two pointers which will help them to understand the subtleties of what they are doing.

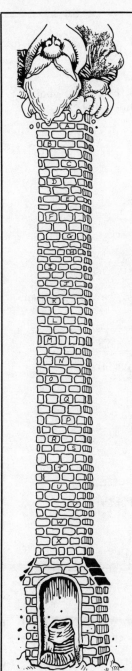

## Alphabetical order 1

Why is alphabetical order so important?

Well, just look at all the things which use it. You couldn't use these if you didn't know alphabetical order:-

- Telephone directory
- Book index
- Yellow pages
- Encyclopaedia

1 Can you think of four more places where you will find things in alphabetical order?
2 On this page there is something *not* in alphabetical order which should be. When you've found it write it down correctly.
3 Now write this out, and fill in the gaps.
   *In a dictionary all the words beginning with _____ come first. Next come all the words which start with _____. At the end of the dictionary come all the words beginning with _____.*

# A B C D E F G H I J K L M
# N O P Q R S T U V W X Y Z

Here are 4 words:

## kick , ball , score , goal

How do we put them in their correct *alphabetical order*?
The first letter of each word is different: *k*ick *b*all *s*core *g*oal.
The order these letters occur in the alphabet is:-

a *b* c d e f *g* h i j *k* l m n o p q r *s*

So the *alphabetical order* is:

1. **b**all

2. **g**oal

3. **k**ick

4. **s**core

4   Here are some names in a school register. Can you put them back in *alphabetical order*?

| NAME | ADDRESS |
|---|---|
| THATCHER , Margaret | 10 , Downing Street |
| KINNOCK , Neil | |
| BOWIE , David | |
| PRESLEY , Elvis | |
| SMITH , Cyril | |

5   Now arrange these words in *alphabetical order*:
   **(a)** cards exhaustion ate brown door
   **(b)** dark go but how found
   **(c)** do just great maybe application pile
   **(d)** fill stare now library punch read knew
   **(e)** reflect way lady assure desperate young exception neither crumb up

6   **(a)** Get a dictionary. Leave it closed in front of you. Now see if you can open it straight away at the section where words begin with the letter *S*.
   **(b)** Now do the same for: *m, d, l, y.*

3 **Guidelines for choice** Suggest that pupils must bear in mind that they should:
   (a) attempt a variety of work, not just 'do poems'.
   (b) tackle things they think will be more difficult as well as easier ones.
   (c) be prepared to be flexible — not everyone can use tape recorders at the same time.
   (d) organize their time so that they can do some work at home on homework night. The teacher cannot set the homework as each pupil is doing something different, but at the beginning of the particular lesson the class should be reminded that they will need to set themselves homework that night, and at the end of the lesson each pupil should be able to write down exactly what they are going to do, for example, 'finish my story', 'read my book', 'write up my poem in neat'. Then the teacher can do a spot check the next lesson to see whether this has been done.
   (e) realize that by the end of the time allotted to the unit, there will be a certain amount of work demanded and if time is wasted earlier then intensive effort will be needed later to meet the deadlines.

4 **Use a record of work** Each pupil should have a sheet on which is recorded each of the assignments tackled, how long it took and an opinion from the pupil as well as the teacher as to its value and what has been achieved. The sheet must be simple enough to fill in, but detailed enough to be informative. These should be filled in during the last five minutes of every lesson as part of the routine packing away. If these are kept in a file on the trolley, then a glance at these tells the teacher straightaway how much has been attempted. It may show that one has been wasting time, another attempting tasks too difficult or another working well within capacity. At the beginning of the next lesson the teacher must remember to have a quick word with such pupils to suggest a goal for that lesson, or the next task to try. Such advice may also be offered as the opportunity arises during the lessons, when pupils request help. Sometimes they can be directed to another pupil for help. In these circumstances the teacher is much more a manager, provider and encourager than a dominating instructor.

# Record of work

| Assignment no. | Title of assignment |
|---|---|

| Date | Time taken |
|---|---|

| Pupil comments | Teacher comments |
|---|---|

## 5 Keeping track of work

(a) Keep a folder for records of work (as above).

(b) Keep a folder for completed work that is ready for marking.

(c) Take in *all* work at regular intervals, perhaps once a fortnight, to check what is happening.

(d) Ask pupils to work on paper rather than in books. Completed work may then be handed in and other work started whilst the teacher is marking the first piece. Otherwise the teacher may well have the pupil's book just when it is needed.

(e) Pupils should have files kept in school so that their work may be stored and not lost.

(f) At the end of the unit use a self-assessment sheet, where pupils are encouraged to assess critically their own performance and decide areas for improvement. Alternatively, a pupil journal or diary may be used for this purpose.

## 6 Presentation

(a) Use plenty of drawings, coloured paper, posters, diagrams to make the work attractive.

(b) Where a worksheet demands a lot of reading, it should be read on to tape, so that a less fluent reader may, with cassette player and headphones, hear it read without the teacher doing so 'live'.

(c) Display work as soon as it becomes available from pupils, and spend time in lessons playing back pupils' tapes to the rest of the class.

## 7 Staffing

(a) Plan to do this sort of work when there may be extra help available — a student, a learning support specialist, another teacher from the department. Joint lessons with another class are easier in these circumstances.

(b) Alert the librarian to likely demand.

(c) Invite to the class a visitor who is willing to be interviewed by pupils on the topic.

Extra, helping adults mix into the work pattern easily and the teacher is more likely to feel that worthwhile activities are taking place even if the pupils have gone to another room.

## 8 Timing

This kind of work is best done in double lessons of 70 minutes or so; in shorter periods a greater proportion of time is spent in giving out and packing away all the resources. It is best to devote several lessons each week over a period of perhaps four weeks to the unit, although the occasional class lesson with everyone working together on one task makes a welcome break, and provides a framework for the rest of the work.

## 9 Examples

A unit for second years entitled 'Beginnings' might contain some of the following assignments:

(a) paraphrasing the first twenty lines of Chaucer's Prologue to *The Canterbury Tales*

(b) reading and writing poems about spring

(c) observing a young baby and how it responds to the environment

(d) prefixes

(e) a video programme on the beginnings of life on this planet

(f) drawing posters to advertise the new sport of hot air ballooning (after research in the library)

(g) taping a piece about 'My First Day at School'

(h) reading stories from Ted Hughes' 'How the Whale Became' and writing their own versions

(i) looking at the openings of novels and trying to suggest what sort of books they are and how the stories might continue

For fourth years, in a unit on 'Male and Female Stereotypes', areas of work, clearly organized and structured, might be as follows:

(a) reading *The Big Switch* by Muriel Box
(b) dramatizing a scene where the wife comes home from work expecting a meal and finds her husband is still doing the ironing
(c) choosing two or three books on a topic from the library, and analysing the illustrations for stereotyping
(d) devising a questionnaire for classmates on different expectations of boys and girls, and analysing the results
(e) reading a passage on the different educational achievements of boys and girls and comparing it with their own experiences
(f) analysing one or more novels they have read recently to see if conventional stereotypes are relevant
(g) comparing magazines aimed at boys and girls to see what conclusions may be drawn about media expectations and manipulations
(h) writing their own views on the issues, or a story demonstrating the effects of stereotyped expectations on boys and girls

Introductory work will be necessary, and feeding in occasional relevant videotapes and materials keeps the topic going, as pupils pursue their own lines within the subject area.

Here are some worksheets for a unit called 'Creatures Moving' which is for first/second years.

The resources used are:

1 *Creatures Moving* — Penguin English Project
2 a collection of other writings called *All Creatures Great and Small*
3 a collection of pupils' writing on these topics
4 general resources of the library, class library and department

## CARTOON FUN

1 **LOOK** at the cartoon on page 28.
  **DRAW** your own mouse or spider cartoon.

**2 LOOK** at the insects on page 26.

**CHOOSE** THREE and DRAW them.

**MAKE UP** some NAMES which really fit the insects.

**3 LOOK** at the picture on page 110.

**GIVE** it a title.

**DRAW** a picture of your own where the animals are in control of men.

**4 LOOK** at page 70.
**DESIGN** a title for the 'Creatures Moving' display using animals in your letters.

**5 COLLECT** as many pictures of animals as you can. Arrange an animal montage.

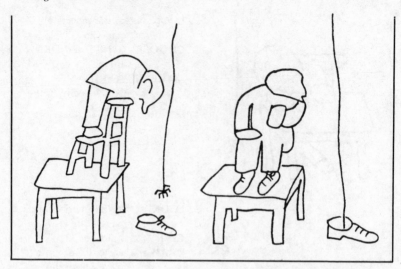

## STORIES

**1 READ**      'Tadpole Time' on page 42 of 'Creatures Moving'.

    **WRITE**      out the words and phrases you enjoyed most.

    **WRITE**      your own story about TADPOLES, FROGS, WORMS, FLIES or any other creepy crawly.

**2 LOOK**      at page 8 of 'Creatures Moving'. The picture tells the story of men helping a fallen horse.

   **CONTINUE** this story.

**Slippery cobbles**

"Ay up, Jack! We'll have to get him up sharpish. He's winded 'imself on these damn slippery cobbles."

"Right-o Harry. Whoa boy, now boy ... it's alright, we're unfastening your harness. Steady now."

Charlie and his son Tom stood watching the

operation, apparently unconcerned about Dusty, the horse, or the delay in their rag collecting.

"You'll not do it that road. Here let me show you," Charlie eventually said irritably.

Harry snapped back, "You just stand and watch, why don't you! We can do without a foreman thank you very much!"

# Endpiece

Since there is no such thing as a homogeneous group in English, *all* classes are mixed-ability, and the strategies and expectations I have described apply to all groups whether theoretically streamed or not. By thoughtfully applying some of these methods to their own situation teachers' perceptions of individuals and classes are changed and will lead them to devise other strategies for themselves which allow the wide experience and talents in any classroom to flourish and *all* pupils to progress.

(With acknowledgements to the English Department of High Green School for the 'Creatures Moving' unit.)

# Recommended reading

*Teaching English across the Ability Range*, Richard Mills, Ward Lock, 1977

*Best laid plans: English teachers at work*, edited Sue Horner, Longman, 1983

*Mixed Ability Teaching*, edited Chris Sewell, Nafferton Books, 1980

*English*, Minns, Fry et al, Ward Lock, 1981

*Every English Teacher*, Anthony Adams and John Pearce, OUP, 1974

*English 8–13*, Gerald Haigh, Temple Smith, 1980

*Continuity in Secondary English*, David Jackson, Methuen, 1982

*The Craft of the Classroom*, M Marland, Heinemann, 1975

*A Probationary Language Teacher's Handbook*, Alan Smalley, Modern Language Association, 1983.

*The English Department Book*, David Marigold, Mike Raleigh and Michael Simons, ILEA English Centre, 1982

*English Studies 11–18: Arts Based Approach* edited by Bernard Harrison, Hodder and Stoughton, 1982

*Encouraging Writing*, Robert Protherough, Methuen, 1983

# 4 Getting them to write

Don Shiach

## Why should they write?

'Grab your readers' interest with your opening paragraph!'; that is a useful piece of advice to pass on to your pupils, so in trying to follow that advice myself, let me indulge in some generalizations. In the sixties, progressive English teachers were intent on establishing the importance and centrality of imaginative/creative/personal writing in the curriculum. The emphasis on imaginative writing in English classrooms was one strand in a more general opening-out of British education in the fifties and sixties which manifested itself in open-plan junior schools and comprehensives oriented towards liberal educational values.

In the English classroom, 'Go forth and write creatively' was the instruction, despite dark rumblings from pre-Black Paperites and Rhodes Boyson clones about airy-fairy 'stuff and nonsense' and 'falling standards'. Hopefully, I can now express the opinion, without being accused of reneging on sacred progressive principles, that perhaps, in the midst of this surge towards creativity, not enough attention was paid to the need to give pupils the tools with which to write well — the skills or craft of writing.

## Pupils' needs

Remember the impassioned criticism of the eight pupils of the Barbiana School in their 'Letter to a Teacher' (Penguin 1970):

> One subject is totally missing from your syllabuses: the art of writing.
> It is enough to see some of your comments you write at the top of

71

your students' compositions. I have a choice collection of them here. They are all nothing more than assertions — never a means for improving work.

'Try to improve your form. Unclear. Try to write more simply. You must have better control of your means of expression.'

You are the one who should have taught all that. The craft of writing is to be taught like any other craft.

That was true when the Barbiana pupils wrote their 'Letter' and it is still true today.

# Here and now

In the last ten years there has been a growing awareness that the mere opportunity to write is certainly not enough to ensure that pupils master essential writing skills and find a personal voice in their writing. Clearly, English teachers are not aiming to produce future legions of professional writers, but writing is one of the avenues through which young people find an identity and a sense of things. In the world beyond school, imaginative and personal writing can no longer be seen as a pursuit carried on by a gifted élite. All over the country, there has been a growth of community writing workshops where ordinary people of all ages write about their experiences, their interests, their environments. Only an embattled élitist like Kingsley Amis could deplore that trend; writers are not born; writers can be, if not exactly 'made', helped to find that writing 'voice' that is in all of us. Every one of our pupils is a potential writer because everyone has something to express.

There is a danger that, with so much flak still flying around about 'falling standards', and with the post-Tyndale and Black Papers hysteria still rattling in a few cupboards, plus the initiatives about absolute standards from the DES, English teachers might be tempted to draw their horns in and play safe with a diet of boring essays, deadly comprehension exercises, isolated skills exercises and other traditional fare. Not that essay-writing, basic skills, summary and study skills ought not to be taught! The debate has always been about *how* these skills should be taught, not about *whether* they should be taught. The polarization between those who were seen to be in favour of imaginative English teaching, with an emphasis on creativity, and those who were for things called 'standards' and 'skills' has probably narrowed. Perhaps it can now be seen more clearly that good writing and the acquisition of skills are interdependent. Teaching so-called skills in isolated exercises is simply no longer good enough. Skills should be taught in an integrated way arising out of the various activities of the English classroom. Competent 'directed' writing arises from the springboard of personal/creative writing.

If you, as an English teacher, are still having to argue for the importance of imaginative/personal writing in your department or school, if you have a Head breathing down your neck muttering Joseph-like imprecations about 'trendy English', be positive in your avowal of creativity. What cannot be seriously contradicted is that a mastery of the more formal writing skills cannot be had until pupils have found a more personal and imaginative voice in their writing.

## Towards a product?

It is axiomatic that pupils should be given a sense of purpose about their writing and that writing in the English classroom should be an enjoyable activity. What easy assertions to make and how much more difficult to make them happen! Later in this chapter, I will be putting forward concrete ideas and strategies about how to make writing both enjoyable and purposeful, but may I make a plea at this point for *products* in the English classroom?

It is taken for granted in art and craft subjects that pupils are working towards the making of an end-product, although the process is naturally also of central importance. There is no reason why in English lessons secondary pupils from first to fifth year cannot be encouraged to think of producing a folder or book of writing centred round a theme or a particular activity. For example, if several weeks' work is centred around the reading and writing of science fiction, pupils could be asked at the outset to think in terms of producing a folder of writing in this genre. After their first effort at science fiction, pupils should be encouraged to make a folder for themselves to house their stories or shorter pieces and eventually a collection. Time should be given in the classroom for the making and decoration of these folders and they should be kept safely by the teacher. New pieces of work should be added to folders only when they have been carefully worked on, after the various stages of drafting, correcting and then re-drafting. Pieces of writing should be illustrated. Anything that enhances the status of the writing process can be used.

Wall displays and class anthologies are the other obvious ways of encouraging an awareness that the 'product' is important. As many pupils as possible should participate — class anthologies should not consist only of the work of the most able pupils. Pupils warm to the idea of writing on carbon, knowing that they themselves can use the duplicator to run off copies of their own work to add to a class collection. Departmental and school duplicators should be used by the pupils themselves for all sorts of sound educational reasons, not least reducing the burden on overworked teachers.

By the end of the school year, pupils can have several 'products' to show from their work in the English classroom. On one occasion, I started the year with a second-year class by doing serial stories, and we produced highly imaginative writing encased in covers made by the pupils and brightened by illustrations. The pupils took great care with the production of these books and the quality of the writing and the enjoyment of the activity were definitely enhanced because of the context and sense of purpose.

Course work is more and more an important element in examination syllabuses. Pupils who need motivating to assemble the required quantity (and quality) of written course work can be helped by using a system of banking files which you, the teacher, keep for safety's sake and to give the writing some extra status.

- Get rid of dog-eared exercise books.
- Make course work look neat, bright and well cared for! It will not only impress examiners but also motivate pupils.

# Who are they writing for?

'A sense of audience'. I cannot remember where this particular piece of jargon came from or who coined the phrase. Unlike some educational terms it does mean something, although, like all jargon that has sunk into the consciousness of most teachers, there is the danger that the glib utterance of the words substitutes for actual practice.

Simply, having a sense of audience means that pupils should have an awareness about whom they are writing a particular piece for — is it for their peers, a general reading public, knowledgeable fans, the teacher, someone in authority, a friend, an employer, total strangers? As far as possible, set writing tasks in a real context and suggest a possible audience.

Following through with the example of science fiction, when you ask pupils to write stories, you could suggest that they are writing for a science fiction magazine read regularly by afficionados of the genre; make sure there are copies of such magazines in the classroom. Or make the 'audience' the class itself; aim to produce an anthology of sci-fi stories.

# Register

Inextricably linked with 'sense of audience', is another term that has achieved status — 'appropriate register'. Again, jargon or not, it is crucial that pupils know that they have to suit language and tone to the purpose and audience of any piece of writing.

Be careful to avoid implying that a very informal, colloquial style is always wrong. I find exercises such as this are useful: Ask pupils to write a fan letter to a 'star' or group they admire. Encourage them to use very colloquial language and tone. Then ask them to use the same register in a letter to an employer enquiring about a job. The inappropriateness will be obvious. Other amusing writing tasks of this kind can focus on aspects of school routine and organization e.g. rewriting school notices/rules/reports in a very colloquial style or as a Radio 1 disc jockey might talk — anything that emphasizes the incongruity and reinforces the need to suit style to context.

It is not always possible to give genuinely 'real' context to writing tasks; writing scripts for a soap opera that the pupils themselves have devised is not 'real' in the sense that the scripts will be transmitted. What is 'real' is the context or medium (radio, television) for which soap operas are written and factors such as the type and size of the intended audience, the characters and plots soap operas usually employ. Use what is familiar to the pupils and build on it.

Factual writing (a broad term covering a range of writing) lends itself to setting real tasks for real contexts — writing letters to comics and magazines, letters to various organizations and firms, written instructions, memos, planning events, making actual routes. There are plenty of real contexts which will involve the pupils and give them a clear concept of the audience for whom they are writing.

### Standard English and dialect

Most pupils speak or know a dialect of English and yet they are seldom asked to write in the kind of language they use at home and among their friends. Their exposure to dialect in stories and other reading matter may be limited so that if they are asked to write in dialect, even in direct speech in their stories or for dialogue in plays, they find it difficult to write down words they have seldom, if ever, seen printed on a page. I believe pupils should be encourged to write in dialect not only in direct speech and plays but in first person narrative and poetry. The richness and vitality of their dialects should be emphasized.

Before asking them to write in dialect, get them to improvise scenes in pairs or small groups, set in familiar settings — shops, launderettes, youth centres, school playground, home. Record the improvisations and play them back; spell the more common dialect words phonetically and write them up on the board. Read some poems and short texts that use their local dialect. If mainstream publishing does not supply this need, then it is almost certain that within your area there is a community writing project printing the work of ordinary people, some of which will be written in local dialect. Then ask the pupils to use dialect in poems, short plays and as direct speech in their stories, still using Standard English as the narrative language. After that, they can attempt to write stories using dialect as the first person narrative.

As well as underlining the richness of dialect, it is necessary to point out to pupils that, in the wider world, it is not always appropriate to use dialect in speech or in writing. This is a sensitive issue, but it is best explained by pointing out that communication must take place in day-to-day interaction and that the use of an unfamiliar dialect may hinder that communication. Improvisation in classroom drama is a good opportunity for underlining the concept of using appropriate tone and language, and you can follow this up with writing tasks that reflect lack of communication because of mixed registers.

# Talk

There is a certain amount of glibness around about the value of talk in the English classroom. It is glib, not because talk is not important, but because much of the 'professional' advice handed out does not seem to acknowledge the difficulty of setting up really profitable talk situations in the classroom from which *every* pupil benefits. To hear some college lecturers and inspectors, one would suspect that all you have to do to achieve excellent talk in the English classroom is divide pupils up into small groups and have a few cassette recorders around to catch the pearls. If only it were that easy!

You have to convince your pupils, and yourself, that time given over to talk in the English classroom is purposeful. Structure the time carefully. On occasions whole class discussion can be more appropriate than discussion in small groups. In group discussions, make the objectives very specific. For example, if you are leading up to the writing of soap opera scripts and you want them to discuss the genre in small groups, do not just leave them with the instruction, 'Discuss soap operas'. You should write a list of topics on the board or on a slip of paper which is given to the group:

- Which soap operas do you regularly watch or listen to?
- Why do you like or dislike particular soap operas?
- Why do you think soap operas attract such mass audiences?
- What features do most soap operas have in common?

Tell the pupils they have a certain amount of time to discuss these questions and that, either they will be expected to report back on what they have debated in class, or you will be round to join in their discussion and hear what they have to say. Encourage them to take notes from their discussions.

It would be idle to deny that difficult classes can make talk in the English classroom wasteful and demoralizing, but talk is an essential prelude to writing (and can be, of course, valuable in its own right). But pupils must perceive its value or they will dismiss it as not 'real' English. If group or class discussion is proving unsatisfactory, at least discuss writing tasks individually with pupils (you will want to do this anyway even if group/class discussion is successful with a class).

## Decision-making exercises

One of the most profitable avenues leading to interesting talk and writing is to set up decision-making exercises for the pupils. This can work well with all ages and levels of ability in the secondary school. Material I have used of this kind includes:

- 1st and 2nd years:
  Choosing a tutor or form group representative. Pupils are given six brief written portraits of young people of their age. A description of their personalities, their beliefs and attitudes and other relevant and irrelevant details are included. Pupils divide into small groups and arrive at a democratic decision about which pupil they would choose as their representative on a school forum or council. The groups' decisions are discussed as a class, then the class votes. Writing about the process of decision-making, explaining why individual choices were made, what details were relevant and what were not, stories and plays based on the six characters — these writing assignments naturally emerge from the talk.
- 3rd/4th/5th years
  (a) Pupils are given portraits of six teacher candidates for a post at their school. Which one would they appoint and why?

  (b) Pupils are given six portraits of candidates in a local or general election, covering the political spectrum. Which candidate would they vote for?

In my experience, decision-making exercises of this kind stimulate interesting discussion and writing of various kinds.

## Starting them off

Talk, in groups, as a class or on an individual basis, is especially necessary to launch less confident pupils into writing. In the lower secondary years, pupils can begin by being asked to write quite short pieces emerging from topics that relate to their interests and culture. These are some ideas that I think work with many pupils:

- **Lists**: Use results of surveys of tastes among young people in various spheres — favourite foods, jobs, hobbies, books, films. After discussion, they draw up their own lists, adding brief explanations for their choice.
- **Howlers**: My favourite howler source is sports commentators. Kids love sending up television pundits. Extracts from the collection *Colemanballs* (Private Eye) can set them off in creative directions.
- **Failures**: Stephen Pile's *Book of Heroic Failures* (Routledge & Kegan Paul) provides amusing tales of comic mishaps that young people can relate to. Again this should lead on to the kind of comic writing many pupils warm to.
- **Advertising**: Advertisements are always being 'sent up' and there are plenty of examples of mock ads in various humorous anthologies: *The Gentle Art of Advertising* by W Heath Robinson, Duckworth. Pupils will enjoy creating advertisements that find new uses for everyday household things, or making exaggerated claims for particular products.
- **Inventions**: Lunatic inventions can involve pupils' imaginations. If Heath Robinson is thought to be too sophisticated as a model, there are numerous other examples of mad inventions available: *Madvertising* by Dick de Bartolo and Bob Clarke, E C Publications.

These are just a few ideas but the common element in all of them is humour. Young people should be given the opportunity to unleash their absolutely natural penchant to debunk, parody and send up all kinds of things.

Humour should continue to be an important element in promoting good writing with older pupils, but in the adolescent years you will want them to write about more serious subjects as well. Yet it is important that the comic, fantasy, even anarchic elements in young people's writing are not totally submerged by a solemn, 'nitty-gritty' social realist school of writing. Of course, their writing should not always suppress the frequently sombre environment and experiences they encounter, but humour is very much a part of young people's strategy for responding to the wider world they are emerging into and this should be reflected in their writing. They will enjoy doing these humorous writing assignments and once they associate writing with enjoyment, there will be fewer cries of 'Oh, not writing again!' in the English classroom.

# Poetry

Familiar strategies to start younger pupils off in writing poetry include shape and acrostic poems, limericks, haikus, epitaphs. Pupils do need basic instruction about how to set out a poem — line lengths, capital letters, rhyming or non-rhyming stanzas. It is amazing how many older pupils reveal in their exam course work that they have not grasped the principles of setting out a poem.

# What kind of fiction-writing?

Start with what is familiar to pupils and build on it. Most young people, and adults, read 'genre' fiction. 'Genre' is a rather pretentious term which again has reached the hallowed status of jargon, but it means, in the world of fiction-writing, novels and stories aimed at a mass reading public and written according to certain structures and formulas. Each genre has its own conventions and styles. Genre fiction usually embraces some of the best and the shoddiest of fiction — writing, for example, in the American detective thriller genre, there is Chandler and Hammett at the top and thousands of pulp writers at the other end of the ladder. As English teachers, I do not think we should be too snobbish about popular forms of fiction. Use genre fiction not only to promote involved writing from the pupils, but to analyse the conventional elements in it and point the way to higher things: start with what is familiar and build on it.

Here is a list of types of genre fiction that are familiar to many young people:

horror (vampires, werewolves, transformation)
supernatural
science fiction

family stories
war
psychic thrillers (psychokinesis, special powers etc.)

| | |
|---|---|
| romantic fiction | sports stories |
| crime | school stories |
| adventure | spies and special agents |
| gang stories | |

The comics and magazines young people habitually read are filled with short stories and serials of these types. Many young people read best-selling novels because they have seen the film of the book, e.g. *The Godfather, The Shining, Close Encounters of the Third Kind*, the James Bond series, *Carrie, Jaws, ET*. Whatever you may think of the quality of these novels, they represent the type of fiction that many young people enjoy reading, so we should harness that enthusiasm in the English classroom. When you are embarking on a section of classroom time centred round a particular fiction genre, have a wide selection of books and magazines of the type in the class library for pupils to borrow for reading in class and in their own time. It is sometimes necessary to demonstrate to pupils that not all English teachers think literature begins with Austen and Dickens and ends with William Golding.

Of course, you should use extracts, short stories and full-length novels as models of whatever genre you are concentrating on, but be careful not to overload the lessons with this approach. Use just enough material in the classroom for you to analyse the conventions and techniques you wish to pinpoint. Encourage pupils to read widely in the genre as homework or in the reading/library period. After all, some of the pupils may know more about these types of genre fiction than you do — they may just not be able to put into words what the conventional components of the genre are. That is where you come in.

You should *build* towards writing full-length short stories — in other words, do not start by saying 'Today we're going to write a science fiction story.' Begin by watching a video of a science fiction film or reading a sci-fi story, or both. Then have a discussion as a class or in small groups about the elements that went to make up the film or story. Be clear in your own mind what features you want to pinpoint at this stage. One example — in sci-fi: the aliens, the alien planet, the use of robots, the technology, the contacts with the aliens, the conflict.

- Use what the pupils can give to you from their previous knowledge of the genre.
- If some pupils are 'turned off' by science fiction, have another card up your sleeve.

- Find out what types of fiction they prefer.
- Cater for individual tastes as far as possible.

After the initial discussion, start building towards writing stories or serials by looking at specific elements. Let us continue with the sci-fi model:

- There are many conventional elements from this genre that you could deal with, so you have to select a few of the more popular and immediate:
- Robots: what are robots? How are they different from computers and androids? Do robots belong purely to the realms of fiction?
- Tell them about Asimov's Laws of Robotics. Ask pupils to create their own robots with individual powers and characteristics.
- What other laws of robotics should there be to govern their use in society? If robots ruled the world, what laws would they make for human beings?

At this stage, you might be satisfied with shorter pieces of writing from some pupils, but if others want to write stories about robots, give them full rein.

- Androids: How are they different from robots? Examples of androids.
- Are androids a real possibility in the future? Should scientists produce androids anyway?
- Create your own android. Which physical/psychological features would be different from human beings? Describe your android in detail.

Again, stories involving androids are an option at this stage. Less confident pupils will be encouraged by asking them to do snippets of writing. Give pupils as wide a choice as possible.

- The aliens: Examples of aliens from bug-eyed monsters to plants of high intelligence. Use familiar examples — *ET*, *Star Wars*, *Close Encounters*. What other kind of alien beings can pupils think of? Create your own extra-terrestrials. Describe them in detail.
- The alien planet: some examples of planets from pages of sci-fi (science fiction illustrations are particularly imaginative). Describe the planet in detail — its atmosphere, its temperature, its surface. Does it have water, mountains, craters? What life is there on the planet?
- First contact: close encounters of the first kind with the aliens. Is it friendly or hostile? How is communication attempted?

All these stages can be supplemented by discussion and dramatic improvisation. For example, groups could act out an encounter of the first kind. Prior discussion about the structure of the improvisation is essential. Too often drama in the English classroom is aimless.

After you have dealt with some of the conventional elements of the genre in this stage-by-stage way, launch the pupils into writing full-length pieces, or, if some have already been doing that, then encourage those pupils to attempt stories in several episodes. The strength of this approach is that you supply a clear structure, and this is particularly helpful for those pupils who find difficulty in starting. It is flexible enough to give full rein to the most fluent writers and, at the same time, helps the less fluent to find their feet.

## Other genres

'Ah, but . . .' I hear you say, 'I don't like SF and neither do some of my pupils.' I have used sci-fi only as a model for this structured approach. The same stage-by-stage structure can be employed in dealing with other types of fiction-writing:

- Spies and special agents: what kind of agents? Who are the villains? What kind of plot? The cliff-hangers! The climaxes! The technology!
- Supernatural: What are vampires? The Dracula Legend. Transformation — werewolves and the Jekyll-and-Hyde syndrome. Ghosts and spirits. The settings. The atmosphere.

There are usually so many conventional elements attached to most popular genres that naturally you can find other headings you would want to deal with. The criterion should be: do these headings or stages help to build towards successful writing within the genre? Do not dwell too long over each stage and avoid an overly academic approach. There is, however, no harm in making critical points about clichés and the use of stereotypes, especially of a racist or sexist kind. Subvert the genres — they are not sacred — and if pupils want to write parodies, encourage them to do so.

# Personal writing

All writing is creative and perhaps all personal writing is imaginative. These categories — imaginative/creative/personal — overlap and merge; it is important, however, that pupils think that their lives and experiences are significant enough to be the subject of writing in the

English classroom. If you have moved to personal writing after a spell concentrating on fiction-writing, then take the opportunity to deal with skills such as the use of person and point of view. Generally, you would aim to include suggestions for personal writing with imaginative and factual writing, but there is a case for spending a section of class time on personal writing by itself.

Autobiography is the obvious starting-point for personal writing. Start again with snippets of writing. Ask pupils to do a family tree and then ask them to describe the members of their nuclear or extended family. Discuss early childhood with them, using short extracts, and lead into their memories of junior schooldays. Family occasions — weddings, parties, funerals, birthdays, Christmas, births — provide a wealth of material. You must use your discretion about how many models — extracts, films, stories — you use; my advice is not to overload the project with material. After all, the pupils' lives provide rich sources and should promote involved discussion. By all means use external stimuli, especially to underline some writing skill or because some piece is especially evocative. Once you have anchored the writing in the pupils' own experience, bringing the topics you touch on up to where they are in their lives now, you can ask them to deal with more abstract topics such as 'hopes', 'fears', 'happy times/sad times'. Make a collection of the pieces and build them into an autobiographical collection in a separate folder.

Move beyond pupils' own lives to writing about the local area and the people who live there. I have already mentioned the wealth of community writing now emerging in many areas. Pupils are impressed by the novelty of reading pieces by ordinary people, non-professional writers, and these models encourage them to write about aspects of their town or neighbourhood that interest them. Of course, you must also use pupils' immediate interests — music, fashion, popular entertainment, hobbies, spectator sports, collecting, for example — as a springboard for more personal writing.

## Integrating the skills

When you are spending classroom time on fiction and personal writing, you should deal with essential skills at opportune stages, integrating the teaching of these with the writing assignments. Most pupils do not pick up by osmosis the skills of structuring and ordering the content of their writing, whether it be imaginative or factual. The skills I am referring to are not the 'first line' of skills of spelling, punctuation, grammar and sentence construction. Clearly, these skills also have to be taught. But the secondary skills connected with the craft of writing must also be specifically covered. These are some of the skills I mean:

**Checklist**

- planning: drafting and re-drafting
- structuring: paragraphing
- openings
- endings
- use of direct speech
- descriptive detail
- dramatization of incident
- climaxes and 'twists'
- continuity
- precision of style
- structuring
- skeleton plots/storylines
- point of view/standpoint
- use of person
- narrative techniques
- pacing

If these skills are taught specifically to pupils on a class, group or individual basis, arising out of the on-going work of the English classroom, then it is likely that you will receive fewer writing efforts that are slight variations on this kind of story-telling:

> 'He did this and then he did that. After that he went there and then he did another thing. Then he . . .'

How do you choose the times to teach these secondary skills of writing in the classroom? Some opportunities present themselves fairly obviously. If you are trying to get over the importance of openings in story-writing, for example in spies or special agent stories, then the structured stage-by-stage approach I have outlined above will allow you to ask pupils to focus on the need to grab the reader's attention from the first few lines — effective openings, in other words. Start by asking them to think about how they decide to read a book in a library or a bookshop; ask them to do some brief research into the openings of novels and stories of the kind you are dealing with. Then give some examples of types of openings to stories: the melodramatic, the descriptive, the straight narrative, the mysterious, the atmospheric, the bizarre. Pupils will want to experiment with openings and some will pursue story ideas from among these numerous attempts to grab readers' attention from the first few lines.

## Planning

You must communicate to your pupils that good writing, interesting stories or factual pieces, do not generally just happen; they are crafted by a combination of skills, a knowledge of which is accessible to everyone. Some pieces of writing come easily and, as English teachers, you would not want to interfere with the natural creative flow that some pupils experience from time to time. But most interesting writing emerges not from something called inspiration, but from graft and craft. If pupils believe that writing in the English classroom is rewarding enough to spend planning and 'perfecting' time on, then you have been getting your message across to them.

As soon as you can in the secondary school, teach your pupils the necessity of these stages in the writing process:

**Checklist**
- making rough notes
- ordering these notes in sequential or paragraph order
- writing a first draft
- discussion and correction stage
- re-drafting and handing in for assessment

I am not stating categorically that every piece of writing need necessarily go through each one of these stages, but there are probably very few that would not benefit from this planning and drafting process. The discussion and correction stage need not always be with you — pupils should read one another's work and advise how to improve it. As far as exam course work is concerned, it is up to the pupil to decide when he or she has decided to submit a final version for assessment. A teacher should surely help the pupil to present him or herself in the best light, and that involves pupils' correcting and reworking pieces after advice from you, as often as it is possible in large classes.

## Structure

The craft of writing need not be taught in a dry, academic fashion and pupils can actually extract amusement from practising various aspects of fiction-writing. For example, when you are dealing with the structure of stories, you should focus on climaxes or twists. Thinking up unusual twists or exciting climaxes can be stimulating to pupils; it does not really matter at the intial stage how bizarre or unlikely these are, as long as the general point about structure is being taught.

Of course, you have to emphasize negative as well as positive aspects of structure. Point out the dangers of long, irrelevant preambles in short stories, a very common structural error in writing at 16+ examination level.

The soap opera is a very useful genre to employ for the teaching of structure in writing. Soap operas rely on tight plotting to sustain interest in the various storylines that are juggled by the writers from episode to episode. Most pupils will enjoy analysing the storylines of well-known soap operas. How different plots involving resident characters are woven into the overall pattern of the serial, how these stories are developed, resolved and new stories take over while others are kept boiling, will not only intrigue pupils but make valid points about plot and storylines. This kind of analysis also reinforces the concept of 'sense of audience' because what the writers of soap operas are doing is directing their skills towards sustaining interest in several stories appealing to different sections of a mass audience.

# Direct speech and dramatization of incident

Direct speech and dramatization of incident are linked skills. Not all pupils understand the need to dramatize particular incidents in stories, rather than dealing with them in the barest of narrative. Exercises within the framework of genre fiction writing that will show the effectiveness of dramatizing particular incidents, using direct speech, should be attempted. For example, some pupils often explain the 'dénouement' of a detective story through the barest of narratives, rather than by dramatizing this conventional stage of the genre by a mixture of narrative, direct speech and description. The difference, obvious to us as English teachers, is not so clear to many of our pupils:

1 **Bare narrative**:
   The master detective by assembling all the suspects uncovered the truth. The butler had committed the murder. The case was closed.
2 **Dramatization**:
   One by one all the suspects entered the room. They all looked anxious; some even had a furtive air. The master detective welcomed them. 'How good of you all to spare the time,' he began politely. 'I have gathered you . . .'

Too often pupils choose bare narrative, rather than dramatization. Make them think about an intended readership: their peers, the school as a whole, the readership of a particular magazine. Look at the relevant models. Show them graphically how tension must be built and readers' interest sustained.

## Pacing and continuity

Pacing and continuity may seem rather sophisticated concepts for even fourth and fifth year pupils, but they are aspects of planning and structure that can be explained and practised in simple terms. We are all familiar with 'rushed' stories where no breath is taken and there is no variation of pace. There is no harm in using this kind of writing as models to avoid. Pacing a narrative is a fairly subtle technique, but you should be able to get over the point that different types of writing need different pacing. Again use incongruity as the basis for exercises:

— Ask pupils to use a breakneck narrative pace in the description of a quiet peaceful scene.
— Get them to employ a leisurely descriptive technique to describe a cliff-hanging situation.

Varying the pace within a story is an even more subtle technique, but the important thing is that pupils grasp that some details can be covered briefly in a story whilst others need dwelling over. Dramatic improvisation is an excellent method of making this point. You can quickly restructure a scene in improvisation by pointing out the need for more introduction of character and story, the excision of unnecessary detail, the ploys of using dramatic pauses and climaxes, or finding an effective ending. These points can be highlighted in drama and transferred to the craft of writing.

## Factual writing

This is a blanket term for discursive, explanatory, transactional and directed writing. Personal writing is a very important stage in preparing pupils for successful factual writing. Too often pupils are expected to make a sudden jump from informal writing to very formal forms of written communication. The process should be gradual. For example, personal writing assignments should ask pupils to express something of their inner hopes, fears, joys, sadness. In these early secondary years, pupils will have opinions about immediate matters — television programmes, films, sport, the local area — and they should be encouraged to express them freely in a fairly informal way. As they mature, their interests will widen and they will form opinions on wider issues.

When you think the time is ripe, start teaching the skills of discursive writing, showing how opinions about important social issues need a more reflective and formal style than the expression of reactions to more immediate personal experience. Demonstrate how discursive essays must have a clear structure: ask them in their planning to list arguments 'For' and 'Against' a particular belief. It is crucial that audience and register are concepts that are dealt with in this context. Use examples of exaggeratedly bad practice to make the points.

Writing reports based on research involve study and language skills that will play an important part in the school's language across the curriculum policy. Pupils should be taught how to use reference books and books in general — using list of contents, chapter headings, indices, headings and sub-headings. Skimming and extracting essential information should be taught within an integrated, meaningful context, not as isolated skills that have little reference to the work going on in the English classroom. Pupils have to be shown how to take notes when listening to someone giving a talk or when searching for information. Encourage them to create their own system of shorthand.

Writing reports, or, for that matter, giving oral reports, requires structuring skills that must be taught. Some study and reporting skills can be taught in the lower school years, but the more formal skills are best taught from the fourth year on.

**Checklist**
**Structuring a report**:
1 Introduction
  Make clear the subject and aims of the report.
2 Headings
  The report must be divided up into sections with clear headings, and sub-headings if necessary.
3 General points backed by evidence
  General points should be made precisely, with specific examples as evidence.
4 Conclusion
  The report should have a definite conclusion: a recommendation, expression of opinion, a summary of the main points — whatever is appropriate.

The majority of pupils have to be taught to present written reports in a structured manner such as the outline above. Again this skill is not picked up by osmosis.

The tasks on which pupils are asked to give reports must be located in the real world and be relevant to pupils. Here are some possibilities:

● Prepare a report for the careers teacher at your school on the kinds of visits and talks you think would be of interest to your year.

- Your year, or the school as a whole, has organized a fund-raising occasion that was poorly attended and lost money. Investigate why this occurred and make recommendations about how to ensure success for future events.
- A local person has left £100 000 to provide leisure facilities for young people in your area. You have been asked by the local council to prepare a report on behalf of your school about present facilities and to make recommendations about how the £100 000 should best be spent.

Giving oral reports based on notes from research is a necessary prelude to asking students to write reports.

# Letter-writing

Tone and register are obviously crucial concepts in letter-writing. In the lower school you will have given pupils opportunities to write personal letters — to friends, as fans, as readers of comics and magazines. They should have learned how to set out letters properly, but further reinforcement of this will be required when you ask them to write more formal letters. Again, find them real tasks to do, e.g. letters to local newspapers, local councillors and MPs about issues they care about. Include opportunities to write general letters of enquiry to firms and organizations. It can be amusing and instructive to write exaggeratedly inappropriate letters of this type. The structure and paragraphing of letters must also be taught.

Writing instructions giving clear advice about how to go about doing something should also be set in relevant situations. Domestic notes, memos, instructions about how to get somewhere — these strategies I have already mentioned. Here again start with what is familiar to the pupils and build to more complex instructional language:

1 Simple:
  (a) Write a brief note to a member of your family explaining what to do with some food you have prepared for cooking.
  (b) Write a brief note explaining to your parents where you have gone for the evening, how you can be contacted and at what time you will be back.
2 More complex:
  (a) Write a short memo to another member of the school committee reminding him or her about some piece of information or some task that has to be done.
  (b) Draw up a detailed plan for a friend who does not know your

> area at all showing how to get to your house by public transport and walking.

3 Longer pieces:

   (a) Describe in detail how to mend a puncture on your bicycle or how to wire up an electric plug for domestic use.

   (b) You are loaning your music centre/video recorder/stereo or any other piece of electrical equipment to a friend. Write clear instructions to this person about operating and looking after the equipment.

As you build from simple to more complex instructions, you should take the opportunity to deal with matters such as precision of style, relevance and structure.

# The reception of writing

How you as a teacher receive and respond to your pupils' writing is clearly very important. More and more exam syllabuses require course work as the most substantial part of the assessment in English. Most syllabuses demand evidence that pupils have mastered the skills of writing in a variety of modes. I do not apologise for once more stressing the necessity of storing the pupils' work, either in banking files for their finished pieces of work or in separate folders containing work centred round themes, genres or types of writing. The method you use to keep pupils' writing is an integral part of the reception of work.

Get the message over as often as possible that the writing is worth keeping, by nagging about it, by spending classroom time on bringing it up to date and putting it in order, and by supplying either banking files, or the materials with which pupils can make their own covers or folders. Make the losing of pieces of writing a serious matter! Show by your own practice that pupils' writing is valuable and worthy of safe-keeping.

With such a volume of writing coming your way from pupils, especially from the examination classes, it is not always easy either to discuss a piece of writing with individual pupils or to write lengthy comments on the paper. However, as far as is humanly possible, you should attempt to respond in a way that is both encouraging and constructive. I have never been much in favour of receiving a piece of English work in these 'bald' ways:

6/10 or 'Good'

Neither says much, if anything. I do not use marks unless I have to for examination purposes, but if you do, I think it is incumbent on you to add specific comments:

6/10    Shows improvement but read the opening side again. Your *PREAMBLE* is far too long. GET RIGHT INTO YOUR STORY. The twist at the end works well.

or

6/10    Good BUT it does *ramble* a bit. Did you plan it? Use *rough* notes, a *paragraph* plan, write a first *draft* and then *re-draft*. Some of your points were forcefully made.

My advice is that in your comment you should find one main aspect of the writing to concentrate on and something encouraging to say as well.

As far as the actual correction of spelling, grammar, punctuation and sentence construction is concerned, you should try to adapt your response to the needs of the individual pupil. The able pupil who has very few mechanical errors and perhaps needs to think about varying sentence construction or extending vocabulary can be seen individually in class time. The pupil who has a sprinkling of spelling and grammatical errors should have these marked by you and, where specific remedial treatment is appropriate, you should attempt to supply it. The pupil who makes many spelling and other errors presents a difficult choice: should you mark all the errors and risk depressing him or her even further, or do you choose to mark only the worst examples or a section of the writing, with the risk that you seem to be condoning many other errors? Some teachers believe that you should not mark any errors in pupils' work, but I have never agreed with that. There is a real danger of grotesque overcorrecting, however. I favour pinpointing specific problems or words, hoping that the focussing on a few errors at a time will be of more help than a 'blanket' approach.

## Record-keeping

You should keep a record of pupils' strengths and weaknesses in writing. This can be in the form of brief notes in your mark book along with a lesson-to-lesson record of what each pupil has been working on (see page 92).

It is especially important in the teaching of mixed ability groups that you keep a record of pupils' classroom activities and specific needs. It may seem burdensome to keep these kinds of notes but the mixed-ability classroom allows you time to make them because, more often than not, pupils are working on different tasks and you will be seeing individuals and groups of pupils. Pinpoint what each pupil requires to improve the quality of his or her writing. Find the time in class to work on individual problems.

| | 1/5 | 3/5 | 5/5 |
|---|---|---|---|
| Alison | extended writing sp. still weak | ext. writing spell. aid. | making report paragraphing exer. |
| James | sci-fi writing | sent. constr. practice | sci-fi skeleton plots |

## Teachers as writers?

I refer back to the Barbiana letter I quoted at the beginning of this chapter. We should as teachers of English be able to teach the skills of writing to our pupils. I believe all English teachers should write themselves, either sharing the tasks you set for your pupils, or writing in your own time. The act of writing imaginatively will remind you of the sometimes complex skills that are involved in the craft of writing. Setting up time for imaginative writing in the English classroom is not enough by itself. Pupils must be helped by you, with the knowledge you should have acquired, to absorb some of the skills they require to write to their full potential.

## Endpiece

Obviously I have been able to touch on only a few key ideas in this chapter. The key points I want to reiterate are:

**Checklist**
1 Make writing enjoyable for pupils by starting with *their* interests and enthusiasms and building on them.
2 Think of ways of giving pupils' writing *status* in the class and in the school.
3 Teach the *craft* of writing. Good writers are taught, not born — in general.
4 Start with personal/creative writing and gradually introduce the skills required for factual/directed writing.

5 Deal with the specific problems and needs of *individual* pupils.
6 Show by your *reception* of their writing and the care you give it that you consider it important.

Yes, I know *exactly* how difficult it is to do all these things successfully! Teachers teach too many pupils with too few resources in sometimes atrocious conditions. Sometimes it seems an impossible task. However, it *is* important to define our goals. I have tried to keep my suggestions in this chapter practical and feasible; too often guidelines for teachers are quite unrealistic, belonging to an ideal teaching world that exists only in the heads of pedagogues. I hope my ideas and strategies belong to the very real world of the English classroom of the eighties and nineties.

## Recommended reading

*Teaching Writing*, G Thornton, Edward Arnold, 1980
*Writing and the writer*, Frank Smith, Heinemann, 1982
*Working with Language*, Barry Fitzgerald, Heinemann, 1982
*Encouraging Writing*, Robert Protherough, Methuen, 1983
*The Development of Writing Abilities 11–18*, Britton et al, Macmillan, 1975
*Understanding Children Writing*, Burgess et al, Penguin, 1973

Many of the ideas and materials mentioned in this chapter feature in the following classroom textbooks by Don Shiach:

*Framework English, Books 1–3*, Nelson
*Framework Examination English A and B*, Nelson
*Now Write On*, Bell & Hyman

# 5 Managing talking and listening

Dr Melvyn Elphee

Twenty-five years ago, when I began secondary school, talk was definitely out. It had been tolerated in the infant school, gradually reduced in the juniors and finally forbidden in the seniors, where talking was equated with disobedience, indiscipline and potential insurrection.

Then came the seventies and with them the liberation of classroom talking and listening as valid, and indeed essential, educational elements. Progressives turned their backs on teacher talk and chalk, written work was reduced in quantity and significance: the age of pen and ink had been replaced by the era of mouth and (hopefully) ear.

At the same time, more traditional teachers took what they felt to be a 'wise affright' at all this oral activity, and continued to avoid what they saw as the horrors of the noisy classroom in favour of a peaceful — sometimes sleepy — teacher-dominated environment.

Now in the eighties the talk revolution has settled down to something more balanced. Oral work now takes its rightful place within the language curriculum of the school, working in partnership with reading and writing rather than in opposition to them.

This is the ideal, at least, to which the role of talking and listening in the modern classroom aspires. This chapter is directed to those who work towards such an ideal, to those who are still rather scared by or sceptical of the whole notion of classroom talk, and to those who have lost patience and interest in any activities which do *not* involve the twin gods of talking and listening: we all have something to learn from each other.

# Why are talking and listening important?

The first thing to establish, for the reluctant, sceptical, confused or curious, is the sheer importance of talking and listening.

In terms of usage, talking and listening outdistance reading and writing immeasurably. There are perhaps a few overworked professionals (including several English teachers) for whom reading and writing represent almost as important channels of communication as talking and listening — though even *they* will actually *do* more talking and listening than reading and writing. But for the rest of society, talking and listening are matters of everyday activity while reading and writing are reserved, increasingly and to varying degrees, for special occasions.

Apart from the symbol recognition of road signs, product markers and essential instructions, a large number of people never read. Occasionally the tax man or the DHSS forces them through the process — though as often as not the reluctant reader in this situation will seek oral explanation from one of the literary minority. Similarly, the written news now takes second place to broadcast news. As for fiction, this is more likely to be transmitted via TV, cinema or video than through the medium of the printed page — whether English teachers like it or not.

As for writing, its importance for a huge percentage of the population has declined almost to extinction. I asked some of my classes to conduct a survey into the writing habits of their families. The vast majority had not written anything over the last year apart from addresses on greeting card envelopes and their signatures. The most common uses for those who had had to write were various forms and brief memos to members of the family, the milkman or a note covering school absence. Only six per cent had written letters and only two per cent considered writing a significant part of their working or leisure activities.

While not wishing to under-estimate the significance of adequate teaching of reading and writing, I do not think they can vie with talking and listening in sheer terms of practical usage. Having looked at what reading and writing are *not* used for, it remains to examine what speaking and listening *are* used for.

Above all, they are favoured for immediacy of communication. At work, we describe a job verbally as we demonstrate physically — how much more accurate, memorable and convincing than a written pamphlet! Messages are now habitually conveyed by word of mouth, either person to person or by telephone, and though they may be confirmed in writing, it is once again talk that has the advantage of immediacy. How rarely most people *write* their opinions, yet just listen at the local pub to hear how often they 'give' them! And even expressions of emotion, once charmingly couched in ardent love letters or carefully worded sympathetic condolences, are now felt to be sincere only in face to face verbal contact.

Finally, speaking and listening have, for the developing adolescent, certain psychological advantages over reading and writing. Particularly among less able or less mature pupils, 'talking it through' gives confidence, where 'writing it down' results in confusion and a sense of failure to communicate. Having said which, there are almost as many of us — adults and children — who find 'thinking with writing' less embarrassing (because more protected and more within our control) than 'thinking through talk', a fact which has been insufficiently recognized in many a modern classroom where the shy and self-conscious can become as scared of talk as the illiterate is acknowledged to be of writing. Even so, the supreme importance of speaking and listening — even for those who do not like it — cannot be sufficiently emphasized. As the HMI paper *Bullock Revisited* (1982) forcibly puts it:

> The primacy of the spoken word in human intercourse cannot be too strongly emphasized. Important though the written word is, most communication takes place in speech; and those who do not listen with attention and cannot speak with clarity, articulateness and confidence are at a disadvantage in almost every aspect of their personal, social and working lives.
> (*Bullock Revisited*. III.6. p5)

Most teachers now would acknowledge that importance. There remains the fear.

# The fear of talk

This is a condition felt not only by many older teachers, who established themselves in the era before 'talk' was regarded as having a rightful place in the curriculum, but also by many younger teachers who feel pupil talk on a wide scale to represent a threat to the control and order of the classroom. Often such teachers command a high level of pupil respect and conduct their lessons with an integrity and conviction which many a more liberal teacher might envy. The recent tendency of educationalists to regard such teachers as reactionaries can hardly be justified and becomes positively dangerous when the teacher comes to see his or her own achievement in this light. This can have two bad effects: firstly, the teacher becomes demoralized and ceases to value his or her positive achievements; secondly, he or she becomes defensive and firmly entrenched in the 'traditional' position, dismissing all talk of 'talk' as 'new-fangled, trendy nonsense'.

If I confess that I started out as such a teacher, excessively nervous and sceptical of the whole idea of 'oral work', perhaps any comparably doubting Thomases will at least bear with me. So many things about talk have been written by those who have never felt the difficulties: I can at least offer the shared experience of one who was not 'born' to classroom talk, resisted attempts to have it 'thrust' upon me, and finally 'achieved' an orally active classroom without losing sight of discipline or, I hope, integrity.

# How does talk affect the classroom?

Yet classroom talk does have certain implications for relationships within the class. The autocratic rule of the despot teacher is replaced by the consenting participation of the pupils under teacher guidance; the battle between teacher and taught dissolves into a relationship of mutual cooperation. That, at least, is the propaganda of the 'talk' movement and a state of affairs with which many of its proponents are happy. Yet in truth, the introduction of pupil talk does not bring about this egalitarian state unless that is what the teacher specifically requires.

The real implication of pupil talk in the classroom is that the teacher can deploy a far greater variety of teaching/learning techniques. Pupils are capable of considerable flexibility in their relationships: they can accept their teacher as dictator, ally, even servant. The teacher does not have to lose control: he or she retains all the advantages of leadership and authority, and gains the virtues of cooperation. The pupils, meanwhile, come to realize their own potential and value through the medium of talk.

This is easier to achieve in schools which have an ethos of pupil cooperation than in those which depend on a rigid code of externally imposed discipline. In such schools, talk is often seen as an opportunity to challenge the artificially imposed restraints and any teacher who fails to conform to those restraints will be regarded as weak. In such circumstances the strategy has to be:

## Checklist

1 Establish authority in accordance with the pupils' expectation of what a teacher should be.
2 From this position of strength, direct group activities firmly.
3 Gradually allow more responsibility for their own learning to devolve upon the pupils.

The important thing is to resist the natural temptation to rush to 3 without achieving 1 and 2. The pupils will simply regard you as incapable of what *they* regard as your job.

Of course, meaningful talk cannot flourish in a hostile, inhibiting environment, but neither can it in chaos. Pupils respond to leadership and guidance: as long as the teacher gives to oral activities the same significance and attention he or she accords to literacy, the pupils will accept the cooperative role in oral work as readily as they accept the instructing role in other fields: the expository and exploratory modes of teaching are complementary, not mutually exclusive.

# Means and ends

The next point of confusion met in oral work within the classroom is over whether such work is to be seen as a means or an end; whether we are concerned to *use* oral work in the exploration of other topics, or whether the development of good oral expression and understanding is to be seen as an end in itself. The answer, of course, as with most such questions, is that it is both. As with writing, talk is a means, yet in order for that means to be satisfactorily achieved it must receive the kind of attention that makes it — at least for a time — an end in its own right.

The simpler use of talk for the classroom teacher is undoubtedly as a means, a vehicle, that can be used for virtually any subject, both within English studies and across the curriculum. As a means, talk can be used for acquisition of information, interchange of ideas, exploration of feelings and experiences, description of processes, analysis and anecdote. For all these, talk has the advantages over writing of immediacy, involvement, flexibility and social interaction. It also has the disadvantages of inexactitude, embarrassment, submission to peer pressure, tendency to irrelevance and evasion of verbal challenges through non-verbal communication (an aspect of 'language' still neglected). Writing and talking are therefore to be seen as mutually complementary rather than as competing against each other — though there are some classrooms where talk has ousted writing almost as disastrously as the written word once conquered the spoken. Working together, talk and writing can mutually extend the pupil's ability to communicate for a wide variety of purposes and situations. Exploring these skills through one medium will actually reinforce achievement in the other.

So far, all teachers may embrace the concept of classroom talk without unnecessary fear. It is when we come to the consideration of the development of talk skills as an end in their own right that dissent is likely to emerge. On the one hand, 'traditional' teachers, determined to develop literacy, feel themselves threatened by the pressure simultaneously to develop oracy; at the opposite extreme, the 'progressives' see talk as natural, spontaneous and free of the need for conscious development. Both stances seem to me illogical. The teacher who perceives a need to teach literacy, rather than merely encourage it, must surely see a comparable need in the field of oracy. The teacher who sees no need for conscious intervention in the development of either must surely be content with a lower standard of communicative effectiveness than is socially or personally desirable. No, if pupils need to be able to talk they need to be able to talk well, 'with clarity, articulateness and confidence', and though practice makes perfect and much may be achieved by practice (i.e. using talk as a means), less will be achieved than if talk is occasionally made an end in itself.

The performing musician does not learn to play his or her instrument merely by playing music — scales and exercises can save time, energy and frustration in the long-run; athletes improve their sporting facility by conscious exercise of separate muscle groups. In learning to write, it is not enough merely to keep writing (unless we are content to repeat the same inaccuracies and infelicities). So, in developing talk, it is not enough merely to keep talking. Work in techniques of questioning, answering, development and phraseology are as valid here as in the more formal world of writing. The place for such direct development of the skills of talking and listening is within the English lesson, just as this is where pupils must learn the skills of reading and writing.

## Talking across the curriculum

The English department may see its task, then, as developing language skills through direct attention and through meaningful practice. It is also its task to encourage the rest of the school to take up and extend this practice function, since this is where the richest and fullest oral development will take place. Scientific experiments, for example, create an excellent environment for the active use of pupil talk. If the silent English classroom is a crime, the silent laboratory is a sin. Similarly, the subjects of practical skill — Cookery, Woodwork, Art, etc — provide ready and relevant material for the importance not only of talk but of accurate listening. Where pupils themselves can carry out some of the direction, opportunities can be opened up for clarification through questioning and a real context created for the development of a precise vocabulary and an appreciation of conventions. Religious/ Social Education, Humanities, Craft, Design and Technology all seem more aware than the counterparts they have replaced of the need to open up a higher level of pupil participation which will come largely through the medium of exploratory talk, while that most neglected of all academic subjects, Physical Education, provides a ready context for discussion, verbal analysis, criticism and description far beyond the grunts, shouts and yells that accompany the average games session.

It is for English teachers to watch the use of English in all these other subject areas, to support where they see good practice, to encourage where they see willingness, to suggest where they see opportunity, and to take some of these areas into their own classrooms where they see that the pupils' experience is not being given adequate opportunity for linguistic exploration. At the same time, the value of quiet must also be appreciated: many craftspersons use the craft as an escape from the pressures of communication — let them! And there are few things in life as engaging as the quiet of a genuinely involved Art class. God forbid that English teachers should set themselves loose on such things!

Perhaps too, this is the place to mention the enormous contribution that can be made to oral communication by extra-curricular activities. In the first place, the voluntary nature of such activities ensures genuine interest and in such an atmosphere even the quietest pupils develop the self-confidence and self-image which are the very foundation of all oral communication. Any school that regards such activities as *extra*-curricular is dangerously mistaken: they are the very life-blood of the curriculum, and those schools which actually incorporate them in their timetable as 'clubs' or 'free choice' sessions provide a far richer soil for the development of oral communication.

# Techniques and strategies

Effective development of oral work demands that for a large part of their lesson time pupils should work in groups. This ensures the fullest potential participation of all pupils. In a full class the brighter or more extrovert pupils give all the responses or become increasingly impatient if they are not allowed to do so. In group work, the shy or slow pupils learn from the others through observation and imitation. The shyness that inhibits some pupils in a full class disappears in the small group. Within the groups there is space for discussion, disagreement and different points of view and everybody has a chance to talk more often and more fully than they would in a full class.

## 1 Desk arrangement

Children grouped around tables make for easier use of oral work and collaboration in general than classrooms arranged with the desks in rows. But time is needed to check that every pupil can easily see the blackboard or any other required focal point. A viable alternative which many teachers have found successful is a large horseshoe, with or without a central island. Even so, many teachers are forced by other constraints to teach in the conventional pattern of straight rows. In this case a routine is needed for moving of *chairs* (not desks!). Make sure the pupils always sit in sensible clusters for talk — i.e. face to face; and watch out for groupings which place one pupil as an 'outsider'. Try to minimize interference from other groups' discussions by spacing the groups with maximum distance in between. Time spent getting such practical matters right is not wasted.

## 2 Pair work

The 'safest', easiest and most controllable form of group work is undoubtedly pair work. Where classroom conditions are cramped, where the discipline of the class is poor or where the teacher lacks confidence, this may be the only form of group work possible. It has many merits:

(a) Pupils can discuss in depth.
(b) 'Troublemakers' can be spotted easily.
(c) Everyone is actively engaged.
(d) It is readily compatible with reading and writing activities.
(e) Shy pupils soon get over the feeling of threat.
(f) It is easily organized in a conventional desk arrangement.

For these reasons, pair work makes a good start to oral and group work.

On the debit side must be considered the following:

(a) Two pupils can soon decide they have finished — in a larger group, stimulus is more likely to be maintained within the group itself.

(b) 'Unpopular' children — those with whom nobody wants to work — can be mercilessly exposed. A small group seems more capable of absorbing its unwanted members than an individual, afraid of ridicule from the whole class if he or she is seen to accept the 'outsider'.

(c) Classes do not always have even numbers. Therefore at least one pair may become a trio with the result that one pupil often feels unwanted. When this is necessary, ensure that it is not always the same pupils left as a trio.

(d) Four people will produce more than twice as many ideas as two! Larger groups provide more material for each member to react to.

(e) Groups of two are often inhibited by the need to get on with each other. They tend to agree on points, where groups of four are more confident in expressing disagreement. This results in a greater complexity of viewpoint.

(f) Some pupils actually feel greater pressure in a pair, where their individual personalities are unavoidably exposed, than in a larger group, where it is easier for them to hide behind a mask. This can be both advantageous and disadvantageous.

(g) Social development and interaction are limited.

Thus although pair work is valuable and should be used to introduce group work and to continue its development, it should not, ideally, be the class's only form of oral work. The following are some activities where pair work seems particularly appropriate:

(a) Giving instructions to a partner, for example:
   • Drawing an unseen diagram from precise instructions
   • Tracing a route on a map according to oral directions

(b) Discussing controversial points which arise in whole class discussion

(c) Discussion of a reading passage (including poetry)

(d) Inventing questions on a passage or book or film

(e) Responding to a series of fairly rapid questions from the teacher where speed of thought is more important than depth (e.g. factual matters).

Where pupils are not good listeners, pair work can be used to enhance this skill if each pupil has to report back the *other's* ideas or information.

# 3 Small group work

In general, groups of *four* provide the best mix of diversity of opinion and equality of opportunity. Vary the composition of the groups in accordance with the task and its purpose, always remembering that the English teacher is concerned with social as well as linguistic development.

Groups can be made up in the following ways:

## (a) Voluntary combinations
This often leads to lively, genuine discussion but can be disappointing for the pupils as well as the teachers since such groups openly express the often tenuous threads of adolescent relationships. Voluntary groupings are more likely to end up with 'nothing to say' (i.e. they don't want to disagree with their friends) or disruption (since the group forms voluntarily, logic dictates that it can dissolve voluntarily!) There is also the danger that one or two unpopular pupils may be left out. Therefore, save voluntary groupings until the class and teacher are fairly experienced in group work, and a high level of motivation is apparent.

## (b) Ability groups
Here the most able pupils go into one group, 'descending' by degrees to the least able — a kind of streaming within the classroom. Although rather against the tide of contemporary thinking, such groups work well in a wide range of activities from discussion of poetry to planning exercises. Pupils are able to work at their own levels and are released from the pressure of 'looking stupid' or 'sounding big-headed'. Often the 'least able' group will produce the most interesting ideas and thus its members gain a prestige and self-esteem they may not find in written work.
*Warning*: Make sure they are *ability* groups and not *behavioural* groups — this is bound to cause trouble! Also, the fact that the groups are selected for ability need not be made explicit, though the pupils are rarely unaware of it.

## (c) Mixed-ability groups
This is the most popular grouping, even within streamed classes. Ideally, it gives the less able a chance to learn from the more able, while the brightest pupils have to develop the need for precise expression in order to make themselves understood. At their worst, such groups result in the 'bright' pupil doing all the work, revelling in his or her own pre-eminence while the others become increasingly convinced of

their own inferiority and the pointlessness of their utterances. Teacher vigilance and intervention are essential where this occurs.

### (d) Arbitrary groups

Names can be taken from a hat. This is good for a social and intellectual mix and brings together a wide variety of viewpoints and attitudes.

Whatever the type of group chosen, it needs a structure and strategy if it is to function effectively. It is a good idea to get the group to begin by appointing a chairperson. A note-taker and spokesperson can also be appointed. This gives everyone a sense of responsibility which ensures serious attention. Some groups will start by leaving it all to the chairperson or allowing the 'scribe' to opt out of discussion. Generally these problems disappear as the groups get more used to working together and become more self-assured. It is a worthwhile exercise for groups to work out their own code of conduct as their first discussion task.

Here is a typical example from a first year pupil:

1 Respect for the leader
2 Sensible behaviour
3 Ignore clowns
4 Everyone must take part in all work
5 If you do something wrong, own up
6 Everyone should have a fair share in what you are talking about
7 If not paying attention, extra work should be given
8 If not suited in group there should be a chance to change to another group

(David Ashman, aged 12)

Small group work always needs an end in view; otherwise motivation soon fails. Sometimes it can be written — even a formal essay, and this is especially useful for older classes who have not been used to oral work and may be 'exam bound'. It ensures that a serious, productive attitude is taken.

On the other hand, especially with younger classes, care must be taken that every oral encounter is not seen as the pleasant preliminary to an unwelcome written task — rather in the manner of old-fashioned school visits. Sometimes there will be a written outcome, often the oral work will spring from reading and may be developed through writing, but talk is also to be valued for its own sake.

Therefore, the proper end of small group work is often a plenary session for the whole class where ideas or findings are pooled. Again, avoid the tendency for this to be a clichéd pattern: if oral activities always follow the same lines they become predictable and boring. Where plenary sessions are used, their organization can be varied:

(a) Each group can state its ideas through its spokesperson. This can be followed by further group work, evaluating the various responses and another class session to reach conclusions — where appropriate.

(b) Alternatively, one group gives a full report. The others listen, comment and add omissions, express disagreements or develop points more fully. This needs some experience on the part of teacher and pupils as it can descend to a free-for-all.

(c) Each group gives just one point at a time. This ensures that every group has — potentially — an equal say and shortens the required listening span for each group. It is, therefore, a particularly good method with less motivated or noisy groups, or where a specific number of 'points' are being looked for.

(d) Each group is dealing with a different topic. Therefore each group has to report in full and the listening demands on the others are high. This method works best with older, examination classes and proves particularly useful in discussion of literature.

## 4 Class discussion

Currently unfashionable in theory but still widely used in practice, class discussion still has a place in the total language experience of the developing child. At its best it has the advantage of a truly communal activity. Many younger secondary pupils are more eager to 'tell teacher' than to talk to their peers, and the class discussion gives the teacher the opportunity to cross-fertilize enthusiasms, to follow interests and to develop such concepts as relevance. The teacher's ability to re-phrase and develop pupil thought will often sharpen communicative awareness and the teacher's position as a role model leads to the widening of the pupils' vocabularies and the extension of their patterns of phraseology. Such discussion is especially valuable *after* group work, where a plenary session gives a sense of purpose and communal sharing to the preceding activities.

The main objections to class discussion are that relatively few pupils are actively involved and that pupil responses tend to be undeveloped, over-simplified and linguistically unchallenging. These objections contain much truth, but two counter-considerations must be brought to mind: first, the poverty of pupil language tends to come from a barrage of clichéd, predictable teacher questions in which the children are really being asked to guess what the teacher is thinking. Therefore pupils are largely *conditioned* to minimal contributions to class discussion. The teacher should avoid this by asking open-ended questions. Genuine thinking is provoked when the teacher poses a genuine problem, one to which he or she does not have a pre-conceived answer.

Secondly, the familiar diagram of the non-participating pupil in class discussion is misleading:

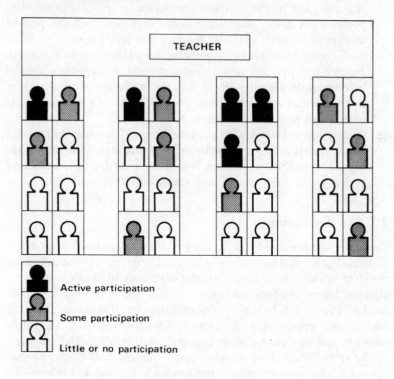

This diagram does not take account of 'internal verbalization': in a good class discussion this can be considerable and those not actually talking are still active in a mental sense which ought not to be under-valued.

The most realistic objection to class discussion is simply a practical matter, for it is one of the most difficult techniques for a teacher to manage. It puts the teacher in the spotlight and makes considerable demands on mental alertness and agility. Pupils easily become bored or frustrated. A 'hands-up' procedure can lead to stiltedness and frustration; a 'calling out' spontaneity eventually produces chaos.

Yet class discussion can be among the most rewarding aspects of the day for both class and teacher. The occasions when it is most likely to work can be categorized as follows:

1 When the *class* is sufficiently involved in a topic to *initiate* the discussion;
2 When it is a logical outcome to work already read, written or talked about in smaller groups. It is quite easy to move from discussion to pair work and back without any break in continuity. This ensures increased pupil participation and lessens teacher centrality effectively.
3 When it is connected with a text which can re-focus attention if concentration begins to wander or interest to flag.

Class discussion is least successful when it is obviously teacher-initiated as an end in itself and has no discernible framework. The teacher sees it as a 'discussion lesson', but the pupils see it as a way of 'not doing any work'.

## 5 The debate and the short talk

The Bullock report is rather dismissive of debates — at one time the only form of 'talk' considered allowable in class:

> A good deal of the oral work we saw in schools suffered from a lack of contact with reality in the sense that it did not carry this conviction of real purpose. Its air of contrivance was apparent to the children themselves, and since their language was answering to no real need beyond that of an elaborate exercise, it has an artificial restraint about it. This was particularly true of the weekly period devoted to lecturettes, 'formal' debates, and mock interviews.
> (*A Language for Life*)

My own experience has been that debates are immensely enjoyed by the pupils. They focus attention and concern in a way that few other activities do, involve everybody in the class, bring about painstaking research and develop a care for effective spoken expression. The divergence of opinion encountered promotes careful listening and sharpens critical and analytical faculties. The exercise can be extended through small group oral work and linked to written work of varying kinds. Any activity which does so much gets my support!

Similarly, the short talk came in for some sharp comments in the Bullock report, though the criticism was less for the medium itself than for its frequently poor management and de-contextualization.

Again, the short talk can be a valuable medium for language development, even when in no particular context other than imparting information, experience or entertainment to the class. What it does need is time for preparation: very few of us could prepare a talk at the start of the lesson and deliver it later in the same lesson, yet teachers (and text books) have been known to ask for such feats of virtuosity!

As long as pupils are talking about something in which they have a genuine interest, most pupils can surprise themselves by their own performance. Even so, the chief drawback of the short talk is that it may remain uninteresting for the rest of the class (one wonders how many of Billy Casper's patient classmates in *Kes* would really have been at all interested in his long talk). Nevertheless, the short talk has its place, though form time (tutorial periods) can often give it a more valid setting than the usual English lesson.

# 6 Potential problems

No matter what form of group organization for oral work you come up with, problems arise.

**Problem (a)**
Pupils don't discuss what they're supposed to, but talk about something else.
**Action**: Don't over-react. Guide them firmly on to the subject through questions, by going round to the various groups. Reward good group feed-back and show disapproval where groups have wasted time. As oral work becomes an accepted feature of the classwork, pupils take it more seriously. A written outcome may be needed until this is established.
**Problem (b)**
Pupils start squabbling/fighting.
**Action**: Deal with this as you would in a full class. It may be necessary to withdraw some pupils from the discussion until they realize they are missing out on something enjoyable. Fortunately, nearly all pupils enjoy oral work.
**Problem (c)**
Silence. Some groups may be very inhibited at first.
**Action**: A few questions from the teacher will usually break this down. Occasionally, re-shuffling of groups may be necessary.
**Problem (d)**
Laziness. Some groups decide to let the other groups do the work.

**Action**: The demand of a written report from such a group usually cures the problem.

**Problem (e)**

Facetiousness.

**Action**: Treat as for a full class, i.e. ignore, crush or ride good-humouredly. The more the teacher makes of it, the more facetious the pupil becomes. Don't over-react.

**Problem (f)**

Wordiness. You are lucky if this is your problem, but it needs tackling nevertheless.

**Action**: Asking for the 'three main points' of a group's discussion will focus expression and provide relevant training in summary. But don't *always* ask for limited summaries: the pupils will just stop talking.

**Problem (g)**

Difficulties with note-taking. This is not usually a problem with intelligent or mixed-ability groups where someone can write fast, but presents problems with younger and less able groups. For them, the difficulty of writing down even simple notes can inhibit discussion and slow things down to a catastrophic degree. Fortunately, these pupils often have good oral recall and can report their discussions without recourse to notes.

**Action**: In general it is better for them to report back without notes than to reduce the fluency of their discussion by nerve-wracking note-taking.

# Registers of language

It is important that pupils' language experience should not be confined to a single register. There are various systems of classification for the registers of the language, but a good working list is:

> the frozen
> the formal
> the consultative
> the casual
> the intimate

Since the 'intimate' register is confined to our nearest and dearest and the 'frozen' is limited to remote public occasions, these may be effectively reduced to three for classroom purposes (though contact with the others should remain through literature and role play).

Ultimately, the most important register is the *consultative* — the mode for inquiry, information and discussion — but the consultative language available is affected by the nature of its *casual* basis (which may vary widely according to social and educational background) and the degree of contact with *formal* language. Since the casual register of language is used widely outside the classroom, the classroom needs to develop formal uses of language if an enriched and effective consultative style is eventually to be achieved. Pupils who use only one register — the casual — for all purposes are ultimately personally and socially disadvantaged. Yet too much of what passes for 'oral work' in today's classrooms is merely 'casual talk'.

To realize this is not to attempt to crush or eliminate that register — much exploratory talk will necessarily be first produced as casual language. But the skilled teacher must elicit a flexibility between the registers so that thoughts which emerge casually may be discussed consultatively and finally formulated formally. One important way of achieving this awareness of registers is through the teacher's own talk.

## Teacher talk and teacher listening

The teacher remains a powerful influence on pupil talk. His or her utterances have a special kind of validity for most pupils. Perhaps the greatest problem facing a teacher in talking to pupils is that of level of expression or register. One school of thought inclined to the view that the teacher should use his or her own language, complete with the vocabulary and sentence structure of an adult intellectual. The assumption was that pupils would have to 'rise' above their own language to that of the teacher in order to achieve comprehension and so vocabulary, syntax and phraseology would be 'up-graded'. In practice, such teachers often exaggerated the academic remoteness of their phraseology with the result that pupils regarded them as merely eccentric and unworthy of comprehension. The old grammar schools typified this approach and many esteemed institutions still do.

The more modern school of thought inclines to the view that teachers must talk with pupils on their own level, getting down to 'where they're at'. This involves the rejection of complex vocabulary (getting rid of big words), a consequent reduction of thought (the teacher can only say what the pupils already understand) and the importation of vogue phrases in order to demonstrate the equality and indivisibility of teacher and taught.

Modern society requires the pupils to be able to operate within a wide range of registers. The same is true for the teacher. The two approaches described above ought not to be mutually exclusive, but part of our response to different situations. There are occasions when we need to be able to talk with the pupils at their own casual level without the annoyance (to them) of alien language, but there are also occasions when they must become aware of more 'formal' registers and the vocabulary appropriate to them. If pupil talk is crucial to the development of casual and consultative language, teacher talk must develop the awareness of formal and even frozen registers, which in turn will enrich the important consultative area.

Teachers who are perpetually casual impoverish child language as surely as those who are perpetually formal restrict it. Both approaches are ultimately socially divisive. The best teachers of language (in any subject) are those who demonstrate through usage its infinite flexibility in a variety of registers and thereby encourage their pupils to develop the same range and control.

Significantly, most of this section has been concerned with teacher talk. How typical of a teacher to neglect his role as a listener! How often we complain that our pupils *won't listen*. Yet at the same time how often we bulldoze over their utterances in a desire to express ourselves. There are no easy steps to developing pupils' listening skills, but there will certainly be none at all unless the teacher shows a genuine willingness to listen to the pupils. Of course this needs strategies just as group discussion among pupils does, but *teacher listening* has to be as consciously incorporated in the lesson as teacher talk. This requires certain classroom conventions: a teacher does not have to listen to ten pupils shouting out simultaneously! There must be understood agreements between class and teacher on appropriate ways and times for the pupil to talk to the teacher.

The following are suggestions from my own experience. Like all rules, a time comes when they are best broken:

## Checklist

(a) No calling out
(b) Pupils to raise hands before they talk to the teacher
(c) No questions at the *start* of the lesson
(d) Hands down while any other pupil is being attended to
(e) Points relating only to the individual (e.g. 'I haven't got a pen') should not be asked in the whole class situation but must wait until individual work is underway.

But whatever strategies are adopted, once the teacher has agreed to listen he or she must do so.

## 'Alien' talk

With the present emphasis on classroom talk there is a danger that pupils — especially those in homogenous groups — may come to see *their* language as *the* language. Classroom talk can thus lead to a narrowing of conceptions and a smug sense of self-sufficiency. It is important, therefore, that some balance is given to this by encounter with and examination of the speech of other races, regions and social backgrounds. Multi-racial schools have an obvious advantage here. Mixed-ability classrooms also tend to widen the social range of language.

Where there are 'language gaps', video and sound recordings involving 'alien' talk should be encountered and discussed. Care must be taken to avoid the sense that the pupil's own language is 'normal' and everyone else's is 'weird'; language experience should foster the sense in which the pupil's own language is but one of many 'dialects' in the broadest sense.

# Resources

1 Portable cassette players
These are cheap, need to be available in large numbers — sometimes as many as eight to a class — and readily available.

Their principle uses are:
(a) Focusing attention in group work/discussion
(b) Interviews and surveys with pupils, parents, members of the public
(c) Creating a 'radio' programme
(d) Listening materials
2 A mains cassette machine of higher power
The modern pupil is used to a good standard of sound reproduction at home and any materials used with a whole class should at least be clearly audible. There are few sounds more insulting than a tiny portable cassette player at full volume attempting to broadcast a group's discussion or radio magazine.
3 Video camera
Most of the activities involving oral work can be video taped with an increase in motivation and interest — especially with older pupils.

**4** Books

Many of the most recent course text-books are sensitive to the real needs of classes in connection with oral work. Particularly recommended are:

*Oxford Secondary English* (OUP), Seely, John
*Your Language* (Macmillan), Healy, Maura
*Words in Action* (Macmillan), Foster, John
*Working with Language* (Heinemann Educational), Fitzgerald, Barry

Nevertheless, the best oral work is done without text-books and it is the teacher, rather than the pupils, who needs book resources.

Four which I have found extremely useful and would recommend as a central core to any teacher's resources for oral work are:

**(a)** Bullock: *A Language for Life* (HMSO)

This Bible of modern language teaching deals with the following aspects of oral work:

**(i)** Exploratory talk as a learning process
**(ii)** Acceptance of accent
**(iii)** Variety of registers
**(iv)** Role of teacher speech
**(v)** Teacher's role of planned intervention
**(vi)** Use of large and small groups
**(vii)** Flexibility in discussion
**(viii)** Development of listening ability
**(ix)** Need for audio-visual aids
**(x)** Role of oral exams
**(xi)** Need for teacher training in dealing with oracy
**(xii)** Need for further research
**(xiii)** Role of drama

The teacher interested in any of these should begin his or her investigations with the Bullock report's succinct, apposite paragraphs, though at the same time Mr Stuart Froome's note of dissent (pp 556–559) also repays attention, particularly his contention that the report placed 'undue emphasis upon talking as a means of learning language'.

**(b)** *Active Tutorial Work* (Blackwell)

Widely known as the Lancashire Project, this consists of five books aimed at developing effective pastoral work in secondary schools with an emphasis on personal relationships. Since this is an area of central concern to English teaching, there is considerable overlap with our work, particularly in the oral area. In schools which are following the project, 'English' effectively has an extra allocation of time and the astute English teacher will find many areas of concern and interest to carry over into the timetabled English lesson.

Where the school has not adopted the scheme, the English teacher will find the Lancashire project a valuable resource unit with its emphasis on pair work, small group discussion, action research, role play and use of visitors — all crucial in developing oral language fully and actively. It is not necessary to follow the project through in systematic steps and some of the sections lend themselves more relevantly to English teaching than others, but in the First Year book alone there is good material on School Rules, Homework, Punishment, Bullying, Putting yourself in someone else's place, How different people behave, Leisure, Friendship, all of which can be enriched by appropriate use of literature, especially poetry, and provide authentic activities for pupils to explore their thinking through their own language.

(c) *Language in Use* by Peter Doughty et al (Edward Arnold)
This loose-leaf book, first published as long ago as 1971, was at the fore-front of the pioneering move towards pupil-centred language. Its stated aim is that 'the pupil . . . can explore, in terms of his own experience . . . his mastery of language. The mastery of language . . . is not simply the ability to say what one means; rather, it is the ability to mean'. It consists of 110 Units, each of which provides an outline for a sequence of lessons, all concerned with the extension of linguistic competence. Above all, *Language in Use* emphasizes — because it does not artificially divide — the links between linguistic and social matters and reinforces the connections between talking and writing. It is thus a compendium of some of the best practice in English teaching. Yet while it provides a framework for class and teacher, there is no straight-jacket: flexibility without chaos is the key-note, and use of the units invariably leads to lively, purposeful classroom work with all fully involved.

(d) *100+ Ideas for Drama* by Anna Scher and Charles Verall (Heinemann)
This is perhaps *the* most useful tool for classes who are inhibited with regard to oral work or disenchanted with school in general. The whole book is one of proven excellence, firmly based on practical experience, but the section on The Spoken Word (Chapter 2) is particularly useful, as it can be used in *any*

classroom without any special resources — other than the pupils themselves. Here are a wide range of attractive activities (Speak Easy, Opposites, Interviews, etc.) and a long list of subjects which stimulate talk. For even less orally inclined classes, the 'Mental Games' (pp 24–27) are an excellent way in. I have yet to meet a class incapable of responding to Word Tennis and this can be the key to more advanced oral work.

# Talking and listening versus reading and writing

To develop listening and talking skills in the classroom is a more elusive, more difficult, less definable task than the development of reading and writing. Brave indeed is the teacher who takes on the challenge, understandable the nostalgia for the past when such areas were avoided or evaded. But there remains for many teachers the feeling of tension between literacy and oracy. Some seek to preserve literacy against what they see as its illegitimate offspring. Others embrace the cause of oracy to the neglect of literacy.

The English teacher's task is to balance the two, and that task will be achieved more easily if we can see oracy and literacy as working together rather than in opposition. Listening and speaking practice clearly and demonstrably enhance writing performance. That much is acknowledged to the point of cliché. But reading and writing also contribute to the development of speaking and listening, and that is an aspect which has been under-stressed. Wide reading gives to the pupil a range of thought, expression and understanding that exploratory talk alone can never achieve; 'thinking through writing' gives order and shape to chaotic, haphazard ideas, which in turn becomes transferred to the spoken medium.

The recent neglect of the contribution of effective literacy towards effective oracy has led to an under-emphasis of another important element in language development: internal speech. Just as we need to express ideas in order to find them, so, as we increase in ability, confidence and maturity, we develop the ability to internalize such thought. A classroom with thirty silent pupils may in fact have as much language generation for each pupil as one where the class is obviously and actively engaged in oral work. It has been a grotesque over-simplification to imagine that *talking* is the only way of developing *talk*: internal monologue has an important part to play and the more complex, mature and difficult the thought processes become, the more essential is this need for *silent* talk.

The Bullock Report recommended that teachers should have 'an explicit understanding of the processes at work in classroom discourse' and 'the ability . . . of extending it' (pp 526/7). What is now needed is further research into the effects of reading and writing on spoken English and the connection between internal and external expression. And when such research is carried out, its findings need to be absorbed into the work of the classroom teacher.

Meanwhile it is not a case of the oral baby and the literary bath water but of a single, whole human being whose need is not for the development of speaking, listening, reading and writing as distinct entities, but of *language* as a whole and indivisible concept.

# Assessment

I have demonstrated the necessity for effective oral communication and some of the ways in which it can be developed in the classroom. There remains the problem of assessment. Not to assess oral English implies a lower status than that accorded to written English. Yet our current procedures for such an assessment remain unsatisfactory.

The Assessment of Performance Unit's *1982 Primary Survey of Language Performance in Schools* includes such tasks as:

- learning how to play a simple board game and then instructing another pupil
- listening to a story and re-telling it
- arguing a point of view in a discussion
- following instructions to make a model
- answering questions on material that has been listened to on tape
- giving an account of a past experience
- describing pictures to a listener
- putting pictures in order to make a story
- listening to an account of a process with reference to diagrams and then telling others about it.

By 1983 some of these were replaced by:

- group discussion and collaboration on a problem-solving task
- extracting and summarizing information to present a case for or against a particular decision
- a science-based task which required pupils to instruct partners in how to carry out a simple experiment, observe the results and hypothesize about the effects they saw.

All of these make excellent and worthwhile classroom activities, but how does one assess them? Even the National Foundation for Educational Research who conducted the research for APU surveys state that 'In order to adopt the techniques developed for application by teachers or for use in national examinations at secondary level further developments would be necessary . . . The more closely we look at pupils' spoken language abilities, the more we realize how complex and subtle the business of communicating is.'

It would therefore be something of a fool who would rush in to assess where even experts tread with caution.

# Endpiece

At this stage in our understanding of oral communication, the classroom teacher is more properly concerned with its development than its assessment. Haphazard grading of oral work, whether formally through grades or marks, or informally through negative comment, may do irreparable damage to a pupil's confidence, which in turn undermines his or her capacity for development of clarity and articulateness. We do not become more beautiful by being told we are ugly, and we do not become more effective as oral communicators by being told how ineffectual we are. In this area of English, even more than the others, success breeds success and a positive assessment is the only possible path to development and enhancement.

# Recommended reading

*Language in Use*, Doughty, Pearce, Thornton, Edward Arnold, 1971
*Working with Language*, Barry Fitzgerald, Heinemann, 1982
*From Communication to Curriculum*, Douglas Barnes, Penguin, 1976
*Understanding Children Talking*, Martin, Medway *et al.*, Penguin, 1976
*They Don't Speak Our Language*, edited by Sinclair Rogers, Edward Arnold, 1976
*Uttering, Muttering*, Edited by Clem Adelman, Grant McIntyre, 1981
APU: *1982 Primary Survey of Language Performance in Schools*, HMSO
*100+ Ideas for Drama*, Anna Scher and Charles Verrall, Heinemann, 1975
*CORT Thinking*, Edward do Bono, Direct Education Services
*Talk: A practical guide to oral work in the secondary school*, David Self, Ward Lock, 1976
*Encouraging Talk*, Lewis Knowles, Methuen, 1983
*Checkbooks: Oral Work*, Roy Blatchford and Melvyn Elphee, Hutchinson, 1986

# 6 Making comprehension interesting

Bill Deller

## Everybody likes it

Comprehension is popular with everyone. Examiners like it because it seems to offer them an objective measure for testing reading progress. Heads in general welcome it because it encourages silence and gives the appearance of 'hard work'. It is popular in the classroom because it keeps the children's heads down and allows hard-pressed teachers a rest from the fray, its only drawback being its appalling tendency to produce marking. (Luckily multiple choice provides a way out of even this disadvantage.) Publishers are happy since 'comprehension' exercises form a major part of profit-making English text books. Even the pupils themselves accept it as a necessary ritual not only in English but in many other subjects as well. The question is — if everybody likes it, what objection is there to doing what we've always done?

## What's wrong with traditional comprehension?

Let's be clear about what we mean by 'traditional comprehension'; typically it is a passage of writing — usually prose — followed by questions which seek to test the reader's understanding of it. In English lessons the passage will most commonly be fiction, quite short (about five hundred words on average) and almost certainly an extract of some kind. The questions will range from the factual (Who did what when?) through inferential (Why do you think X did so and so?) to evaluative questions (Was X right to do so and so?). Usually the emphasis of the questions will be on the factual side, or will require the picking out of words or phrases from the extract and reformulating them in order to answer the questions. The answers will generally be written in complete sentences.

There are a number of problems with this method, but the fundamental one is that the activity just described does not correspond very closely with what good readers do when they read a text. There are a number of reasons for this:

1 In 'comprehension' exercises the reader is seen as passive, reading to answer someone else's (usually the teacher's) questions.
2 The passage itself is often of little intrinsic worth; that is, nobody would read it except to answer the questions which follow.
3 It is possible to answer many of the questions by referring to single words or phrases of the original without understanding the passage as a whole.
4 It places the reader in a test situation. The aim is to locate 'correct' answers to be rewarded by a tick.
5 The passage plus questions is used so frequently in many different subjects that it becomes a habit not connected in the pupils' minds with 'real' reading.

By way of contrast a mature reader goes about things very differently.

# What good readers do

Mature readers (like you as you are reading this!) engage in the following activities:

1 They actively interrogate the text to seek the meaning in the writer's mind.
2 They compare what the writer is saying with their own experience both of life and of language.
3 They adjust their reading approach in accordance with the purpose for which they are reading (e.g. skipping dull bits in a novel or closely reading word by word the insurance policy after the bath has overflowed).
4 They delay 'the put-down moment' and can tolerate a high degree of incomprehension while they are searching out the meaning.
5 They adjust and revise their views in the light of what they read.

Good reading is much more a matter of the brain than the eye. It is not unlike talking to someone — a rapid flickering between what the other person is saying and our own thoughts. We cannot therefore teach reading by mechanistic sets of exercises; we can only teach reading by reading, by having as wide and varied experience of the activity as possible.

# Reading for pleasure

If what I say is true, it follows that the first priority for any teacher of English is to encourage as much reading for pleasure as can be arranged. Nowadays children have innumerable claims on their attention, so books must be vigorously 'sold' to them. It is no good just feebly admonishing them to go to the library; we must make concerted, continual, efforts to imbue them with the reading habit. Nobody will improve his or her reading beyond a certain point unless there has been recent experience of the pleasure to be gained from the activity. It is essential to have good books available in the classroom; the teacher must talk enthusiastically about books he or she has read, and encourage children to do likewise. A book shop is essential as is a regular time in English lessons for individual reading. More than any exercise, however trendy or superficially attractive, it is regular, pleasurable reading, unaccompanied by writing demands, that will improve children's reading comprehension.

# Where do we go from there?

Assuming your school has a working method of ensuring that as many children as possible are reading as much as possible, what does the teacher of English do next? Before I try to answer that question with practical ideas for the classroom, a few points of principle must be understood:

1  Reading is a unitary ability — that is, it cannot be broken down into a hierarchy of separate sub-skills which can be individually exercised and tested. (In other words it is no good teaching children to, for example, skim quickly through a text to pick up the gist, and then go on to teach the skill of scanning a text for specific information as if the two activities were totally distinct from each other.)

2  Confidence and flexibility of reading is best nurtured when children are given the opportunity to *talk* about a text in pairs or small groups. This allows for tentative suggestions, the expression of puzzlement, confusion or disagreement, the sort of exploratory talk which is not often possible in large groups or when working in isolation from others.

3  As comprehension activities will be only a small part of the
   children's reading in English, the passages chosen for such
   activities must be worth reading, as far as possible complete in
   themselves and not mere lifeless extracts. My own view is that the
   bulk of such passages should be literary in nature because it is
   literature that demands the subtlest and most sensitive kinds of
   reading. Too many comprehension books these days seem to
   consist of endless memos, forms and encyclopedia extracts, but it
   seems to me that if you can read a poem adequately you are in a
   good position to cope successfully with the reading demands of
   'real life'.

# Eight ideas for starters

We are now faced with a class of children. We hope that they are
reading for pleasure and that our discipline is sound enough to
venture a little way from the routine passage-plus-questions, worked
on by pupils in isolation from one another. Let us imagine that they are
in the first or second year of the secondary school. How do we go
about increasing their confidence and their capacity to read maturely?
The first thing is to build confidence by demonstrating how good they
already are at decoding a text. This can be done in several ways:

1  Take a passage and 'doctor' it so that there are an increasing number
   of mistakes in it. These mistakes can be in spelling, word order or
   meaning. Such a doctored passage might look like this:

> 'It is wonderful how quikly wee are able to rede. Ur eyes wizz
> the over paeg and our brians pik up the meening even iff al the
> wrds ar up mixd and the spelings are rong. It show wat brllant
> thingis our brians are . . .'

The majority of children will be able to read this quite easily,
particularly in a group, and the point that should be constantly
driven home to them is how marvellous the reading process is and
how adept they are at converting little marks on the page to
meanings in the head, even if obstacles are put in the way.

2  Another way of demonstrating the brain's capacity to extract
   meaning from print is to leave gaps in a text (cloze procedure).
   There are various ways of doing this; a starting point, particularly
   with less confident readers is to leave out words for which there are
   a limited number of possible 'fillers'. Such a passage might read:

> 'I will not put _____ with all this noise,' shouted Mrs Brown angrily. 'Sit _____ and get _____ with your work. Immediately the class went very _____ and the children sat up _____ in their seats. 'That's _____,' said Mrs _____.' I do like _____ children.'

If you do this sort of exercise in pairs and then report back to the whole class it is possible to discuss which suggestions fit best in the blank spaces. Again the point to stress is how creative yet accurate is the reader's brain.

3 A third starting game is to arrange sentences to read right to left instead of left to right and then invite the children to read them. Here are five examples:

> **(a)** nosrep revelc yrev a ma I kniht I.
> **(b)** seye neerg dna liat yrruf a sah tac ruO.
> **(c)** etal emoh evirra I fi yrgna steg mum yM.
> **(d)** .EP dna yhpargoeg era stcejbus etiruovaf yM.
> **(e)** gninrom yadrutaS yreve noisivelet eht hctaw I.

Children find it quite fun to try this and the interesting thing is that some poorer readers are able to succeed as quickly as better readers. I suspect it may be because poor readers read slowly almost letter by letter, so starting from the right doesn't handicap them as much as it does more fluent readers. For all the children the point of the exercise is to show them how used their brains are to the left–right pattern (after all many world languages do read right to left) and yet how quickly they can adapt to a strange system. Some children even become quite good at writing right to left sentences of their own. Another variant of this game is to arrange sentences up and down the page as in the following poem. Again it's a popular activity to get the pupils to make their own top to bottom poems (see example on page 123).

4 A fourth game is to rewrite a passage, missing out all the vowels so that it looks like this:

> Mrs Cod bgn t wlk wy. Hr thn lps wr st n sml. Helen rn ftr hr. 'D y knw nythng bt Ldy Jane?' sh skd. 'Cn y tll m bt hr?' Helen wntd t hr mr bt Mrs Cod snppd hr lps sht. Myb sh wsn't n th md fr chttng . . .

**Rain**

| | |
|---|---|
| wh | w |
| en | e |
| t | ar |
| he | e |
| r | in |
| ai | cl |
| n | in |
| is | ed |
| f | t |
| al | o |
| li | fo |
| ng | rg |
| i | et |
| n | w |
| lo | ha |
| ng | t |
| c | a |
| ol | mi |
| um | ra |
| ns | cl |
| | e |
| | it |
| | i |
| | s. |

*Top to bottom poem*

This can be fairly hard to read so it is advisable to choose an easy passage, at least until they get used to it. The underlying point is similar to the other games — to give youngsters confidence in the brain's power to puzzle out meaning.

5 Word search games can be an aid to reading confidence and working together in groups. In this idea a subject is chosen — first names or football teams for example — and the names are disguised in amongst random letters on a grid of squared paper. The readers have to pick out as many of the hidden words as they can. At first, or with less confident readers, it may only be possible to devise word searches where the hidden words can all be found by reading left to right on a single line but there is no end to the complications you can build in. Hidden words can be read up and down, diagonally across the squares, even backwards. Here is an example produced by a pupil.

## NAMES WORDSEARCH

## HOW MANY OF THESE NAMES CAN YOU FIND?

| | | | | |
|---|---|---|---|---|
| ANNE | TRACEY | JUSTINE | WENDY | NATASHA |
| NICOLA | JENNIFER | MARCIA | KAREN | CHRISTINA |
| LISA | MICHELLE | FIONA | ANDREA | VICKI |
| DIANNE | ZOE | SHARON | JULIE | JACKIE |

| O | C | M | P | I | O | T | O | P | H | E | R | M | O | Y | T | E | R | R | Y |
|---|---|---|---|---|---|---|---|---|---|---|---|---|---|---|---|---|---|---|---|
| R | N | R | Q | M | P | I | C | J | G | W | Z | A | F | X | Q | S | E | A | N |
| A | L | A | N | X | Q | C | M | R | I | S | T | R | K | R | R | I | M | A | J |
| H | T | O | L | R | R | B | R | S | F | T | U | C | D | Z | E | A | A | W | U |
| A | P | M | O | M | N | C | I | M | V | E | V | I | I | D | R | J | J | I | L |
| M | I | C | H | A | E | L | S | D | C | W | L | A | V | K | K | K | U | K | I |
| J | I | F | Q | B | H | G | T | Y | E | A | S | K | A | R | O | N | S | J | E |
| E | S | C | V | I | C | K | I | U | T | R | L | Y | D | Y | K | Z | T | G | N |
| N | P | V | K | P | H | U | N | G | A | T | O | I | F | J | W | K | I | H | S |
| N | E | B | Y | E | R | Q | A | B | L | J | A | C | K | I | E | A | N | G | I |
| I | T | W | L | A | L | J | U | N | I | O | R | X | V | X | H | J | E | B | M |
| F | E | R | L | X | G | L | K | U | Z | M | S | A | E | S | T | F | S | U | O |
| E | R | F | I | C | P | S | E | M | D | C | L | Q | A | R | T | T | R | E | N |
| R | O | E | B | D | N | N | R | L | B | O | C | T | D | V | J | V | K | S | C |
| C | H | A | R | L | E | S | E | Z | C | A | A | D | M | W | P | A | U | L | E |
| F | A | I | U | K | R | E | D | I | O | N | N | E | E | L | I | E | C | D | W |
| I | S | O | N | F | A | N | N | E | A | B | J | C | I | X | G | R | O | F | E |
| G | I | P | O | P | K | G | H | W | Z | O | E | B | L | Y | K | D | Q | D | N |
| H | L | E | O | R | I | I | J | G | W | H | M | L | U | A | Z | N | Y | V | D |
| A | N | D | R | E | W | F | J | O | H | N | M | H | J | T | R | A | C | E | Y |

| | | | | |
|---|---|---|---|---|
| ANDREW | ALAN | JULIAN | CHARLES | TERRY |
| JAMIE | SIMON | MARK | BRUNO | PETER |
| GRAHAM | DEREK | DAVID | JUNIOR | BILLY |
| MICHAEL | PAUL | JOHN | SEAN | STEWART |

The word search highlights the reader's ability to scan jumbles of letters in order to find meaningful sequences. It is also fun to do. Crosswords are another interesting variation.

6 To show that reading is a 'real' activity, that we do it all the time often without thinking, and also that the reader can spot the context of a piece of writing from only a very few clues, it is useful to make a collection of writing seen in the course of a single day or even in the course of a single journey. Here is a sample collection made in and around school:

---

(a) NO SMOKING ALLOWED
(b) This must be the offer of the year — unrepeatable prices.
(c) Unions Reject Government Plan
(d) Unusual events are to be expected tomorrow as Mars, your birth sign, is approaching Venus.
(e) John needs to concentrate much harder if he is to improve his spelling and punctuation.
(f) Inter City Savers are incredibly low. 2nd Class fares available daily on selected trains from London to hundreds of destinations.
(g) In case of emergency press the red button and wait until the machine stops.
(h) All visitors should report to the office (ARROW)
(i) Coleman Street no. 4–16 even.
(j) Answer question 1 from Section A and three other questions. You have 1½ hours to complete the paper.

---

The pupils are then asked what each piece of writing is about, where it might be found and who it was meant for. They can then make similar collections of their own to try out on other groups.

7 A more sophisticated exercise of a similar kind is to collect short extracts from different kinds of books and get the children to guess the type of book the extract is taken from and what it might be about.

Some may be non-fiction, e.g.

---

Stir in the milk, add the salt, pepper and grated cheese. Bring slowly to the boil, taking care to avoid the mixture sticking to the pan.

---

or

125

> To remove the needle valve first unscrew the four bolts which
> secure the float chamber cover. Detach the float itself, taking care
> not to damage it as you do so.

Others may be obviously aimed at a particular type of reader,
e.g.

> Now when the King heard that no one was to be found in all the
> kingdom who could solve the secret of the magic clock, he was
> so angry that he decreed that all his courtiers should wear black.

Yet others may be from a recognizable type of fiction, e.g.

> Nobody noticed the thin shabby man who climbed slowly up the
> three flights of rickety stairs to the top floor of number 37
> Avenue des Foches. People were too busy arranging the long
> strings of coloured flags that would greet the President as he
> drove by later on that day.

or

> Quite suddenly Karen noticed somebody gazing at her. She tried
> to concentrate on her typing but at last she was forced to look
> up. It was Peter; he had come back to her.

8 On a similar line it is a good group exercise for children to cut from
magazines, posters and labels pieces of writing which give the
reader just enough clues for him or her to decipher the message.
Each group makes a large and colourful wall display for other
groups to read. Part of such a display might look (in black and
white!) like the illustration on the opposite page.

We are now in the position that our pupils are, we hope, reading for
pleasure and have been enlivened and encouraged by reflecting on
their own reading expertise, using these introductory games. The
problem now is to build into the whole English programme regular
opportunities for the development of active reading.

## Keeping it going

It is all too easy for the hard-pressed teacher faced with exam and institutional pressure to slide back into the extract-plus-questions model of comprehension. Individual teachers of English, or better still, whole English departments, should try to develop a variety of reading activities involving pair or group work.

The following ideas and examples will I hope be useful in that process. The list makes no claim to originality or completeness. Many of them are now finding their way into published material. Any device to encourage good reading can become a trap if used unimaginatively, or too often. No device can compensate for a sympathetic teacher who reads widely and can establish good working relationships with his or her classes. That said, here are the ideas.

## 1 Questioning a text

Even if the teacher wishes to stick pretty closely to the traditional comprehension pattern, it is still possible to depart from it in various fruitful ways.

## (a) Open-ended questions

These can break the habit of ploughing through a long list of rather tedious questions before you get around to matters that require a higher degree of thought or involve a consideration of the passage as a whole. You set only three or four questions on the passage (often a poem will lend itself to this sort of treatment) to which there is no right or wrong answer. The children can discuss their answers in pairs within a fairly strict time limit. It is up to the teacher to decide whether the answers should be written down, but a report back to the whole class may do the job equally well. The sort of questions you can ask are:

---

(i)   What is a good title for the passage or poem? (You may want to give a few suggestions yourself to start them off.)

(ii)  What sort of person do you think the writer of this story/ poem is? (You may want to give a series of guiding questions about the writer e.g. what age, what sex, what occupation, what hobbies do you imagine, what do you think he or she looks like? etc.)

(iii) If the writer of the poem/story walked through the door now what would you expect him or her to say; or what would you want to say to him or her?

(iv)  If you had written this story/poem what bits would you have left out and what bits would you have added?

---

These are obviously only suggestions but the vital point is that many answers should be possible and that the questions should be sufficiently off-beat to provoke discussion.

## (b) Variations on the usual multiple-choice questions

This is a way of loosening up the comprehension process. At a conventional level a series of statements can be prepared about a piece of writing which the pupils have to mark true or false. Better is to ask children to respond to statements which express opinions about the text. These statements can be biased, partly true or contradictory; the pairs or groups are set the task of discussing the validity of each one or, better still, of listing them in order of relevance or importance. Later reporting back to the class can be the occasion for establishing a consensus of opinion for the whole group. A skilful set of statements about a piece of writing, dealing perhaps with the characters in the piece, the style of the writing or the author's opinion or intentions, can often give hesitant readers something definite to focus their discussion on.

## (c) Making up questions

Another improvement on routine comprehension. After reading a short story or poem, pupils are asked to make up a few questions the answers to which they would genuinely like to discover. The group swap questions and prepare answers to each other's questions. One problem with this method is that a group may devise questions designed to catch another group out or concentrate on low-level questions like the meaning of words or trivial factual points. One way round this is to discuss with the whole class beforehand the type of questions it is possible to ask of a text. Establishing a distinction between questions requiring a literal understanding of the words on the page (*on the lines*), questions which require an ability to comprehend implications of the writing (*between the lines*) and questions which involve the reader's own opinion or evaluation (*beyond the lines*) may be necessary to clear the path for fruitful questions. Any structure is better than nothing. Here is the guidance I wrote for a third year class recently after they had read a Bill Naughton short story about a fight in school.

---

When you have read the story carefully think of some interesting questions which other people in the class will have to answer. Your questions must be like this:
(i) Two questions on the meaning of particular words.
(ii) Two 'checking questions' about what actually happens, e.g. where did the fight take place?
(iii) Two questions on why someone involved does or says something, e.g. why does the narrator of the story feel pleased when the crowd moves back?
(iv) Two 'filling in' questions where the writer doesn't actually give you the answer in the passage but you can guess the answer if you read it carefully, e.g. which boy had been in fights before?
(v) Two 'opinion questions' where you have to say what you think about something in the passage, e.g. Do you think that children should be allowed to fight to settle arguments?

---

## (d) S Q and R

A useful habit derived in part from SRA work-cards. A chapter of a book or complete booklet is presented to pupils who rapidly Survey it noting as many clues to its content as possible (for example, cover, blurb, illustrations and sub-headings.) These initial impressions are then discussed and Questions raised as to the likely content, relevance or bias of the material. Pupils then Read the passage closely, considering possible answers to their own questions. This technique can be useful for developing alert reading of non-fiction material.

## 2 Tinkering with a text

One good way of getting young readers into a text is to alter it in some way so they are forced to speculate, make decisions and discuss the possible meaning of the text. If a piece of writing has bits missing or is printed in the wrong order, for example, it is no longer possible for readers to gaze passively at it, hoping the meaning will leap out at them from the page with no effort on their part.

### (a) Cloze

This is perhaps the best known and easiest way of tinkering with a piece of writing. The essence of the method is to remove pieces from a text — single words, phrases or whole chunks — and invite readers to supply their own words to fill the gaps. The great advantage of the technique is that it compels the reader to 'enter' the text in a way that routine comprehension does not. The danger I have found, apart from it getting boring if you do it too often, is that pupils often imagine that there is a single 'correct' answer whereas the method's value is in the process of discussion as pupils offer their alternatives. On many occasions they come up with answers equally valid and interesting as the words in the original passage. There are several variations on the general idea.

(i) Single words are deleted from the text. You can do this randomly, or every seventh or tenth words, but a better way is to take out words which are critical to the meaning of the piece. At the early stages you can list the deleted words at the end of the passage. Later you can leave the choice completely open.

(ii) Later still you can delete words and phrases, the substitutions for which require a high degree of stylistic or aesthetic discrimination. At this sophisticated level pupils have to justify their choice rather than simply slot in 'answers' from a limited range of alternatives.

(iii) Another way forward is to delete whole chunks of a passage — complete stanzas in a poem or several paragraphs in a piece of prose — and require pupils to speculate on the missing sections. You can be really radical and include only the first and last sections of the piece, leaving the readers to guess what the whole thing might be about. This is a good way of introducing pupils to the reading of a story or poem, because they have generated interest in it before they read the whole thing.

**(iv)** Yet another variation is to replace bits of the original text with inferior alternatives. The readers have first of all to detect where the original has been tampered with and then to re-work the text to bring it back to what the original might be like. This works well with poetry and it is quite fun putting in various kinds of inferior lines into a well-known poem!

## (b) Prediction

**(i)** This is another common technique, indeed something good English teachers have been doing for years. A story or poem (it is best to start with something that has a strong narrative line) is read or presented in instalments and pupils are invited to predict what will happen next, using clues in the instalment they have just read. At a simple level you can choose a story in a genre that signals clues to the reader in a very obvious fashion (horror stories for example). You can then work up to narratives where the development of the plot is related to the characters of the protagonists. You can even ask questions like, 'What should X do next?' compared with, 'What do you think X will actually do?'. A method of presentation that works well is to prepare the instalments of your story beforehand and present them in the form of a booklet, each page of which consists of the instalments plus any questions you want to ask. In this way the whole story can be read in small groups. Most children play the game and don't turn over the page until they have discussed the previous questions.

**(ii)** Story completion is very similar to prediction except here pupils have to complete a story or poem having been given the first part only. This can range from using the story beginning as primarily a stimulus for their own writing without much regard for the original, through to giving them the bulk of an original piece with, therefore, a more limited number of suitable endings. In the discussion that follows the writing, attention will be drawn to how well the endings fit the beginning in terms of plot, characterization and style. Another rather jolly variation on this idea is to give pupils the start of very well-known story — 'Little Red Riding Hood', for example — and ask them to complete it in as different a way as possible from the original.

**(iii)** Letter-sequences is another more advanced prediction idea, in which pupils are given a letter which could be the start of a series. A letter of complaint from a neighbour about noisy parties is a possible example. One group predicts what the reply might be and passes it on to the next group who think of an appropriate response and so on over a sequence of about six letters. Although difficult to organize the results can often be entertaining.

**(iv)** Stock responses — the teacher selects material which is inherently predictable. Possible areas are advertising copy, political speeches, bureaucratic exchanges of various kinds, Christmas cards, letters of excuse, thanks or condolence. Pupils are given the first part and asked to complete it in an appropriate style or register. Obviously this is an exercise for confident readers and writers but it is surprising how well groups can perform as long as they are familiar with the social and linguistic conventions involved.

## (c) Sequencing

This involves jumbling up the paragraphs of a piece of prose or the stanzas of a poem and asking pupils to arrange them in a sensible order. One way to do this is to make copies of the text and cut it up into pieces. (This can be inadvisable if the class is over-lively or difficult.) Pupils should then be alerted to the syntactic and semantic devices writers use to give coherence to their writing. In practice it is a more difficult exercise than it at first seems. It is best to start with writing that has a clear logical order, like sets of instructions or recipes, or a strong narrative framework with plenty of cohesive devices evident in the text. Despite its problems this idea is very fruitful in that it draws readers' attention to whole texts and how they are put together.

Another way of doing the same thing is to present pupils with an unparagraphed (or unstanza-ed) piece of writing and invite them to split it up into a pre-determined number of sections making their breaks where they feel the text demands it.

# 3 De-mythologizing the text

One of the difficulties that less confident readers often experience is that they are overwhelmed by print. They expect to be bored or confused by much of the material they encounter in schools and so never learn to use a text for their own purposes or to develop strategies for coming to grips with it. The following exercises are designed to diminish writing's power to intimidate.

## (a) Errors and mistakes

As a start, pupils can be presented with a text containing a number of simple errors of fact. It is helpful to choose a subject they know something about — a hobby or leisure activity for example. The next stage is to include errors of argument and to alert readers to non-sequiturs, exaggeration and bias.

## (b) Bias and opinion

This leads naturally on from the previous activities. A good method is to take a contentious piece of writing — a newspaper or magazine article for instance, and ask groups to underline first all the facts in the piece and then (in a different colour) all the opinions. As readers increase in confidence it is possible to set up quite subtle discussions on the way relevant facts may be left out by the writer, or presented in a distorted way. Pupils can produce their own versions of the material written from an opposing point of view.

## (c) The implied reader

All texts, however bland or authoritative, have an implied view of the person reading it. Pupils can be given a number of texts, if possible on a similar subject, and from the evidence of subject-matter, lay-out and style, guess the intended audience of the writing. To start with it is best to ask specific questions — e.g. What age is the target audience? What knowledge or beliefs does the writer assume? Is the writer trying to entertain, help or brow-beat the reader? Good sources for this sort of exercise are advertisements, magazines or official documents.

## (d) Difficult vocabulary or syntax

Groups may be given a passage or poem containing words they are not likely to understand. It is important to stress beforehand that this will be the case so that they do not become despairing or resentful. They should be encouraged to use the context to guess the meaning and only use a dictionary as a last resort. As they increase in confidence they can discuss the necessity or otherwise of such vocabulary and syntax. In the end one hopes they will be able to make judgements about jargon, inflated writing and obfuscation. Having grasped the point, groups are often capable of producing parodies of an original or converting simple statements into unnecessarily obscure versions (e.g. Given the straightforward injunction, 'Be quiet', groups create such pomposities as, 'It would be most advantageous if all school students in the immediate vicinity were to desist from all forms of verbal communication . . .!) There are all too numerous sources for this sort of exercise — specialist magazines (especially computer magazines), school reports, gas board final demands, school text-books, etc.

## (e) Different versions

In this exercise pupils are presented with different versions of a poem or piece of prose and asked to comment on the differences between them. It may be necessary if various drafts of a poem are not available for the teacher to write a simple prose version of a poem to compare with the original. Different translations of the Bible or other classic texts can also be used successfully. A variety of newspaper accounts of the same event is another useful approach. An interesting variation, if you can find material, is to compare factual and fictional treatments of the same or similar episodes.

## 4 Ways of reading and responding

A poor reader does not vary the speed and attention of his or her reading. A good reader is more flexible, reading according to the nature of the text and his or her purposes. Unfortunately, traditional comprehension encourages inflexible reading and the readers' response is invariably tied to the written answers they are required to produce. The following exercises are aimed at breaking this vicious circle.

### (a) Problems, judgements and mysteries
The idea is to give pupils a text which requires them to make a decision or judgement of some kind. Ones I have tried include the following:

- An imaginary court case with witness's statements, reports from the police and other details. Pupils are the presiding magistrates.
- The problem pages of a magazine (suitably edited) with pupils having to come up with answers to the problems.
- A car accident report with different accounts of the events and pupils put in the position of insurance assessors deciding how to apportion blame.
- The biographical details of prisoners applying for parole — pupils are asked for their decisions.
- Job applications with the letters, references and testimonials of several candidates — pupils make the appointment.
- A 'whodunit' mystery where pupils have to guess the guilty party.
- Well-known mysteries like Flannan Isle, the Bermuda Triangle or the Marie Celeste story — here pupils have to suggest an explanation.

The advantage of all these is that the pupils are reading for a specific purpose with a definite outcome at the end, using the evidence of the texts in front of them. Equally good (and easier to arrange) is to have a wide selection of literary texts which invite readers to make judgements on the actions and behaviour of the characters involved.

## (b) Drawings, diagrams and cartoons

This gets away from the inevitable written answer. Children are asked to present some aspect of the text in a visual form. An idea for this is a story to be converted to cartoon form with a picture for each stage of the narrative. An alternative is to illustrate a scene or character including as much information from the text as possible. Diagrams can be used to depict relationships or the development of the plot. For non-fiction pieces pupils can re-assemble information in the form of a table, drawing or flow-chart of some kind. (The Schools Council Project based on the University of Nottingham, 'Reading For Learning in the Secondary School' has developed a wide range of such activities called DARTS — Directed Activities Related To Texts.)

## (c) Skimming and scanning

In order to encourage pupils to vary their reading strategy, a passage can be read and readers asked to jot down a single sentence impression within a time limit that prevents them ploughing slowly through the whole thing. Another method is to present a number of longish texts and ask pupils which ones would be most relevant to a given subject of task in hand. The point to stress is that it is perfectly legitimate, indeed necessary on occasion, to skim through texts without reading each sentence. For scanning (looking for particular facts or details) you can use timetables, charts, small ads., or telephone directories, again with a strict time limit. A more advanced exercise is to ask groups to marshall evidence from several sources to present later to a particular audience.

## (d) Changing the form

Pupils can be asked to use their understanding of a text in their own writing or better still in drama, role-play or talk. The events of a story can be presented in the form of a newspaper article, short play, news bulletin, radio or TV programme. Characters can be interviewed about their actions or several characters from a book can improvise a conversation; key events may be dramatized for performance. A story can be transposed to a different setting or given a twist (e.g. *Macbeth* as a gangster film or *Lord Of The Flies* with girls only on the island). A member of the group can become the writer of a story with the task of defending the text while the rest of the group voice criticisms or questions. On the non-fiction side some texts are ideal for this approach, recipes or instructions for example, (I've used origami and knots!) because the test of comprehension is whether you can do what the instructions, or whatever, describe.

The aim of all this is to get away from the idea that the comprehension of a text always involves written, or indeed oral 'answers'.

# Endpiece

Over a term or a year's work school readers should experience a wide variety of different kinds of text (though the emphasis should, as I have said, be on literature). In this way attention can be drawn to the different kinds of reading required. An example of such a variety might be:

## Checklist

1 Fables or parables that demand reading as a whole; then the ability to grasp and reflect upon the 'message'.
2 Several information books to be read, skimmed, scanned or rejected for some specific purpose like giving a talk to the rest of the class.
3 A number of poems presented perhaps in some of the ways I've suggested.
4 The close study of several short, densely argued passages, starting possibly with the small arguments in logic to be found in introductory philosophy texts.
5 Sets of instructions to be performed, perhaps done in cooperation with other subject teachers.
6 Forms and official documents for functional comprehension with the aim being not just to get pupils to fill in forms successfully but to consider the content and presentation of such material, the readership it assumes and the possibilities for improving it.
7 A range of novels and short stories read individually, in small groups and as a whole class, with only some of the work taking written form.

With a diet like this, most pupils would, I suggest, be able to increase their reading ability more effectively than with regular doses of traditional comprehension exercises. No teacher would want to use all these ideas at once, of course. A modest start with a class one gets on well with is probably the best way forward.

The vital point is that our methods of improving children's reading should be brought much more in line with what we now know about the way mature readers actually tackle print: that reading is an active, flexible, questioning activity, engaging the totality of the readers' experience both of language and of life.

# Recommended reading

*Twenty-Two Ideas for Variety in Comprehension Work*, Mike Taylor and
Bill Deller in 'New Directions in English Teaching', edited A
Adams, Falmer Press, 1982

Many of the ideas contained in this chapter are translated into
classroom practice in *Comprehension*, Checkbook Series, Hutchinson,
1985

# 7 Getting it 'right'

Chris Bridge

## What is right?

Before you can 'Get it right' you have to know what *is* right. The answer to that question is not only philosophical it is also political. That is no reason for not tackling it here. Indeed each teacher of English has to tackle this question if they are to teach basic skills at all. But, having said that, the practical classroom applications begin on page 142 and you are welcome to skip this section. However, I hope you will come back to it because thinking the problem through has given new confidence to myself and my colleagues to teach accuracy in a purposeful and supportive way.

### My Mum says you're wrong

The issue was speech punctuation and the catalyst was a freckled girl who was waving her book in front of my nose. The book was open at a page of model speech punctuation that I had written on the board as a guide for their writing. They had copied it down. This child had gone home and showed it to her mother who disagreed because I hadn't used 66 and 99. I had stuck to a typewriter formation (". . .").

It is only one example of the confusion that occurs because we all use a language without a formal set of rules for its usage. It is incredibly easy to think that our way is 'The Right Way' and when pushed for an explanation we say it was because we were taught like that. Try it for yourself. Here is a piece of work. Mark the mistakes of ENGLISH and then read on.

Snow. Snow lying as crisp as meringue over the landscape. Inviting the feet to quickly sink themselves into its fastness. And somewhere out there many less noises to dull the edge of consciousness. Such silence is rare and only the first snowfall of the season invites it, welcoming it back into its ancient and rightful place so that our thoughts can be turned in again on themselves. There is magic in that moment and with it comes a longing that such peaceful times could be more frequent.

So, what did you think of that piece of child's work? I am going to work on the basis that it is a practice GCSE piece in order to highlight the problems we face. At this stage I want to pose questions rather than to suggest answers.

1  Take that first word 'Snow'. Can it be a sentence on its own? It is an excellent opening to a piece of creative writing. My favourite novel 'Bleak House' begins with the single word sentence, 'London.' Its second paragraph commences, 'Fog everywhere.' But neither is a sentence if, by definition, a sentence has to contain a finite verb.

How then can we mark 'Snow.'? Do we say something like this? 'It's all right to use a single word sentence; in fact I rather like it; but I wouldn't use it in the exam. You don't know what the examiners will think of it.' Have we even got time when marking to weigh up such an issue?

2  'Snow lying as crisp as meringue over the landscape.'
I find that a pleasing sentence but again it isn't one. Yet do we stifle the creativity if we mark it in red ink? circling it many times in order to protect them from an imaginary examiner's wrath. (Yes, you *can* use a question mark in the middle of a sentence.)

3  Did you change the full stop to a comma after landscape? I would. It is the easiest way out even though the longer sentence you create has no finite verb in it. Worse it has a split infinitive which is always wrong, or is it?

4  'And somewhere out there many less noises to dull the edge of consciousness.'
The one rule every child knows from the Primary School is that you cannot begin a sentence with '*And*'. Why not? Most 'good' authors do when it suits their purposes. I find this beginning acceptable, but we still have no finite verb. You will, of course, have noticed that it should be *fewer* noises: *less noise* but *fewer noises*. Turn on the radio or the TV and you don't have to listen very long to hear that rule abused. How do we mark it? Do we bow to the inevitable and no longer teach it?

5  'Such silence is rare and only the first snowfall of the season invites it, welcoming it back into its ancient and rightful place so that our thoughts can be turned in again on themselves.'
At last we have a finite verb. The problem here is the comma. It is 'OK' but it isn't as good as a colon would be.

6  'There is magic in that moment and with it comes a longing that such peaceful times could be more frequent.'
I chose to finish with this long sentence which needs a comma or a semi-colon in front of the *and*. Do you agree? There is after all no rule.

I think we would all welcome such a piece of writing. It shows sensitivity; an engaging use of words, e.g. *fastness*; a talent for observation; and a reasonable progression through the ideas. It is the work of someone who communicates at a sophisticated level. The whole object of punctuation is to aid communication. Teaching and marking such sophistication is like negotiating a minefield.

The minefield is made more dangerous by the existence of those who are certain. This is where the problem becomes political. I hope you will forgive two stereotyped portraits of people who do no service to English teaching.

The first I always visualize as over fifty years old. He (I am not being sexist: it usually is a he) looks back nostalgically to the days of parsing rather in the way that others of his generation do to the summers of childhood; always longer and hotter than those of today. 'Why don't we teach them Grammar?' he demands annually. 'Précis never did me any harm,' he continues. It soon becomes clear that he equates exquisitely neat handwriting with Godliness and accuses me of 'lacking standards'.

The other stereotype is a figure of the sixties, bearded or kaftaned. These people care little for handwriting. Accuracy can be seen by them as the fascism of the middle class language. 'What matters,' they claim, 'is the authenticity of the statement.' They nurture creativity at the expense of everything else. Even 'grammar' is divisive and spelt with a small letter.

I am sure that you will be quick to argue that those portraits are cheap ways of putting over the weaknesses of both sides without the balancing strengths. I would argue, however, that there is a pedant in all of us. I had a colleague once who told the pupils that it was bad manners to split a word in half at the end of a line. That they added the hyphen made not the slightest difference. The split word was taken by that teacher as a personal affront. We all know those who eradicate the split infinitive. What are our own pedantries? I confess that I am a one-inch-from-the-margin-at-the-beginning-of-each-paragraph person. The problem is that you cannot solve the diversity of modern practice by mere pedagogy.

## All change

Nor can you ignore the fact that the language is changing rapidly. I said earlier that the BBC tended to abuse the distinction between *less* and *fewer*. Is that abuse or is it a change in the language? How many shop signs use apostrophes? What has happened to the subjunctive? The range of modern practice is wide.

**Take speech punctuation:**
Most paperbacks punctuate speech with single inverted commas. James Joyce as early as *The Portrait of the Artist as a Young Man* was using no speech marks but introducing speech with a dash. We still teach double speech marks.

**Take letter writing:**
The typewriter has changed the layout of the letter. Informality has frowned on 'Dear Madam'. Even *The Times* prints letters beginning 'Dear Sir' and ending 'Yours sincerely'.

**Take paragraphs:**
Books often begin paragraphs with a three letter gap. An examination board prints passages in its exam papers beginning at the margin and with a one line gap separating paragraphs.

**Take the hyphen:**
This useful punctuation mark causes more laughs when it is omitted or wrongly placed than any other. Even if it is the shared laughter of the literate against the less literate we can all enjoy the man who confused 'extra marital-sex' with 'extra-marital sex'. There was also a school which proudly claimed that its pastoral-care system allowed for the formation of 'a lasting base-relationship between every child and his tutor'.

To sum up — teachers of English have the difficult job of teaching their subject against the background of no coherent set of rules and a changing language. Their task is not made any easier by the way that the question of basic skills has become a political issue. How does all this affect schools?

It is not enough for each teacher to formulate his or her own rules and teach them in isolation from other teachers in the English Department, or even in isolation from other teachers who use written language. How often have you set out your own stall for a particular aspect of punctuation only to be told, 'Last year we didn't do it like that.' As my subject is *Basics* I will begin with the basics.

# 1 Presentation

### Handwriting
We all know the children whose writing is poor because they do not form their letters properly. The teacher who wants to help must give

advice on how to form letters. We all have different handwritings. How can we advise without having first agreed on a school policy? By this I do not mean a single style that we teach to all but rather a single style that we teach to all *whose handwriting is below standard*. Here I would argue that handwriting is important because it encourages pupils to have pride in their work. I would also add that it is useful to agree a style with the feeder primaries if you can. Surely this is much better than a child being told by one teacher to use loops and by another to cut them out.

### Setting out work
This is trivial to us perhaps, but I don't think it is to the pupils. They often have to learn several styles to fit several teachers who can each be fierce in the defence of their own way of doing things. By trying to cope in isolation we often confuse and such confusion is *not* useful.

What I have said about handwriting and setting out work applies equally to other areas and we should not underestimate its importance. The realities of working within schools insist that we cannot be idealistic but must be willing to compromise. The teacher who 'throws a fit' when her pupils do not write on the top line has to be accommodated. The teacher who tells pupils to leave a line between paragraphs needs to get together with the teacher who insists on a three letter gap. These are all matters where agreement should be possible and mutually beneficial to the school. If you can organize such ideas into a pamphlet available in all classrooms (even if it is only English classrooms) then so much the better.

Here is an example from my own school's pamphlet called SNAGS (Skills Needed At Glossop School).
Copy it if you like but I recommend the process of working out your own. The care with which you go through the process will be a good guide to how well it is used afterwards.

# SNAGS I

## Presentation

Neat handwriting is not the only way in which you can show that you care about your work. The way you present your work helps it to be both clear and interesting to read.

Here are some points to follow:

**(a)** Leave at least a one-line gap between one whole piece of work and the next.

**(b)** All headings and the date should be underlined.

> Examples: <u>Friday 1st February</u>
> <u>The Preparation of Carbon Dioxide</u>.
> <u>The Classification of Living Things</u>.
> <u>Substances from the Sea</u>.

**(c)** Begin writing at the left-hand margin, not half an inch in from the margin.

**(d)** Rather than risk squashing a word in, it is far better to waste a little space and start the word on the next line.

**(e)** Always write on the top and the bottom lines but do not use the bottom line for headings.

**(f)** Use paragraphs.
A *paragraph* is a group of sentences about the same subject. (But in special circumstances you can use one-sentence paragraphs.)
Paragraphs are used to split up a solid mass of writing and so make it easier to read.
Every hand-written paragraph after the first one must begin one inch or 2.5 cm in from the margin so that it is clearly recognizable.

**(g)** Use capital letters correctly. They have four main uses:

**(i)** Every sentence must begin with a capital letter.

**(ii)** All names of people and places must begin with a capital letter.

**(iii)** The letter 'I' when it is on its own and means *me* is always a capital 'I'.

**(iv)** Capital letters are used for days of the week and months of the year.

> Examples: *Let's go back to Glossop with Kevin and Steve.*
> *What am I going to do?*
> *London is where Karen lives.*
> *Next Monday will be the first of May.*

**(h)** Try not to break a word at the end of a line. As you write, look ahead towards the end of the line, and if you are in any doubt start a new line. It is better to leave a bit of space wasted at the end of a line than to crowd the last few letters together because you have run out of space.

However, if you do have to break a word at the end of a line, bear these points in mind:—

(i)    A hyphen should be used to link the two main parts of the word that you have broken. It must then be placed immediately after the letters that you have written at the end of the old line, and never at the beginning of a new line.

(ii)    Try to split a word into *syllables that you could pronounce*. So you would write 'quan-tity' and not 'qua-ntity' because it is hard to say 'ntity' on its own.

(iii)    You should never split a syllable. So if you get to the end of a line and want to split a word such as 'strengths' the answer is that you just cannot. If you have begun to write a word before realizing that there is not room for it all, you should just cross through the letters that you have written and start the word again on a new line.

(iv)    You should never split a word that is a person's name, however long it may be.

(v)    For further guidance we recommend 'Collins English Dictionary', which shows how to split every one of its listed words.

## 2 Punctuation

This is much more difficult to deal with. It is also more important because it is an essential ingredient of communication. Indeed you can argue that clear thinking and clear punctuation go together. In schools at the moment confusion created by the teaching of several different approaches to punctuation is neither the only problem nor the worst one. Because it is such a minefield I fear that we often abdicate responsibility and try, through marking, to clear up the mess after it has happened. My feeling is that punctuation needs to be taught.

What are the problems?

1 There are few universal rules and a wide diversity of acceptable practices.

2 The pupils we teach are at different stages. Some first years are

writing sentences that cry out for semi-colons. Some fifth years are still only writing basic sentences.

3 Whichever formula we arrive at must satisfy the examination boards and be applicable to both formal and informal modes.

4 We must be able to explain the structures, and that means that some grammatical grasp is necessary.

Surely this calls for the agreed formulation of a developmental punctuation framework: one that uses simple concepts to explain simple structures and grows more complex as both written skills and grammatical understanding develop together.

This is our answer to the problem. It too comes from SNAGS, the pamphlet we wrote for the pupils to use and, crucially, share with their parents.

## Punctuation framework Part One

## SNAGS II

---

### How to write clearly

If your writing is properly punctuated it will be easier to understand. Writing that is not properly punctuated will be hard to read and hard to understand. It may be misleading or even meaningless. If you understand punctuation you will have a better understanding of what you read. You will also be able to read more quickly. See how you get on with reading this passage:—

> *the great white shark waited unknown to the surf rider only ten feet below him if he had looked down he would have seen the fish but his eyes were fixed on the horizon searching for the next wave the fish sensed him and moved upwards the man paddling his hands gently on either side of his surf board waited for the right wave to ride on the fish whipped its tail and shot upwards ready to strike at the flimsy surf board at that moment the wave came*

### Sentences
What is a sentence?
(a) A sentence is a group of words that makes full sense on its own.

---

(b) A sentence begins with a capital letter and ends with a full stop.

(c) Each sentence needs to have a verb, a doing word, in it.

(d) A full stop at the end of each sentence marks the place where you have to pause when reading out loud. If you don't pause at each full stop, what you read will not make sense.

Example:—

> The great white shark waited unknown to the surf rider only ten feet below him. If he had looked down he would have seen the fish but his eyes were fixed on the horizon searching for the next wave. The fish sensed him and moved upwards. The man paddling his hands gently on either side of his surf board waited for the right wave to ride on. The fish whipped its tail and shot upwards ready to strike at the flimsy surf board. At that moment the wave came.

The passage is now much easier to read. Because it is now easy to understand, it is possible to read it with enjoyment.

**Pausing in the middle of a sentence**

We have said that you must pause at the end of a sentence if what you are reading is to make sense. There are also times when you must pause in the middle of a sentence if it is to make sense. This kind of pause is most often shown with a comma.

Look again at the piece about the white shark. Without any commas the first sentence could mean the surf rider was ten feet below the shark!

But if we put in two commas then the meaning becomes quite clear:—

> The great white shark waited, unknown to the surf rider, only ten feet below him.

Here is another place where a pause is needed:—

> The fish whipped its tail and shot upwards, ready to strike at the flimsy surf board.

The passage has a sentence in it that still needs two commas added. Can you see where the two commas should be? The answer is a little further on.

If a sentence contains a clause that is an essential part of its meaning then you do not mark it off by a comma or commas.

Examples:—

*The pupils who worked hard got very good exam results.*

*I have read the book that you lent me.*

But if a sentence contains a clause that is not essential to the meaning — that is, a clause that could be left out without seriously affecting the message of the sentence — then you must use a comma or commas.

Examples:—

*I live in Glossop, which is a town in North-west Derbyshire.*

*My pupils, who did not all work hard, got exam results that ranged from excellent to disastrous.*

*The man, paddling his hands gently on either side of the surf board, waited for the right wave to ride on.*

In the last two sentences you have seen how a pair of commas in a sentence serves to cut off a group of words, in the way that brackets do.

## Teaching the punctuation framework. Part One

Simple sentence punctuation needs reinforcing and there are two main ways in which this can be done by teaching and by marking.

### Teaching

There is a time-honoured strategy to emphasize the rule that, 'A full stop at the end of each sentence marks the place where you have to pause when reading out loud . . . if what you read is to make sense.' Borrow an offender's book and read it out to the class pausing only when you reach a punctuation mark. Ham it up. Take a deep breath at the beginning; go purple; accuse the child of attempted murder! If the class are laughing then you are winning.

### Play the sentence game

Split the class into two teams. In turn each person in each team has to say a single sentence. If it is not a sentence or if it is two sentences the other team win a point for a correct challenge. It sounds as if they will only produce stock, hack sentences but the way to score is to try sophisticated sentences and produce false challenges which score two points. Use disputed sentences to write up and explain and discuss.

**The wrongly punctuated piece**
This is also time-honoured but I would like to suggest a refinement. When you choose your piece for the board try to make it highlight one aspect only. If you go back to the white shark passage, there is one sentence where you need a comma to make sense of the sentence. Try for passages where full stops are crucial. For example,

> You must lock the door in the first place you need to be sure that your house is safe.

A phrase like 'in the first place' can belong at the end of the previous sentence or at the beginning of the next.

**Marking**
Here we need to balance the need to make pupils aware of their mistakes with the equally important need of not deeming them to be failures by applying a plethora of red ink. I recommend the following strategies:

*Enabling them to put the mistakes right*
Too often when we add the punctuation for them the result is that they do not learn from it. How are they to be helped to learn? I ring five or six key punctuation mistakes in each piece of work which I mark. This puts the onus on individuals to go back over their last piece and think about what was wrong either with the punctuation mark they used which is inside my circle, or with the space inside my circle which should contain a punctuation mark. When the next piece of work is ready to be marked you look back to check on the previous corrections. This approach works much better if you spend time at the beginning of each year laying it down. It works even better if it is part of a departmental or a whole school policy.

*Creating a focus by split marking*
I rarely give marks out of ten because I teach mixed-ability. However, I do use the CAP systems:

C means Content.
A means Accuracy.
P means Presentation.

This enables me to focus the individual on their own weaknesses. You can then do a blitz on punctuation by making the A mean punctuation accuracy. This has an important by-product — it is very useful information when it comes to writing reports.

149

## Punctuation framework Part Two

## SNAGS III

### Joining up short sentences

Look at these two sets of sentences.

> *I got a bus into Manchester. Lynda met me at the bus station. We went into the buffet for coffee.*

> *Stanley washed up. He made the beds. He hoovered the stairs. He fed the goldfish.*

You may feel that the sentences in each set ought to be joined together to make one long sentence: their meanings are closely connected, they are very short and when they are separated by full stops they seem jerky.

There are *five* main ways to bring together what could be written as separate sentences.

**1 You can use the word 'and'**
Examples:

> *I got a bus into Manchester and Lynda met me at the bus station and we went into the buffet for a coffee.*

> *Stanley washed up and he made the beds and he hoovered the stairs and he fed the goldfish.*

(Or we could leave out the repeated 'he' and write:

> *Stanley washed up and made the beds and hoovered the stairs and fed the goldfish.*)

What we now have is still not completely satisfactory. It is not good to use a number of 'ands' to join a number of short sentences. Usually two short sentences joined by one 'and' are enough.

**2 You can use one or more commas followed by an 'and'**
Examples:—

> *I got a bus into Manchester, met Lynda at the bus station, and we went into the buffet for a coffee.*

> *Stanley washed up, made the beds, hoovered the stairs and fed the goldfish.*

(a) One of these sentences has a comma before the 'and' while the other one does not. The simplest way to decide whether a comma is needed like this is to read the whole sentence out loud and ask yourself, *'Do I pause* at that point as I read it out?' If your answer is 'YES' then probably you need a comma. In the next two sentences we need a comma after the word 'rain'. The lack of a comma makes the sentences harder to understand on a first reading.

Examples:

(i) *I shall go out into the wind and rain and I hope you can keep a good fire going till I get back.*

(ii) *I shall go out into the wind and rain and hail a taxi if I can see one.*

(b) What you must *not* do is join sentences by using commas *and nothing else*.

Examples:

*Stanley washed up, made the beds.*
*Stanley washed up, he made the beds.*   WRONG
*Stanley washed up, he made the beds, he hoovered the stairs.*

These examples would be right if in each sentence we used 'and' instead of the last comma.

## 3 You may need a better word than — 'and' — a word that says more

Examples:

*I got a bus into Manchester and met Lynda at the bus station though she had flu.*

*We went to the buffet and I had a coffee, but Lynda didn't want anything.*

*I chatted with Lynda until she said it was time to go for her train.*

## Notes

Other words often needed for joining short sentences to make one long sentence are: *if, because, when, while*.

Often it is right to place a comma before these joining words (which are called *conjunctions*), especially where you need to show a break in the sentence or to make it easier to understand at first glance — as we have pointed out in the Notes on (1) and (2). Very often 'but' needs a comma before it, because at that point the direction of the sentence changes — as in the foregoing example with 'but'.

**4 You can use one or more semi-colons, possibly followed by an 'and'**
Usually the semi-colon is used when the short sentences being joined are *closely linked in meaning*.

Examples:

> *I got a bus into Manchester. Lynda met me at the bus station; we went into the buffet for coffee; then we made our way to Lewis's.*
>
> *Stanley washed up; he made the beds; he hoovered the stairs and he fed the goldfish. (Here the repeated 'he' <u>cannot</u> be left out.)*
>
> *The heat of the early sun told me it was going to be another beautiful day. I took a shower; I dressed quickly; I had a cup of coffee and some biscuits. It was half past seven now. I set off on foot towards the town centre. I felt on top of the world. I drank in the early morning smells; I revelled in that symphony of sounds that means a whole community of machines and people is once again coming to life. I crossed the Central Gardens. The dew was still heavy on the grass, even on those patches that the sun had already reached.*
>
> *And then as I came out of Central Gardens I caught sight of Keith. He was walking slowly; he was looking down at the pavement; he didn't see me.*

(Those sentences joined by semi-colons belong together because their meanings are closely linked. None of the other sentences belong together in the same way.)

**5 In certain cases you can use a colon**
The colon can be used rather like the word 'because', to show that you are going to give a reason for what has gone before.

Example:

> *Stanley felt pleased with himself: he had washed up, made the beds, hoovered the stairs and fed the goldfish.*

The colon can also be used to show that you are going to give details of what has just gone before.

Example:

> *You'll be my general handyman: I'll want you to keep things tidy and you'll be in charge of all repairs.*
>
> *It was the worst holiday we've ever had: the sun never came out once, the beds in the hotel were damp, and the locals were a bunch of miserable tightfisted swindlers.*

(The foregoing sentence is an example of both uses of the colon: as often happens, the part of the sentence that comes after the colon both *gives a reason* for the preceding statement and *gives details of what has been mentioned*.)

## Teaching the punctuation framework Part Two

The marking strategies of Part One still apply but here are some new teaching hints.

Create a situation where you can concentrate on punctuation to the exclusion of everything else. A good way is to buy a class set of 'The Beano' and focus on the Roger the Dodger story. (Your money will be well spent as they are also useful for speech punctuation exercises.)

Instruct your class to retell the story in their own words but using all the spoken words. Tell them to include all the relevant detail but also to use the fewest possible words. This will compel them to think about how they retell it to the exclusion of all other considerations. *At this level punctuation is about choices*.

The story I used was one involving Roger and his friend the crow. In the first frame Roger takes two coathangers from his mother's wardrobe, leaving her dresses on the floor. In the second frame Roger assures the reader that he knows some dodges with coathangers which he urges us in the third frame to watch. In the fourth frame he sends a coathanger, like a boomerang, to pick up a stick of rock being eaten by another child. The boy threatens revenge in frame six so Roger uses a coathanger to make a quick getaway by hooking it over a clothes line and sliding down the line. In frame nine he comes to a halt and is too frightened to look down. In the tenth frame Roger's parents have discovered the mess in the wardrobe and in the final frame, realizing that Roger is the culprit, his father advances on him, slipper in hand saying that he's in the ideal wacking position: hanging in fact only inches from the ground, but too frightened to look down.

That is my version. Three pupils from a mixed-ability third year class will illustrate the differences in approach that can then provide a focus for discussing quality. I've cut the passages so that together they retell the whole story as a single sequence.

---

**Roger the Dodger Take One**
'Ah, these are what I am after,' says Roger.

'I just managed to get past him to get the two coathangers,' said Roger.

'I think I shall do some good dodges with these coathangers,' said Roger.

**Roger the Dodger Take Two**
He saw a boy eating sweets and said, 'Watch this one readers.' He threw a coathanger at the boy, 'Just like a boomerang.'

The coathanger hooked on a stick of rock and the boy yelled, 'Yowl, my stick of rock.'

The coathanger brought the rock back to Roger.

'Dodger I'll get you for that,' yelled the boy.

**Roger the Dodger Take Three**
'Not if I can make a quick getaway' says Roger looking at a garden's sloping lawn with a washing line from the top to the bottom. He hooks the coathanger onto the washing line and slides down the line. 'Yahoo, just like a commando,' he says.

Then the line snags and he stops. 'Aw no I've stopped and I'm too scared to look down at the drop.'

Meanwhile . . . 'My dresses, who took the coathangers?' says Roger's mum.

'Roger, I shouldn't wonder,' snaps Roger's dad.

Roger is still dangling on the washing line too scared to look down at the drop.

---

The first passage uses (in its whole length) only two joining words. The second is more sophisticated. The third is the most successful because it best exercises choice over sentence structure. That choice has been partly created by the use of more detail. Perhaps we need to teach the need for detail parallel with the need for sentence variety.

The group as a whole then went on to create a booklet with advice on how to join sentences. This was designed to hang on the classroom wall to instruct others and to introduce them to choice. Their joining devices include:

| | |
|---|---|
| but | however |
| a dash | a semi-colon |
| three dots | before |
| meanwhile | after |
| thus | hence |
| therefore | or |
| which | as |
| in order to | in spite of |
| although | when |
| so | |

I once caught myself standing at the front of the class saying, 'At your age you ought to begin using more semi-colons.' It was the expression of my deep inadequacy as far as the more advanced punctuation goes. The problem remains because I do not know which comes first: the semi-colon or the need for it? I do now teach the above rules for colons and semi-colons and encourage pupils to use both: by marking, by pointing out examples that need the use of either, and by spotting them in the writing of others. Such punctuation marks are, as my third years found, a way of saying more by using fewer words. The colon and the semi-colon are among the most disputed rules in English. Our version is not the only possible one but it will work and be accepted. Only when they know the basics can they really employ choice to create diversity.

# 3 Spelling

Even in streamed classes spelling will have to be taught on a mixed-ability basis. Some people can spell; others can't. It is not a function of intelligence. It seems more closely linked with visual memory, but in each grouping there will be those the teacher labels (or who label themselves) as people who cannot spell. Of course they can spell many words. It is not an either/or situation but the label is important if we are to help with their problem because it encapsulates a self-defeating pessimism. We have to provide strategies to overcome the problem and the labelling.

## Teaching strategies

**1** *Handwriting*
Handwriting is important because the visual content of knowing

how to spell is so important. If a child's handwriting is poor then the letters will be badly formed and the words will not make clear shapes. Indeed we all know children (and adults) who deliberately create hybrid letters in order to avoid looking a word up, to see if it is spelt with an e or an a for instance. There is a link therefore between poor spelling and poor handwriting which we have to take seriously. That is why, as I have already said, secondary schools need a handwriting policy.

**2** *The spelling mistakes which are not*

We can cut the problem down to size at once by taking out a whole group of words which are often labelled as spelling mistakes and which are in fact homophones used in the wrong circumstances. I am talking now of words like *their, weather, know, too, right* and *off*. There is no point in labelling these as mis-spelt when they are in fact WRONG WORDS. So if you mark spelling mistakes *sp*, these wrong word mistakes should be marked *ww*. At least then the student will know how to deal with them because they cannot be learned as spellings are. Wrong words need to be studied in pairs or groups. Spellings should be learned singly.

When we have marked a word as being *ww* how does the pupil respond? Just as with punctuation mistakes these must be acted upon by the pupil. The wrong word and its real meaning should be written at the bottom of the piece and the real word substituted.

**3** *Homophones*

These can be taught in fun ways. Every class should be given the opportunity of compiling a long list. It should be possible to fit 150 single words on a class list. This will alert them to the problem. With some the pronunciation of words which are not in the strictest sense homophones will help. *Of* and *off* do not sound the same as each other or as *have*. Decline the verb *of* for them!

Write this up on the board:

    I of
    You of
    He or she ofs
    We of
    You of
    They of

They might get the message, but teaching like that raises two problems. The first is that many of the children I teach do say, 'I could of'. By making them spell the phrase, 'I could have' we are substituting our dubiously superior language in place of their supposedly inferior kind. In the written form do we have an alternative? The problem is more acute in an oral exam.

The second problem with declining *of* is that whatever we write up on the board tends to be seen as received wisdom. That is why I am uneasy about using the blackboard too often when teaching from passages with mistakes in. Invariably the pupils spend longer studying the mistakes than the right ways of writing. The overhead projector is a much better tool for this kind of work: it is quicker because you write smaller; it allows the class to help by doing the corrections on the OHP for you; and it lacks the aura of infallibility.

How can we help them to solve their own homophone problems? Why not use a booklet approach? The class can even write it for their own use. Whoever writes it, we need to provide pupils with the means to be more accurate and the motivation to use those means.

Here is a possible page:

# SNAGS IV

## Learn the difference between

**1 There and their; where and were**
*THEIR* shows belonging.

*WERE* is a verb. Here is a mnemonic: WE
WERE
READY
*WHERE* and *THERE* and *HERE* are all to do with *places*.
*HERE* and *HEAR*        Mnemonic: You *HEAR* with your *EAR*.

Example:
   *I can't hear anything here.*

**2 NO and KNOW and NOW**
Example:
   *Did you <u>know</u> there was a 'k' at the beginning of 'knowledge'? <u>No</u>, but I <u>know now</u>.*

**3 KNEW and NEW**
Example:
   *We all <u>knew</u> that; tell us something <u>new</u>.*

**4 TO and TOO**

Mnemonic: *'Too'* is the last word with an *extra* 'o' that has the meaning of as well, or *extra*, or too much of something.

Examples:
> *This fine weather is* too *good to* last.
> *She wants* to *go* to *the party* too.

**5 OF and OFF**

Example:
> *This jar* of *jam smells as if it's gone* off;

**6 RIGHT and WRITE**

Example:
> Write *these words on the* right *side of the board: that's* right.

4 *Marking spellings*

Unless you are wanting to make a point about carelessness don't mark any more than five mistakes per piece of work. There is a practical and a philosophical reason for this. The practical reason is that five is just about the optimum number to be learned by a pupil at any one time. The philosophical reason is that we want to boost the self-image of the weak speller. If this worries you your department should send a letter out to parents explaining this policy. Such a letter will head off complaints and indeed build up the image of the English Department in the eyes of parents as a Department which thinks about and implements a common policy amongst its teachers.

*Which five errors do you choose?* Not the first five. Preferably choose five which form a pattern of some kind. Mark them as spelling mistakes and then spell out the key mis-spelt section, especially if it is a word in its own right, either above the word or in the margin. This will help the speller to focus on the wrong part of the word which will, in turn, help the pupil to learn that word. Here are some examples:

5 *Learning from mistakes*

Spend time teaching the whole class how to learn spellings. Writing the word out five times is an ineffective way. If you have no way of your own, try the following way. Better still make it department policy so that it can be taught to all pupils in the first year. Make it part of the letter to parents and ask them to help.

## SNAGS V

**Learn spellings**
- If you have spelt a word wrongly and that word has been corrected for you, *you must learn it*. There are many ways to learn spelling but this is the best way. It is in seven short stages and it works.
- Find — write out — check — copy over and sound out five times — cover — write out — check.
  (1) Find. Look over each piece of work that has been marked. Find the words that you have spelt wrongly and that the teacher has spelt for you.
  (2) Write out. Write the word out correctly spelt on a spelling page in the back of your book.
  (3) Check. Go back to the page you were copying from. Check *letter by letter* that you have spelt the word correctly. It is worse than useless to learn wrong spellings.
  (4) Go over the actual letters of the word you have written down *five times*. As you go over the letters sound the word out in your head, so that as you copy it you can hear the sounds that the separate syllables make. When you have done all this the word will look like this

  *separate*

  (5) Cover. Cover the word with your other hand.
  (6) Write out. Write the word out without looking at it. Sound it out in your head as you do so.
  (7) Check letter by letter that you have learned the word. If you have followed this method you will have learned it.

- Your teachers will normally help you by giving you only five words to spell at once. Once you have learned a word, practise it by using it again.
- This way of learning spellings will become easier as you get used to it. It will help you. Use it. Don't learn more than five spellings at once. It is best to use this method little and often.

- If you organize yourself to learn one spelling a day and keep to it you will make your spelling much better in less than six months.

**6** *The spelling rules*

I don't find these very useful in the classroom as there are too many exceptions. There are some schools which even teach the incomplete form of some rules. How can you spell 'weight' if you don't learn the last line of the *ie* rule: 'Whenever the sound is a long *eee*'? I do use the rule of doubling a consonant after a short vowel to set the class off on a search for examples. This can not only reinforce the spelling rule but also introduce them to new words.

**7** *Building words up*

Many words will be better spelt if the speller takes the word back to its base word:

- *Cigarette* is a small *cigar* and they would not spell cigar with an e.
- *Cupboard* was for *cups*.
- If you first think of *busy* you will get the *s* and the *i* the right way round in *business*.
- *Definitely* comes from *finite*.
- It is worth spending time building up word families (not only to help spellings). *Circle* is a good word to use: circle, circling, circuit, circulate, circulation, circumstances, circumstantial and even circumcise.

**8** *Introduce new words*

When you deliberately or inadvertently introduce a word that is unfamiliar to some of the class then do not just say the word once.

- Pronounce it several times
- Explain the meaning clearly
- Write up the spelling and comment on any patterns within the word.
- Patterns in words are most important when learning spellings.

**9** *What to do in class when someone asks you to spell a word*

    (a) Offer the dictionary. This isn't a wonderful approach as it is too slow. Children are reluctant to use dictionaries and they rarely learn from looking words up.

    (b) 'Try the word on this piece of paper and I'll check it for you.' This approach is much more effective especially as you can often praise them for getting part of the word right. You may also be able to devise an on-the-spot memory-helper for the bit they got wrong. If you can organize yourself well, the piece of paper with the words on can then be a useful list for any class teaching of spelling that you have in mind. But I would like to stress again that class teaching is not always applicable to spelling.

# 4 Grammar

## What is the object of it all?

A teacher came round to talk to the parents of one of her pupils. The pupil herself answered the door.
Teacher: Where are your parents?
Little girl: They was in but now they is out.
Teacher: 'Was in . . . is out' where is your grammar?
Little girl: In the front room watching the telly.

Many a true word is spoken in jest. In this joke we side with the little girl. She has answered the question and made her meaning quite plain. What purpose does it serve for the teacher to use the word *grammar*? In these circumstances, none. The pupil does not understand the concept. She might well have understood a straightforward correction of her statement but the teacher does not offer that; and the little girl does what she can to understand the teacher.

Of course it is not that simple, but when considering how we approach grammar we need to know what the object is. If the object is to allow children who already use their language well to have a clearer understanding of its structure then we need to teach grammar. It is implicit in all that I have said about knowing the rules before you break them. If the object is to improve accuracy by teaching grammar then there are shortcuts, because grammar is considerably more complex than correcting a few mistakes.

In the section on complex punctuation we referred to the word *clause*. In writing *SNAGS* we found that we needed to refer to the following grammatical terms: the parts of speech, finite verb, tenses, phrase, clause, subject and object. As well as those recognized terms, we invented a new one: the supporting clause. This refers to the words about *who* was speaking and *how* they were speaking and is useful when discussing the punctuation of speech. Speech is then split up into two parts: the spoken words and the supporting clause. We used this and the other terms because they are precise and therefore a shorthand way of describing the process. The difficult question thus arises as to whether this terminology is useful to the pupils and at what stage it should be attempted.

Here is another sample from SNAGS:

## SNAGS VI

**Finite verbs**

A finite verb is limited by subject and tense.

Look carefully at the following sentence:

*Feeling very curious and wondering if his sharks were thirsty, Stanley tried to tip a bottle of beer into the fish tank.*

In this sentence, there are two *finite verbs*: *were* and *tried*. Each of them has a subject (his sharks, Stanley), and is in the past tense (it is quite clear that these events have already happened).

There are three other verbs: *feeling*, *wondering* and *to tip*. None of these is a finite verb. None of them shows completely clearly the tense (whether the event is past, present or future). To be classed as finite verbs they would need to show completely clearly their tense and subject.

The following example is not a sentence because none of the verbs is finite.

*Two middle-aged vampires eating pomegranate sandwiches and planning to pour nitric acid over their English teacher . . .*

If you added 'looked out at the garden' it would then be a sentence because 'looked' is a finite verb.

If you changed 'eating' to 'ate' and 'planning' to 'planned' it would then be a sentence because both are finite verbs.

When I ask a fifth year group what a finite verb is only a few have a clue. (The same would be true of adults, even of English teachers.) When I ask the same group what is wrong with the sentence about the middle-aged vampires they can all sense that something is wrong, and given time they will say that it does not seem finished. To call the missing ingredient a finite verb is merely icing on the cake, but then I like icing on cakes and some of my pupils want to know about grammar. Such icing involves several other terms as ingredients: verb, subject, tense. To explain it properly involves the same developmental approach to teaching grammar as we have to teaching sentence punctuation. In fact the two should be developed in tandem. The grammar can then be used to reinforce an already partly mastered skill.

Once we have decided on *when* to teach grammar we need to discuss *how* to teach it. The following checklist offers some suggestions:

## Checklist

- Teach it in small doses.
- Deal with one concept at a time and give each concept time to develop.
- Fit in your teaching of the parts of speech with the needs of the Modern Languages Department.
- Play classroom games: for example, in small groups each pupil names a noun or an adjective and is counted out if they name one that someone else has used.
- Use the collage approach to sentences with the names of each part of speech under the word.
- Teach grammar to the whole class. Because it is slow and logical use a pretence, for instance a problem that has arisen with one person, to go over the concept with the whole class.
- Take your time and make sure that *you* (!) fully understand the term *before* you explain it.
- Once a grammatical term has been taught then use it. If they all know what a pronoun is, then the line of poetry that is giving problems because no one has yet identified the pronoun becomes much easier to deal with.

There is obviously a place for teaching grammar in all secondary schools but that place needs defining. In a sense grammar, although rarely at the forefront of the English teacher's concerns, is always there in the background to be relied on even if it is not often remarked on — like the grandma in the joke, watching the telly.

# Taking the pressure off . . . how to help them avoid mistakes

In common with many other schools we use work journals. The purpose of the work journal is to allow pupils to comment on the teacher's teaching and the work they are asked to do. Because we want authentic statements we promise not to mark the spelling and the punctuation in the work journals. And they aren't any the worse for that! Mistakes can take care of themselves. Taking the pressure off *can* work to improve accuracy.

But no single idea will work on its own, especially if you don't structure it. There can in the end be no split between content and accuracy. Both are a part of the logic of conveying meaning. Surely the ideal is that when our pupils put pen to paper they are striving to create meaning which can be readily understood. It is important that they do not see accuracy as an extra, demanded by pedantic English teachers. Three central strategies, then, for healing the gap between accuracy and content.

### First, give pupils time.

This is especially important in the second and third year when pupils should be moving away from mere flow to more careful planning and structuring of their work. If you give time for a rough version then pupils have the time to make choices which is the key to improving writing. If the work is for presentation in a pamphlet or for the wall, then the onus is on them to 'GET IT RIGHT'. Not because their teacher will splatter it with red ink if they do not but because we are valuing their work by displaying it; and they will in turn see accuracy as being more important.

### Second, encourage pupils to write in groups and to read each other's work in progress

This can lead to group correcting. You gain every way. You have less marking and the marking you do is more rewarding. You maximize learning. You create an audience for them. The work on the walls is bright and encourages others. On parents' evenings you put on an automatic display to boost the departmental ego. Perhaps most important of all: you have time in class to do some on-the-spot correcting and encouraging. You can give out the dictionaries and go over the SNAGS examples.

### Third, promote the drafting of written work

Drafting is the best way to encourage choice and diversity in pupils' writing. Begin by a general warm-up session before they start writing. As part of the warm-up I ask them to create some of the detail that they will use. In the example which follows pupils had to write a monologue by a person over eighty who now lives in an old folks' home. Jessie began with the name of her old person, Edith Lawton, and some details from Edith's past life. She then wrote her first draft, in rough, on old computer paper. (I use computer paper because there is no chance of it being anything but a rough draft.) Next I asked her to pick an interesting phrase from the piece as her title. Finally she had to cut the piece by one third before presenting it.

Here are both the first version with the crossings out and her final version. Notice that the cutting involves her breaking rules and yet the piece is peculiarly alive because she *has* broken rules. All her changes are improvements. She is actively making choices from the position of a firm understanding of the rules. Her command of the basics has enabled her to use diversity . . . and that is the aim of the whole process of 'getting it right'.

MONOLOGUE                    SUMMERSHADES

EDITH (sits at the window, with a blanket covering her legs, swollen wrists dangleing over chair arms)

Yes ~~Ethel we had great fun that day~~, climbing trees stealing apples, splashing about in the pond at the bottom of our garden. Oh! Summershades was a lovely house. Sitting up on the hill ~~with little Alice~~ and eating breakfast, ~~with the sun browning our legs~~. Sledging down in the Winter with ~~Joe,~~ Bob and Alice.

Oh dear Frank ~~bought~~ me a ring and I lost it the very same day. ~~The only reason he bought it me was because I kept weaving those hapenny rings from slot machines and kept getting sore fingers. For that he bought me a gold ring and I lost it.~~

(Begins to exercise fingers bending and stretching them, wriggles her toes)

~~Oh yes dear, I remember when Joe used to collect me from work in the bus~~ and he used to make all the passengers wait while he walked me up our drive way. Yet none of them minded ~~because he was such a kind hearted man~~.

( Clasps hands together)

165

Wonder what we'll have for dinner hope its soup, don't like to have to chew that tough meat ~~they have here~~. Not like ~~my~~ Grandmothers farm. Fresh meat, home baked bread and cream ~~whenever we wanted~~. Eggs and bacon in the morning, with thick delicious milk. Not like the milk we get here, watered down.

~~Only mother could get Daisy out of that field~~, never seen a cart horse so big. Mother would go in with a sugar lump ~~call her over~~ and she came ~~trotting eagerly to her~~.

---

### Summer shades

EDITH (Sits at the window, with a blanket covering her legs, swollen wrists dangling over chair arms.)

Climbing trees, stealing apples, splashing about in the pond at the bottom of our garden. Oh, 'Summershades' was a lovely house. Sitting up on the hill and eating breakfast: sledging down in winter.

Oh dear, Frank brought me a ring and I lost it the same day.

(She begins to wriggle fingers, bending and stretching them, exercises feet.)

Joe used to collect me from work in the bus. He used to make all the passengers wait whilst he walked me up our drive-way.

(Clasps hands together)

Wonder what we'll have for dinner. Hope it's soup. I don't like to chew that tough meat. Not like grandmother's farm: fresh meat, home-made bread, eggs and bacon in the morning with creamy, thick, delicious milk. Not like the milk we get here — watered down.

Only mother could get Daisy from the field, soft old thing.

'Nurse! Nurse! I want to go to the toilet.'

*Jessie Clarke*

# Recommended reading

*Mark My Words*, Tony Dunsbee and Terry Ford, Ward Lock, 1980

*Teaching the Basic Skills in English*, Don Smedley, Methuen, 1983

*Teaching Spelling*, M Torbe, Ward Lock, 1978

*The West Indian Language Issue in British Schools*, V K Edwards, Routledge & Kegan Paul, 1979

*Awareness of Language: An Introduction*, Eric Hawkins, CUP, 1984

*Languages and Dialects of London School Children*, H Rosen and T Burgess, Ward Lock, 1980

*Becoming our own experts*, The Vauxhall Papers, Schools Council, 1982

*Finding A Language*, Peter Medway, Writers and Readers/Chameleon, 1980

*Man Made Language*, Dale Spender, Routledge & Kegan Paul, 1980

*Language Study, the teacher and the learner*, P Doughty and G Thornton, Edward Arnold, 1973

*Checkbooks: Spelling*, Martin Tucker, Hutchinson, 1984

# 8 Working with poetry

Terry Gifford

## Poetry and parents — why poetry matters

'My own anxiety is that in the concentration of attention upon numeracy and literacy insufficient care will be paid to certain other absolutely basic needs.'

John Watts

One evening each year, parents whose children will be coming to Yewlands Comprehensive School as a 'new intake' attend a meeting in the comfortably carpeted music room. They pass displays of poetry and pictures or photographs in the corridors. Each half-term for the last year they have been receiving a copy of *Yews News*, a free school publication of two folded A4 sheets, the centre one of which contains writing by pupils from first to sixth form, often in the form of poems. As Head of English, I have this crucial opportunity to give them an understanding of what we are doing, a sense of our approach, an indication that we will deliver what they expect of us, and a chance to gain their support as partners in the education process. As I wait, armed with a poem by a fifth year boy, I wonder what they are thinking of all that poetry, knowing that spellings, grammar and exam results will be matters that, quite rightly, will also need comment from me.

The Head refers to the partnership idea, which cues me in. I must be brief and straightforward.

'Hello, I want to start by talking about you, the first educators of your children, and then about us, what we're doing in the English

Department and why. You have already taught your children a lot, and although they are about to come to secondary school you will still have a vital part to play in your children's growth in the really important aspects of their thinking, feeling and behaviour. It won't seem like it at times, I know! But there are two practical ways in which you can help us develop parts of their growth in what is called English on the school timetable.

'We know that each individual child's understanding of what is going on around them is personal to them and grows from their individual way of expressing it. Whether they are dealing with their own dreams, their first experience of a computer or the pressure from their friends towards joining in certain mischief, they need to talk or write about it to find out how they feel and what they think. You will know that a lot of this goes on at home. They have already come to the age when they will be testing out opinions, ways of feeling, ways of understanding on you. It is quite simply through talking and listening to other people outside school that in the next few years your children will grow up as people. And of course it won't always be convenient or easy! But we shall, whether we like it or not, be drawn into the process of talking and understanding both in school and at home. Let's all use this to help feelings and thoughts grow through your child's individual expression.

'I mentioned a book of poetry being taken home, and you'll have seen some displays of children's writing on the walls of the corridors. You'll see more poems when you go into the English classrooms. I don't want you to think that we do nothing else! Stories, novels, plays, tapes and debates are not always best displayed on the walls! But I do want to give you an idea of what we're trying to do in English and how we're doing it by explaining what lies behind our working with poetry.

'You'll be anxious to know how our teaching is going to give your children the best chance to get qualifications and a job. Part of that anxiety will be based on the hard facts that not all children will be able to get high qualifications or a job. Even those in work in the future will not necessarily keep it for all their lives or for all of the week. Our exam pass rate is above the national average. Last year only three out of fourteen 'A' level English candidates failed, and half the group gained the top three grades. Our record as a school in helping our students get jobs is good.

'However our students will become not only workmates but also parents, friends, neighbours. The education of the feelings was never more important in a society that is under stress. The growth of children into people with a secure sense of themselves has never been more important. The writing of poetry will not achieve this in itself, of course, but you can see that it has a part to play in the development of a confident personal view of the world and in the education of a sensitive, alert person. The writing of poetry brings together feeling and thinking. The exercise of the imagination is not separate from the development of opinions. An expression and arrangement of images of reality shows an attitude towards that reality.

'We're told that the workers of the future will need to be adaptable to cope with fast changing technologies. Flexibility, initiative and divergent thinking away from traditional patterns will be needed in the world your children will live in. Poetry is not the only educational tool that will help develop these qualities but you can see that its exploring and its discovery of ways of feeling and thinking will be useful. I'd also like to develop a critical curiosity in your children's attitude towards their future world.

'And then there are the other basics. Poetry, more than other forms, demands precision in choice of words, accurate punctuation and careful spelling if it is to communicate the writer's intention to the reader. Spellings which need to be corrected after a first draft will be added to each pupil's personal spelling list which forms the basis of their individual learning about spellings.

'Finally, I always like to give parents a sample of the goods after all my sounding off about our intentions. So I ask you to imagine a fifth year boy who is more interested in motor-cycles than English, and who probably sees himself as a pretty unsentimental character. His last English teacher is on maternity leave at present. She brought her eight week old baby into the classroom last week and this is how Dean Wade saw baby Michael Sellars:

**Michael Sellars**

Eyes like pies,
Lips like chips,
Ears like spears,
And a head like a bed.
He wriggles like a worm,
His hands are like an action man's,
His skin is soft and pale.
His finger nails are
Like pin heads.
The veins in his head are like a road map.

*Dean Wade*

# You've written your first poem

'We used to do it as a punishment when we were talking.'
(first year pupil quoted by Ray Tarleton in *English in Education*, Autumn, 1983)

'I can't write poems,' children often say, even after they have written them quite successfully once or twice. Only regular practice and the teacher's devising ways of celebrating the quality of the work will result in 'I can't write poems' being heard less in the classroom. But how to get over the first hurdle of actually writing the first poem? 'Today we're going to write a poem' is what I avoid saying. I simply take the class through a series of stages at the *end* of which I can say 'Today you've written a poem!'

First we might go out of school on a walk, preferably through a park, during which pupils are asked to collect just one small object that can easily be brought back to school without destroying any part of the environment! Alternatively children can be asked to bring something small to school or to choose from a collection assembled by the teacher. As each pupil sits with their object in front of them I give an instruction to the class, and go round helping people who have 'stuck', expressing genuine delight and surprise at some of the marvellous things being written. I emphasize the tentative spirit of the exercise and move on fairly quickly from one stage to the next.

The following is a step-by-step guide to what I ask pupils to do:

1  List down the left-hand side of the page words to describe the:
   shape of the object
   texture of the object
   smell
   colours
   how the parts fit together
2  Make comparisons for as many of these words as possible using 'like', 'as though', 'as if'.
3  Choose one of these comparisons to turn into a summary statement: 'It is a . . .'
4  Make notes to describe the place one metre around where you found it, then standing further back the sort of place more generally.
5  Write your rambling thoughts about how it got there, the story behind it.
6  What does it make you think about? What does it represent, symbolize for you? What message does it leave you with?

7 Write a rough draft of a poem, based on these notes, words, and ideas. Do not necessarily follow this order, start where you like, with an idea from the middle of your notes perhaps. Avoid rhyme at the moment. Write in sentences for most of the poem. Choose active words rather than lots of words ending in -ing.

8 For the next stage I take any first draft from a pupil who offers it to me. I write the first lines on the board just as they are written, e.g.

> As we walked on the stony winding path
> The mist quickly rose up like the smoke
> of a burning fire.

I then show how this can be spaced out just as the phrases are spoken:

> As we walked
> On the stony winding path
> The mist quickly rose up
> Like the smoke
> Of a burning fire.

Finally I show how spacing can give dramatic impact to key words:

> As we walked on the
> Stony winding path
> The mist
> Quickly rose up
> Like the smoke of a
> Burning fire.

After considering these alternatives, Russell's final draft printed in *Yews News* reads:

> As we walked on the stony winding path
> The mist quickly rose up
> Like the smoke of a burning fire.

9 I ask for a final draft using spacing for the best effect of the words.

10 We illustrate, illuminate the MS, blue-tack them all onto the walls, display the objects, then walk around matching poems to objects and selecting those we like. (My own poem is usually then criticized for trying to be too clever!)

These stages have produced for each pupil his or her own descriptive poem, some parts of which will usually have surprised them. Certainly they will be impressed by some of the poems up on the walls round the room by the end of this process. Incidentally, have no fear of asking which poem is liked best because, even if there is one outstandingly popular poem, in my experience a lot of other poems will also be acclaimed. The reading out of bits that are felt to be 'good' by pupils can be a great celebration at the end of the session. Then there is the possibility of using the poems for an assembly or as a reading for another class.

The major elements of this ten-part process of poetry writing can form the basic pattern of all forms of poetry writing whether reflective, narrative or experimental. Making notes of words, ideas, feelings, images, followed by a first draft that gets the words flowing, leads on to a sharpening of the words and expressions, and finally a couple of drafts that explore the possibilities of the rhythms created by shape or form. Reading aloud helps get the feel of the form as it affects the reader's eye and understanding. The emphasis should be on precision of choice of words and ideas. From this, the power of suggestion from the way those words are spaced will be sensed increasingly by the writer.

Good habits established early allow for greater flexibility and complexity later. Writing mainly in sentences, and punctuating the poem, just as you would for sentences of prose, help to avoid a lot of children's misunderstandings about writing poetry and show that it is about helping the reader understand the writer's suggestions. Choosing words which rhyme is very difficult if you have also to choose the best, most accurate and suggestive words in the early stages of writing. Similarly the power of active verbs and positive forms of expression are to be encouraged at first in order to avoid those rather wet lists of self-indulgent feelings which children can assume to be what writing poetry is all about.

Finally the spirit of writing should be one of an interesting exercise, a little imaginative adventure which may lead to something exciting or may lead to something fairly straightforward. It is difficult to set out to write a good poem. The spirit of the enterprise needs not to be intimidating or precious, although the results can sometimes be valued for just those features! It is a case of 'let's have a go and see what we've got only at the end', recognizing that some exciting things might be appearing on paper in the room at every stage of the process.

# Ideas for writing poems

'To teach English is to seek the elucidation and celebration of the self through the art of symbolization.'

Peter Abbs

## Starters

I have increasingly come to feel that exercises that are set not only provide practice but can 'accidentally' unlock the needs of the psyche and produce an important poem that has explored a hardly conscious preoccupation. A number of adult writers set each other projects in this way. Teachers have been forcing exercises upon pupils for years, but they know that the best work comes from the most telling starters. For two workshops with sixth formers which were organized by visiting writer David Craig he set the following:

1 'You are struggling to gain a foothold. Finally, after much effort, you only just make it.'
2 'You come home and all is not as you expected it to be. Write as a character who is the opposite from you in all respects: age, sex, etc.'

An exercise in exploring extended metaphors began with the following instruction:

'Sometimes poems can develop one image or idea, exploring its implications, seeing where it leads. Taking one of the following, make yourself extend it, taking it as far as you can:
    The playground is a whale's back.
    The road is a throat.
    Your house is a ship.'

## Write in the city

An arts centre right in the centre of the city provided a base from which people went out for an hour collecting images of the city in words which they noted down and brought back. They were then asked to go through the following exercises:

1 Choose one particular place providing an image and note what it was that struck you about it.
2 List words that describe its sounds, smells, feel, colours, touch, shapes and patterns.
3 Choose three of these words and add comparisons.
4 Using some of the words written so far, write one sentence that tries to sum up this place or image, e.g. 'Like an urban gypsy's skirt, the ragged bill-board dances the colours of the city's nightlife'.

5 Write a snatch of dialogue that might be overheard in this place.
6 Note a personal reminisence that this place brings to mind.
7 Using some of the above material, or going back to something else you want to explore, begin the first draft of a piece of writing.
8 Consider what form it will finally be written in, and make a second draft.

**Choose a summer tree**
In preparation for a poem about a tree chosen on a visit to a park or in the school grounds, pupils were given this worksheet:

These questions are to help you produce unusual but accurate images and ideas. *Look* at your tree for *each* question.

1 Make a free description of what strikes you about your tree in your own words.
2 (a) List words to describe the way the branches hang or stand.
  (b) Use those words to complete this sentence. 'The branches...'
3 List words to describe the leaves from where you are.
4 Make a comparison for the shape of the tree. ('Like . . . something')
5 Words to catch the movement of this particular tree in the wind.
6 Write at least two sentences about whether the tree fits in or stands out from its surroundings. What is it *like*? Does it remind you of anything standing just there in that way?
7 What would be the ideal setting for your tree? Describe it.
8 What is the character of this tree? What impression does it give? If it were a person what sort of person would it be?
9 What would be its main mood?
10 What colour would be its favourite?
11 If it sang what sort of voice would it have?
12 What sort of song would it sing?
13 If it could speak what would it have to tell? What would its one sentence be?
14 What would you want to say to that tree about itself?
15 If it were not a tree but a bird, what sort of bird would it be?
16 If it were not a tree but an animal, what sort of animal would it be?
17 If it were not a tree but a machine, what sort of machine would it be?

**Using films**
Films provide ready-made visual images that can successfully provide

175

the material for writing poems. If you are reading *The Midnight Fox* with first years as a class novel a film on foxes might well be available from the LEA Audio-Visual Aids Centre, delivered to school free of charge. Do not be afraid to order films intended for Biology or Geography teachers! If you are discussing nuclear weapons with fifth years and have a TV documentary on video it may provide suitable images for exploring some personal thoughts and feelings in a poem before the debate is underway.

When screening a film for this purpose I do so with the sound off first, talking pupils through the first stages of note-making, basically listing words to chart a sensate response to images of impact: movement, shapes, colours, feelings evoked. Secondly, I reshow the silent film asking pupils to add items to their notes: comparisons, thoughts, symbols, associations. Finally, I run the film with the sound on asking pupils only at this stage to note any information that particulaly strikes them, and sounds that seem significant to them. These notes then form the basis for a poem which may be simply descriptive, or may explore an association, or may consciously explore something overtly symbolic in the images seen. The following poem was produced after watching a film on 'The Life Cycle of the Toad':

### Toad Princes

God, that Toad is there again,
Bothering me.
What does it want me to do?
Let it sleep on my pillow,
Eat at my table?
Should I kiss it?
Maybe it will turn into some handsome Prince,
But I am no Princess.
That Toad turned Prince would still bother me.
I have no time
For Toads or Princes
And the bother they bring.
I want to get on with my life.
But Toads and Princes stand in my way,
Confuse me, jump in my path, love me.
It's unfortunate that I need them so much.

*Emma Hall*

## Museum loans

The ability to produce a fox in a glass case when reading *The Midnight Fox* with a class, or a mounted kestrel to look at closely and catch something of Billy Casper's enthusiasm for the bird when reading *Kes*, is not necessarily impossible. Our local museum has a schools loan service, with free delivery and collection, all for the effort of a phone call. These resources are worth finding out about since they can obviously provide fascinating starting points for writing poetry. A catalogue of items for loan is provided for each school so that what is available can easily be scanned.

## Sports poems

Intense experiences often come from concentrated physical activity and there is no reason why these should not be celebrated in poetry. Particularly interesting work may arise after pupils have been experiencing a sport for the first time. My own form of third years took part in four outdoor activities as part of the school's annual residential experience. Stephen had never been in a canoe before and on the evening of the day of his first experience he wrote the following poem which is interesting for its struggle with language, despite its control of structure:

### The Experience of Canoing

Like a Rowntree's jelly,
I began to get into the canoe.
Scared that I would be a rolling barrel,
I started as slowly as I possibly could.
My feelings were not with me,
I could feel them flying away.
But gradually, more machine came into my body,
And the idea of body and muscles came to my senses.
I swiftly deteriated the facts that I was scared,
And I smoothly began canoing.
Faster and faster like the Orient Express.
Splash after splash went the water.
Like nothing was going to stop me.
Full of confidence.
I went faster and faster, faster and faster, faster and faster.
Until I became,
A rolling barrel.

*Stephen Coldwell*

## Poem models

Adrian Henri's 'Love is . . .' provides an example of the fact that the quality of a model will be reflected in the quality of the writing which follows it. Adrian's poem is not intended to be taken seriously and neither has the work which I have had from pupils following his format. A less mechanical format which provides deeper openings for exploration is to be found in Miroslav Holub's poem 'Man Cursing the Sea' (*Voices I*). The best models are obviously the best poems, but to use them regularly as models can become mechanical. Here is a cursing poem by a third year based on Holub's poem:

### Cursing Smoke

She watched the twisting smoke
from the cigarette
until her eyes stung and ran.
She hated that smoke
and cursed it
like this:
    Innocent, clean, whiteness
    concealing the black death
    that hangs there.
    Immitating the fluffiness of clouds
    to coax its real dirty, sooty way
    to you.
    Its swirling grace and
    Snow White loveliness
    carry decay and poison.
    A hateful, evil, murderer
    in a cloak of beautiful white.
Yes, deceiving
with twining threads of
silk-like softness.
With gentleness of floating feathers.
Just until it has you.
Then, laughing, it changes
back to its true
oily identity.
Smoke that cannot get to you
dances away in fright,
staying only to pollute
and infect the air.
You have me now
clever smoke.
Why did I let your plan
work on me ?
Now I don't think
I'll ever be
rid of you.

                                 *Kelly Broomhead*

**Haiku**

The examples in *Voices I* led me to Harold G Henderson's *An Introduction to Haiku*, (Doubleday, New York, 1958). This little paperback contains many witty examples of haiku suitable for use in school. I used the form to create a sequence of mood poems by describing at different times of the year the same clump of trees seen from the window of a classroom in which I taught. Here are three examples (which do not keep to the 5,7,5 syllable pattern):

24th November —
   At the last attempt of the day
   In the clarity of death
   Sun fires a corner of holly.

1st December —
   Frosted coral, thin-boned
   Waits at the bottom of the
   Motionless sea of space

19th January —
   Three cornets of ice-cream, topped
   By thin wafers : bushes take
   The strain, trees strain the wind.

*Terry Gifford*

**At the art gallery**

Collections of posters, prints, slides and photographs need not preclude the use of 'live' art. These days municipal art galleries are under pressure to demonstrate their usefulness and often have an education officer with whom you can discuss the possibilities in the year's programme of exhibitions and activities for your English teaching, and poetry writing in particular.

**Reflecting on experiences**

A real success in developing an enthusiasm and sense of the usefulness of poetry writing will be reflected in pupils bringing to school poems written at home in order to explore their own personal experiences. Of course this will never happen for some pupils so I sometimes ask for a poem to be brought back after a holiday break which reflects on some, not necessarily very recent, experience. I was making this invitation after discussing with a fifth year class D H Lawrence's poem 'A Winter's Tale'. Lorraine brought back a poem which I would like to print in full because it is an invaluable resource and a fine poem:

### Experience

The sky
Was light purple, and there was
A thin grey mist on the mountains.
It was cool,
And we sat, Jenny, Michael and I and we sang
Softly into the wind
And our voices came back clear.
And then the cow began to cry, but
Softly,
As if she wanted to hide her pain
We watched her and she lay down under an oak.
And Jenny and I both looked at Michael
Anxiously.
But he said, 'It's all right'.
And I said, 'Are you sure?' and Jenny said 'Be quiet,
He should know'.
And then her cries came louder and I sensed
Her pain, and Michael laughed because he saw
Our eyes were wet.
And then the cow stood up
And heaved, and then we saw two hooves appear.
I looked at him, then, strangely shy,
Looked down.
And Michael said, after we'd watched her for
A while.
'It's no good, she can't do it by herself.
We'll have to catch her,
Then you
Can help me help her'.
'Yuck', said Jenny.
And I thought the same,
But didn't say so.
He chased her and I stood and held the shippen door,
While Mike and Jenny slowly drove her in.
I tied her up.
The concrete walls sent echoes of her cries.
I looked at him and questions glinted in his
Pale blue eyes.
He said to Jenny, 'Fetch a rope.
No, wait. Fetch two. Lorraine you help me
Pull.'
He tied a rope around one hoof.
I tied my rope around the other, but
It slipped, the slime had forced it off.
I pulled

A face. 'I hope it's not as bad as this for us.'
The ropes were tight and Michael whispered
'Whisht, Polly, Whisht, Polly. Good girl,
To me he said,
'Pull down.
Not now.
Pull
When she heaves.
Pull now.'
And then her body seemed to swell and then
The head came out.
The eyes were closed and on the mouth was blood.
And Jenny turned away and I just looked.
'A bull', he said, and I said 'How d'you know?'
'Shut up', he said, 'and pull'.
The body came.
The hind legs, crossed, came out in front.
He looked at me and laughed, I think
Because my hair was in my eyes
And all my face was all screwed up
Like some old
Apple.
And as I looked into his eyes
The cow came second
And I slipped.
I knelt there on the bloody, slimy floor
And pulled
And cried,
Because I found my strength
And that of Michael and the cow
Were not enough.
Then Jenny saw my tears because she came.
Love overcame disgust
For her, too.
She took my rope
with me.
As Polly strained we pulled.
She heaved, her body swayed. I held my breath.
It dropped.
Onto the hard, cold stony floor
And splashed us all
With blood. The afterbirth
Hung, swaying, from the trembling cow,
As on the floor the calf lay still.
'It isn't dead?' I said, and shook with sudden
Cold.
'It must have hurt it, falling on the concrete floor.'

'Oh no!' He laughed. 'It's like the doctor slapping you
When you were born.'
And I felt angry, for he'd made me feel
Just like a child,
Now I have learned so much, and felt more
Adult
Than I ever had before.

*Lorraine Whiting*

## Wallpaper poems

A roll of wallpaper blue-tacked to a wall, white side outwards, is hard to resist. I just write a line and pass on the felt-tipped pen to someone else asking them to add a line and pass the pen on to someone else ... The following poem was written at a workshop for probationary teachers and stands as a serious reminder to all of us:

The first years of teaching
are like
throwing snowballs in summer,
eating ice-cream in a fridge,
a waterfall,
being Yosser Hughes
(and Yosser Heaney)
male and pregnant,
chewing water,
breaking in wisdom teeth,
dropping pebbles in a chasm,
being an extra in *Zulu*
trying to turn off a very loud alarm clock that you can't quite reach,
picking your teeth with a large pole,
reading graffiti with the light off,
standing in a puddle with holes in your wellies,
writing with a felt tip that keeps running out,
knitting with slippery slime.

*Sheffield teachers*

# Engagements with texts

'First encounters in the classroom should deliberately hold back formulation, should back away from anything that is not tentative and partial.'

D W Harding

All of the following activities can be used with pupils across the secondary age range to promote engagement with poetry texts being studied in class.

1 **Anthologies** Make an anthology of six poems you like. Write an introduction which says in at least two sentences why you have chosen each poem. Quote one line or phrase from each poem and say what you like about it. Swop anthologies.

2 **Five questions** Choose a poem. Read it carefully then write five questions to which you would genuinely like to know the answers in order to help you understand the poem. Swop with a neighbour and answer the other person's questions as best you can. Discuss your answers together. 'Earth-Moon', the final mysterious poem in Ted Hughes' *Moon-Bells* is the kind of poem I choose for this purpose.

3 **Sequencing** You have been given three poems on the same theme or that have something in common. Arrange them into a sequence for a reading. Read them aloud to a friend. Ask the friend to guess why you put them in that order. Explain your own reasons for the sequence.

4 **Graffiti board** In a group of four read and discuss together two selected poems. You have a graffiti board (a sheet of white card) to record your responses, thoughts and opinions aroused by these poems. You have felt tipped pens of two colours. Think about how you will use these two colours. You must write down some lines from each poem. You can use arrows and boxes if you want to show how things relate to each other or are grouped. Poems 13 and 14 in *Voices II* work well for this.

5 **Ratings** In pairs read poems 86–93 in *Voices I* and discuss the extent to which the writer admires or dislikes the creature in each poem. Mark a scale along the long edge of a piece of paper with '+10, Likes a lot' at one end and '-10, Dislikes a lot' at the opposite end, marking off the units in between. Now write the title of each poem where you think it should go on the scale.

6 **Remake a poem** In an envelope are the cut up lines of a poem called 'Lineage' by Ted Hughes (*Crow*, Faber, 1970). Use them to make your own poem by putting them in order, leaving spaces where you want to. When you are ready, stick them on to a piece of paper to show other groups. When you have stuck your lines onto the page, add the word 'because' to any three lines and complete the sentence by writing on the page. (For further work on 'Lineage' developed as an induction into sixth form English see my chapter

'Creative Responses in the Sixth Form' in *English Studies 11–18: an arts-based approach*, edited by Bernard Harrison, Hodder and Stoughton, 1983).

7 **Themes** There are certain dangers in using poems as 'evidence' when following a theme or discussing an issue. The poetry can become a quarry for 'content' and the full celebration of the poem as poetry can be neglected. If used carefully, however, a poem can make an important, delicate, contribution. A fourth year class had been comparing a South African embassy propaganda film about the 'homelands' with a TV documentary about the eviction of Africans to the homelands and the human effects of the policy of 'separate development'. We then read 'Telephone Conversation' by Wole Soyinka (*Voices III*). This turned the attention of our work towards racism in our own country. The wry bitterness of the poem I have always found to be a powerful powder keg for pupils' responses.

# Visiting writers

'I thought we were in for an hour of poetry, but we were in for an hour of laughs!'

4th year boy on Mike Rosen's visit

## Devising a programme of visits

The timing of visits by writers, the reasons for inviting them, the brief given to them and the funding for these visits throughout the school year can all be very much an *ad hoc* business. We recently tried to rationalize our planning and funding of visiting writers and performers, including trips out of school to arts events. After discussions in the English department we produced a carefully argued paper recording our work in this area over the last few years and its benefits, and setting out how we might plan a programme for the following year. It is a plea for extra money aimed at the senior management group. When you distribute a paper like this to all the agencies in the LEA that might be helpful you get known as a school that will take visiting performers. We have been asked to take a writer 'tomorrow morning' to fill a gap in a tour that was already funded. We found that we had first refusal on bookings being made for writers coming into the area. Our Neighbourhood Arts Group used our school as a venue for other schools and adult groups to see visiting performances. It pays to have produced a rationale and to publicize it.

# Arranging a visit

## A few tips:

1 The grapevine is the first way of finding out what different writers have to offer, with which age groups they work best and in what sort of situations. Your English adviser should be able to offer some suggestions.

2 Addresses of writers are available from The Poetry Society, 21 Earls Court Square, London SW5 (tel: 01–373–7861) or their publishers.

3 Go to local poetry readings, form your own impressions and talk to the writers. Find out about the publicity of these readings from the literature office of your regional arts association.

4 Write to or ring a writer to fix a date six months in advance if you want to get the best day of the week for your school's timetable.

5 Complete an application form for the subsidy which is available from your regional arts association. They will pay travel expenses and half the fee (currently £60 for a half day session) after a report on the visit has been received from the school.

6 Order the writer's books for the department or the school library, and the school bookshop.

7 Clear with the Head teacher and other staff any necessary timetable rearrangements.

8 Send a full brief to the writer together with details of any transport arrangements.

9 Begin any preparations you intend to undertake with the pupils: reading selected poems, compiling requests, listing questions, collecting their own work to send to the writer *ahead* of the visit.

10 Make final reminders to other staff about any timetable changes. A notice should go up on the staffroom noticeboard mentioning the visiting writer's credentials. Display a selected poem or two in the staffroom. (Have these signed at breaktime during the visit.)

11 Arrange with the school office to have payment and travel expenses available.

12 On the day of the visit do not forget to get a few school copies of books signed. Take some photographs of the writer with a group of children. Ask permission to publish a poem later alongside the children's.

13 Write your report for the regional arts association, or ask some children to do so, before you forget. Put a copy in the staffroom and the Head's office.

**14** Most writers will respond to children writing to them, or sending work after the visit, with a note of thanks.

## Using visiting writers

Your choice of writer and the brief you give them can, with experience, serve a particular purpose in your work with a group of children. Here are three examples of what I mean.

**1 David Craig** was asked to demonstrate the process of drafting from examples of his own work. I also knew that his poetry often explores abstract ideas through concrete imagery. The writing of a particular sixth form group tended to remain abstract and I wanted David to show how it could work better as poetry, rather than stated thoughts, if it used physical images. The group were also reluctant to re-draft their work. David's reading to this brief was followed by a workshop on the theme of 'footholds'. Jo Anne's poem illustrates the success of at least the abstract/concrete part of the brief:

### Gaining a Foothold

Pulled
In ever decreasing circles
Towards the whirlpool of Insanity.

Drowning,
In the sea of stupidity,
I grab the branch of knowledge.

It snaps.
But at least now I have something
I can float on.

*Jo Anne Knights*

David Craig's poetry deserves to be more widely used in schools. *Latest News*, Journeyman, 1978 and *Homing*, Platform Poets, The Grove, Gisburn, Lancs, 1980)

**2 John Agard** was born in Guiana and was on a reading tour for the Commonwealth Institute. He brought into our all-white school a celebration of the forms and qualities of a culture that was new to the fifth formers who experienced his performance. He performed dialect poetry of his own, played a tape of Linton Kwesi Johnson reciting to reggae, played a Guianan flute to my reading of one of my poems, and cleverly orchestrated the students' use of Guianan percussion instruments and a coffee cup whilst he read a poem by one of the group called 'The Blacksmith'. In the last ten minutes of the lesson Julie wrote:

**The Man**

A wondering man
A wonderful man,
A man filled with art and creation,
A man with ambitions
To fill the heads of children with ideas
That take them from the dull humdrum world
To show them a world full of colour, music, poetry and art.
Yet he shows them reality.

*Julia McHale*

3 **Mike Rosen** is again an entertainer as much as a poet — I wanted to engage him for a dull time of year to give as many pupils as possible a lift. Usually I avoid making large audiences for visiting poets; the intimacy of talking to a writer from the security of your own form group is what I usually try to provide. Mike Rosen performed to whole year groups in the hall. I had just intended some fun with poetry, but I had bought some small sets of Mike's books beforehand to send him a few requests for readings from pupils who I thought would get a boost from being associated with a wicked incident in one of his poems and from being named at the mass reading. After Mike had gone his books were, of course, in great demand all over again.

The Poetry Secretariat's Writers in Schools Scheme provides finance for a publication to follow the two visits by the writer.

# Celebrations — poetry in the life of the school

'The final stage of the art-making process lies with the audience, in their response to and evaluation of the art that has been produced. Do the forms embody the secrets of their own hearts? . . . Or is it sham? Ego writ large?'

Peter Abbs

## In the classroom

Work displayed on classroom walls should be used as part of the resources in the room. Some time should be spent by children walking around when a new display goes up. Children should be directed to look at someone else's work at appropriate moments in their own work, perhaps to see how someone has used spacing to good effect, or developed an idea throughout a poem, or simply to find something they like and talk about it to a friend.

A booklet of work can be exchanged with another class in the same year. Children are often eager to read the work of friends in other classes and can readily find bits they like. Brief discussions of each other's work needs to start from this positive, celebratory spirit and can then move into a helpful discussion of bits that do not quite work. A class or group workshop of this kind can be useful at the drafting stage. It helps if the teacher has a piece of writing to contribute to the workshop.

Performance in the classroom can be both enjoyable and extending with a little planning. A third year class had recently been having some fun with rhyme and reversals of earth-bound normality by writing moon-creature poems after looking at Ted Hughes' moon-creatures in *Moon-Bells* and *Poetry In The Making*. They gathered in a circle with their final copies. I compiled a list of titles and authors on the board and asked them each to compile a shortlist of poems they liked as they were listening to them. I announced each poem and the pupils read their own. I had made a tape of readings of just three of the Hughes poems backed by music from the BBC Radiophonics Workshop record. This tape I played at different points in the performance. The final discussion of the poems that people had shortlisted was as much a celebration of the work as an evaluation of the performance itself.

If you are happy singing, you can use this to introduce poems. Singing is sometimes regarded by children as not 'real work'. They might not realize that they are doing an oral comprehension on the riddles in 'Scarborough Fair'. The *Voices* books have some tunes at the back which it is worth taking the trouble to learn over the years. My second year class had a Hallowe'en lesson in which we told stories about 'trick or treating' escapades, discussed and rehearsed a class singing of 'The Lyke-Wake Dirge' and worked out some eerie, bone-rattling percussion effects with instruments from the music department. All the time the turnip was circulating with a spoon (from the Domestic Science Department). When the lantern had been made we did a candle-lit performance of 'The Lyke-Wake Dirge' for the second year class next door.

A simple but very effective celebration of poetry in the classroom is to read the same four poems aloud at the beginning of each lesson for a fortnight. Have the pupils each select a poem they like, hear them all, then vote on the four poems to be heard during the following fortnight. Ask pupils to delay discussion of responses until the end of the fortnight, so that changes will have had time to take place in the hearing and appreciation of the poems, as well as perhaps in the readings.

## In the corridors

Use colours and patterns to get work read in displays around the school. Give displays a heading that challenges the passer-by:

'You wondered what it was like at Hesley Wood Camp? 3/4 tell you the Terrible Truth!'

'Did you see Mrs Sellars' baby in school recently? Here's how Michael Sellars looked to 5/7'

'Can you guess which animals are described here by riddling 2/2?'

'Was one of these Valentine's rhymes written for you?'

Photographs, pictures or posters help to attract readers. Poster poems made by a collage of cuttings can be very effective on a wall in front of a big space. Of course, all corridor displays need maintenance and should not stay up too long. Make sure also that there is some work on display next to the staffroom door. It all helps when asking for extra money for the department or cooperation in breaking from the timetable yet again.

## Assemblies

I never find any difficulty in getting assembly time to celebrate pupils' work. Poetry needs a little thought in preparing for a performance to a large audience. There is a limit to everyone's concentration on intensive writing such as poetry if it is only to be heard. A performance called 'Poems of Mystery' by a third year class combined visual and sound effects with clarity of communication. All the class were involved in the performance of eight poems written by themselves, inspired by posters of Jan Pieńkowski's silhouette images. A large number of them were in a band which had composed in the class's music lessons atmospheric music and effects to accompany the poems. The poems were read by eight readers. Three of the more difficult poems were shown on an OHP. An easel stood at the front and clipped onto it was a title page and the eight posters which had been the inspiration of the poems. The pages were turned upwards and over the back of the easel to reveal the next image before its poem was read.

The posters I have been collecting for years. They included some illustrations by Jan Pieńkowski from *The Kingdom Under The Sea* by Joan Aiken (Puffin), Rousseau's 'Carnival Evening', and some posters advertising exhibitions at local art galleries with the words trimmed off. The latter is an excellent source of images which come regularly to our art department.

'Poem of the Week' was an idea taken up by our Head of Sixth Form. Students each took a turn at selecting the poem which was read out at the weekly meeting and mounted for the week in the Sixth Form Common Room. Simple celebration was all that was attempted in this exercise, but the discussion which arose in the common room later often touched important issues.

## Make a tape

You only need to find one member of another department who will collaborate with you on one project to improve the quality of what you offer as a teacher quite memorably.

If the result of collaboration is a tape, you have made a valuable and unique resource. A class had been investigating the experiences at work of one member of their family. This had involved interviews, reports, story collecting, the radio ballad 'The Big Hewer', and finally, after a singing of the splendid song 'Poverty-Knock' (*Folksong In England*, A L Lloyd, Paladium, p. 328) each pupil wrote a work-song on this model to express their feelings about their work. In music lessons they worked on a performance and finally taped them. The same music teacher orchestrated a class performance with percussion of one boy's 'Amulet' poem based on Ted Hughes' poem of that name in *Moon-Bells*. The tape of this is a marvellous celebratory expression of the qualities in the boy's poem.

## Publications

Our Pupil's Pages in *Yews News* which was referred to at the beginning of this chapter gives us a half-termly publication of current work. It is easily compiled because it is both sides of a single A4 sheet turned on its long edge and folded once. It is free to all pupils and parents. Schools must give funding and secretarial support to the celebration of good work. The investment is easily returned in goodwill, respect and more good work. The responsibility for Pupil Pages is part of the job description of a post holder in the English Department.

When a particular unit of work has produced remarkable results it is good to make a one-off publication. Some local authorities provide Print Units which will help teachers get good quality design and production of pupils' work, especially if it is to become a resource for the school or the authority. Your English adviser will know about this. It is valuable also to include an example of the stimulus material, and most writers will be only too delighted if asked for permission. A simple, stapled, flat A4 publication called 'Could This Be Love?' was based on a programme in the BBC *Speak* series.

One sample from 'Could This Be Love?' might be a useful example of what can be opened up by good quality material, in this case Abse's 'Not Adlestrop' and Shakespeare's Sonnet No. 129:

**The Rugged Truth**

Did he love her or lust for her?
What did he really feel?
She knew the answer,
The rugged truth.
But her love for him was deep.

She was just another damsel
Falling for man's hateful lust.
She must kill her love,
And face the fact
That behind that handsome, smiling face
Was the stony lustful stare.

Her love, and his smiles would soon vanish
Like the summer heat.
She would hate and he would lust,
And then it would be too late.

She had to face the rugged truth.

*Anonymous Fourth Year Pupil*

## Special events

There are often opportunities to celebrate poetry through readings, tapes or songs in the special events of the life of the school. It could be the odd reading by a pupil punctuating the Christmas carol concert, or a couple of readings at a meeting of parents. Or you could organize a special poetry evening for parents, perhaps based on the publication following the visits of writers from the Poetry Secretariat's Writers in Schools Scheme. It is a formula which works even against the expectations of the pupils.

191

## Cultural celebrations outside school

'You don't have to go to the Brothers Grimm, or to this or that Book of Beautiful Tales. Great story tellers are amongst us. Sometimes we call them parents', writes Mike Rosen in *Becoming Our Own Experts*, studies of language and learning made by the Talk Workshop Group at Vauxhall Manor School, 1974–79, (available from the ILEA English Centre, Sutherland St. London SW1). Schools in multi-cultural Britain contain children who hear, chant, sing poetry in their home culture whether in the street, in their grandmother's house, at the Mosque, family weddings, at the Gaelic Mod or at the disco. Teachers of poetry have hardly begun to tap this source or tune into these celebrations. Mike Rosen goes on to list forty aspects of kids' culture 'as it exists between young people in schools'. This list which ranges through proverbs, songs, celebrations and feasts, provides food for thought for a teacher of poetry.

One particularly expressive use of a cultural form is recorded on a tape accompanying the Open University Inset Unit P5/30/CN, *Children, Language and Literature*. A seventeen year old boy who provides a DJ and disco service is a 'toaster', an improvisor of words to the rhythms of reggae music. His 'Young Warrior Toast' on this tape is similar to the cultural form made well known by Linton Kwesi Johnson. But most remarkable is a reggae performance by nine year old Jennifer Hughes of Santley School, London. Her poem, 'Voodoo Doll', was written after a school trip to a museum. Here perceptive teachers have drawn from oral tradition a cultural form that is a fine vehicle for this girl's expression of what that Voodoo Doll means to her. Borrow the OU tape from your local teachers' centre; it represents for me a new direction for teachers of poetry in multi-cultural Britain today.

# Recommended reading

*I See A Voice*, M Rosen, Hutchinson, 1981
*Poetry in the Making*, Ted Hughes, Faber, 1967
*Does It Have To Rhyme?*, Sandy Brownjohn, Hodder & Stoughton, 1980
*What Rhymes With 'Secret'?*, Sandy Brownjohn, Hodder & Stoughton, 1982
*Poetry Workbook*, Eric Boagey, University Tutorial Press, 1977
*Teaching Poetry*, James Reeves, Heinemann, 1958
*Understanding Poetry*, James Reeves, Heinemann, 1965

*An Introduction to Haiku*, Harold G Henderson, Doubleday, New York, 1958

*English Studies 11–18: an arts-based approach*, edited Bernard Harrison, Hodder & Stoughton, 1983

# 9 English and drama

Nigel Toye

## Why use drama in English teaching?

Drama, when not specifically 'Theatre Studies', *is* English work.

- It particularly gives contexts for speaking and listening, two core English activities.
- It provides situations to promote reading and writing, the two other central concerns of English teaching.

Most vitally, drama brings the creative spark to talk. When students adopt the roles central to the issue under consideration, the language possibilities are abundant. For example, ask students to frame questions as interviewers of a character from a book and you will find that most students respond more readily, think more creatively and understand more clearly than if they were to discuss the character in a theoretical way.

This 'acting out' need not involve 'acting' in the sense of performing. It does not require the techniques for being another person complete with unusual accent, mannerisms and stage effects. It essentially requires the student only to adopt a new position and to think how he or she would behave in that new framework. The technique is not to rehearse and perform plays, but to set up a situation to be worked through then and there. Preparation may be desirable, but not practice.

## Organization and control

Many English teachers feel that drama presents inordinate organizational and control problems. In fact it can produce fewer problems than much English teaching if the interest is there and a few simple guidelines are followed. The drama work needs:

— control
— cooperation
— security for the individual

**Guidelines**

1 Start your first drama work with a class where you already have a good working relationship.
2 Vary the work and start inexperienced classes with very clear structures.
3 State the rules at the beginning, especially if you are in a large space pupils are not used to working in, e.g.
   — prohibited areas in the hall should be indicated
   — no running unless instructed to
   — no simulated fights
   — soft shoes or no shoes are required
4 Have a clear control signal when work is likely to be properly noisy
   — for example the sounding of a tambour or cymbal, which requires instant stillness. Play games to test the group's responses to it, games like 'move and freeze'.

Always define for yourself the aims of the drama work.

(a) Decide what oral skills or language development a group needs to work at.
(b) Decide what work is appropriate, useful, possible.
(c) Decide on the strategy to employ in starting the work.
(d) Plan the stimulus, detail, materials, e.g. decide on the area, theme or character of the book you wish to explore.

You might also wish to encourage

— listening
— the ability to organize and recount experience
— the use of more formal speech
— the writing of letters, correctly laid out
— the development of logic in argument

So plan stages (b), (c) and (d) accordingly. Sometimes work with the class as a whole, at other times break into smaller groups of fours or fives.

# Drama and literature

Drama can be extremely useful as a support to work on literature, at all levels. This work is *not* the acting-out of books, not the dramatization of the stories, but the exploration of character, theme or style. At the pupils' desks in an English classroom drama can provide opportunities to study the set text or class reader from new angles.

*Note*: I have not given specific age groups for the ideas and examples which follow. They obviously refer to secondary school children, but the flexibility for any piece is considerable. The relevance to age can be shifted by classroom handling, modifying specific input of the raw material, yet retaining the same basic idea.

The aim of what follows is to present to the English teacher unfamiliar with drama techniques a short compendium or resource bank of practical ideas that can be used in the teaching of literature.

## Character study

Pupils question a character from a book about incidents, relationships, attitudes, or motivation. This can be done with the book partly or completely read. Pupils are asked to prepare questions — making notes on paper — they wish to ask a key person. They can do this preparation on their own, in pairs, or in groups.

### Questioning the character 'in role'
**Technique 1**: *Billy Liar* (the play version), by Keith Waterhouse and Willis Hall[1]
Asking questions of Billy Fisher to try to understand why he behaves as he does.

(a) **Q** 'Which girlfriend do you prefer?'
**A** 'I like them all in a way, but I prefer Liz because she's free and has an imagination.'
(b) **Q** 'Why do you lie?'
**A** 'I don't really lie. I like to spice up people's lives by inventing interesting things about them. I can't help it if people haven't got a sense of humour.'
(c) **Q** 'Why are you so lazy, like not going to work on Saturdays?'
**A** 'Don't you believe me either? I just forgot which Saturday it was. I can't help it if they get angry about it. They don't pay me enough anyway.'

These are samples based on work done on the play version of the story showing the sort of answers which can be easily improvised from a knowledge of the text.

Who answers the questions? If the class are inexperienced at this sort of work it is a good idea for the teacher to take Billy's 'part'. The teacher tells the class what is going to happen (the questions having already been prepared): that when he or she sits in the seat at the front he or she is Billy who has come along to help with their work on the book. Classes soon pick up the convention. When the teacher leaves the seat he or she will be coming out of role.

Some students will volunteer to take on similar roles at the front. The 'character' can be 'played' by a pair or small group of students, who can discuss how to answer and can help each other. The teacher can then become one of the questioners, giving him or her the opportunity to raise new issues and follow good ideas from the students. Answers can feed interpretation of the book and produce further questions, especially if students think the 'character' is evading the issue, as a character like Billy might very properly do. Questions can be asked on any aspect of a book, or take readers beyond it into related themes. Useful discussions can arise on the authenticity of the answers — as with evasive ones where Billy's own self-delusion can become clear. Tape the questions and answers if you can so that you have a ready-reference for further discussion.

**Technique 2**: *The Wind in the Willows*, by Kenneth Grahame
Toad might be asked about the way he treats his friends; his love of cars; his unreliability; what he would do if he could do anything he wished.

The interviews can be given a more specific purpose to guide the questions.

* * *

**Class asking questions 'in role'**
**Technique 3**: *The Silver Sword*, by Ian Serraillier
The class are told that they are newspaper reporters at a press conference to interview the children after their adventures. The 'children' sit at the front and answer prepared questions. The reporters ask questions and take notes in order to:

(a) Write a news story for the next edition of the paper to be headlined 'Children Defy Death'.
(b) Write a more descriptive 'feature' article giving a considered and detailed account of the children and the trip.

This single exercise highlights two differing styles of writing, practises the skills of listening and note-taking, question and answer techniques, and tests the pupils' knowledge of the book. 'Characters' can be given questions beforehand to prepare and 'research' answers from the book. The exercise can be done in the whole group, in small groups (of four or five) with tape recorders, or in pairs.

\* \* \*

**The 'trial' as a format in drama**
This is an example of a more formal setting that is useful as a structure to 'examine' many characters.

**Technique 4**: *Of Mice and Men*, by John Steinbeck
George is on trial for the murder of Lennie. A formal court with judge, jury, prosecution, defence, witnesses etc. may be set up, or more simply the class is divided into prosecution and defence groups. They prepare their cases, and questions based on the events of the book, to present to the judge. They decide which witnesses to call and in what order. Curly might be questioned about his part in events, his jealousy of Lennie, his neglect of his wife; Slim might give evidence to show the motives for George's actions; George can be asked about the events in Weed, his relationship with Lennie, Lennie's state of mind, his strength; Candy could testify to the closeness of the two friends and the 'dream' they all shared.

Thus the central issue of the relationship is considered and the attitudes of any number of characters. The conclusion is likely to be that the killing is humanitarian. The class still has to face the dilemma of the 'punishment' for such a 'killing', which, although not the central concern of the book, can lead to vital discussion.

In a similar manner to this Toad, of *The Wind in the Willows* could be tried — or Claudius in *Hamlet*, or Macbeth, depending on the age group of the class.

\* \* \*

**Dramatizing consciences of characters**
**Technique 5**: *Terry on the Fence*, by Bernard Ashley
Terry, the main character, faces a delicate choice when he is forced to steal radios by Les's gang. Does he shop Les or go along with the theft? Will they believe he is innocent anyway? The two sides to the argument can be given to two groups of students to present as a morality play, where a 'Terry' is subjected to the two sides, who make their cases as strongly as they can, calling on the 'gang' or his mother and father to speak.

**Technique 6**: The pressures on Kino can be dramatized and emphasized similarly, using *The Pearl* by John Steinbeck. The decision of what to do with the pearl can be debated in the context of what other characters would do or want Kino to do.

\* \* \*

**Linking books**
**Technique 7**: The work on *The Silver Sword* can be extended by having the class set up a series of 'famous escapes'. The stories of a number of escapers can be produced as a number of interviews, taped and subsequently written up. *Walkabout*, by James Vance Marshall and *The Wooden Horse*, by Eric Williams, are appropriate for this approach, and can be introduced using extracts from each and having the characters interviews based on those. Further 'programmes', which is what the tapes often become, can be based on students' own experiences (e.g. 'Nearly a Nasty Accident') or they can be invented. The radio programme format gives further scope for oral work for the interviewers/presenters, and further 'programmes' might be devised to explore other character links — e.g. 'Famous dreamers': Billy Fisher, Toad, Walter Mitty, Tom Sawyer — followed by the class's very own 'dreamers'.

\* \* \*

**Pair discussions**
For many books and plays pairs of 'characters' may be set up to improvise around the text to test understanding and develop insight. There are many pairs of characters in literature that this approach can be used to explore.

**Technique 8**: *Our Day Out*, by Willy Russell (from *Act One*, edited by David Self and Ray Speakman, Hutchinson)
Set the class, in pairs, the following task:

'One in each pair of girls is Mrs Kay and the other is Carol. Of the boys' pairs, one is Mr Briggs and the other Reilly. Here are two possibilities:

(a) They are discussing the outing two weeks later.
(b) They meet two years later, look back on the event and discuss what happened in between.

Start all the pairs to work simultaneously by counting them in. Allow them five minutes. Then discuss what happened in each pair. Consider the attitudes displayed, the material the pairs improvised and the variations they managed to develop. Only *look at* pairs improvising if the group is experienced enough.

\* \* \*

## Presenting material from a novel
**Technique** 9: *Cider with Rosie*, by Laurie Lee (or any other book steeped in a particular setting or period)

Set groups to collect material from the novel on aspects of childhood at that time: school, home life, entertainments, transport, etc. Each group, as the authorities on that facet of the book, presents its findings as a joint lecture, or as a prepared interview with one of the group, or even as someone from the era. This can be linked with contrasting research on 'Childhood Today' with interviews carried out with brothers and sisters, parents and other peers outside the classroom.

\* \* \*

## Character quotes
Different approaches to character studies can be developed as follows:

(a) Put an empty chair in a space in the room. The character is imagined to be sitting in the chair. Alternatively someone can sit passively there to represent him or her.
(b) Set groups of six to work on different characters from the book or play. They select quotations from the book to sum up the character. They arrange these in a chosen order.

The group stands round the chair and delivers their quotations, presenting the study to the rest of the class.

Here are some variations on this approach:

1 The students speak about or to the character in the role of other characters in the book or play, quoting and/or improvising as they think the character would, to present different attitudes to the character.
2 The character in focus can have the opportunity to reply, even engage in dialogue with each in turn. Or he or she might only be allowed to voice thoughts.
3 Different groups of students can present alternative views of the same character for subsequent appraisal and discussion.

These are extremely useful and effective techniques in studying literature at examination level, particularly in dramatizing the differing views embodied in a question.

## Technique 10: From an examination paper:
' "A clever rogue"; "a drunken fool"; "a loveable old man". Which of these descriptions of Sir Toby Belch in *Twelfth Night* seems to you the most appropriate?'

Three groups can represent one each of these views, using the characters and quotes most appropriate for each. The approach for the presentation must be biased, the balanced view being considered by the class at the end and conclusions drawn.

For a looser, more fictional build-up of a character, imagined characters can be added: colleagues, relatives and acquaintances from the focus character's background.

**Technique 11**: *Billy Liar*, by Keith Waterhouse and Willis Hall
For a characterization of Billy Fisher, Shadrack and Duxbury, Billy's employers, or Rita's brother, all of whom are mentioned in the play but do not appear, could be 'called' in addition to the main characters. Comments from them could be based on what we know from the play: the employers talking of Billy's thefts and his laziness; Rita's brother talking of the way Billy treated his sister. Decisions about this would be made by the group *and* the preparation for him or her would be their responsibility.

**Technique 12**: *Z for Zachariah*, by Robert C. O'Brien
Mr Loomis can be built up more as a character by using the background material from the book as a basis for 'people' from that past. They would speak of him as they knew him before the disaster. Thus understanding of the background is checked and ideas about the character and his motivation tried out.

\* \* \*

**Exploring situations or themes**
**Technique 13**: *The Thirty-Nine Steps*, by John Buchan

The class are set the task of working in groups to prepare the material for a talk, lecture, written paper on the 'ingredients of a mystery story'. They are introduced to the idea as if they are experts on the genre who are to base this talk on *The Thirty-Nine Steps*. They work together to list the elements and put them in order of importance, with each group then presenting their findings to a symposium on the subject. They can, of course, cite other books (which can be limited to real examples or the teacher may allow invented 'mystery stories' to be used). Examples produced from *The Thirty-Nine Steps* might include:

— a mysterious stranger
— a code to break
— death threats
— deaths
— mysterious opponents
— disguises

— physical stress
— chases
— suspense

The symposium is chaired by a non-expert (a good role for the teacher) who constantly asks questions about anything he or she does not understand.

**Technique 14**: *A Kestrel for a Knave*, or *Kes*, by Barry Hines
The class is divided into groups of social workers, teachers, youth employment officers and parents (four or five to a group) to consider Billy Casper's case. They have to examine the problems from their own point of view and make recommendations for the future in order to avoid some of the problems Billy faced or posed. They are given fifteen to thirty minutes to do this. The youth employment group look particularly at the interview in the book (and might set up an alternative interview). The parents consider his mother's behaviour, as would most of the representatives. The teachers consider how best to help someone like Billy in the future. The report with recommendations is then written up and presented by each group, and debated to arrive at a conclusion.

Such case studies are one way of approaching a large number of books with 'problems' in them — for example, *A Taste of Honey*, by Shelagh Delaney and many of Dickens's novels.

Another approach is to appoint *investigators* who can study the effects of loneliness and isolation as evidenced in books such as: *Z for Zachariah* by Robert C. O'Brien, *The Diary of Anne Frank*, *Day of the Triffids* by John Wyndham, *Lord of the Flies* by William Golding, *Robinson Crusoe* by Daniel Defoe.

(a) The expectations of the class are discussed.
(b) The evidence is prepared and discussed (characters questioned).
(c) The conclusions are drawn and written up.

*Committees of Enquiry* can also be convened about a number of issues or themes, e.g. the evidence of prejudice in *To Kill a Mockingbird*, by Harper Lee. In this example each of the characters can be 'graded' on their signs of prejudice.

\* \* \*

**Extended case study**
**Technique 15**: The use of language for propaganda can be examined in conjunction with *1984*, by George Orwell.

**Aims**: to learn about the use of words to create bias, to manipulate opinion, to direct thinking.

The class become trainees at 'The Ministry of Truth'.

(a) Tasks are set to them working in pairs or solo to produce 'campaigns' extolling a new lottery, praising the Thought Police.
(b) The use of 'Newspeak' in the book can be studied as a guide.

With one extract only as the 'kick-off', rather than a study of the book, the work can be broadened by having the unit working for the school, local town council, the current national government, a business, or a television network.

**Teacher in role**: As with the character work already mentioned, the teacher can help set the tone, direct the work and design input most effectively by taking on a role him or herself. When it is negotiated with the students first this can be a very powerful tool. See *Dorothy Heathcote: Collected Writings on Education and Drama* edited by Liz Johnson and Cecily O'Neill, *Dorothy Heathcote: Drama as a Learning Medium* by Betty Jane Wagner or *Drama Structures* by Cecily O'Neill and Alan Lambert (all published by Hutchinson) for discussion of teacher working in role.

For this 'Ministry of Truth' project I took on the role of Training Manager, and thus introduced the new recruits to their work. We had already read extracts from *1984* and discussed them.

'Welcome to the first seminar as recruits to the Ministry Training School.'

I called a roll with official titles: 'Ministry recruit No. 273.'
I introduced slogans from *1984*, displaying them large in the class:
'War is Peace'
'Freedom is Slavery'
'Ignorance is Strength'

I explained the importance of these and went on to the idea of 'right thinking' and the making of Black/White and vice versa. Our unit was working in 2004.

'Our study will be based on archive material from 1983, which we will examine as propaganda and make propaganda out of.'

● At any point I could drop role, as they could, to discuss the truth of something or the direction of the project.

We re-wrote various 'truths' of the time at which we were working. For example:

> we 're-structured' unemployment out of existence
> we re-wrote the Falklands War so that it was a failure
> we boosted Channel 4 to the most popular television channel
> we made school the most popular pastime

- As source material we examined propaganda, bias and fabrication in newspapers from the '1983 archives' dealing with cheque-book journalism, the press and Royal Family stories. (Advertising is another useful resource.)
- The students chose areas of 'control' they wanted to work in on 'graduating', such as:
  > entertainment for factory workers
  > history
  > news
- Another member of staff, in role as Training Executive, gave the pass/fail results. (If you can engineer the involvement of another member of staff in role it can raise the credibility of the drama considerably.)
- The results were arbitrary, in no way based on the quality of material produced, commitment to the 'Ministry' (which did vary within the group), contribution in class etc.

The students were confused by this and tried to rationalize them. I did it as the final part of the work and, out of role, explained the arbitrariness. That led to a discussion of how much they wanted to 'pass', their attitude to marks, exams and the way they could be misled themselves.

*Note*: Make sure you explain the purpose, approach and your role in the drama to the students at the beginning. Make a CONTRACT with them, seeking their interest and cooperation. This is vital to all work of this sort.

\* \* \*

### Introducing a book before reading
The aim of 'introductions' is to engage interest in the book and to raise points to look for in the reading.

**Technique 16**: *Lord of the Flies*, by William Golding
Before mentioning the book, start with this situation:

> 'You have been stranded on a desert island.
> What would you do?

What would you need to survive?
How would you organize yourselves?

Pupils plan ideas for organization, food, shelter, defence, warmth, exploration, escape in groups of four or five and are then set the task of uniting their efforts in one, large class group, and produce a set of priorities. (Ten minutes in groups, twenty minutes as a class.) The teacher's role is to observe only. 'There are no teachers or adults with the party.' The teacher makes notes about how they handle the situation so that a subsequent de-brief can consider the relative success and failure and the reasons for this. Issues like leadership, cooperation, trust, equipment will arise and lead naturally into the novel.

Other novels lend themselves to this type of lead-in, for example:

*The Day of the Triffids*, by John Wyndham
*On the Beach*, by Neville Shute
*Ash Road*, by Ivan Southall

For a novel like *The Day of the Triffids* one important decision to be made is the 'where do we settle?' A large map of your area can focus ideas for this. Another approach could be 'You have a number of helpless, injured people. How many do you help and how?'

These examples can be successfully handled in an ordinary classroom, with desks moved or chairs put in a circle for some work. However, other types of work need more space. Seek the use of the Hall, drama studio or other space.

\* \* \*

**Introducing story-lines**
A method of whetting the appetite before reading is to write out the bare outlines of a number of scenes from a book on separate cards, and then to give one card to each group of students and ask them to mime or act out the sequence. 'Clues' like characters' names can be substituted by letters. The groups show their scenes in a random order and the class try to make sense of the 'story' by putting them in the right order. Groups must not compare cards.

**Technique 17**: This is one way to introduce Shakespeare to lower forms, e.g. *Macbeth*.

**Group 1**    A and his wife, B, welcome a king C and his son, D, to their home. As C sleeps, after a meal with A and B, A murders him. D flees in terror. A and B celebrate.

**Group 2**    A becomes king. His wife, B, is pleased for him, but A is worried that his friend, X, knows a secret he does not want anyone to know. He hires Y to kill X. Then he feels safe.

**Group 3**   A is a bad king so D gets a friend, E, to plot his overthrow. E is especially keen to do this as revenge for A's murder of his wife, F. D and E advance on A's castle and surround it.

**Group 4**   King A and his wife, B, are besieged in their castle by D and E. B cannot sleep at night because she has a bad conscience. B kills herself. D and E attack the castle, and E kills A. D is proclaimed king.

Each group performs its piece (mime is the best method at first), and the class is asked to try to establish the correct sequence and who the common characters are. They then act it out in sequence.

Similar work can be done with *Animal Farm* by George Orwell using the windmill building and destruction sequence.

\* \* \*

**Tableaux**

**Technique 18**: With space available the class can form tableaux or still pictures, using students, to illustrate character relationships or themes from books. The teacher can initiate and enable the setting up of tableaux (or groups of students may devise their own) to represent:

(a) the 'sides' in *Romeo and Juliet* or the factions in *The Crucible* by Arthur Miller

How the characters are grouped, where they stand in relation to each other, whether they face towards or away from another character can symbolize a great deal. Tableaux can also represent:

(b) the stages of Buck's career in *The Call of the Wild*, by Jack London where a student represents each owner or human Buck meets. What each character is doing in statue form symbolizes that character's treatment of the dog.

(c) The characters from the same book or from *The Long and the Short and the Tall*, by Willis Hall can be arranged on a three-dimensional scale of responsibility, from 'highly responsible' to 'irresponsible'; the decisions are made by one or a group of students; the decisions must be justified.

(d) The theme of 'pride' or 'jealousy' from *King Lear* could be represented by focusing on one character and having the consequences represented in tableau form.

(e) The stages of Braithwaite's winning over of his class could be

represented in a series of tableaux, based on *To Sir With Love*, by E
R Braithwaite.

Always give a time-limit but be sensitive to the groups' requirements.

* * *

**Poetry and drama**
Drama can be used as a way of thinking about poetry and material can
be worked on employing some of the techniques already mentioned.

**Technique 19**: *Meet My Folks*, by Ted Hughes
This group of poems can become the focus of Character Represen-
tations. Having read the poem, the class, one at a time after some
preparation, speak as people who have met 'Brother Bert'. Each
explains what happened. Or each describes a visit to 'Uncle Dan's'
house. This can be done in pairs, one to another. Students can describe
how they trained to become an Inspector of Holes based on the poem,
'My Father'. Such an inspection can be dramatized.

Stage two is to set the students to versify, in a form imitating Hughes'
originals, the ideas they have begun to articulate.

In the same way, poems by First World War poets can be used as a
basis for:

- War correspondents' reports, where the figurative language of the
  poem has to be 'translated' into more factual style.
- Archivists' researches in the year 2000 to piece together a picture of
  that earlier period.

# Drama and language

## Discussions

Carefully directed, drama can lead to more thought in preparation for
discussion of controversial issues, the adopting of opinions other than
the students' own, the use of registers new to the students and greater
awareness of alternatives.

**Example 1**: Cast groups as town planners, housing developers, local
residents, young house buyers, and town councillors. They meet to
discuss the plan for a densely-packed estate of houses on derelict land
in the town. Provide each group with outlines of their position on
cards at the beginning; allow time for them to prepare their cases.
Provide a map with the estate marked.

**Example 2**: The discussion of experimentation on animals might be approached similarly. Cast groups as the RSPCA, Cancer Researchers, the Animal Liberation Front, a pharmaceutical firm, or a cosmetics firm. Adopting this kind of approach, students can be required to take on a cause they do not believe in personally and to make a convincing case of it.

## Simulations

**Example 3**: *Town Council Meeting*

Set up the room as a committee room. The students chose which area of the town they represent (get a map of wards).

— The class becomes the council.
— Issue official-looking agendas (with a letter heading if possible). Put them in folders on the desks before the students' arrival.

Agenda for the full Council Meeting on . . . . . . (correct date)

1 Apologies for absence.
2 The minutes of the previous meeting (append an invented set).
3 (a minor local issue)
4 (ditto)
5 To consider the recent petition from the young people of . . . . . . asking for more facilities for youngsters in the town.

— Append to the petition any newspaper reports available on the issue, or write and duplicate one.
— Work through the agenda. Have key officials chosen from the group.
— Give the 'councillors' prior warning of the main issue beforehand, or not, and give most time to the central complaint (a double lesson of one to one and a half hours).

The class must discuss it formally as the council might, as adults, not as the young people who are asking for the facilities. Any proposals, letters to be sent from the council, research, canvassing of opinion can be taken on as English work and the project extended as the teacher wishes. The teacher must be prepared to respond to the council as various people giving them problems to solve, e.g. as the district council applying spending cuts; as a local resident complaining about the local youth club, thus threatening one facility. These can be fed in as letters or memos.

Choose the central issue as one which is of interest to the class you use this simulation for. I used the 'facilities' issue with a group of non-academic fifth years. The local press was full of the 'petition', letters from our own youngsters, and the local council was taking an interest. So the issue was 'real' in one sense. I put the students into the 'council' position to get them to treat the points from a different viewpoint.

Other aims for that group were:

- to enable them to become more confident speaking within the group.
- to provide a context for writing that had more material and more motivation than usual.

Obviously, it has taken more than one piece of drama to move towards the first aim, but the second followed well from the work. The group soon began to pick up ways of addressing each other, the need to speak through the chair etc. Over two hour-long council meetings a number of decisions were made to write letters to the youth club, local organizations, schools. These were later written as part of a follow-up lesson.

**Example 4**: *A convention of double-glazing salespeople*

The class are asked to use their 'experience as successful members of our sales force' to define the best strategies for selling.

(a) Write name, sales area, recommended approaches for the company.
(b) The convention considers the recommendations. Students will suggest ideas such as: product quality, a pleasant soft-sell approach, know your product, good aftersales service, good literature.

A campaign is planned, training methods re-appraised, a market survey outlined (use of language is vital here). An advertising watch-dog body is set up as another follow-up. This can lead to a consideration of selling and advertising.

**Example 5**: *School staff meeting*

**Aims**: to consider school from a different viewpoint; to face negotiating the solution to a problem.

**Stages**: the school is drawn up on a plan by consensus:

(a) A name is chosen for the school.
(b) Teachers choose and state their subjects.

(c) The meeting ... problems raised ... rest of the work depends on the 'problems'.

Problems might be raised by the students in role such as:

How to combat truancy
How to combat vandalism
How to raise money for a major development
What type of punishments to use

**Possible developments** — contacting parents
                            — writing the school guide
                            — planning a trip
                            — planning new courses

**Example 6**: *A meeting of experienced police officers to consider the image of the police in the community*

**Aim**: to examine how words create images, define and limit our view of others.

**Stimulus**: Cartoon figures of a policeman.

**Input**: Teacher's role is as Chief Inspector, convenor of the meeting. Possibly use a second teacher as a consultant with knowledge of the effects and influences of 'image'.

**Stages**:

(a) Talk to outline the 'problem' and state the aim of the meeting to suggest ways of improving image.
(b) Discussion of unhelpful stereotypes sparked off by cartoon.
(c) 'Experiences' of the police officers attending the conference are given. Groups 'act out' some examples, 'police officers' taking the role of the members of the public.
(d) Names, unhelpful words defined. (Small groups report back.)
(e) Working groups assemble proposals.

*Note*: The above examples are based on my own ideas and classroom experiments. I have only given the first stages in most cases as the individual class will provide particular development possibilities and require specific, local input. Next I give an account of a more extended example where the direction was influenced by the students' decisions. It was set up for a group of third year students.

**Example 7**: *A conference of experts*

**Aims**: to encourage the group to take more trouble over written work;

to concentrate on the idea of being good at something; to work as a whole group; to introduce an interest in words.

**Initial stimulus**: the short story *The Hitch-hiker*, by Roald Dahl, using the idea in the story that a pickpocket who is proud of his skill calls himself a 'fingersmith'. Teacher is in role as conference organizer.

(a) All conference attenders have been invited because they have a special skill. Each decides what that skill is. The teacher is 'an expert conference organizer' (or alternative).

(b) New names are invented for each skill: the organizer is a 'Meeting Master'. The words that might be used to help make up composite titles are discussed and names chosen, such as:

writer — word maker
musician — note artist
artist — colour king or artwright
dart player — target ace
cook — taste maker

A list of attenders and skills is drawn up and distributed.

(c) Skills are discussed in pairs and some demonstrated in mime. An outline of each skill is written. A list of words associated with the skill is produced.

(d) A memento from each expert's career is produced and talked about in pairs, before some volunteers talk to all of the conference. The memory is written up.

(e) The advice to give to would-be experts is discussed and the points noted for an advice pamphlet.

(f) A press conference is held to brief one press representative (another member of staff?) about the purpose of the conference. This purpose has been decided as 'the promotion of the recognition of skill as valuable'.

Students handle this briefing while I am not present. The teacher/'reporter' writes his or her report which is 'published' back to the conference.

(g) Conference final session (had lasted five one-hour sessions so far, which we decided to call five days).

Open question to the conference: What do we do now to carry the conference work further?

**Proposals**:    An annual conference
Regional committees to promote recognition of skills
Advertising

> A television programme
> A magazine
> A committee

(We followed up the committee, regional committees and magazine in particular.)

**(h)** A commitee is elected. They meet separately with an agenda made up of the items raised for future action. An Association, 'Experts Unlimited', is formed.

**(i)** Regional committees are formed, each with one main committee member. (The geography department did some input on regional perception.) Regional policy is discussed.

**(j)** Magazine contributions are agreed on.

**(k)** Final task — regional committees submit projects for their areas to view for a limited number of grants offered by the 'government' to the association.

**(l)** Grants are allocated. The magazine is produced.

**Example 8**: *Examinations*

**(a)** Set up the fifth year group as its own examination board to set the papers for an examination at English 'O' level.

**(b)** Discuss sample 'real' papers. Decide what is required. Discuss exam criteria.

**(c)** Each 'examiner' submits sample essay questions, writes questions on the passage agreed for the comprehension. These are discussed and the composite papers made up.

**(d)** The papers are sat by another group (another group within the class, or outside it).

**(e)** The answers are marked and the results discussed.

This can make pupils much more aware of the process of an examination and what is required of them.

*Note*: Many of these examples are based on the formula of 'a meeting'. Such gatherings are a natural situation to employ since they include the whole class in a common initial focus with no one threatened, yet can be sub-divided later should the work demand it.

## Interviews

Try students as interviewer and interviewee to help build confidence.

**1** Job interviews

(a) Start with pairs interviewing each other (situations and questions should be planned).

(b) Teacher plays employer (and employee on occasion).

(c) Enlist the help of an outsider (a teacher the students do not know well, a parent, a sample employer) at a later stage.

2 Vary the interview diet and boost the confidence for other role play and improvisation. This sort of pair work can be very helpful as warm-ups for drama generally.

— Parent/teacher: the child is a problem and the parent is not expecting complaints.

— Boss/employee about job progress: set up special 'news' from one or other of the roles; for example: Tell the boss, separately, that he or she will announce redundancy halfway through; or tell the employee to raise the idea of a wage increase.

— At the Citizen's Advice Bureau

— Television interviews — politician
                                        — celebrity
                                        — the person in the street

*Note*: Media interviews can be a useful input in many of the pieces that are the concern of this chapter. They can challenge positions, review material, check the grasp or understanding of individuals.

Other interview situations:

— lawyer/client
— policewoman/suspect
— policeman/victim
— traffic warden/motorist
— doctor/patient

**Approaches to interviews**
It is useful to have at least some pairs report back at the end of the interview to the teacher and the rest of the class. This is useful as a check and can take work further if the teacher questions them in role; e.g. as the superior officer asking for a report from his constable and then questioning the suspect further after his or her statement.

Start all pairs at the same time by counting them in. Do not let them rehearse it. Give separate information to all of the As or all of the Bs. For example:

Tell both that the patient goes to the doctor with a stomach pain. The interview starts after the examination has been carried out.

213

Tell A/doctor that the patient has nothing wrong, is a hypochondriac, but that 'you feel it is necessary not to be too harsh, so you prescribe a harmless settling agent'.

Tell B/patient that he or she thinks the doctor is always making light of serious illness, that he or she thinks there is something more to this than just a pain.

Some pair work can be carried out by volunteers in front of the class. The outcome can then be discussed.

The issuing of separate information to participants can be vital to add the spark of spontaneity, true improvisation. (John Seely's book *In Role* gives useful examples of pair and group work based on separate instructions.)

Attitudes can be given, surprise facts, secrets for later disclosure. If the information is given on cards the same situation can be set to a number of small groups at the same time. The pieces are not discussed, apart from the basic set-up, but are developed on the spot. Differences between groups using the same material can be revealing.

# The contribution of drama to creative/personal or discursive writing

There are two main advantages in basing personal and creative writing on drama:

(a) The 'acting-out' has what one colleague of mine describes as a 'concretizing' effect that no ordinary discussion with or exhortation from a teacher has. This colleague found drama invaluable in realizing detail even when the focus was an examination essay. She used the essay title, 'A story which takes place in one setting'. The drama consisted in thinking up and exploring a range of possible stories for the 'one setting' context. The detail acted out contributed greatly to the perception of detail in dialogue, description and character when writing.

(b) Much of the writing feeds back into the drama. This immediately makes it more valuable, having a wider audience and influence.

Here is a summary of related writing possibilities:

1 Evaluating the drama itself in a diary piece can be a valuable exercise. Here is an example from a diary written as a reaction to the above work on the police and image: (the 'sketches' were the demonstration pieces about 'experiences').

'As soon as I walked in I did not know what to expect . . . I enjoyed myself expressing views and began to feel like a policeman . . . apart from Claire and myself and a few others no one else contributed enough. As soon as the lesson finished we returned to normal, but it took a while to get back to being me . . . Miss B. said when we were doing our policeman sketches she noticed a lot of stereotype public. They were really exaggerated and I agree. I played a hard lad and that was over-the-top a bit. I doubt very much if people would stop a police officer in the park and say 'what are you going to pick on me about now?'

(13 year old pupil)

We were able to discuss 'police' stereotype views of the public as a result of this.

2 The student may write as the role, councillor, expert, etc. at any point in the work, to clarify thoughts and feelings, to relate events, or to communicate to others in order to initiate action.
3 The student may be required to write a report, letter, or longer piece of reflective writing.
4 A news reporter writes the news item. The class might become a newspaper office with all the students as staff.
5 Writing may take place after the drama stimulus. Many of the above examples could lead to imaginative pieces, discussion essays, character studies.
6 Notes have to be made, letters of enquiry written as part of the preparation.
7 Drama techniques can provide creative writing exercises, e.g.

**Story starters**: Work in pairs, A and B.
Each think of an opening line for a story.
A starts, B adds to the story, A continues and so on.
Do likewise with B's line.

*Or*: A and B swap their original lines so that it is entirely the other's responsibility to work the story out. The ideas can be acted out by the pair; they play all the characters. The ideas can then be shaped in writing.

# Points to remember

1 It is the teacher's task not only to plan but also to assess and evaluate the work. The book *Learning through Drama: the Schools Council Drama Teaching Project* (10–16), by McGregor, Tate and Robinson

(Heinemann), is helpful on this. See pages 124–7 particularly for questions such as:

— What kinds of learning are being emphasized/developed?
— How clear are aims and intentions?
— Is the teacher sufficiently flexible to allow unexpected learning possibilities to occur?

They also list questions for the student's evaluation of work.

2  Teacher in role. This must be used with care, but is a powerful way to influence work from the inside. Slip in and out of role to suit the work as you and the students become used to it. Make sure the teacher's role is not always the dominant one. Give students the opportunity to lead.

3  Create a secure structure. Be comfortable with the work yourself and the students will be too.

4  If the group are busy working, always be ready, watching, listening, to intervene, to help, to direct the course of the work to be most challenging. Letters, memos, private instructions are good ways of influencing the direction without stopping the work. Here is a letter I wrote to an application from part of a 'television company'. They wanted to use a current TV series on their channel but I wanted them to evolve an idea of their own. They wrote to 'ITV' (the teacher), requesting to use the programme. I replied:

> Dear Sir,
> Regarding your request for a licence to screen . . . . . . . . we find ourselves unable to release any episodes of this programme in the near future while we are screening it ourselves.
>     Yours faithfully,
>
> (ITV Programme Licensing Manager)

The 'programme executives' who received this then had to fill their schedule another way.

5  Reinforce each achievement: discuss each problem. For example:
    Ask for suggestions to solve problems.
    Discuss one group's difficulty with the whole class.
    Use material supplied by the students as much as you can.
    Accept all ideas, but help the less acceptable ones to be modified or eased out.

6  Be prepared to fail. Drama lessons are as variable as any teaching, but no more so. Try to see where the remedy lies. Try a new strategy.

7  Problems

(a) *The isolate*. In many groups there are students who do not fit. This is not an easy problem to solve, although it helps if in pair work there is a convention of revolving partners, pairing randomly, having the flexibility to have a three. It cannot be a permanent solution for the teacher to work with the student concerned. Make involving everyone an aim of the work for the students as well as the teacher.

(b) *The shy student*. If there is a reaction against drama from such a pupil, it is usually because of too much emphasis on showing work to the class. Take the focus off product on to process. Help the person find confidence as part of a whole class working. Make contribution voluntary or carefully supported by questions from the teacher in role. Have each student responsible for only certain points, and even then in pairs rather than singly.

(c) *The exhibitionist*. The emphasis on 'not showing' will help this problem too. Divert this student's energies into contributing within the class rather than in front of them. Help him or her learn control in showing, and give roles that demand more than simply comedy. Reward his or her achievements in other areas of the work by giving other sorts of responsibility.

# Aids for drama

## 1 Games

If you are lucky enough to have a space to work in games can be a great help:

(a) to warm the class up, get rid of energy that might be unproductive, to mix groups together and help group feeling.

(b) to help concentration and trust.

Two good books on games and exercises are: *The Gamesters' Handbook*, by Donna Brandes and Howard Phillips (Hutchinson); *100+ Ideas for Drama*, by Anna Scher and Charles Verrall (Heinemann)

## 2 The visits of Theatre in Education Groups

A group like 'SNAP People's Theatre Trust', who are based in Hertfordshire, are especially good. Their work on English examination texts is particularly relevant as they work without scenery or elaborate costume and run a workshop after the performance. The characters answer questions in role and can motivate students to work in the same way.

3 **English and drama advisers**
They will put you in touch with theatre groups or with teachers of English who can help with developing your work.
4 **The National Association for the Teaching of Drama or your local drama teachers' association**
For courses, evenings about drama. Many teachers connected with such groups are English teachers and not drama specialists, so do not be daunted by the prospect of doing some drama yourself.
5 **A photocopier to produce materials.**

# Recommended reading

*Learning Through Drama*, McGregor, Tate and Robinson, Heinemann, 1977

*Drama and the Whole Curriculum*, edited by Jon Nixon, Hutchinson, 1982

*In Context*, John Seely, OUP, 1976

*In Role*, John Seely, Edward Arnold, 1978

*Dorothy Heathcote: Drama as a Learning Medium*, Betty Jane Wagner, Hutchinson, 1979

*Drama Structures*, Cecily O'Neill and Alan Lambert, Hutchinson, 1982

*Gamesters' Handbook*, Donna Brandes and Howard Phillips, Hutchinson, 1979

*Drama Without Script*, Susan Stanley, Hodder & Stoughton, 1980

*Exploring Theatre & Education*, edited by Ken Robinson, Heinemann, 1980

*Approaching Classroom Drama*, Rosemary Linnell, Edward Arnold, 1982

*Making Sense of Drama*, Jonothan Neelands, Heinemann, 1984

*Drama as Education*, Gavin Bolton, Alan Lambert, Rosemary Linnell and Janet Warr-Wood, Heinemann, 1976

*Gamesters' Handbook 2*, Donna Brandes, Hutchinson, 1984

# 10  Fiction in the classroom

Gervase Phinn

## Reading for pleasure

Reports and research studies confirm that many children find little pleasure in reading, that there is a disturbingly large number of young people who have either failed to establish or have abandoned altogether the reading habit by the age of fifteen, and that the one common feature shared by adult illiterates is their failure to realize that reading can be a source of pleasure. And yet there cannot be an English department in the country which does not include, in some form or another,the encourgement of reading amongst its aims. Why then is there such a rift between this stated aim and the reality of what is actually achieved in the classroom? Perhaps it is because many teachers of English approach the teaching of literature as they have been taught it: working tediously through the text spotting the literary devices, explaining difficult words, summarizing scenes and dictating endless notes on imagery and character — rather than exploring with the pupils the wider meanings of the poem or novel.

In this chapter I shall suggest a number of strategies which reconcile reading for pleasure and the demands of the external examinations, and which foster a love of reading while recognizing the importance of some intensive study.

## A reading environment

'Our study has shown convincingly that the provision of books by the school plays an extremely important part in children's reading.'
(*Children and their Books* Schools Council Research Study. Frank Whitehead et al)

Surrounding pupils with an attractive, interesting and varied range of fiction is the first step in encouraging the reading habit. This provision of books need not be limited to the school library — each English classroom could become a 'branch' library stocked with bright, glossy-backed paperbacks by good modern writers such as Paula Fox, Betsy Byars, Stan Barstow, Roald Dahl, Aidan Chambers, Joan Lingard, Jill Paton Walsh, Penelope Lively, Philippa Pearce, Robert Westall, John Christopher, Geoffrey Trease, Bernard Ashley, Jan Mark, Peter Dickinson, James Vance Marshall, Alan Garner, Leon Garfield, Paul Zindel, Vera and Bill Cleaver, Judy Blume, Robert Cormier, Farrukh Dhondy, Robert Leeson and the many other writers who appeal to children.

Storage, distribution and security can present the teacher with problems. Sets of novels are easy to check before being distributed but single copies are less easy. One method of organizing classroom libraries is to display the books on open shelves and/or display racks. Every member of the school is then issued with a ticket (different in colour from the school library ticket) which can be used in any of the English rooms where the libraries are in operation. The English rooms can be left open for pupils to borrow and return books at any time during the day. Pupil librarians are then responsible for issuing books during breaks and lunch-times and a member of staff can keep a watchful eye on things during the week. Each new book added to the 'branch' library can be recorded in an accession register for that particular room, and this will give a quick guide to members of staff who wish to check which titles are available and which are missing.

Giving pupils easy access to good fiction and the freedom to choose what they wish to read plays an important part in encouraging reading for pleasure. Since many children do not come to school eager to read, it is vital that we should expose them to books which arouse their interest and develop a love of reading.

In the present economic climate the idea of providing such a large and varied selection of books might seem fanciful. It is becoming increasingly difficult for the Head of English to make a part of the book allowance avaliable for the purchase of fiction for class libraries since much of the capitation has to be spent on examination texts for the fifth and sixth years. But we should not let the spending of a dispropor-tionate amount of the book allowance on expensive examination texts go unchallenged. We should provide books equally for all pupils and perhaps make the provision of books for the 'reluctant' readers more of a priority.

# Reading aloud

'The child who enjoys being read to learns to love books.'
(*Bruno Bettelheim*)

Having provided such an environment of books in the classroom the next consideration is the teacher. How can you, as an individual, promote reading? It is axiomatic that the teacher must set out with the clear intention of making books enjoyable. Reading aloud is one of the most effective ways of ensuring that pupils enjoy and appreciate a novel or short story or poem and there needs to be a clear commitment of time to this activity.

Once a short story or novel which is appropriate for a particular class has been chosen, then the teacher's reading of it will be the most important factor in its success or failure. Few of us have entered the profession trained in the techniques of reading aloud to children and yet mastery of this skill is an essential qualification for all teachers. To perform the reading of a story successfully these points are worth bearing in mind:

## Checklist

1 Prepare the reading in advance. You may wish to abridge certain passages to suit the audience or re-tell parts of the story in your own words. You need to know what happens in order to change your voice to suit the characters and the mood, to note when to pause and when to quicken the pace.
2 Be sensitive to the audience and remain so throughout the reading.
3 Create a relaxed and informal atmosphere in which to read.
4 Make the reading unhurried so that both you and your audience can fully appreciate the story.
5 Animate your reading in your voice and face, bringing the words to life, converting them into people and events, feelings and thoughts. If the reading is mechanical and devoid of pace and rhythm it is no more than spoken print.
6 Do not read for too long. After about twenty minutes or so, pause for comment and discussion. Choose an exciting moment to break off, so that pupils will be eager to resume.
7 But do not stop too often for explanation and questions; this will spoil the pupils' enjoyment.

A great emphasis should be placed on reading aloud to children, especially in mixed-ability classes where the less able may not yet have the skills to cope with particular texts. There is a case for reading aloud to the ablest pupils too, where the teacher's ability to read the story well can bring the writing to life. The poor readers need even more especially to hear written language orally presented. Hearing a story well read will introduce these pupils to the real pleasure which can be derived from literature; it will extend their own reading range, help develop their taste and strengthen their ability to come to terms with more difficult language and more demanding literature.

# Handling reading performances

There are a number of ways of handling the reading 'performance' in the classroom.

## Fourteen short stories for reading aloud

Read a complete short story in a double period. Follow the reading with a class discussion or discussion in small groups, or encourage the children to reflect on the story and use it as a starting point for writing their own short stories and plays. On occasions, say nothing afterwards — the teacher and the pupils merely enjoy the experience. Stories which are written simply, with rounded characters, dramatic incidents, plenty of suspense of humour, and which have an immediate appeal include:

'The Ransom of Ted Chief' (O'Henry)                    (younger classes)
In *Short Stories of America* compiled and edited by Glyn Humphreys (Nelson 1965)
This short story which is typical of the writer's style, develops through a series of very amusing incidents centring around the kidnapping of little Johnny Dorset — 'a two-legged skyrocket of a kid' — who makes the kidnappers regret their rash action.

'The Pond' (Nigel Kneale)                              (older classes)
In *The Gruesome Book* edited by Ramsey Campbell (Piccolo Books 1983)
Nigel Kneale wrote the Quatermass serials and one of the most terrifying supernatural stories ever filmed: 'The Stone Tape'. In this sinister tale of a man who kills and stuffs frogs there is a gradual build up of tension to the horrific and ironic ending.

'The Fib' (George Layton)                              (younger classes)
In *The Fib and Other Stories* by George Layton (Knockout Series, Longman 1979)

This vivid, realistic and extremely funny story, based on an incident in the writer's childhood, describes a young boy's meeting with his football hero.

'William's Version' (Jan Mark)                                    (all ages)
In *Nothing to be Afraid of* by Jan Mark (Puffin 1980)
Written by the author of the prize-winning novel *Thunder and Lightnings*, this superbly funny little story is about William who surprises his granny with a gruesome version of a well-known tale.

'The Cocoon' (John B L Goodwin)                          (older classes)
In *Some Things Strange and Sinister* edited by Joan Kahn (Bodley Head 1973)
A chilling tale about Denny, a strange boy obsessed with collecting moths and butterflies. Well-written with a cleverly delayed and unexpected ending.

'My Oedipus Complex' (Frank O'Connor)                   (older classes)
In *Friends and Families* compiled by Eileen and Michael Marland (Longman Imprint Books)
A warm, sensitive, superbly-written story about little Larry who resents the return of his father after the First World War.

'The Most Dangerous Game' (Richard Connell)               (all ages)
In *Short Stories of America* (as above)
A short story full of suspense and graphic detail which keeps the reader guessing to the very end. The quiet, ordinary opening gradually builds up to a frightening conclusion. The man-hunt through the jungle shows this writer at his very best.

'Flowers for Algernon' (Daniel Keyes)                     (older classes)
In *Best SF Four: Science Fiction Stories* edited by Edmund Crispin (Faber and Faber)
A fascinating, highly original and humane account, written in the form of a diary, about a feeble-minded man who undergoes a series of brain operations and develops a super-intelligence.

'Nine-Thirty Start' (Julie Byrne)                             (all ages)
In *I Want to Get Out* edited by Aidan Chambers (Macmillan Topliners 1971)
An amusing but only too painfully true account about examination nerves.

'The Landlady' (Roald Dahl)                               (older classes)
In *A Roald Dahl Selection* edited by Roy Blatchford (Longman Imprint Books)

A deliciously unnerving tale typical of this prolific writer of short stories. Bizarre and frightening at one point, amusing at the next, with a macabre twist at the end.

'Late Night on Watling Street' (Bill Naughton)          (older classes)
In *Short Stories of Our Time* edited by D R Barnes (Harrap 1963)
Like all stories by Bill Naughton this account of the murder of a policeman is powerful, realistic, dramatic and very readable.

'The Secret Life of Walter Mitty' (James Thurber          (older classes)
In *Modern Short Stories* edited by Jim Hunter (Faber & Faber 1974)
A classic short story by one of the most popular humorous writers. Thurber's humour often has its more serious implications but it is always amiable and sympathetic. This immensely entertaining account about the dreams of an ordinary little man, has often been imitated but never equalled.

'The Destructors' (Graham Greene)          (older classes)
In *Twentieth Century Short Stories* edited by D R Barnes (Harrap 1973)
Boys will recognize the enjoyment of destruction in this disturbing account of how a gang systematically destroy an old man's house.

'Chutzpah' (Jan Mark)          (all ages)
In *Hairs in the Palm of the Hand* by Jan Mark (Puffin 1981) and *Aces: Bold as Brass* (Hutchinson, 1984)
A frighteningly realistic and extremely funny account of an intruder who causes havoc in a comprehensive school.

More will be said about the use of short stories in the classroom later in this chapter.

## Eleven passages for reading aloud

Reading exciting passages from novels is a particularly effective device for stirring demand; 'that little piece of pie,' writes J Gillespie in 'Juniorplots', 'so good that it tempts one to eat the whole concoction.' Arresting extracts might include:

The fight scene between Lennie and Curley in *Of Mice and Men* (John Steinbeck) Chapter 3 (Heinemann Educational New Windmill Series)

Michael's First Confession in *One Small Boy* (Bill Naughton) Chapter 9 (Macgibbon and Kee)

The opening chapter of *The Crane* (Reiner Zimnik) (Translated from the German by Marion Koenig) (Macmillan M Books)

The kidnapping of Jessie in *The Slave Dancer* (Paula Fox) Chapter 1 (Macmillan M Books)

The arrival at the castle in *Frankenstein's Aunt* (Allan Rune Pettersson) Chapter 3 (Hodder & Stoughton)

Jamie's arrival home from borstal in *The Green Leaves of Nottingham* (Pat McGrath) Chapter 1 (Hutchinson Educational)

The first day of the apprentices in *A Ragged Schooling* (Robert Roberts) Chapter 17 (Fontana Collins)

Mr Johnson's first lesson in *Danny Jones* (Andrew Salkey) Chapter 3 (Bogle-L'Ouverture)

Kit's arrival at Wethersfield in *The Witch of Blackbird Pond* (Elizabeth George Speare) Chapter 3 (Puffin Books)

Carlie's first night at her foster parents' home in *The Pinballs* (Betsy Byars) Chapter 2 (Macmillan M Books)

At the Disco in *A Crime for the Family* (Dulan Barber) Chapter 1 (Macmillan Topliners)

The opening entries from *The Secret Diary of Adrian Mole aged 13¾* (Sue Townsend, Methuen)

## Twenty-four novels for reading aloud

A novel could be serialized over several lessons or several weeks. Novels which can be dealt with in this way might include:

### Younger classes

*Thunder and Lightnings* (Jan Mark)
(Heinemann New Windmill Series 1978)
A light-hearted, lively and entertaining novel about the friendship of two boys. It appeals to younger classes because of the raciness and humour of the style.

*Conrad's War* (Andrew Davies)
(Hippo Books Scholastic Publications 1978)
An enormously funny, energetic and readable novel following the adventures of a boy obsessed with war. One day Conrad finds himself transported into the thick of the fighting — driving a Centurian tank,

then flying on a bombing raid over Nuremburg and finally master-minding an escape from Colditz.

*Empty World* (John Christopher)
(Puffin Books 1977)
A virulent plague sweeps the world and Neil is left alone to fend for himself. A chilling and original science fiction story which sustains the excitement until the very end.

*The Cay* (Theodore Taylor)
(Heinemann New Windmill Series, 1973)
Set in the Dutch West Indies, this controversial story explores the relationship between a young white American boy and an old West Indian sailor, who are shipwrecked on a deserted island. The boy is blinded by an injury and is forced to overcome his prejudice and rely on the old man. The account of the survival and particularly the fierce hurricane, provide a powerful and moving story of developing understanding.

*Gowie Corby Plays Chicken* (Gene Kemp)
(Puffin Books 1979)
The central character in this compelling, easy-to-read and amusing novel is a monstrous child ('I just have enemies') who makes everyone's life a misery. The story is told by the little monster himself in a lively, refreshingly funny and often quite moving narrative. Into his life comes Rosie, a large, energetic, good-natured but rather bossy black American girl who reforms him.

*The Robbers* (Nina Bawden)
(Heinemann New Windmill Series 1981)
A vivid, gentle story about friendship and loyalty. Philip, a likeable but rather precocious boy, goes to live in London with his father and step-mother. There he meets Darcy, a lad from the other side of the canal. The plot sounds very ordinary but it is a subtle and sensitive study of relationships on a number of different levels set against a background of crime.

*Friedrich* (Hans Peter Richter)
(Heinemann New Windmill Series 1978)
Friedrich is a Jewish boy growing up in Nazi Germany. He befriends Hans, a Gentile. The characters of the two boys and their growing understanding of each other and their respective backgrounds is authentically handled and very believeable. These are real boys living against a background of violence and intolerance. *Friedrich* is an exciting and poignant account, simply written with great emotional power; it is also a strong indictment of racial hatred.

*The Devil on the Road* (Robert Westall)
(Puffin Books 1978)
A fast-moving, powerful and highly original story centring around John Webster who is transported back to the time of the witch-finders.

*Jet, a gift to the family* (Geoffrey Kilner)
(Puffin Books 1976)
When the West Indian Reynolds family buy the greyhound Allegro, it seems a poor investment until she presents them with an unexpected gift: a black puppy which they name Jet. The tensions, loyalties and humour within this closely-knit black family are convincingly handled and the detailed description of the training and racing of greyhounds is vivid and realistic.

*Ghost in the Water* (Edward Chitham)
(Puffin Books 1973)
When Teresa and David discover a curious inscription on a gravestone in a local churchyard it excites their curiosity and they determine to discover the mystery surrounding the death of the young girl. A readable, fast-moving novel of mystery and surprise with good characterization and sense of atmosphere and place.

*The Cybil War* (Betsy Byars)
(Puffin Books 1981)
A lively, amusing and sensitive story about adolescent love. Simon goes on a date with Harriet because she is bringing along Cybil with whom he has been in love since third grade. But his best friend Tony has developed an interest in Cybil and the war for her affection is on.

*Walkabout* (James Vance Marshall)
(Penguin 1959)
Mary and her younger brother Peter, the only survivors of an aircrash in the Australian desert, have to overcome strong feelings of racial prejudice when they are rescued by an Aborigine boy who feeds them and guides them to safety. An original and haunting novel with excellent characterization and exploration of the developing relationship between the white children and the black boy.

*Playing Beatie Bow* (Ruth Park)
(Puffin Books 1980)
A prizewinning story of the supernatural about Abigail who finds herself taken back in time to a place which is foreign yet strangely familiar. A compelling, exciting and sometimes horrifying account in which the dialogue is vivid and the plot a series of tense moments.

*The Trouble with Donovan Croft* (Bernard Ashley)
(Puffin Books 1977)
Donovan, a West Indian boy, loses his ability to speak when his
mother suddenly returns home to Jamaica and his father is forced to
have him fostered out with a white family. The relationship between
Donovan and his new foster brother Keith is explored sympathetically
and the author catches successfully the flavour of an old, inner city
school.

**Older classes**
*The Wave* (Morton Rhue)
(Puffin Books 1981)
This powerful, thought-provoking and convincing account is based on
a true incident which occurred in an American high school. Ben Ross
tries an experiment with his history class in an attempt to explain the
strong forces of group pressure which gave rise to Nazism — an
experiment which goes disastrously wrong.

*It's My Life* (Robert Leeson)
(Fontana Lions 1981)
When her mother leaves home one day and disappears without a trace
and she is faced with looking after her father and brother, Jan comes to
realize the pressures which made her mother walk out. Through
humour, insight, splendid plotting and crisp dialogue, the author
enables us to live through the series of crises with Jan.

*The Upstairs Room* (Johanna Reiss)
(Puffin Books 1980)
A Jewish family in German-occupied Holland are forced to separate
and go into hiding. Ten-years-old Annie and her elder sister spend
over two years in the cramped, dusty attic of a remote farmhouse
hardly daring to leave it and totally dependent on the kindness and
courage of the farmer's family. This tragic, moving and very readable
story is based on the author's own experiences hiding from the
Germans as a child.

*A Pair of Jesus Boots* (Sylvia Sherry)
(Heinemann New Windmill Series 1975)
Rocky tries to pressure his friends into crime, aping the exploits of his
admired older brother Joey. A well-written realistic and absorbing
novel.

*Under Goliath* (Peter Carter)
(Puffin Books 1977)
A young working-class Protestant boy befriends Fergus, a Catholic,

but their friendship falls victim to the divisions of bigotry, unemployment and social injustice which exist in Northern Ireland. A rather grim novel but splendid for initiating lively classroom discussion.

*See You Thursday* (Jean Ure)
(Puffin Plus 1981)
Marianne's best friend has moved away, her teachers are getting at her for being immature and then her mother announces they are to have a lodger — and a blind one at that. When a young, gifted musician moves into the spare room and turns out to be intelligent and amusing and independent, Marianne's prejudice is swept away. A warm, sensitive, realistic and readable novel which explores well the relationship between the two main characters.

*Roll of Thunder, Hear my Cry* (Mildred Taylor)
(Puffin 1977)
A most moving and dramatic novel set in Mississippi at the time of the Depression. The characters are richly portrayed, particularly Cassie, the self-willed, independent black girl.

*The Chocolate War* (Robert Cormier)
(Macmillan M Books 1978)
The setting of this disturbing and absorbing novel is a private Catholic American high school. The Assistant Headmaster tries to raise funds by dragooning the boys into selling boxes of chocolates. In the school is a secret society led by the corrupt and vicious Archie Costello who forces the pupils to carry out ingenious assignments. The novel has intelligence, reality, superb characterization and builds up to a horrifying climax.

*A Temporary Open Air Life* (Christopher Leach)
(Macmillan Topliners 1974)
Dave has just left school and determines to achieve more in life than his father who has worked at the same tedious job for over thirty years. His ambition is to get away from the 'rat-race' but then his father dies suddenly and he is faced with a dilemma. A realistic, punchily-written and thought-provoking novel.

*Basketball Game* (Julius Lester)
(Penguin)
It is Nashville in the 1950s and fourteen-year-old Alan, who is black, moves with his parents into a white middle-class neighbourhood. Alan becomes friends with the girl next door but it cannot last. A very readable, sensitive and searingly truthful novel.

# The classroom project

Many teachers recall as pupils the set book: *White Fang*, *The Thirty-Nine Steps*, *Prester John*, *Greenmantle*: those dark, green-covered hardbacks written in cramped print, reluctantly read around the class until thankfully finished. Then such novels were often subjected to the abuses of summary practice, vocabulary testing, inane comprehensions, exercises in spelling and punctuation and literary devices — activities which were hardly likely to stimulate reading for pleasure. Such an approach to the novel is still 'slow and hard to lay to rest'. But there are many alternatives to this kind of approach. One way is for pupils to undertake a project of a literary nature: a study of science fiction stories, an analysis of an author or genre, the making of a child's picture book, a comparison of women's magazines, a critical look at advertising, the study of children in novels or the adaptation of stories for television. Such an approach need not be limited to the upper forms — several full class projects can be undertaken with first and second years.

One such project was tackled by a third year mixed-ability group which devoted itself to the reading and studying of the novel *The Machine Gunners* by Robert Westall. The novel is set in Tyneside during the winter of 1940 when the German bombing raids were fierce and relentless. Chas McGill has a prized collection of war souvenirs and is always on the lookout for items to add to it. When he discovers a crashed German aircraft with the machine gun intact he cannot believe his luck. With the help of two friends he removes the gun and the ammunition and starts off an exciting chain of events involving his family, school, the police and the Home Guard.

From the novel were developed a variety of different listening, talking, reading and writing activities. The resources used were the fiction and non-fiction books in the school and classroom libraries and a selection of books, materials, maps, pictures and 'Jackdaw' folders borrowed from the History Department. In addition, a selection of paperback novels relevant to the project were purchased and available for loan.

Further resources were brought in by the pupils, and by the second week of the project we had amassed an amazing variety of wartime bric-a-brac to equal Chas's collection described in the novel. This collection included medals, flags, POW identity discs, cap badges, photographs, bullets, tins of powdered food, newspaper cuttings, comics and a variety of model tanks and 'planes. The most prized item was a notebook full of poems, accounts and copies of letters sent home, written by a soldier on active service abroad.

The novel was serialized and took about a month to read. The remaining weeks of the half term were spent on related activities. These included:

## Talking and listening

1 The pupils had discussions in small groups about the novel, some with the teacher's help, others without. Many areas were covered in these informal discussions including:

  ● What special problems were faced by people during the war?
  ● Which parts of the novel did you enjoy the most and which the least?
  ● Which characters did you like the best? Give reasons.
  ● How does the novel compare with war stories on television and in comics?
  ● What is your attitude to the violence in the novel?

2 The class divided into small groups for improvised drama based on certain episodes in the novel:

  ● The discovery of the wrecked German 'plane
  ● In the Anderson shelter
  ● The headmaster investigates
  ● A visit from the police
  ● Fatty Hardy's road block

3 Homework assignments included talking to grandparents and older relations, anyone who remembered anything interesting about the war. Pupils were asked to make a tape recording or jot down notes and be prepared to tell the rest of the class any stories or anecdotes.

4 Individual pupils prepared short talks on certain aspects of the novel, some selected by the teacher, others chosen by the pupils themselves. One member of the class talked about the bombing raids in the area where his grandparents lived, while two girls gave an account of the fashions of the time. Two pupils combined their efforts to present an illustrated talk about war comics while another member of the class, who had read the sequel — *Fathom Five* — agreed to outline briefly the later exploits of Chas McGill. The process of sharing experiences is valuable in that members of the group create and extend interest in the project.

This activity can prove less successful when the pupils lack the skill necessary to prepare and give a talk which will hold the attention of the class. An alternative method is to break the class into small friendship groups and ask them to prepare a taperecording of some interesting topic related to the project. This might include readings from the novel, material from radio and television and short dramatizations.

## Reading

1 Pupils who so wished could continue with silent reading for part of the week. Although many pupils selected from the wide range of novels related to the project, there was no compulsion to do so.
2 A visit was arranged to the city library where a librarian took the class on a tour of the entire building including the lending and reference sections, the local history library, the archives, record and tape department, repair rooms, film theatre and where the newspapers and periodicals were microfilmed. Of particular interest were the archives where the pupils were shown original documents, photographs and newspapers relevant to the project.

## Writing

A wide range of writing tasks was undertaken which demanded responses in different styles: short stories, poems, letters, book reviews, plays, newspaper features, requisition orders, police statements, wireless broadcasts, transcripts of court hearings and so on.

## Other activities

1 The class divided into small groups and during the library period when all the reference books were available, each group produced a short quiz which was duplicated and given to the other groups later in the week. Questions were asked relating to aspects of the novel: the Blitz, rationing, conscription, the Home Guard, prisoners of war, freedom fighters, the Hitler Youth, the Luftwaffe, the Wehrmacht, the Geneva Convention, Quisling, billeting, etc.
2 A general class discussion centred on the cover illustration of the novel. In the 'Puffin' and the 'M Books' editions the jacket design by John Williamson depicts a purple sky full of bright blue explosions and streaked by white searchlights. Silhouetted is the town, a number of barrage balloons and the creeping figures of Chas and Cem pulling the 'bogie' in which is concealed the machine gun. We discussed the significance of the colours and the arrangements of the scene, then the pupils were asked to design their own covers.

3  An extensive display based on the work done by the group covered the classroom walls. In addition to the pupils' own work were poems, war posters, photographs, drawings and newspaper articles.

Such a means of studying a novel is more powerful, attractive and worthwhile than the often monotonous and meaningless drudgery of working through a class reader or set text. This approach gives children more opportunities to give life to print, through class and group discussion, dramatizations, original writing, re-telling of interesting sections and displays of work. Such an approach moreover offers an important way of enlarging the child's critical understanding and appreciation of the writer's craft.

## Study sheets

Teachers who do not have the time to involve pupils in an extended classroom project of the kind described above can devise something more modest in the form of study sheets for use with the novels and short stories read in class. These study sheets are relatively easy to produce and might include, in addition to the more traditional questions on plot and character, a brief review and various interesting ideas for working with the novel. Pupils might be asked to write a letter to or from a character in the story, or to dramatize an incident, or to re-write scenes from the novel from a shifted viewpoint.

If every English teacher in the department agrees to produce a number of these study sheets an extensive bank of material will form for use with the sets of novels.

Study sheets might take the form of the following example used with fifth years reading *A Crime for the Family* by Dulan Barber (Macmillan Topliners).

---

*A Crime for the Family* **(Dulan Barbner) (4th/5th Year)**

**Review**
A readable, fast-moving, simply-written novel centring around Colin Radnor, a sixteen year old whose parents split up after many years of marriage. Life becomes very frustrating for Colin at home and at school and when he finds that his father has left to live with another woman he is driven to a foolhardy course of action. The events in the

---

novel are exciting and the characters natural, set up without
false glamour yet with an understanding that does justice to a
complex plot.

**Activities**

1   Read Chapter 1 again (pp 7–28). Write about an argument at
    home in which you have been involved.

2   Describe the thoughts and feelings of Sarah Radnor as
    she sits alone in the kitchen after her husband has
    walked out.

3   Write the conversation which might have taken place
    between Sarah Radnor and her mother the Sunday after
    (see pp 20–22).

4   Read the letter on page 43 from Colin's Year Tutor, Miss
    Dolby, to the School's Welfare Officer, Miss Preston.
    Write the reply.

5   Write a letter from Miss Dolby to Mrs Radnor regarding
    Colin's truancy and poor attitude to work in school.
    Arrange an appointment for her to see you.

6   Improvise (or write out as a short play) the interview
    which takes place as a result of this letter.

7   Imagine Jenny keeps a diary. Write entries for:
    (a) the night of the disco (pp 16–19)
    (b) the day of the robbery (pp 88–97)
    (c) the day she visits Colin in hospital (pp 111–112)

8   Improvise (or write out as a short play) the scene where
    Mr Goldstein tells Mrs Radnor that, because of her
    frequent absences and arrival late for work, she is
    dismissed.

9   Here is a report slip for Colin's School:

```
┌─────────────────────────────────────────────────────┐
│              HOLLYBUSH ROAD SCHOOL                    │
│                                                       │
│  Subject .......... Ability .......... Effort ......  │
│                                                       │
│                                                       │
│                   Teacher .....................       │
└─────────────────────────────────────────────────────┘
```

    Complete reports for several of the subjects Colin takes.

10  Read pp 60–63. Write a story called 'My First Date'.

11  Miss Dolby sends for Jenny in an effort to find out why
    Colin is absent. Write an account of the conversation.

12 Read again the part of the novel where Colin tells Sparrow he cannot go through with the robbery (pp 97–102). Improvise the scene.

13 Imagine that Colin has agreed to help Sparrow and Jacko break into the shop. Describe the events which follow. Begin your account:
'There it is,' whispered Sparrow, pointing to the old shop on the corner of Dunster Road.

14 Write a short newspaper account of the robbery.

15 After the attack, Colin is interviewed by the police. Write out his statements about the events which led up to his injuries.

16 Two weeks after Colin is released from hospital Dulcie meets Sarah Radnor in the supermarket. Write a short account of their meeting.

17 Continue the story. Begin by writing out the last paragraph of the novel. You might consider:
(a) Does Colin's relationship with Jenny continue?
(b) Does Dick stay with Dulcie or return home?
(c) Are Sparrow and Jacko out for revenge?

Devising tasks such as these means a shift away from the tightly-controlled, teacher-directed analytic response. It does not, however, lead to a casual approach, lacking in intellectual rigour; it simply means that the interpretation is expressed more creatively. Responding to such tasks in this way will allow novels such as *A Crime for the Family* to survive as a source of pleasure in a way which much of the traditional teaching cannot hope to do.

# Using short stories in the classroom

Some mention of short stories was made earlier in the chapter. At this point I would like to consider their use in the classroom in a little more detail.

The selection of short stories now available for the teacher is extremely wide. There are stories from different cultures, in varying styles, of contrasting moods; there are sad, funny, provocative, strange, horrible, romantic, frightening tender stories by writers ranging from Roald Dahl to Doris Lessing, from Kate Chopin to Sean O'Faolain, Saki to Bill Naughton. The approach to the study of these stories can be varied. On occasions one might read a story in a double period without any follow-up discussion or written work. Another time the reading might be followed by work in small groups or with the full class where the pupils might be given a series of questions for discussion:

- What part of the story remains particularly in your mind?
- Do the characters seem realistic?
- Does the story make you think in a different way about some aspect of human behaviour?
- How does the writer bring the story to its climax?
- Is the writer expressing any of his or her own ideas and opinions through any of the characters?
- Does the story help you to understand any better the world around us?

The short story, by its very brevity and simplicity of construction, is often more suitable than the novel for initiating discussion and encouraging pupils to think aloud and explore the implications of the narrative.

One rather different approach is to omit to read the end of the story. The pupils then break into small groups to consider a 'suitable' conclusion. Follow-up discussions will vary greatly. Some groups will spend half an hour arguing about the ending while other groups will come to an agreement in less than ten minutes. (The latter can be directed to other aspects of the story.) Casette recorders can then be given to the groups and the discussions taped.

At the beginning of the next lesson the various alternatives can be heard and discussed. Each group can then be given the dozen or so sentences which conclude the story. These will be in random order and the pupils will have the task of rearranging them into some sequence which makes sense. There are likely to be several 'acceptable' versions and the final decision in favour of one will be based on ideas of style and structure.

# Improvising drama from fiction

'Improvisation can provide a physical context for the printed word to come to life. . . . There are countless occasions when written words are illuminated by being placed in a real context, which drama can help to realize.'
(*The Bullock Report*)

Drama activities, particularly improvisation, can offer invaluable opportunities for investigating themes and situations met in the printed text, and can generate an enormous amount of enjoyment and commitment for the literature in pupils. A practice which reflects this possible correlation of improvisation and literature pointed to in the Bullock Report, involves supporting the reading of a novel in class by a number of drama sessions. This helps the pupils arrive at a clearer and more sensitive understanding of the various themes, ideas and concepts explored in the novel.

For example *The Milldale Riot* by Freda Nichols (Ginn & Co 1965) could be introduced to a third year class by a drama session. This simply-written, very readable novel is set at the time of the Industrial Revolution and describes vividly life amongst the poor at that time. Two pauper children — Harriet and Nick — escape the filthy and primitive conditions of a coal mine to search for a better life in the large industrial town of Milldale where many new factories and mills have been built. But the town is dark, squalid and violent. Harriet finds work in a cotton mill where working conditions are little better than they were down the mine. Nick fares worse. Kidnapped by a cruel and drunken chimney sweep, he becomes a climbing boy whose job it is to clean the filthy narrow flues of the large houses. Life does improve for the two children and after many exciting and sometimes amusing adventures, they are rescued by the kindly Mr Anderson.

The novel might be introduced by a drama session beginning with mimed exercises in response to the teacher's account:

1 You wait — quietly, nervously, trembling with cold — outside the huge iron gates of the mill.
2 The chief overlooker, Mr Richardson, arrives, opens the heavy iron gates and motions you to follow.
3 You enter the 'blowing room' of the mill. All around you is activity — a mass of moving pulleys, clanking machines, noisy machinery. You stare in amazement.
4 You follow the overlooker into the 'carding room'. The noise is deafening. You cover your ears and move on.
5 Next is the 'draughting room' where the atmosphere is hot and dry and oppressive. You begin to cough.
6 You arrive at your place of work: the 'winding room'. Some workers are feeding cotton lumps into long metal cylinders, some are collecting bits from the floor, some are stuffing wadding into huge rollers and others are carrying heavy bales to the 'weaving room'. Two overlookers are checking your work.
7 You are set combing the fibres. It is hot, tiring and thirsty work.
8 A bell rings. The machines are silent. You relax and wipe the sweat from your face. It is time for your one meal of the day.

Following this mime session the class might break into small groups: managers and overseers, the workers, the mill owner and his family, and the sequence can be repeated and continued with the entry of the mill owner and his daughters — richly-dressed, proud and authoritative figures who examine the cloth, stare coldly at the workers and walk condescendingly around the factory. The workers confer. Someone must approach Mr Higgins and ask for a fair day's wage for a fair day's work. Bert Jenkins agrees and walks nervously towards the plush office. He knocks lightly on the door. Mr Higgins looks up in surprise. From here the pupils could add simple dialogue involving the improvised conversation between worker and boss. This could be followed by some discussion about how the drama has developed so far and what the pupils felt they had gained from the sessions. They could be asked specific questions such as:

- Do you think Higgins would have reacted as shown in the improvisation?
- Could Jenkins have handled the situation better?
- How do you think the workers would have reacted on hearing of Jenkins' dismissal?

And questions of a more general nature:

- What for you was the value of these sessions?
- When were you most involved? How?
- When were you least involved? Why?
- Did the sessions help you to undersand any better what life must have been like in the mill?
- Any other comments or suggestions?

The next stage might be to devise a set, making a plan of where the owner's office, the overlooker's desk and the various machines would be. Some sessions of rehearsal might be undertaken to prepare the short improvisation for showing to another class.

There are a number of points worth mentioning concerning the value of this kind of approach for encouraging sensitive reading. In improvising their own exchanges, the pupils come to realize the dramatic nature of the novel. Furthermore they 'live through' the experiences in the episodes in a way more immediate and compelling than a straightforward reading of the text. The pupils become involved as participants projecting themselves into assumed roles and imagined situations, and are thus led to insights and discoveries about the novel they might not otherwise experience.

# Using television and radio

'We do know that television serializations often stimulate children to read books.'
*('Children and their Books' Schools Council Research Study. Frank Whitehead et al)*

Much has been written about the supposed detrimental effect that television viewing can have on reading. It seems clear that television is a formidable competitor with books for the attention of children, and yet it can be harnessed in the cause of fostering an interest in reading. Many excellent television adaptations and the films of books which are frequently screened can provide a strong incentive for pupils to read them. Following the broadcast of such serials as *The Machine Gunners* and *Break in the Sun* or the films *To Sir, With Love* and *Kes*, it is sensible for teachers to be alert to the opportunity this presents and display the novels (which often have the familiar television stills on the covers), discuss the adaptations and encourage pupils to borrow the books.

Adaptations of novels can be the subject for detailed study. Pupils can explore in what senses the screen versions are different from the original novels, they can examine and discuss the treatments and presentations, study the ways in which the two media work and consider the problems of adapting a novel or short story for the screen. Working in small groups they might be asked to consider:

1 How well does the director capture the atmosphere of the novel?
2 Which parts of the screen version are significantly different from the original episodes in the novel?
3 Why do you think the director decided to make such changes?
4 Which details in the novel does the director emphasize and which does he or she consider less significant?
5 Which episodes/characters do not appear in the dramatization? Why do you think they were cut?
6 How well do the actresses and actors portray the characters in the novel?
7 Are there any parts included in the television version which do not appear in the novel? Why do you think they are added?
8 Any other comments?

Pupils might take this a step further and write their own radio and television scripts. The BBC and IBA Education Departments are always willing to supply material on writing for television. The material can be discussed and pupils set the assignments to adapt a short story of part of a novel. This kind of writing demands roughly drafting out the script, re-writing, cutting down and building up.

Pupils can be given a series of suggestions for laying out the scripts:

**Radio (Notes for pupils)**
1  Give yourself a wide margin of about one third the width of the paper. This will be for the speakers' names and any rough production notes.
2  Everything which is not spoken should be underlined.
3  Write speakers' names in capital letters.
4  FX indicates sound effect.
5  A radio adaptation is only sound. Don't write: 'Sunlight lit up the whole room.'
6  Avoid using too many characters.
7  Avoid using a narrator but if you must make what he or she has to say clear and brief.
8  Sound effects can be used for the setting of the drama: a noisy school corridor, street sounds, country noises etc.
9  There is greater freedom on radio to use a lot of scenes. The writer is not limited to a few sets as in a television play.
10  Scenes begin and end with fading. Music could be used to begin and end your adaptation.

When the script is completed select a producer, nominate a pupil to be in charge of sound effects, and assign parts to the actresses and actors. After a few rehearsals you will be ready to record your play.

**Television (Notes for pupils)**
1  Use only the right-hand side of the paper, leaving space for the producer to make notes.
2  Speakers' names, directions and descriptions are all written in capitals. Only the actual words spoken are written in lower case.
3  Do not include too much dialogue. Television, unlike radio, is visual and facial expressions can often make dialogue unnecessary.
4  Do not use too many characters. Television is a medium which uses close-ups.
5  The characters must be clearly established and their relationships with others.
6  Scenes should be kept to a minimum.

The adaptor needs to do a good deal of groundwork: careful reading and re-reading of the text, making rough drafts, organizing and structuring the material, writing the first version, cutting and adding sections for the sake of clarity, watching for repetition, revising and polishing. These activities demand comprehension skills of the highest order and an understanding of character far deeper than that elicited by the 'O' level 'crammers'.

One word of caution concerning the use of television adaptations: while it is quite acceptable to ask pupils to watch the television version at home, to study a recording in the classroom does infringe the law of copyright. The definitive legal position and a full statement of concessions can be found in: 'Copyright Clearance, a practical guide', by Geoffrey Crabb (Council for Educational Technology)

## The reading teacher

'This question makes clear, I hope, the essential prerequisite for happily successful teaching and learning of literature: Who can teach reading who does not himself love books?'
(*Trevor Dickinson*)

If as teachers we hope to encourage our pupils to read avidly and widely and with enjoyment, we must ensure that it is matched by our own professional commitment. We must know the types of books which interest particular pupils and be in a strong position to recommend appropriate titles. The school day is hectic and keeping abreast of recent publications and new books is extremely demanding on our time. One answer may be to share the reading within an English department. Over the holidays the English staff might agree to read several novels each and on returning to school be prepared to discuss what they have read at a departmental meeting, and share with colleagues the successes and failures of particular approaches to specific novels and short stories used in the classroom.

Just as non-reading children are made by non-reading parents so the problem is compounded by non-reading teachers. Unless our pupils see us enjoying reading and hearing us talk with enthusiasm about books, it is hardly likely that such pupils will become 'hooked on books'.

## Recommended reading

*Introducing Books to Children*, Aidan Chambers, Heinemann 1973
*Teenage Reading*, edited Peter Kennerley, Ward Lock, 1979
*The Effective Use of Reading*, edited Lunzer and Gardner, Heinemann 1979

*Reluctant to Read*, edited John L Foster, Ward Lock

*The Child and the Book*, Nicholas Tucker, CUP 1982

*Books and Reading Development*, Jennie Ingham, Heinemann 1982

*On Learning to Read: the child's fascination with meaning*, Bruno Bettelheim and Karen Zelan, Thames & Hudson 1982

*Developing Active Readers: ideas for parents, teachers and librarians*, edited Diane Monson, International Reading Association Press

*Running a School Bookshop*, Peter Kennerley, Ward Lock, 1978

*Young Fluent Readers*, Margaret Clark, Heinemann, 1976

*Now Read On*, R Dixon, Pluto Press 1982

*Copyright Clearance, a practical guide*, Geoffrey Crabb, Council for Educational Technology

*Ms Muffet Fights Back*, Rosemary Stones, Penguin 1984

*Reading and Righting*, Robert Leeson, Collins 1985

# 11 Literature for examinations

Paul Cheetham

'Good teaching of English, at any level, is far more than the inculcation of skills: it is an education of the intellect and the sensibility. . . . In teaching English we are teaching pupils to think clearly, to be self-aware and to be responsive to their experience of the world of people and things about them.' (*English from 5–16*, DES publication 1984)

## Introduction

'I read English at university, and I'm glad to say that I haven't read a single book from that day to this.' However apocryphal many such statements may be, there is no doubt that lurking in the back, and sometimes the forefront, of every English teacher's mind is the fear that in teaching literature he or she is in danger of killing stone dead the pupils' interest in both the text under examination and literature in general; that the tedious drudgery apparently inseparable from detailed preparation for examinations will replace the comprehensive appreciation and enjoyment of a work of literature.

This chapter suggests ways in which both these aims — detailed understanding and overall appreciation — may be achieved together; indeed it proceeds on the assumption that the realization of the second aim depends upon the realization of the first. My own experience — and that of many other teachers — is that these two activities, essential for success in examinations, also form the basis of any true literary appreciation. So although this chapter is headed 'Literature for Examinations', I would not wish to make any significant distinction between teaching for that purpose and the general teaching of literature.

# PART ONE

## English Literature at 16+

Almost every pupil at this stage reads some English literature, and the majority of them will sit some form of examination at the end of the course. For English teachers this presents both a great opportunity and a great challenge. It means that both texts and teaching methods for the whole ability range must be considered. The establishment of the GCSE examinations required the examination groups to spell out their aims and objectives. These reveal a common purpose in the examining of literature at 16+:

### Aims

- To stimulate and develop an interest in and enjoyment of literature.
- To promote a sympathetic, critical and imaginative response to a wide range of literature.
- To encourage the individual study of areas of personal interest.

### Objectives

Candidates will be required:

- (a) to demonstrate first-hand knowledge of prose works, plays and poetry;
- (b) to demonstrate understanding of the texts studied;
- (c) to show evidence of a thoughtful approach and response to themes and ideas in the texts studied;
- (d) to comment in an informed and personal manner on significant features of the texts studied, such as plot, characterization, setting and use of language.

How can the English teacher best prepare pupils to achieve these objectives while satisfying the aims?

## Novels

For many English teachers the teaching of novels, even the shorter ones, can frequently prove surprisingly difficult. It is not always clear why this should be so, though I suspect that it may have something to do with vagueness about what teacher and pupil are supposed to be doing with the book.

The approaches described below have been found useful in reducing these problems and increasing the participation and enjoyment of both pupils and teachers. They can be well illustrated in operation on three frequently set texts, *Kes* by Barry Hines, *Of Mice and Men* by John Steinbeck and Roald Dahl's collection of short stories, *Someone Like You*.

## Kes

*Kes* has instant appeal to adolescents, who find it easy to identify with many features of Billy Casper's life. There is little difficulty in getting pupils to reconstruct Billy's account of events such as his argument and fight with MacDowall (pp 74–7); [all page references are to the Penguin edition], the PE lesson (pp 86–108) or his persecution by Jud (especially pp 127–152). This appreciation of Billy's life and problems can be deepened by a close examination of his 'Tall Story' (p 73), which brings to light a number of other grievances in his life, only lightly touched on elsewhere, or by analysing the state of mind which takes him to the abandoned cinema (p 156) and his reflections as he sits, alone and disconsolate, in the derelict building (pp 158–160). A more demanding task is to ask pupils to put themselves in the position of some of the adult characters in the novel. These projects can be either written or dramatized:

(a) the conversation between Mr Gryce and his wife at the end of the school day, based on pp 46–58;

(b) a conversation between Mr Farthing and his wife in which they discuss the problems of pupils such as Billy;

(c) a staffroom discussion after the PE lesson between Sugden and another member of staff (Mr Farthing?) about Billy;

(d) Jud's account of the day's events to a friend in the pub later the same evening;

(e) Mrs Casper's account of her family problems to a neighbour, sympathetic or otherwise.

In this way pupils have to look closely at how characters speak and behave; they become aware of the whole question of point of view, and they are encouraged to expand their imaginative horizons.

## Of Mice and Men

The immediate appeal of *Kes* to British schoolchildren obviates the need for any kind of introduction. The same is not true of Steinbeck's *Of Mice and Men*. Although familiar, via television, with American films, for the majority of contemporary British pupils this means material of the *Starsky and Hutch* variety, which is some way removed from the Western, ranch-based culture from which *Of Mice and Men* springs. I have also found that the story seems to have little immediate appeal to some girls. Before launching into the book there needs to be some discussion with the class about Westerns and about the status and predicament of women in that male-dominated society. The showing of a classic Western film, such as *High Noon* or *Butch Cassidy and the Sundance Kid* can provide additional useful background material — as well as an entertaining afternoon. Such a ground-clearing approach opens up the book to a much greater degree than if one approaches it 'cold', and significantly enhances the pupils' understanding and appreciation of it.

There are a number of passages in the book which would benefit from detailed examination, but I shall confine myself to one — the extract in Chapter Four from the point where Curley's wife comes to Crooks's room, looking for her husband, to the end of the chapter (pp 81–8 in the Heinemann New Windmill edition). Like several other passages it can easily be performed as a dramatized reading, with members of the class taking parts and the teacher acting as narrator. It also gives rise to a number of questions of both the localized and the general variety. Examples are:

(a) What have we learned so far about Curley's wife?
(b) What does this extract tell us about her?
(c) How does she feel about Curley?
(d) What is her attitude towards other men?
(e) Why is Candy so angry?
(f) How seriously does he believe in his claims about having his own place?
(g) Does Candy strike you as impressive or merely pathetic?
(h) What does the episode tell us about Crooks?
(i) In what ways is Lennie's behaviour in this scene typical of his behaviour throughout the novel?

Discussion of most of these questions inevitably impinges on some of the central issues raised by the book and makes them relevant to the pupils' own lives and experience.

# Short stories

### Someone Like You
Collections of short stories, such as *Someone Like You*, have an obvious appeal to the reader daunted by the length of the average novel and they offer equally valid opportunities for insights into human nature and personal relationships. Take *Lamb to the Slaughter*. This story can be

read out loud in less than a quarter of an hour, after which the pupils can be asked to analyse Mary Maloney's attitude and feelings in the first part of the story. What clues are there that her sense of well-being is not shared by her husband? Is the reader made aware of this before she is? If so, what is the effect of this? At what point does she begin to suspect that there is something wrong? Why are we not told why he is leaving her? Is this a merit or a defect in the story? How are we meant to react to his behaviour? Is her reaction realistic? Analyse her state of mind immediately after the murder. Is she fully responsible for her actions? Is there any reason to believe that she is, in any sense of the word, mad? Would a court of law find her guilty of murder?

Additional written assignments could be:

(a) Imagine you are Patrick Maloney driving home from the office, thinking about what you are planning to tell your wife and anticipating her reaction; *or*
(b) Imagine you are Mary Maloney lying in bed that night, reflecting on the evening's events and planning for the future for herself and her unborn baby.

All these questions provide ample material for discussion, and some can develop into heated boy–girl exchanges! They may also, of course, touch on unhappy experiences in pupils' own family lives. Teachers, therefore, need to consider whether in certain circumstances such exercises may be helpful or traumatic.

# Longer novels

The books examined so far have the advantage of brevity and ease of language. Different problems arise in the case of longer and more complex novels which have traditionally been set for O-Level, such as Victorian novels like *Oliver Twist* or *Jane Eyre* or modern classics such as *Nineteen Eighty-Four*. Unlike the shorter novels, they defy reading *in toto* in class, yet clearly some direction is necessary. Pupils need some guidance, at least in the early stages, about what to look for, particularly in a type of literature with which they may be unfamiliar.

### Nineteen Eighty-Four

Thus, in studying *Nineteen Eighty-Four* the teacher needs to draw the pupils' attention to the key features of the book. In Chapter one, for example, the teacher should point out the irony of the contrasts between the grandiose claims made by the regime and the squalid nature of life enjoyed by the average citizen. There is the central notion of the inversion of reality, conveyed by the paradoxical naming of the ministries and the three slogans. There is the traditional figure of the bogeyman, Emmanual Goldstein, whose function is to divert and release the fear and hatred which might otherwise focus on the domestic system of government (this might in turn provoke a discussion of modern governments' use of bogeymen). There is the image of a new religion, conveyed by the woman who mutters 'My Saviour' in response to the image of Big Brother and bows her head in prayer, and there is the introduction of novel notions like 'Newspeak' and 'Thoughtcrime' which merit some explanation and should provoke discussion about the complex relationship between speech and thought.

This essential function on the part of the teacher need not militate against simultaneous pupil involvement. For example, groups of pupils could be commissioned to compile notes and produce a combined summary for class consumption of the following features of life in 1984, as described in Part I of the book:

(a) Material (i.e. living conditions);
(b) Political (i.e. the whole political organization of the state);
(c) Intellectual (i.e. how (b) affects the individual's intellectual life);
(d) Linguistic (i.e. Newspeak and its effects on (c));
(e) Personal/emotional development under such a regime.

The study of a book of this length and complexity should include brief chapter summaries, occasional tests and quizzes, notes and discussions on characters and relationships, notes on various images and themes which run through the book, and debates about democracy and totalitarianism, revolving round such critical questions as 'Could it happen here?' 'Has it happened anywhere?' It would also offer an opportunity for more enthusiastic pupils to engage in some literary detective work by discovering what Orwell himself said about his novel in his letters and by unearthing early reviews of the book. (These have been conveniently collected by Bernard Crick in his biographical study *George Orwell — A Life* (1983)).

# Drama

The study of a play is probably the aspect of work which presents fewest problems for most English teachers. Reading the play in class necessarily involves pupil-participation, and there is obviously wide scope for discussion about characterization, direction and so on. Such generalizations, however, are easily made. What do they amount to in practice? To answer this question I propose to suggest some schemes of work relating to two very different plays, *The Long and the Short and the Tall* and *Julius Caesar*.

## The Long and the Short and the Tall

*The Long and the Short and the Tall* is both readable and concerned with such important issues as attitudes to authority, the behaviour of people under stress and the ethical question of killing an unarmed prisoner. It was also the subject of an excellent television production which was made for schools and is thus available for use without any infringement of copyright. The play demonstrates excellently for pupils of all abilities a crucial issue in the teaching of drama, namely the part played by dramatic form and convention in bringing the central issues to our attention. As a means of assessing both the pupils' grasp of the issues and their awareness of dramatic features one might, for example, isolate p 29 (all page references are to the edition published by Evans Drama Library) and ask the following questions:

(a) Why is all interest centred on Macleish and Bamforth?
(b) What is indicated by the fact that Bamforth only comes 'slowly to attention'?
(c) What do you think is the purpose behind the pauses in Mitchem's speeches to the patrol?
(d) What does Macleish mean when he says 'I had occasion to reprimand . . .'?
(e) What is Mitchem's answer to Macleish's last statement?
(f) In the end how is the identity of the man revealed?
(g) Examine the different ways in which Mitchem asserts his authority over the patrol in this scene.

Questions (a), (e) and (f) are relatively low-level questions, merely testing factual recall, as is the vocabulary question (d). The other three questions are more sophisticated, (b) requiring the pupils to read between the lines and relate Bamforth's behaviour on this occasion to his general attitude to Johnstone throughout the play, while (c) and (g) test the pupils' sensitivity to dramatic effects, differences of tone and the varied use of language.

There are other projects which can relate to the play as a whole:

## Before reading the play
1 (p 3 — Programme note) *Singapore*. Find out as much as you can about it — where it is, its early history, its economic and military importance, what has happened to it since the war, etc. Give a brief account of its history, accompanied by a

sketch-map. (Parents or grandparents may be able to help with this, as well as encyclopedias, atlases and other reference books.)

**After reading the play** (NB You will probably find the 'Production Note' most helpful after you have finished the play.)

2 Give a fairly brief (5–10 lines) description of each member of the patrol, covering both personality and physical description. You can use your imagination here, since there are few clues to physical appearance in the play, though you should try to make the description, especially of the face, appropriate to the personality of each individual. (If you have watched the video-recording of the play, compare your own mental picture of the character with the actor's actual appearance, manner and behaviour.)

3 Imagine you are Evans *or* Smith *or* Whitaker. Write a letter home, in which you describe the other members of the patrol. Remember to write in character and include some touches about yourself and family.

Thus Evans might be writing to his girl friend (see p 21), or Smith might be writing to his wife and asking about the children (see pp 22–23). In particular you should say what you think about Bamforth. Here again your attitude to him will depend on who you are. Whitaker's attitude towards him is likely to be very different from Evans's.

4 In Act One, Mitchem, as the leader of the patrol, is faced by a number of crises — the quarrel between Macleish and Bamforth (pp 28–31), the discovery that the Japanese are very close to them (pp 34–6) and the question of what to do with the Japanese prisoner (pp 39–40).

Taking any two of these episodes, discuss Mitchem's qualities as a leader. How decisive is he? Does he reassure the other members of the patrol? Is he fair? Is he a good disciplinarian? Would you care to serve or work under someone like him?

5 Johnstone is consistently in favour of killing the Japanese prisoner, (pp 39, 41, 44); Bamforth is at first (p 39), and Mitchem's attitude varies. In pairs discuss the arguments for and against killing a prisoner in these circumstances. Afterwards write up the arguments on both sides and finally come to a conclusion as to what you think the correct decision would be in such a situation. (You should consider the conversation between Mitchem and

Macleish (pp 54–8) and the argument between Mitchem, Johnstone and Bamforth on pp 75–6).

6   After the patrol has been wiped out the unit's commanding officer is required to write a detailed account of each man for regimental records. Putting yourself in his position, write the reports for Mitchem, Johnstone and Bamforth. These reports should cover their family circumstances and upbringing. You should therefore use your imagination and you may wish to consider some of the ideas in the production note, for example the suggestion that Bamforth may have had 'an unhappy family life' (p 6), or that Mitchem's 'experience of personal relationships has been bitter' (p 7).

7   Imagine you are the wife, mother, sister, daughter or grandmother of any of the dead soldiers. You have learned in some detail about the events in the jungle and you are asked to write for a newspaper (or record for radio) your views about what happened and the part your relative played in these events. Did he act as you would have expected him to? Are you proud or ashamed? What are your feelings about the political and military situation which led up to this episode?

8   Expanding on the idea behind question 6 above, compile a complete dossier of any one or all three of these characters. The dossier would include such things as school reports, social worker/probation officer reports, newspaper articles giving accounts of sporting achievements and/or criminal behaviour, e.g. fighting or a drunk and disorderly incident. You might also include a recommendation for a military decoration for bravery.

9   Imagine that the patrol returns safely to base, though not without losing some of its members. As a surviving member of the patrol write an account of the whole experience from start to finish, *either* in the form of a letter home, *or* as an official report, *or* as a conversation with your friends back at camp.

10  Put yourself in the position of the Japanese prisoner and describe the whole episode from his point of view from the time of his capture up to just before his death. Remember that he speaks no English, but try to convey his reaction to the different characters, based on the way they treat him.

11  Bamforth is probably the most complex and interesting character in the play. Give a detailed account of his attitude towards war, the army, authority, violence, killing and the prisoner. Do you find

him a sympathetic or unsympathetic character? Do you think we are meant to like or dislike him? Is it surprising that he is the one member of the patrol who defends the prisoner's right to life?

12 Imagine that one member of the patrol survives the shoot-out at the end and spends the rest of the war in a Japanese prisoner-of-war camp. Years later he and his wife visit Singapore on a package holiday, and on a trip up into the jungle re-discover the hut where it all happened. Acting as the survivor or his wife, write an account of the whole experience, *either* in diary form, *or* as a letter home, *or* as an article for the local newspaper. (You could get useful additional information from a travel agent's brochure, which you might also be able to use to illustrate your piece of writing.)

13 What does this play say about war? You may find the conversation between Mitchem and Johnstone on pp 58–9 particularly relevant to this question, but you should also consider the way in which each of the characters reacts to the situation in which he finds himself.

**Julius Caesar**

Shakespeare confronts us immediately with the problem of the language barrier, a significant stumbling block for many pupils. Modern editions of the plays, printed for the most part with glosses and explanations on the facing page are, of course, very helpful, but this arrangement can prove a snare and delusion, because the explanation of individual words or expressions can still leave the passage as a whole partially or even totally misunderstood. There is therefore little alternative but to proceed on the assumption that a first readthrough of the play will give only outline comprehension but that a second much more detailed — and periodically tested — readthrough will be necessary to ensure a full comprehension of what the play is really about.

The teacher's initial fear is that such a procedure will prove inexpressibly boring for everyone. Although I do not think we should be too apologetic about requiring able pupils to be on their academic mettle and show a reasonable degree of intellectual pride and curiosity, there are various strategies which break up or disguise the tedium which almost inevitably attends even the most enthusiastic examination and explanation of the language. Examples of such strategies employed on *Julius Caesar*, are:

(a) *Act I, sc. ii*: the teacher gives the pupils a note which reads as follows:

(i)    A long and important scene, which falls into four sections: 1–24: our first view of Caesar and ominous reference to the Ides of March;

(ii)   25–177: Cassius' attempt to enlist Brutus' support in some form of conspiracy to overthrow or remove Caesar;

(iii)  178–214: Caesar's return and expressed reservations about Cassius;

(iv)   215–end: Casca's account of events and Cassius' final reflections on Brutus.

1    Rewrite in modern English ll. 36–62, taking care to illuminate any obscurities in the original.

2    It is clear from Cassius' words in ll. 25–177 that he has given much thought to the question of how best to approach Brutus and enlist his support. In the light of his speeches in this scene, imagine yourself in Cassius' place *before* the scene, reflecting on your feelings about Caesar and working out how best to tackle Brutus on the subject.

3    Look at ll. 164–5. Putting yourself in Brutus' place at the end of the scene, consider your feelings and position in the light of Cassius' speeches and Casca's account of Caesar's behaviour.

(b) Act II, sc. i: the teacher distributes a note to the pupils which reads as follows:

(i)    Brutus' soliloquy (ll. 10–34) is a crucial stage in the play. Write a paraphrase in modern English, taking care to identify his main reason for joining the conspiracy.

(ii)   By a careful examination of ll. 77–85, 114–140 and 166–180, consider Brutus' attitude towards conspiracy in general and this conspiracy in particular.

(iii)  What evidence is there that Brutus is an idealist rather than a realist?

(iv)   What evidence is there in this scene of a change in the relationship between Brutus and Cassius, compared with their relationship in Act I, sc. ii?

(v)    Why does Shakespeare end the scene with the conversation between Brutus and Portia? Does this in any way alter our view of Brutus, the conspirator?

(c) Act III, sc. i is almost 300 lines in length. On the assumption that the class numbers about 30, the teacher divides the scene into sections of approximately 20 lines, then, getting the pupils to work in pairs, asks them to rewrite their sections in modern American changing the names as appropriate. (Thus Brutus may become Butch, Cassius Casey, Rome Chicago and so on).

253

(d) (i)   A front-page newspaper account of the death of Caesar. The piece should be written in the style appropriate to different types of newspaper, whether they choose to reproduce the Roman equivalent of, for example, *The Times* or the *Daily Mirror*.

(ii)   A leading article for the same (or possibly a different newspaper) reacting appropriately to the assassination. (Most pupils of this age are unlikely to be familiar with leading articles, and the task will have the additional merit of increasing their awareness of the function and power of newspapers.)

(e) *Act IV, sc. iii, ll. 1–236.* Again the teacher organizes the class into groups, this time of 3, dividing the extract up into sections of about 25 lines each. The idea here is that one of the 3 acts as the director, instructing Brutus and Cassius in how to play that particular section of the quarrel scene. Thus instructions could be expected to include tone of voice, volume, facial expressions and other gestures. This will necessarily involve examining the language closely for its precise meaning. Finally each group acts out its section of the extract.

(f) (After finishing the play) Imagine that Brutus and Cassius survive the battle of Philippi, are captured and brought back to Rome to stand trial for the death of Caesar. Each pupil is required to write any one of four speeches:

(i)   the prosecution speech against Brutus;
(ii)   the prosecution speech against Cassius;
(iii)   the defence speech for Brutus;
(iv)   the defence speech for Cassius.

In order to give substance to the speeches, pupils will need to re-examine any or all of the following scenes: I,ii; I,iii; II,i; II,ii; III,ii; IV,iii (ll. 18–22); V,v (ll. 67–75). A selection of pupils could then be asked to deliver their speeches in class.

## Poetry

If plays are seen by most teachers of English as one of the easier aspects of their work, the teaching of poetry, particularly to the 14–16 age group, is frequently regarded as the most difficult. In a sense this is a little surprising, since poetry presents few problems to younger children, who are automatically and naturally attracted to the rhymes and rhythms which characterize much of the poetry to which they are exposed from the time they start listening to and learning to recite nursery rhymes.

Something seems to happen to many of our pupils between the ages of about 12 and 14, which leads them to regard poetry with suspicion, as a form of literature which is unnecessarily obscure and all too often remote from them in terms of diction and content. Part of the problem may be that much modern poetry, which has tended to make up the bulk of the poetry anthologies which have become popular in recent years, is indeed rather difficult. Another problem is that we often approach a poetry lesson in complete isolation from the other literature that we may have been reading with a class.

It may therefore make more sense to attempt to relate the poetry to the prose literature. Thus a class which has finished *Kes* could look at a number of poems about birds, such as Jon Silkin's *Death of a Bird*. Similarly a natural follow-up to *Journey's End* or *All Quiet on the Western Front* would be to examine a number of war poems. In this way we can begin to de-mythologize poetry, to encourage pupils to see that it has no less validity and importance to them than prose literature but that it operates in a different way. And this is, of course, the second part of the problem: how do we teach poetry in such a way that it becomes something other than a verbal jigsaw-puzzle or bizarre kind of game?

**Cynddylan on a Tractor**
Let us suppose a teacher has just finished reading *Cider with Rosie* with a class and decides to exploit the rural connexion by examining R S Thomas's well-known poem *Cynddylan on a Tractor*.

> Ah, you should see Cynddylan on a tractor
> Gone the old look that yoked him to the soil;
> He's a new man now, part of the machine,
> His nerves of metal and his blood oil.
> 5 The clutch curses, but the gears obey
> His least bidding, and lo, he's away
> Out of the farmyard, scattering hens.
> Riding to work now as a great man should,
> He is the knight at arms breaking the fields'
> 10 Mirror of silence, emptying the wood
> Of foxes and squirrels and bright jays.
> The sun comes over the tall trees
> Kindling all the hedges, but not for him
> Who runs his engine on a different fuel
> 15 And all the birds are singing, bills wide in vain,
> As Cynddylan passes proudly up the lane.

After an initial read through, the success of the session which follows will depend in some measure on the speed and enthusiasm with which the teacher tackles the questions!

(a) What is the effect of the opening word 'Ah'?

(b) What is the tone of the first line? Is it one of admiration? If so, on whose part?

(c) What is the effect of the word 'yoked' in l.2?

(d) Is the tone of the line merely narrative or tinged with regret or relief?

(e) What is odd, even contradictory, about ll.3 and 4?

(f) What is suggested by the use of the words 'curses' and 'obey' in l.5?

(g) Is anything implied by the 'scattering' of the hens in l.7?

(h) How genuine is the expression 'as a great man should' in l.8?

(i) In what sense is he 'a knight at arms' in l.9 and in what sense is he different from the traditional image conjured up by such an expression?

(j) What is meant by 'the fields'/Mirror of silence' in ll.9 and 10?

(k) What is the effect of the reference to 'foxes and squirrels and bright jays' in l.11?

(l) What is meant by 'Kindling' in l.13 and what is the effect of the word as used in this context?

(m) In what sense is the 'engine' his in l.14? Is it merely that he now goes to work on a tractor?

(n) Why are the birds' 'bills wide in vain' in l.15?

(o) In gaining his tractor, what has Cynddylan lost?

(p) What is the effect of the word 'proudly' in l.16?

(q) What is the poet's attitude towards the experience he describes? Is Cynddylan to be admired, pitied or deplored?

(r) Is this a poem about Golden Age rural romanticism? If so, does that imply that it is unrealistic?

(s) Finally, and to tie it in again with Laurie Lee and *Cider with Rosie*, is there any reason to think that Lee would have been sympathetic to the general message of this poem?

As a postscript to this examination of the poem, pupils could be asked to write a detailed prose paraphrase of it. This should have the effect of revealing to them — if they have not already become aware of it — the concentration, distillation and allusiveness that are among the hallmarks of poetry.

Another aspect of poetry which we may tend to neglect, thus contributing to our pupils' alienation from it, is humour. There is the risk that poetry tends to become associated with solemnity and high seriousness. Useful antidotes to this are such collections as *The Mersey*

*Sound* (Volume 10 of the Penguin Modern Poets series), which has a range of poems suitable for a wide spread of ability. A poem such as 'Little Jonny's Confession' rarely fails to entertain and has the additional merit of needing little, if any, follow-up. We should not, after all, lead our pupils to regard every piece of literature as merely the preliminary to some kind of question and answer session, and there is a lot to be said occasionally for distributing a set of poetry books, inviting every pupil to choose two or three which they like, then listening to them read their choices in turn, with at most the occasional question 'Can you tell us what you liked about that poem? What made you choose it?'

## Chaucer

Finally, a brief word about teaching Chaucer. At this level his immediate appeal is principally to those pupils who have an interest in language and its development. Certainly the emphasis in examinations is on establishing that candidates have fully understood what they have read. As with a Shakespeare play, therefore, there is no alternative but to work through the text, to ensure complete and detailed comprehension of what Chaucer is saying. That having been said, however, there is the obvious danger of leaving the pupil with a rather limited view of what Chaucer has to offer. We must therefore provide the pupil with some justification for studying Chaucer, other than the bland and unconvincing statement that he is 'the father of English literature'. We must, in other words, demonstrate that Chaucer's work, though firmly rooted in an age and culture remote from our own, frequently possesses the subtlety and wisdom of all great literature.

This, in fact, is not as difficult to do as it might at first appear. In *The Pardoner's Tale*, for example, the Pardoner's hypocrisy in railing against the sins of gluttony and drunkenness is implicitly hinted at by the fact that he tells his story in a tavern. As for the story itself, the universality of its application is enhanced by the anonymity of the three revellers. The identity of the old man affords endless scope for speculation, and Chaucer's skill as a manipulator of our emotions is demonstrated by the fact that, whereas we might be expected to feel some instinctive sympathy with the youngest reveller, knowing that his own companions are planning to kill him, such sympathy is swiftly dissipated by the disclosure that he is plotting an even more horrible end for his colleagues. Finally, the teacher can point out the skill of a storyteller who, by careful but apparently casual preparation, is able to proceed to the dénouement of his tale in a mere ten lines. *The Pardoner's Tale*, in short, offers ample scope for the teacher who wishes to demonstrate the sophistication that lies behind Chaucer's apparent artlessness.

# PART TWO

# English at A Level

As with English at 16+, before looking at the teaching of the subject, a logical preliminary is to quote a typical statement of the aims and objectives as identified by one of the major examining boards, the University of London Board:

## Aims

To encourage an enjoyment and appreciation of English Literature based on informed personal response and to extend this appreciation where it has already been acquired.

## Objectives

(a) Knowledge: of the contents of the books and where appropriate of the personal and historical circumstances in which they were written;
(b) Understanding: extending from simple factual comprehension to a broader conception of the nature and significance of literary texts;
(c) Analysis: the ability to recognize and describe literary effects and to comment precisely on the use of language;
(d) Judgement: the capacity to make judgements of value based on close reading;
(e) Sense of the past and tradition: the ability to see a literary work in its historical context as well as that of the present day;
(f) Expression: the ability to write organized and cogent essays on literary subjects.

## An introductory course

The majority of A-Level boards require the study of seven or eight texts and most students have two years in which to cover this material. The first term of the course therefore offers the teacher an excellent opportunity for some background work, to broaden the students' range of literary experience and go some way towards helping them to meet objective (e) above. An introductory course, which should aim to cover the three main literary genres, could look something like this:

(a) A survey of the novel from its beginnings up to the present day. Students would be expected to read, discuss and write about a representative selection of novels, such as a late eighteenth or early nineteenth century novel (e.g. *Joseph Andrews* or *Pride and Prejudice*), a Victorian novel (e.g. *The Mill on the Floss*, *Great Expectations* or *Tess of the D'Urbervilles*), an early twentieth century novel (e.g. *Sons and Lovers* or *To the Lighthouse*) and a contemporary novel of their own choosing by authors such as Paul Scott, J G Farrell or Muriel Spark). It would clearly be helpful for students to be issued with a reading list which would both give them a sense of chronology and assist them in their selection.

(b) A brief survey of the development of tragedy and comedy in the theatre. The first component could begin with a reading of a Greek tragedy, preferably Sophocles' *Oedipus Tyrannus*, which could be followed up by a note giving the essence of Aristotle's critique of tragedy, which has been the starting-point for most subsequent criticism of the genre. This could be followed by the reading of a Shakespearean tragedy, and the course could end with a modern play, such as *Death of a Salesman*.

Comedy could begin somewhat later with a Restoration comedy, followed by a comedy of manners, such as *The Importance of Being Earnest*, and conclude with a modern play by an author such as Tom Stoppard or Michael Frayn. An interesting means of dovetailing the tragic and comic components of the course could be provided by following a study of *Hamlet* with a reading of *Rosencrantz and Guildenstern are dead*.

(c) A survey of English and American poetry through the ages. This will necessarily be highly selective but should include some study of the sonnet form (including the writing of sonnets by the students themselves), the Metaphysical poets, the Romantics, some later nineteenth century poetry and some contemporary poetry.

A course of this nature, as well as being inherently interesting and stimulating, provides A-Level students with a literary perspective and a context into which they could then place the texts which are set for detailed study.

# Novels

## Our Mutual Friend

At A Level, the teaching of the novel, particularly the long Victorian novel, set by some boards, occasionally as an absolute requirement, frequently presents teachers with the greatest difficulties. How, for example, does one set about teaching *Our Mutual Friend*? It is highly unlikely that few, if any, members of an A-Level class have ever tackled anything approaching a 900-page novel before, and they invariably — and understandably — find the prospect daunting. A brief introductory note about Dickens's life, writings and particular pre-occupations is an obvious starting-point, but how does the teacher then guide the students through the book in such a way that they do not become overwhelmed by the sheer mass of detail?

In the early stages of the examination of a book such as this, detailed guidance is necessary, and progress is likely to be slow. Students have to be taught what to look for in an author and a style of writing with which most of them will be unfamiliar. Let us take the first two chapters as an example (all page references are to the Penguin edition).

When we are first introduced to Gaffer Hexam, the most noteworthy feature of his presentation is that it is a series of negatives: 'He had *no* net, hook or line, and he could *not* be a fisherman; his boat had *no* cushion for a sitter, *no* paint, *no* inscription . . .' (p. 43). This simple stylistic device sets the keynote for the chapter as a whole, which is designed to generate an air of sinister mystery. The second important feature in the chapter is the reference to money — and attitudes to money — a motif which runs as a central strand through the novel. Thirdly, and more obviously, there is the contrast between the language, manner and attitudes of Gaffer Hexam and his daughter, Lizzie.

Chapter Two provides a total contrast, though with an important common element in the form of money as we are introduced to the 'bran-new' and symbolically named Veneerings. Students need to be aware of the satire in the chapter, which is a characteristic feature of all the sections of the novel dealing with this particular stratum of society. Its superficiality is brought out in two ways, first by the brooding presence of 'the melancholy retainer' and by Dickens's brilliant use of the mirror as the vehicle for presenting the assembled company, who are all seen as mere 'reflections' and thus largely insubstantial and two-dimensional characters (pp 52–3). The same procedure is likely to prove necessary for several more chapters, as the teacher draws students' attention to important recurrent motifs, such as the dust-heaps and the river, to Dickens's use of setting and his way of presenting characters.

But there is a limit to the amount of path-finding that is necessary or desirable. Up to this point all that the students can reasonably be asked to do on their own account is to make brief chapter summaries, as an aid to recollection and a means of finding their way quickly around the book. Henceforth, however, they should be much more closely involved. One way in which this can be done is for the teacher to break down the individual sections of the novel by themes, and allocate each theme to a group of students, directing them to the relevant chapters. The students work separately, pool their notes and one person reports their findings as a whole. Thus Book II of *Our Mutual Friend*, for example, could be broken down as follows:

(a) Education and Charley — chapters I, VI, XV.
(b) Bradley Headstone — chapters I, VI, XI, XV.
(c) Lizzie Hexam and Jenny Wren — chapters I, II, V, XI, XV.
(d) Money — chapters III, IV, V, VII, VIII, XIII.
(e) The Boffins and the Poor Law — chapters IX, X, XIV.

After each section of the novel has been dealt with in this fashion a number of topics could be set for general class discussion and/or essay-writing, for example:

(a) 'Dickens's attack on Charley Hexam's education is unfair and ill-informed.' Discuss.
(b) 'In his treatment of Bradley Headstone, Dickens simply lines himself up with Eugene and Mortimer.' Discuss.
(c) 'Lizzie Hexam and Jenny Wren are too grotesque to be true.' Discuss.
(d) What are the main points that Dickens is concerned to make about money and attitudes to it in Book II?

Such an approach to the novel stands a good chance of striking a reasonable balance between the attention to detail and the awareness of a writer's aims and methods which are both prominent among the examining boards' objectives listed at the beginning of this section.

One final word on teaching the novel at A Level. One of the teacher's principal responsibilities is, wherever possible, to unearth material relevant to the particular circumstances of writing the book. In the case of *Our Mutual Friend*, for instance, Dickens's original plans for the book are available and constitute a rich field for class discussion as one observes the writer at work, proposing an idea, then changing his mind and highlighting what to him are the critical features of the book. Thus one could have an interesting discussion on the subject of names, for example, why the eventually chosen 'Bradley Headstone' is so much more appropriate than 'Amos Headstone' or 'Amos Deadstone', which were his first two versions of the name.

## To the Lighthouse
In the case of many other novels, diary entries can illuminate a writer's intentions and significantly help students in their appreciation of a novel. Virginia Woolf's diary entries concerning her novel *To the Lighthouse* shed a good deal of light on her aims. For example,

14 May 1925: This [novel] is going to be fairly short; to have father's character done complete in it; and mother's . . . and childhood; and all the usual things I try to put in — life, death, etc. . . .

30 July 1925: I think I might do something in *To the Lighthouse*, to split up emotions more completely . . . [Discussion point — what do you think she meant by that?]

5 September 1926: At the moment I'm casting about for an end. The problem is how to bring Lily and Mr Ramsay together . . .

13 September 1926: This last lap, in the boat, is hard, because the material is not so rich as it was with Lily on the lawn. I am forced to be more direct and intense. I am making more use of symbolism . . . [This should go some way towards placating those students who repeatedly accuse English teachers of an obsession with symbolism!]

There are also illuminating comments on the novel in her letters to friends.

This is merely one example of the way in which some preliminary research on the part of the teacher can prove beneficial to students, most of whom are unlikely, for a variety of reasons, to acquire this background information for themselves.

# Drama

The study of at least one Shakespeare play is the one compulsory component in all A-Level English examinations, and so the teaching of Shakespeare is the main focus of this discussion about the teaching of drama in general.

As the examining boards' objectives make clear, precise knowledge and understanding of the text come high on the list of priorities, a not unreasonable requirement, since a correct understanding of the text is a necessary pre-requisite of an appreciation of the play as a whole. Since A-Level examiners are entitled to look for evidence of greater sophistication and a more scholarly approach at this level, the teacher's first responsibility is to ensure a detailed understanding of the text. The time spent on this may vary quite considerably from play to play. For example, the complex language of *King Lear* is likely to require more extensive exegesis than the relatively straightforward language of *The Tempest*.

## The Tempest

We are still talking, however, primarily about the teacher's function. What should students be doing at this stage to help themselves? Guidance such as the following on *The Tempest*, for example, is an obvious, though frequently neglected, starting-point:

1 *After* we have finished examining a scene in class:
   (a) Write a brief scene-summary;
   (b) Consider the overall purpose of the scene and its position in the play;
   (c) Examine what it reveals of any significance about the characters involved, their relationships, motives, etc.;
   (d) Ask yourself any other relevant questions about the scene and attempt to come up with some answers, on such subjects, for example, as imagery.

   These notes, particularly (c), should include *brief* illustrative quotation.

2 *Before* the next class read ahead, consulting the notes as appropriate.

   An example of the sort of thing I have in mind under **1** would be the following notes on Act I, sc i of *The Tempest*:

   (a) The play opens at sea with a storm in full fury. We soon learn that the King and other nobles are on board. The scene ends with every indication that the ship and all on board are doomed.
   (b) The setting clearly provides a dramatic opening to the play, but, given the title of the play, the brevity of the scene and the fact that there is no other storm in the play, it may be worth dwelling on other possible significances of the title. Thus it may, for example, symbolize a stormy condition — of a nature and for reasons yet to be identified — in the minds of some at least of those on board. It also offers an opportunity to examine people's different reactions to a dangerous situation.

(c) The scene tells us something about Gonzalo, Sebastian and Antonio. Gonzalo may be somewhat tiresome in certain respects, but he appears in this scene to be an incurable optimist and invaluable comforter. Three times in the scene he seeks to reassure himself and his companions by referring to his confidence that the Boatswain is born to die on dry land — 'His complexion is perfect gallows' (29–30). By contrast Sebastian and Antonio have little else to offer but abuse and insults:

Seb.    A pox o' your throat, you bawling, blasphemous, incharitable dog . . .
Ant.    Hang, cur! hang, you whoreson, insolent noise-maker (40–3).

The contrast could scarcely be more marked, and for a religious audience it would be all the more striking and shocking that men who believed themselves to be on the verge of death should indulge in such vituperative language. Such an idea would be reinforced by ll. 51–5, where Antonio and Sebastian alone of all the passengers, apparently, decline to join Alonso, Ferdinand and the crew at prayers.

(d) No obvious questions spring to mind at this early stage of the play, with the possible exception of the question whether there is any signficance in the fact that Gonzalo is the most prominent character in the scene. There is also the fairly obvious point that even kings are insignificant and powerless when placed at the mercy of the elements. This could be related to our later perception of Prospero's powers, particularly if we see him in a quasi-divine light.

Similar treatment of other scenes will, of course, necessarily be much more extensive.

## Othello

The next problem is how to break up the remorseless and, it must be admitted, at times tedious examination of the text by devising projects which will focus the students' attention on the more general issues raised by the play. There is a natural fear that in examining the play act by act, the piecemeal approach may lead to a distorted view of the play as a whole, but this problem is more apparent than real. The following projects could quite validly be devised for Act I of *Othello*.

(a) What justification can be found for Iago's hatred of Othello?
(b) What evidence is there in Act I of racial prejudice in Venice?

(c) From the way in which Othello speaks about himself, what initial impression do we form of him?

(d) What does the language used by Iago tell us about the character?

(e) What is the basis of the relationship between Othello and Desdemona?

These projects could be handled in a variety of ways. Thus, while (d) lends itself most naturally and profitably to treatment in writing, (a) could take the form of an inquisition of Iago, played by one of the students, by other members of the class, basing the enquiry on his remarks to Roderigo in scene i and his soliloquy at the end of scene iii; (b) could take the form of a group of students calling Iago, Roderigo and Brabantio to account for the language they use in relation to Othello, and comparing it with contemporary racist language; (c) and (e) could be dealt with in the form of group or class discussion.

The conclusions reached in the course of these projects may have to be revised and adjusted in the light of the play's subsequent development, but they are nonetheless valid at the time and can make a significant contribution to the overall appreciation of characters and themes. If one were, for example, to dramatize a psychiatric examination of Iago in prison at the end of the play, it would be crucial for both Iago and the examining psychiatrist(s) to have kept close track of the soliloquies in which Iago has periodically attempted to justify his behaviour and give an account of his motives.

Once we move away from Shakespeare, we are relieved of the primary responsibility for ensuring close textual knowledge, but there is no doubt that the study of other plays — and of other literature in general — can only benefit from the habit of careful reading thus developed.

## Death of a Salesman
To take a very simple example, in a play such as *Death of a Salesman* no attentive student can fail to notice that within less than 10 lines Willy Loman says of his son, Biff, first that he is 'is a lazy bum' and then 'There's one thing about Biff — he's not lazy', thus pinpointing at an early point in the play one of its central features, the perpetual oscillation and confusion in the Loman family between myth and reality. This is merely one illustration of the crucial lessons that the A-Level student should have learned — that a careful reading of any text is an essential pre-requisite to a proper appreciation of it and that arguments need to be supported by textual reference.

Once such principles have been established, the teacher can explore the issues raised by *Death of a Salesman*, such as

(a)  How far can Willy Loman be regarded as a casualty of the system, a
     victim of the American dream, and how far is he responsible for
     his own shortcomings?
(b)  To what extent is Biff guilty of his father's death?
(c)  Is Linda to blame for colluding with Willy's avoidance of
     reality?
(d)  Is Happy another potentially tragic figure?

In a play of this nature it is consistent with the whole dramatic
approach to ask individual students to take on the persona of a
particular character, immerse themselves in it and argue their position
on these and similar questions. We can ask the character playing
Bernard to state just what his feelings are about the whole Loman
family; and ask Charley whether his attitude to Willy is entirely
consistent, whether he admires him or pities him, whether he really
wants to help him or merely patronizes him. There is scope here for
much animated discussion if the students have done their homework.

# Poetry

### Wordsworth
The difficulty of most of the poetry set at A Level must involve the
teacher, particularly in the early stages, in more direct teaching than in
either of the other two literary genres. If we imagine, for example, that
the set work is a selection of Wordsworth's poetry, the teacher has to
begin by giving the class relevant extracts from Wordsworth's Preface
to *Lyrical Ballads*, so focusing their minds at the outset on some, at least,
of Wordsworth's aims and preoccupations as a poet. This could then
be followed by a quick reading of Books I and II of *The Prelude*, drawing
attention to Wordsworth's particular apprehension of Nature and his
view of his debt to it, as evinced by such lines as

> 'Fair seed-time had my soul, and I grew up
> Fostered alike by beauty and by fear'

> (Bk. I, 301–2)

This preparation will enhance the students' appreciation of poems
such as 'Tintern Abbey', the Lucy poems, 'Michael', the 'Immortality
Ode' and many others. They could be encouraged to make a collection
of relevant extracts from *The Prelude* for the purpose of subsequent
cross-reference to the shorter poems.

All this, however, is no more than a basic first step; merely to hang the label of 'Nature Poet' round Wordsworth's neck is simplistic and unhelpful, tending to lead students to regard him as a vaguely lovable eccentric who has nothing to say to anyone who is not familiar with the Wye Valley or the Lake District. The task then is to explore with the students the development of Wordsworth's thought, as conveyed by poems such as 'Tintern Abbey', from a simple, but vitally important, sensory appreciation of Nature to a mystical, spiritual apprehension of the world. This journey brings out the crucial paradox that although spiritual understanding is critically dependent, in the first instance, on the senses, the final contemplative state achieved by the poet is independent of them; when

> '. . . the breath of this corporeal frame
> And even the motion of our human blood
> Almost suspended, we are laid asleep
> In body, and become a living soul.
> While with an eye made quiet by the power
> Of harmony, and the deep power of joy,
> We see into the life of things.'

(Tintern Abbey, 43–49)

When the complexity of Wordsworth's thought has been examined and explained in this way the student is equipped to tackle such poems as the 'Immortality Ode', 'Resolution and Independence', or the 'Elegiac Stanzas suggested by a picture of Peele Castle'.

**Keats**
The poetry of Keats, to take another Romantic example, presents fewer difficulties for most students. If a collection of poems and letters were set, as it frequently has been, at A Level, an obvious starting-point for the teacher who wanted to involve students straight away would be one of the Odes, preferably 'To Autumn', albeit at the risk of some chronological dislocation. A class on this poem can be based on the following questions:

(a) Look carefully at the language of the opening stanza — what is its effect? How is this achieved?
(b) What is the effect of the run-on lines?
(c) Look at the rhyme-scheme — what is unusual about it?
(d) Why do you think Keats chose to employ an 11-line stanza, whereas the other great odes have stanzas of only 10 lines each?
(e) Identify the three figures in the second stanza; are these real people, or personifications of autumn? What is the difference?
(f) What picture of autumn is presented in this stanza?

(g) What is the effect of the vowel sounds, particularly in the last line?

(h) Why does Keats bring in the reference to spring in the last stanza?

(i) In what way does the mood of the poem change in this stanza? How is this effect achieved?

(j) What sort of progression is there in the poem as a whole?

The hope is that, in a question and answer session of this kind, the students will become aware of the subtlety that lies beneath the more obvious linguistic appeal of the poem, that the poem looks both ways, first of all back to summer and finally forward to winter. In so doing they will, at this early stage in their study of Keats, become aware of a central notion which they will repeatedly come across in other of his poems, namely that the celebration of the beauties of this world is inseparable from an awareness of their transience.

Thus what begins as a rich and sensuous evocation of the opulence of autumn, full of life and action, turns almost imperceptibly into a lament for its passing, with the shift in emphasis conveyed by the accumulation of words such as 'soft-dying', 'wailful', 'mourn', 'sinking', and 'dies'. This approach to Keats should capture the interest of most students with any sensibility to literature.

**Milton**
Finally, some words on Milton, since some examination boards make a point of regularly setting one or two books of *Paradise Lost*. The first major point is that since few students nowadays have any familiarity at all with the Bible, it is essential for the teacher either to produce copies of, or ensure that the students have acquainted themselves with, the first three chapters of the Book of Genesis. The second difficulty with Milton is the complexity of his syntax. Finally, there is the problem of frequent classical allusions, inseparable from the epic tradition.

In spite of these hazards, it is frequently gratifying to see how much satisfaction quite average students can derive from Milton, provided he is studied at a fairly late stage of the A-Level course. They find themselves swept along by the language and forced to examine seriously, possibly for the first time, theological and ethical questions about the nature of Good and Evil. The presentation of Satan and the account of the Fall invariably give rise to animated discussions about determinism, free-will and our ambivalent attitude towards evil. In short, contrary to many people's worst fears, the study of *Paradise Lost* often proves enjoyable and stimulating for teacher and students alike.

# Practical criticism

As most examining boards at A Level require their candidates to undertake the critical appreciation of a piece of poetry or prose, students need training in this particular skill. Some of this takes place incidentally in the course of the study of the texts set for examination, but there is also a need to give specific and detailed guidance on an area of work which frightens many students, particularly when they are confronted by unseen passages for criticism.

## The criticism of poetry

When asked the question 'What is poetry?' Dr Johnson replied, 'Why, Sir, it is much easier to say what it is not. We all *know* what light is, but it is not easy to *tell* what it is.' This is an obvious starting-point for any examination of poetry criticism, and the teacher could stimulate a discussion on the nature of poetry by providing students with a list of suggested answers to the question, such as the following:

1 The difference between genuine poetry and the poetry of Dryden, Pope and all their school is briefly this: their poetry is conceived and composed in their wits, genuine poetry is conceived and composed in the soul. (Matthew Arnold)
2 If poetry comes not as naturally as leaves to a tree it had better not come at all. (John Keats)
3 I wish our clever young poets would remember my homely definitions of prose and poetry; that is, prose = words in their best order; poetry = the *best* words in the best order. (Samuel Coleridge)
4 If we may be excused the antithesis, we should say that eloquence is *heard*, poetry is *overheard*. (John Stuart Mill)
5 Poetry is the record of the best and happiest moments of the happiest and best minds. (Percy Bysshe Shelley)
6 Poetry is the spontaneous overflow of powerful feelings, it takes its origin from emotion recollected in tranquillity. (Wordsworth)
7 Poetry is something more philosophic and of graver import than history. (Aristotle)
8 Poetry is certainly something more than good sense, but it must be good sense at all events; just as a palace is more than a house, but it must be a house, at least. (Coleridge)
9 What is poetry? The suggestion, by the imagination, of noble grounds for the noble emotions. (John Ruskin)
10 Poetry is a kind of ingenious nonsense. (Isaac Barrow)

11  Poetry is a comforting piece of fiction set to more or less lascivious music. (H L Mencken)
12  Poetry is the achievement of the synthesis of hyacinths and biscuits. (Carl Sandburg)
13  Poetry is that stuff in books which doesn't quite reach to the margins. (Anon schoolchild)

The teacher could then involve the students in the poetic process by means of a cloze exercise on a poem. This can be done in a variety of ways and for a variety of purposes, to assess and enhance the pupils' sense of rhyme or rhythm, or to test their stylistic awareness. To take a simple example, copies of T S Eliot's *Morning at the Window* could be distributed with certain words omitted, and the class invited in pairs or threes, to fill in the gaps. A variant of, or an addition to, this exercise is to produce three alternatives for each missing word and require the students to justify their preference. The exercise would look something like this:

Read the following poem, from which a number of words have been omitted:

> They are (a) breakfast plates in basement kitchens,
> And along the (b) edges of the street
> I am aware of the (c) souls of housemaids
> (d) despondently at area gates.
>
> The (e) waves of fog toss up to me
> (f) faces from the bottom of the street,
> And tear from a passer-by with (g) skirts
> An aimless smile that (h) in the air
> And (i) along the level of the roofs.

1  Suggest words to replace the blanks.
2  Select — and justify your preference — from the following alternatives:
    (a)  washing, rattling, clattering
    (b)  trampled, muddy, dismal
    (c)  sad, lost, damp
    (d)  gazing, groaning, sprouting
    (e)  brown, thick, dense
    (f)  ancient, forlorn, twisted
    (g)  draggled, muddy, tattered
    (h)  hovers, wavers, quivers
    (i)  disappears, vanishes, evaporates

All of this, however, is relatively light-hearted stuff, merely designed to break the ice and start the students thinking about what poetry is. There is still the need for the teacher to give much more precise guidance on how to set about criticizing a poem. The first thing is to emphasize that what a poem says — the content — is inseparable from how it says it — the style. All too often one finds students writing a critique of a poem which falls into two distinct parts, the first a discussion of the poem's content, which merely amounts to a prose paraphrase, the second an account of the stylistic devices employed — or sometimes even *not* employed — by the poet, as though the student had a checklist of terms such as 'assonance', 'onomatopoeia' and 'oxymoron' which somehow had to be mentioned, if only to remark on their absence from the poem. As a result one is sometimes driven to wonder whether many students fully appreciate the object of the exercise, which is to demonstrate not merely an understanding of what the poet is saying, but an awareness of the poet's intention and of how he or she achieves the particular effects.

The first pre-requisite of any critique is several careful readings of the poem. The critique itself should begin with a brief summary of the poem's overall meaning and impact. This need consist of no more than a few lines but should establish at the outset that the student has grasped the poet's purpose. It serves as a launching-pad for the next stage of the operation, a detailed examination of the poem, in which the student explores the poet's train of thought, commenting at the same time on the way in which technical features such as alliteration, the rhyme-scheme, the length of syllables, etc., assist the poet's purpose. The process in which the student is involved is one of continuous questioning: why did the poet choose this particular form of sounds? If there is alliteration or onomatopoeia, what purpose does it serve? What is the poet's attitude to his or her subject matter? And perhaps most important of all — and sometimes the most difficult to determine — what is the tone of the poem?

It is the last point which should serve as the main feature of the closing paragraph of the critique, in which the student should seek to bring together the various strands of the argument and sum up not only the poet's aims but also the student's own response to the poem.

An example of this procedure in action would be the following brief critique of Philip Larkin's poem 'Afternoons':

**Afternoons**

Summer is fading;
The leaves fall in ones and twos
From trees bordering
The new recreation ground.
In the hollows of afternoons
Young mothers assemble
At swing and sandpit
Setting free their children.

Behind them, at intervals,
Stand husbands in skilled trades,
An estateful of washing,
And the albums, lettered
'Our Wedding', lying
Near the television:
Before them, the wind
Is ruining their courting-places

That are still courting-places
(But the lovers are all in school),
And their children, so intent on
Finding more unripe acorns,
Expect to be taken home.
Their beauty has thickened.
Something is pushing them
To the side of their own lives.
*Philip Larkin*

This is ostensibly a poem about the actions of a group of young mothers who take their small children out to play together in the afternoons, but the poet takes advantage of the occasion to make a much more general and sombre point about what is happening to the lives of these young women.

Both the title of the poem and its first line have a symbolic application. Time is passing, and the women's youth is fading like the summer. Their loneliness and isolation are reflected in the leaves which fall 'in ones and twos', and the afternoons are described as 'hollow'. The regimentation implied by the word 'assemble' is contrasted with their setting free of their children. They are like jailers who are themselves much more imprisoned than those for whom they care.

In the second stanza their remoteness from their husbands who stand behind them 'at intervals', and the staleness of their marriages are both emphasized, as is the drabness of their lives, with the deliberate exaggeration of 'An estateful of washing', reflecting how it must feel at times to these young mothers. The wedding albums have given way to the television, thus 'lying' in both senses of the word.

As the second stanza merges with the third, we see that the whole idea of courtship has passed on to the next generation. Their children are absorbed in pursuits appropriately associated with the notion of starting out on life, searching for 'unripe acorns' and automatically making blithe assumptions about their mothers' responsibility. As the women are now at the mercy of the requirements of their husbands and children, the poet concludes with the sad reflection that the centrality of their own lives has been correspondingly diminished.

This, then, is a bleak and melancholy poem in which the poet eschews conventional stereotypes about the maternal and domestic contentment of the lives of mothers of small children, to reveal a more sober picture of their isolation, lack of freedom, their passing youth and uncertain future.

## The criticism of prose

Much of what has been said about the criticism of poetry applies, to a greater extent than is frequently realized, to the criticism of prose. The major difference between the two is that, since the prose writer is free of the poet's self-imposed constraints of form, rhyme, etc., the critic will be more concerned with the writer's general use of language (which will include such features as the rhythm and length of sentences, repetition, sounds, the cumulative impact of words, the effect of paragraphing and dialogue, characterization, and authorial point of view) than with the more precise technical features of poetic diction.

As an example, let us look at the opening paragraphs of the passage in *Great Expectations* when Magwitch returns to reveal himself as Pip's benefactor. (It is too long to print here but the extract I wish to examine runs from the third paragraph of Chapter 39 down to the point where Magwitch says 'I wish to come in, Master.')

A criticique of the passage might run as follows:

This is a highly dramatic piece of writing, in which a very deliberate and careful piece of scene-setting serves as the ominous background to a conversation in which the author's sense of puzzled and anxious amazement is strongly contrasted with the ease and assurance of his mysterious visitor.

The opening paragraph establishes a dismal, troubled and wild atmosphere, initially by the repetitions of 'stormy and wet, stormy and wet; mud, mud, mud . . .' followed by the ferocity of the adjectives and verbs — 'furious, stripped, torn, gloomy, violent' and culminating in the closing words, that this day 'had been the worst of all'.

The second paragraph enhances this effect by emphasizing Pip's isolation and suggesting that his position is both exposed and threatened. The gusts of wind are like cannon-fire and his lodgings are compared to 'a storm-beaten lighthouse'. To the image of a siege is added the oppressive blackness of the night, caused by the lamps being blown out and only intensified by the vivid picture of the sparks from the barges' coal fires 'being carried away before the wind like red-hot splashes in the rain'.

Pip's blithe indifference to the symbolic significance of this violent weather is emphasized by his detachment from it in reading, but his detachment is disturbed first by the reflection on the flawed sound of the church clocks striking eleven, and then by the dramatic 'footstep on the stair'.

The disclaimer which begins the next paragraph 'What nervous folly made me start, and awfully connect it with the footstep of my dead sister, matters not', is deliberately designed to have precisely the opposite effect; all too soon it is to matter a great deal, and the stumble on the stair reinforces the reader's sense of Pip's unease.

The whole of the conversation which follows shows Pip consistently at a disadvantage in relation to his visitor. He can do nothing but ask questions, while his visitor's confidence is in marked contrast with Pip's bewilderment. The inexorability of the destiny that is about to overwhelm Pip is conveyed by the relentless progress of the visitor — 'And the man came on', and the drama of the occasion is conveyed by the way in which he moves briefly in and out of the spotlight of the lamp.

Pip's bewilderment at his identity and behaviour is wholly at odds with the visitor's implied assumption of a relationship between them, indicated by his closing word 'Master'.

To sum up, the background against which the action and conversation takes place is a crucial element in the whole passage, as it suggests to the reader a threat to the narrator's essential calmness and sense of security. In this way Dickens brilliantly gives us a double perspective, as it were, on a particular event: the narrator, who provides us with all the information, feels no more at this stage than 'a stupid kind of amazement', while the reader has a much stronger sense of impending disaster than Pip himself.

## Alternative syllabuses

Finally, a word about the option offered by some boards at both GCSE and A Level, allowing centres to devise their own syllabus as an alternative to one (or possibly more) of the papers set by the board. This is a very attractive option, allowing teachers a high degree of autonomy in the texts they choose, and it has been enthusiastically exploited by a number of teachers. If an English department is dissatisfied with its board's syllabus, it is well worth enquiring whether an alternative of this kind is available. It is important to bear in mind, however, that devising and being responsible for the marking of the internal component are both very time-consuming operations, and a department would be well advised to think carefully before committing itself to this extra burden.

## Endpiece

Some readers who have reached the end of this chapter may have been disconcerted by the scarcity of references to examinations. To these I would simply repeat my view, expressed at the beginning of the chapter, that there is no significant difference between the teaching of literature generally and teaching for examinations. I therefore hope that most, if not all, of the approaches I have suggested will have the dual effect of enhancing pupils' examination success and increasing their general enjoyment of literature.

## Recommended reading

*The Criticism of Prose*, S H Burton, Longman, 1973
*Teaching Shakespeare*, Veronica O'Brien, Edward Arnold, 1982
*Critical Approaches to Literature*, David Daiches, Longman, 1984
*Understanding Poetry*, James Reeves, Heinemann, 1980
*Writing*, Linda Cookson, Hutchinson
*Checkbooks: Literature* Roger Lewis, Martin Pugmire and Gill Pugmire, Hutchinson, 1986
*The Cool Web* Margaret Meek *et al.*, Bodley Head, 1977

# 12 Assessment

David Allen

'Without evidence you cannot hope to shun the path I trod'

Jacob Marley to Ebeneezer Scrooge

## What is marking for?

'Marking' is to the English teacher almost a badge of office, an occupational component that sets English teaching apart from all others. A burden it often is — largely self inflicted by such practices as 'a piece of writing each week' set to each class and thus to be read and marked by the teacher. It is certainly the regular evening occupation of the English teacher. Yet what is the purpose behind this orgy of self-discipline? Who is it for?

The answer to that seems obvious, perhaps, but the 'marking' is not done just for the student-writer. It is done for the Head, the parents, the adviser, and so thoroughness is an essential, since gaps demonstrate laziness and lack of professionalism, especially if there is no clear rationale for *lack* of complete thoroughness. This exercise of speaking to several audiences at once resembles school report-writing where the language is so nicely judged for form-tutor, pupil, Head and parent that it is not really appropriate for anyone. It is my contention that 'marking' is a code of behaviour that tries to satisfy so many people that it fails to do the central job of helping the pupils to improve as writers.

## Responding rather than marking

The very term 'marking' points up the confusion at the very centre of the enterprise. It implies a teacher imprint on every piece of a student's writing. It implies, further, a sign of judgement on it, out of ten, or a grading. Most crucially it implies a supposed connection between such 'markings' and the progress of the student-writer, a connection which more and more teachers are now questioning.

The problem lies in a model of operation that is summed up by the inadequate term 'marking'. I want to put in its place the term 'response' and to look at ways in which the teacher responds to writing so that the writer can do something to improve. This implies the need for a clear rationale, for explicit exchanges, for clear agenda between teacher and child.

Of course many English teachers will argue that the most important kind of intervention is the word in the ear, the conversation with the writer. A realist would accept, however, that unless such encounters are organized, built into routines, they do not happen as often as we would like.

## Look at the messages you give

Any response we make to writing means something to the writer. Even *no* response carries its own message to the writer about the worth that you give to the writing. Whether you put the writing on the wall, tear it up, publish it, tick it, criticize it in public, read it aloud, have a quiet word of praise — each will carry its own meaning to the writer. What we want to emerge in the writer is a clear intention to work to improve some aspect of the writing task *and a clear idea of how to do it.*

### Snakesalive

My book is about a Girl who thinks she can be somewhere else and something else while her body shell is still where she was before. She thinks she can change into birds, butterfly's, and worms, etc. She meets a man [doesn't] round about eighty years of age. He dgs'nt have a family and a Jhome. And he sleeps in a park every knight. Monica (the girl's name) takes the old man by tripping, to an old friend of his on a beach riding the waves. Later on they tripped off too. When they were young the old man wants to stay, were he is and the Girl Monica tries desperately to make him go back to the real life. They both get back Monica, the girl looked at the old man. he was middle aged and not old but gregory was still in this daze called tripping. Monica went home and never saw him again. ✓

7/10 A good beginning, a little confusing in the middle

It follows inevitably that the response must bear in mind a detailed knowledge of the student's personality and behaviour as writer (it is obvious that one cannot think about response to writing without some sense of what writing is to the writer). Let us look at some real examples of children's writing to which the teacher has responded, and ask ourselves the questions:

1 What is the message to the child?
2 What help is given to the child to improve?
3 What is the likely response of the pupil?
4 What would *you* do with that piece?

Initially, this seems to be a very good example of a conscientious teacher working hard to no good purpose. It has all the signs of the teacher marking as she reads, correcting any errors that she noticed in the process. Not surprisingly the finished piece is fragmented and does not read easily. If the writer were to benefit from this attention he would have to reconstruct the piece. Of course he did not, which means that that effort went to waste except that

— the pupil feels noticed
— the parents see work 'marked'
— the Head sees evidence of thoroughness

The mark of 7/10 means in usual school terms better than satisfactory, so there is no need to panic, to work to improve. The comment not untypically balances faint vague praise with faint vague criticism. There is no clear indication of where *precisely* the quality or flaws are to be found.

1 **What is the message to the child?** My guess would be: that writing is mainly about avoiding mistakes but that nothing need be done when mistakes are made. Secondly it seems to say that there is no point in looking closely at the marking.

2 **What help is given to the pupil to improve?** There are clear indications to the writer about correct versions of written English, but since the teacher corrects them there is no need for the pupil to do so. The grade is encouraging and might lead to improved morale, but the comment is not specific enough to indicate what should be repeated, what avoided in future, and there is also a confusion implanted in the writer's mind. The 'good beginning' probably means that it explains the point clearly and economically to someone who has not read the book. However in the context of correcting, the writer might think (and in this case did) that it means the first part was 'good' merely because it had no mistakes.

*What matters in the end is not what the teacher intended but what the child understood*. If the child is to develop as a writer the steps needed to improve must be available *at the point of writing*. No amount of good intention on the part of the teacher will bring that about if it is confusing and vague.

3 **What is the likely response of the child?** Probably vague satisfaction and indifference. Nothing much has happened and any attempt to say something in the writing has not met with any response. Perhaps he will feel slightly encouraged, but not encouraged to say more in writing.

4 **What would you do with that piece?** I can only speak for myself here, but it seems clear that I *must* respond to the meaning in the writing, and I would want to open up a dialogue about 'tripping', since this seems crucial to the story and to the review. Perhaps I would write 'I have not read the book, but I find "tripping" a strange idea. Can you explain to me what it is and why it is called that? Do you find the book enjoyable?' Depending on the child's normal writing behaviour I *might* ask that the central section — 'Monica . . . waves' — be rewritten so that the clear version can be seen. But the change to the phrasing should be done by the writer, not merely copied out after correction. It seems clear that this writer does not check after composition.

A useful distinction that the writer needs is 'composition', the forming of the meaning, and 'transcription', the final organization into the conventions of writing for others. A major drawback of writing only for teacher is that the neglect of conventions is not seen by the student writer as making any difference to the effectiveness of the message (particularly when there is no response to that message). This writer would benefit from an *explicit* model of the stages of a piece of writing and this ought to become a specific and unvarying focus for attention in the coming weeks. Indeed, it would help if this 'agenda' were written down either in a notebook or in a simple record system. This 'agenda' in turn becomes a focus for attention when reading later writing, and for any comments that are made.

Let us look at a second example from a different teacher, asking ourselves the same four questions:

1 **What is the message to the child?**
   - Meaning does not matter.
   - I have read this.
   - Only spelling and punctuation count.

## Travel to Space

We started the count down 10, 9, 8, 7, 6, 5, 4, 3, 2, 1, 0, the count down was over we were on ~~are~~ our way to pluto. We were 15,000 feet up and we let our little booster rockets go. When we were 17,000 feet up we let our main booster go. The ship was solo. It took us five days to reach the actual planet but on the way we saw lots of other things. We put our ~~special~~ made space suits on and went out. We stepped up on the planet and started to take samples. I found a rock orange in __colour__ and it had a glowing centre. I put it in a space bag the bag ~~started~~ to sizzle. I went back to the ship and put it in the special freezer. I told my ~~friend~~ what I had found. His name was John. We stuck around for a bit, then we decided to set off. We radioed in to ~~base~~ for the landing on the way back. We saw lots of other things on the way, like Saturn and it's rings of dust around it. When we went near to the moon we were so happy to be near earth. ~~then earth~~ earth kept getting bigger and bigger. ~~as we got closer.~~ When we landed we couldnt get out because the ship would be to hot from ~~bursting~~ through the ~~atmosphere~~. We sat in the cock-pit. We brought the rock out that we had found and a large cheer went up.

### Corrections ✓

| | | | | |
|---|---|---|---|---|
| our | special | colour | friend | |
| our | special | colour | friend | |
| our | special | colour | friend | finally |
| our | special | colour | friend | finally |
| our | special | colour | friend | finally |
| our | special | colour | friend | finally |
| | | | | finally |
| base | base | atmosphere | atmosphere | finally |
| base | base | atmosphere | atmosphere | |
| base | base | atmosphere | atmosphere | |

- Avoid words whose spelling you do not know — you will be penalized if you do not.
- Write less — it avoids spelling mistakes.

2 **What help is given to the child to improve?** There are demands to copy out spellings in correct form, but there is no help with the regularities of English spelling. The assumption is that spelling is learned purely by sighting — the whole of learning by patterning (families of words) is ignored.

3 **What is the likely response of the child?** This writer would probably write less since there are no benefits to be gained except in self-satisfaction. (There is internal evidence here of a certain relish in the writing, a tasting of the words appropriate to the story which *might* sustain the writer through indifference.) The writer would certainly avoid risky spellings and thus risky words, which is unfortunate since development in all language requires extension and risk.

4 **What would you do with that piece?** This piece demands commendation —for attempted precision of vocabulary ('little booster rockets' 'the ship was solo' 'a glowing centre' etc); for narrative sequence; for successes in painting pictures for the reader (in spite of the teacher's crossing out of 'as we got closer', the whole sentence 'Earth kept . . . closer' conveys growth and movement very effectively); for a neat end ('a large cheer went up'); for taking risks, which is much more important than making mistakes. There is a need to improve spelling but that should be done by the writer developing strategies of search, check, matching *during the writing* process, not several days later, as in this case. Children more readily check and correct if there is a normal routine of sharing their writing in pairs before final submission.

In general what matters is how the writer sets about writing, how he or she behaves, rather than what success or failure is achieved. We need to look more closely in our response at what the writer is trying to do and how he or she sets about doing it. We need to offer more usable models of how writers work. We need to avoid the rush to judgement that all too often characterizes teacher response to writing.

**Conclusion**
In looking at these two examples I did not want to imply that the practices of the two teachers are piously to be condemned (the two teachers are hard-working and well-intentioned and their practices are wholly typical of English teachers at large) except in so far as they are manifestly ineffective and are based on untenable assumptions about writing development.

'Travel to Space' was written eighteen months *before* 'Snakes Alive' by the same writer. His writing *has* become shorter, less risky. He has withdrawn from relishing his writing. He does not see writing in school as for *his* purposes at all. Yet when he writes at home — letters, stories, for himself or his younger brother — he does see the need to plan and rework his writing. At school he is well conditioned into a once-and-for-all approach, with little revision of thought. No one takes any notice there of what he is saying, so why say it better? All this is a sad neglect — above all of the possibilities of developing what is, in essence, writing as thinking. I want later to offer approaches that teachers have found effective in engaging the thinking of the child-writer.

## What messages am I conveying over time?

I want to extend the scope of the enquiry by looking briefly at two examples of response over longer periods of time. Again the messages we give to children are clear and when they are cumulative they can be effective. I believe that the role of the teacher can be very beneficial, but can also be damaging. There are, therefore, two questions to be asked:

1 Can we bear to look at our messages over months?
2 Can we afford not to?

First, here are the written responses (there were some oral responses not here documented) of a third teacher to another very different pupil over 42 pieces of writing.

## A teacher's responses to a pupil's writing

( ) indicates a mark was given
— no response
1 Good ( )
2 18/30 Be careful about your spelling. Otherwise quite a good effort.
3 A good selection, but you need to concentrate on writing in sentences ( )
4 Good work ( )
5 It isn't really a good idea to write whole essays in direct speech — especially when you don't punctuate it ( )
6 A good attempt. Good. Keep Trying ( )
7 Do try to remember to use speech marks ( )
8 ( )
9 Some interesting parts but you must take care with basic punctuation.

10     Some good answers which show an understanding of the passage ( )

11     —

12     ( )

13     ( ) Project

14     Untidy, you can do better ( )

15     —

16     ( ) Your story does not quite fit your headline

17     Good ( )

18     You have become very confused with all this speech. If you are not sure how to punctuate conversation properly, do not use so much ( )

19     ( )

20     ( ) This seems very muddled because you have not divided it into paragraphs.
Avoid using so much speech if you are not sure how to write it.

21     ( ) Quite interesting
Do try to write in paragraphs

22     —

23     ( ) You must take more care with spellings

24     ( ) You must take more care spelling and sentence construction

25     Some interesting ideas — but you must be careful with your spelling. Sometimes it lets you down ( )

26     Again your ideas are very good, but your spelling often lets you down

27     A good effort — but you really must write in sentences ( )

28     —

29     —

30     ( )

31     ✓ ( )

32     ( ) Some good ideas, but you must take more care with spelling and presentation

33     Some good ideas, but you must think more carefully about setting your work out ( )

34     ( ) Some very good ideas in the essay. If you have time to copy it out again you will get a better mark.

35     ( ) ✓

36     ( ) You have spent too much time retelling the story

37     ( )

38     ( )

39     ( ) ✓

**40** ( ) ✓
**41** ( ) ✓
**42** ( ) ✓

If we dare collect the evidence and dare look at it closely what do we see? What emerges is a kind of nagging, repetitive and imprecise. There are no helpful patterns that emerge, only a niggardly unenthusiastic drip. Of course it may be very difficult to enthuse or be precise with this pupil.

The teacher is very concerned with the writing of her pupils, very keen to submit it for publication (a *very* positive response for those whose work is submitted). She was not aware of the drift of her remarks over time until she collected them together. It was only when she came to see the evidence of her own response that she became aware of the effect she might be having. It was very courageous to look but the insight gained was priceless because what it stressed was the impact *on one individual*.

## Teacher as writer and reader

An essential preparation for response, I believe, is that the teacher should write. This can be an occasional, or habitual, attempt at any writing task set to the children, or it can be a more private occupation. I am convinced of the need for this, not least because it demonstrates to the children that writing is a normal activity, not one just inflicted by school. When you are writing, you can no longer mark as if writing were easy, as if mistakes are easily avoidable. Above all, you cannot ignore the fact that writing is an attempt to *say* something, first to oneself, then to others.

As an adjunct to this, many teachers are now aware that children rarely see an adult struggling to write, making the sort of choices that any writer has to make. Write *with* them and *for* them explaining to the class why this word is used, why that, what is rejected and *why*. This 'modelling' of the ebb and flow of the writing process shows the normality of the struggle, of writing as behaviour; in which a piece of writing is never complete, only stopped; in which writing is thinking how to mean; in which reworking and re-drafting, planning and revising are essential components. All these in turn are components in the model of intervention and response that I am proposing.

# How to give a response that helps

1 **Respond first and foremost to the meaning — that is what the writing exchange is all about.**

It is feedback that tells the writer whether or not the meaning has been conveyed. It is that feedback that confirms or denies whether the writer has something to say to others. It is only if I feel I have something to say to others that I persevere in the effort of writing.

No teacher, I believe, ever sets a writing task and says 'I shall totally ignore any meaning in what you say. You will have no feedback about the efficacy of your message'. Yet this is the message our marking can easily carry if we do not put meaning first.

2 **Give some feedback to the writer about specific successes on a specific task.**

Avoid vague generalities. You need to show the writer where *exactly* has been the success, the progress, whether in phrasing, spelling, punctuation, vocabulary, shaping or story, character delineation or whatever. You can, of course, point out where there has been some success beyond the task set; it is unfair and in the end dispiriting to point out failure or weakness which is not related to the task as originally discussed.

3 **Avoid reacting to new items which take your attention during the marking.**

If mistakes emerge which were not part of the original focus for the writing and which need attention, save them up for later.

4 **In discussing the writing beforehand, give a clear but limited focus to the writing, a purpose, an audience and an aspect of correctness to be given most attention.**

Every writer has to concentrate on some things and not others. It helps concentration if there are not too many. I suggest two or three at most, one concerning the focus of interest in the writing (creating suspense, persuading your father you understand a major political issue, etc). and one concerning the technical aspects (paragraphing, full stops, etc). Much corrective marking assumes quite unrealistically, that the writer can internalize, even if willing, a whole range of mistakes to avoid next time.

5 **There should be a connection, clear to teacher and student, between task, marking and the development of the individual student.**

This involves a running negotiation between the teacher and the student, discussing the connection and individual focus. There is little point in the teacher having a clear idea of the connection if the student has not. The pupil should play some part in choosing the particular focus for concentrated attention. This may last several weeks, and needs to be in the writer's mind at the point of writing (which includes the thinking and revision stages). It also needs to be retained in the memory of the teacher, so that response can in turn be focused on the 'agenda' that has been decided. I find useful a collection of small cards for each class on which I keep a record of the agreed agenda (dated) which can be consulted by teacher and student. Incidentally this record card can be used to note briefly other useful information about books read, successes in oral work, problem areas etc.

6 **Response should relate to a record of the child's progress in specific items.**

The 'agenda' should be a developing one with a note included on the card (and on the child's writing or in oral conversation) about signs of progress.

7 **There should be follow-up to response.**

The suggested use of an 'agenda' and keeping a record means that follow-up is more likely. However, it clearly cannot happen every week, so the follow-up should be more thorough when it does take place; here a broader view can be taken of writing progress, with the writer invited to suggest new topics, new items for the 'agenda'. It is at these interviews that a sense of progress can be conveyed. Recent work in reading development has suggested that 'reading consultations' are more fruitful than 'having them read'. I suggest that 'writing consultations' are more fruitful than detailed marking of every piece, which suggests that the next guideline should be:

8 **There should be a regular (but not weekly) programme of writing consultations**

9 **Response should help the writer to improve this time or, at the latest, next time.**

Some of the interventions we make should be *during* the writing (still following the 'agenda') so that the writer has a chance to progress on the spot. Immediate feedback on detail is better than delayed — it is more likely to be acted upon.

## Kinds of response

The range of comments by teachers can be quite narrow. Many of us find ourselves writing a bland vague commendation followed by an imprecise niggle.

Compile a list of the types of comment you might make, and share it with the children so that they can be much more aware than they usually are of what the teacher is trying to do in making a comment (This takes practice and discussion but is very well worth doing. It leads to an increased involvement of the writer, a more reflective attitude).

The list might look something like this:

1 *Proofreading*
   This can be a helpful kind of response where the writer is apprised of this in advance, where it is tied to a clear purpose (Proofreading is a final stage response before publication. If there is no further reworking it is a waste of time, a damnation without point).
2 *Pointing out a major flaw*
   (something to avoid in future)
3 *Pointing out an important success*
   (something to repeat in future)
4 *Indicating the effect on the reader*
5 *Showing what can be done to improve*
6 *Extending the writer's thinking on the content*
   ('Would the argument be the same if . . .?')
7 *Showing how errors affect clarity and communication*
   'Missing out the second set of inverted commas made it seem as if you meant . . .'
8 *Inviting self-correction*
   'I think you should look again at the section marked . . .'
9 *Inviting a response to your response*
   (a dialogue)
10 *Pointing out the needs of the reader*
11 *Reassurance about something attempted without full success*
   ('The dialogue didn't quite ring true, but the attempt nearly came off. Worth trying again')
12 *Acknowledging that writing is difficult*
13 *Indicating awareness of the time taken, the difficult choices made, of word, phrase, etc.*
14 *Suggesting help is sought from others*
   ('I think Frances has some good ideas on this')
15 *Setting up wider readership*
   ('Will you let me show this to A.M. in the fourth year?')
16 *Suggesting an alternative way of going about the writing task*
17 *Sensitivity to the purposes of the writer*

This list is far from exhaustive but it does show that there are alternatives available. They amount to the responses of a reader who is aware of the writing task from the inside, of writing as purposeful, risky, rewarding and problematic.

## How the student sees it

An underlying theme in this chapter is that it is what the student-writer perceives of the process that matters, not the sophisticated array of wisdom that may or may not reside inside the teacher's head. More teachers are realizing that, in order to operate effectively on the development of writing, they need to understand the perceptions of the pupils about writing and about the role of the teacher. These indicate where they stand, the baseline for any development. As Margaret Donaldson has reminded us from the standpoint of research in psychology, we perform in ways deeply affected by how we perceive the task in which we are engaged. Writing is an activity bound by questions of purpose, sense of progress, audience, motivation, register, choices, etc. The very detail of the writing is affected by what we think we are doing. Similarly, they are all affected by *not* understanding what we are doing. If we are to pay more than lipservice to the idea of 'individual attention' we need to know more about what the individual thinks of the whole process. This finding out may be by discussion or in written form. Either way a number of aspects should be included.

One teacher used the following as a questionnaire:

1 What are our strengths and weaknesses in writing? Give yourself an honest mark from A to D for the following (A=very good, B=good, C=not bad, D=not good):
   Spelling _____ Handwriting _____ Punctuation _____.
   Story writing _____

2 Do you expect your teacher to mark *all* of your mistakes? Why?

3 Do you prefer a mark, grade or comment from the teacher? Why?

4 Do you expect your teacher to comment on all the good things you do? Why?

5 Do you read through *all* of your work when it is marked? What do you look for?

6 What do you do when you see your mistakes? (a) ignore them (b) read them but do nothing more (c) read them and decide to

improve (d) read them and feel fed up (e) see your teacher and talk about it.

7 Do you think your writing has improved in the last year?
8 When you write *who* do you think you are writing for? If you think there is more than one, make a list.
9 Does the marking in your book help you? If not, say why.
10 Do some teachers mark better than others? If yes explain how.
11 What do you think you could do to improve your writing?
12 How do you think your teacher could improve your writing?
13 Do you enjoy writing? Please say why.
14 When do you enjoy writing most and least?

This is a very courageous approach to take and one which is likely to lead to shifts of understanding, in pupil and teacher. It is essential that once such a step is taken, action is also taken upon the information revealed. If the dialogue begins in this way, the dialogue has to continue in other forms. It is then unlikely that the predictable orthodoxy of 'marking' can continue (though it should be retained as part of the repertoire).

## Widening the repertoire of response — variations on a theme

For instance, it becomes necessary to involve the student in the process of choosing the kind of response that is to be made and to put the student-writer more often in the position of reader and responder. There are many ways of doing this, but if these shifts of focus are to become permanent features of the learning in writing, there have to be built-in, regularly used procedures.

1 It is helpful to ask one or two pupils per week to wait for comments until you can discuss with them *what you would have written* in response to a piece of writing. The discussion would cover the fairness, the balance of your response, any omissions etc. Only when the comment is agreed is it written. It may then be signed by the student as agreed and so becomes a composite view.

Most pupils are unpractised at such responses and can be overawed by the expertise of the teacher. They need help in framing their thoughts into appropriate language (I have found that they need no training in honesty of response) and the same criteria would apply to pupil response as apply to teacher's — Is it helpful, does it lead to improvement?

One stage of the journey to reflexive thinking about their own writing is to ask them to comment on what they think has happened between two drafts of a piece of writing, a sophisticated but essential exercise in looking for evidence of improvement, and a revelation to the teacher of active criteria.

One group of children who had written a poem and re-drafted it wrote as follows:

- Not much change from my first draft. Not a very good ending. He does not say much about his future or his thoughts.
- I think that this poem is very good but the first draft is better and I would give a merit point for it. I could do better by not making so many mistakes and some well good words.
- I think I could improve my work if I didn't do to much crossings out. And I think I should write more neatly. The first draught is better than the second one.
- Very fluent some things better than in first draft. Better words could have been used. Overall a very good poem, i.e. helper = assistant.
- These words are good but *gone* I should find another word to use — disappeared, vanished. Good the way it ends with a prayer.
- I know that I should write words so they have stronger feelings. I should miss words out so it shouldn't read like a poem. I should use original words instead of small words. My second draft is better than the first because I have put more feelings into it.
- B — Quite Good but could do better by using better words. e.g. good sad poor feelings.
- Better because it doesn't rhyme. Improved; good use of vocabulary i.e. opportunity — change words in last verse could be improved on. Dreadfully — really.

What might strike you at first is that many of the comments could have been written by a teacher. Far from invalidating the approach, this constitutes a mirror to our own practice and a revelation of the student's thinking. Yet again we have a basis for discussion, a point from which to move.

2 Another way to involve the student is to select, say, five pupils per week who are asked to specify how they want their writing treated — no annotations, comment only, comment on good things only, punctuation only, help in drafting. The contract is that the teacher will respond as asked and the student must take note *and show how they have taken note*. Afterwards, the student can, in turn, comment on how helpful or otherwise what they chose to happen was, and whether they want the same treatment again.

3   A development of this is to involve other students in responding along specified lines. This takes the whole process one stage further into the hands of the writers, where much of the time it ought to be. The oscillation between the role of the writer and the role of reader can only be beneficial to both.

4   Sometimes more than one source of help can be built in, in the following way: In groups of four to six, the writing of the group members is passed around clockwise for silent reading and written comments, which may be directed to a specific or more general point. In due course, the writing returns to the writer, who in turn reads the comments made and makes a comment on them. Discussion then ensues. (Many teachers have found that asking students to read writing aloud in pairs can lead to a dramatically increased awareness of the needs of the reader, and a greater revision.)

5   Further group discussion can take the form of looking at a piece of writing by another student, but the rule is that only positive supportive comments can be made — what the writer has done well — no negative comments are possible. This kind of discussion can be wide ranging in its focus or it can at other times be concentrated — for example, on the words that are spelled *correctly*. This has the effect of stressing the achievement in the writer, a useful model to be internalized, in place of the model that most children (and adults) have concerned with deficiency and failure. A similar approach can be taken with a writer whose self-image is of a poor speller. Good spelling is at least partly a matter of confidence, and evidence of success is wholly appropriate.

6   Looking at progress between drafts is necessary. Beyond that, students need to look at their writing over weeks, months, years, and be invited to note development. It will help if at first the time between the pieces of writing is quite long, as development can be very attenuated and fragmentary. Nevertheless, a student needs to see development — for motivation and self-image, but also because the habit of looking at evidence of development enhances perception of the whole process of writing, which in turn enhances the capacity to make appropriate choices of approach, vocabulary, tone etc. The assumptions that there ought to be progress and that it is possible to find evidence reflect helpfully back into the dialogue between student and teacher over the pieces in progress.

7   A joint look by two students, one the writer, at four pieces develops a discussion of apprentices — extend the procedure to a departmental meeting, and the insights gained into implicit criteria at work in the department, understanding the nature of progress,

and increased awareness of the needs of the students can only be enriched.

# Endpiece

What I hope emerges from the kinds of activity I have suggested is a pattern of reponse to student writing that is very different from what actually happens much of the time. It draws together the elements of good practice and presents a coherent, practical way forward to making response more sensitive, more individual, more appropriate — and more effective in developing the writer. If that isn't the aim of the whole enterprise, I really do not know what is.

(With acknowledgments to Mike West and Andy Trembath)

# Recommended reading

*Assessing Children's Language*, Andrew Stibbs, Ward Lock, 1979

*Children's Minds*, Margaret Donaldson, Fontana, 1978

*Development of writing abilities, 11–18*, James Britton *et al*, Macmillan, 1975

'Just a tick is hopeless', Essay by Barbara Zussman in *Language Policies in Schools*, Ward Lock, 1980

*Mark My Words*, Tony Dunsbee and Terry Ford, Ward Lock, 1980.

'Real writing, real writers', Ann Baker in *English in Education*, 15, 3, ed. Mike Torbe, Elizabeth Laird, OUP, 1978

'Responses to written work', Barrie Wade in *Educational Review* 30 (2) 1978

'Some considerations when marking', Leslie Stratta in *English in Education* 3, 3, ed. Elizabeth Laird 1978

*Writing and the writer*, Frank Smith, Heinemann 1982

*Writing – Teachers and Children at work*, Donald Graves, Heinemann 1983

# 13 Supporting the slow learner

Brigid Smith

'Education is identical with helping the child realise his potentialities.'

*Erich Fromm*

## Expectations

The most important thing that a teacher can do to help a student with learning difficulties is to adopt a positive, expectant attitude towards the student's eventual success. If we view our students as 'failed' and deficient in certain necessary skills, and if we are only concerned to diagnose, test and grade to a supposed norm, then the students will accept our assessment of their problems and give up on us.

If, on the other hand, we see our task as seeking to develop the potential of each individual, believing them to be students who have not yet found their way into reading and writing, then we will start our teaching from a different premise. We will accept that such students have stories to tell, ideas to communicate, feelings to express and we will see our task as facilitating that communication and actively look for ways in which to help these students fulfil their potential. We need to know how to help. We need to have some understanding of the processes underlying competent reading and writing and of the strategies for effecting improvement. Above all, we need to be able confidently to communicate that knowledge to students having difficulty in school, and to ensure that, across the school in all subjects, consistent and supportive approaches and teaching attitudes are offered to the student. How students feel about themselves as learners is crucial to their eventual success.

We have a system which:

'Persuades the child on the one hand that he cannot read and write and on the other that he has to . . .'     *Mina Shaughnessey (1977)* or as Jason, aged 14 puts it:

> 'Some teachers don't even know about, don't even take the bother . . .
> just like, because we've got something wrong with us like not very
> good at reading or spelling they take us for like an idiot sort of thing.'

We need to reverse students' expectations of failure and to give them learning experiences which will convince them that they *can* learn and that what they have to offer in the classroom is valuable and valued.

# Matching needs and resources

Identifying students in the average English class who need help, and working out how best to meet their needs in literacy, obviously differs from school to school. The organization of positive help for those with special needs is always fraught —contingency comes up against principles, expediency against idealism. To identify the kinds of needs that might occur and possible ways of meeting those needs requires discussion and cooperation between English Department, Special Needs Department, Pastoral Staff and the member of Senior Management whose task is the organization of resources and personnel.

The plan below tries to cover most needs and to suggest possible economic ways in which such needs might be met. It is a blueprint for discussion rather than a prescription for action.

In addition to this, English and Special Needs Departments can produce a booklet for the support of departments across the curriculum covering the ground of this chapter and making possible a consistent *school* policy towards some of the technical skills of English — spelling, handwriting, presentation of work, marking, homework, drafting/re-drafting. Such a booklet would act as the basis for inter-departmental discussion about language issues beyond the needs of those with difficulties in reading and writing and encompassing more than the technical skills. At the same time it will give non-specialists a feeling that there are things they can undertake in the classroom which will consolidate and encourage success in their pupils and give them a feeling of confidence in dealing with students' special needs in literacy.

## Identifying special needs

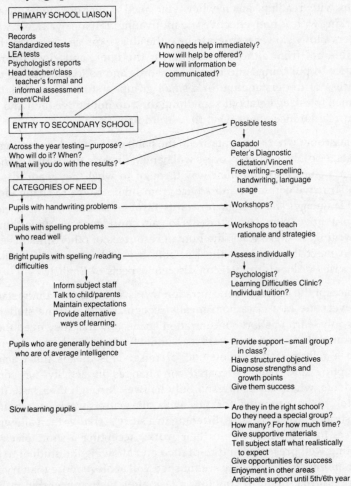

PRIMARY SCHOOL LIAISON

Records
Standardized tests
LEA tests
Psychologist's reports
Head teacher/class
   teacher's formal and
   informal assessment
Parent/Child

Who needs help immediately?
How will help be offered?
How will information be
   communicated?

ENTRY TO SECONDARY SCHOOL

Across the year testing – purpose?
Who will do it? When?
What will you do with the results?

Possible tests

Gapadol
Peter's Diagnostic
   dictation/Vincent
Free writing – spelling,
   handwriting, language
   usage

CATEGORIES OF NEED

Pupils with handwriting problems ———————→ Workshops?

Pupils with spelling problems ———————→ Workshops to teach
   who read well                                              rationale and strategies

Bright pupils with spelling /reading ———————→ Assess individually
   difficulties

Psychologist?
Learning Difficulties Clinic?
Individual tuition?

Inform subject staff
Talk to child/parents
Maintain expectations
Provide alternative
   ways of learning.

Pupils who are generally behind but ———————→ Provide support – small group?
   who are of average intelligence                        in class?
Have structured objectives
Diagnose strengths and
   growth points
Give them success

Slow learning pupils ———————→ Are they in the right school?
Do they need a special group?
How many? For how much time?
Give supportive materials
Tell subject staff what realistically
   to expect
Give opportunities for success
Enjoyment in other areas
Anticipate support until 5th/6th year

# Classroom organization

Whatever method of organization of resources is current in the school, there are still likely to be many English teachers who will have to cope with teaching students with special needs in the ordinary classroom in either a mixed-ability or setted situation. How best can classroom and teaching resources be organized to meet the needs of these students?

Flexibility of movement, groupings and time spent on tasks will help to integrate such students. Allowing weaker readers to work with a good reader, and giving group work on written texts boosts the confidence of the weaker ones and is a good way of sharing resources. Help with reading, given when you need it by someone you are working with, is both effective and motivating. Talking over ideas with others allows slower learners to hear the ideas expressed in a way that is different from either the teacher or the book, and gives them a chance to put things into their own words and so to consolidate the process of understanding. In a small group, a student also has the chance to ask again about something they do not understand and so gain reassurance about what they are doing.

A classroom where students are in the habit of sharing their writing at all stages of the writing process will benefit the less able writer, giving them a chance to find their way through to what they want to say. Constructive comment and advice from others helps to shape ideas and language. The struggle for clarity through sharing writing is very helpful in enabling such students to gain confidence in saying things in writing. In these ways, the human resources of other students can often meet the needs of the less able better than specially written exercises or kits for practising discrete aspects of English.

To accept the different concentration levels and ability to understand of everyone in a classroom means recognizing that some students can only learn in short concentration spans, and that they need their learning structured into easily assimilable steps, each step keying into a relevant and understood premise. This means the teacher accepting and being prepared for changes in activity for some students, when others are still only halfway through their task. It is better to be prepared for this with alternative work — reading, illustrating, word patterns, listening to a story — rather than allowing others to be interrupted in their work. Accepting a short piece of writing well presented and re-drafted and allowing the student to do something else when they are finished will achieve more than trying to pressurize them to continue a task after their concentration has been exhausted. A variety of activities could be on hand to fill this gap.

## Individual or small group activities for the slow learner

- Learning spellings: on cards — test each other; spelling derived from student's own writing
- Cloze comprehension (see page 310)
- Workshop activities particularly Ward Lock's Secondary Remedial Workshop — good reading/comprehension activities — self correcting

- Story retells — as strip cartoons, flow charts, series of illustrations
- Acting out ideas/story and recording on tape recorder
- Reading plays onto tape recorders — try Tempo plays (Longman) Spirals (Hutchinson) Star Plays (Longman)
- Listening to stories: taped and listened to on headphones, helps reading speed — have first three chapters of some books on tape to help reader into the story.
- Silent reading: have plenty of easy, interesting short books to encourage sustained, silent reading
- Worksheet/tape/practise for simple language work
- In addition, any teacher who takes on board the idea of drafting and re-drafting written work, discussing, conferencing between students or with teacher, will find that the class will be at different stages of work at different times allowing for a good deal of flexibility in organization and timing.

## Physical organization of the classroom

If you have the chance to organize your teaching space and resource it, there are further ways in which you could help yourself to meet the needs of slower students:

- **Chairs and tables** which move easily into groups.
- **An area of low stimulation** — a study booth or sheltered table to help the student with very poor concentration when he or she is engaged on a writing or reading task.
- **Accessible bookshelves** with a large variety of reading material including magazines, local newspapers. Box or stand with short easy-to-read books.
- **Bookshelf containing young children's books of the best kind**: e.g. Sendak's *Where the wild things are*, Burningham's *Would you Rather?*, the 'Anno' books without text. These books, contextualized with leaflets, booklets and posters about the importance of reading to small children, can be used both when talking about learning to read and as references when writing books for younger children. In this way, all students have an insight into the importance of books in the parenting situation and some students get the chance to catch up on missed literary experiences from childhood.
- **A reading corner** — easy chairs, carpet, plants, paintings and poems etc on the wall. This sounds ambitious, but it is surprising how many classrooms could fit in such a corner without too much difficulty.
- **Word lists** on the wall relating to work in process — words grouped

according to how they look e.g.

| | | |
|---|---|---|
| search | tomb | burn |
| searing | sombre | urn |
| earth | | furniture |
| heart | | turning |

- **Wall space** for displaying work
- **Noticeboard** which has information, jokes, cartoons, complaints etc on it — a good source of purposeful reading
- **Other resources**
  Tape recorders/earphones
  Books and tapes
  Tapes and worksheets
  Games, puzzles
  Workshop boxes
  Word boxes/word lists relating to current interests
  Simple dictionaries and short word lists along with ordinary dictionaries

Some of the above ideas will help to turn the classroom into a place where activities can be carried out sometimes as a class, sometimes in a group and sometimes on an individual basis. In this way, coping with a variety of learning needs is made easier.

# Reading

Some understanding of the reading process, rather than a reliance on the product (i.e. how the student is reading) is necessary if teachers are to view reading as an on-going process rather than as a learned skill which one can either do or not do. We are all 'learning readers' in different situations and it is the *kind* of reading material that we are using that dictates our reading strategies.

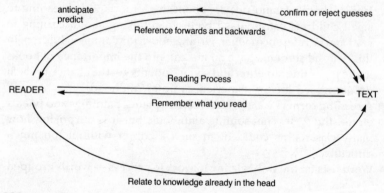

This simple model looks at the various processes involved in reading. Over-emphasis on one aspect can result in a partial understanding of what reading is about. An example of this is eleven year old John who, when asked what he did when he came to a word he couldn't read, replied:

'I sound it out. And every time I sound it out I get it wrong!'

John is seeing reading as a strictly decoding process, matching sounds and letters. When this strategy fails, as it inevitably must, he has no other strategies to fall back on. John needed to know that reading is basically communication and that he has resources already available to him to help him in his task. John already brings to reading his previous knowledge of stories and of book language, his understanding of how language works in oral communication, his knowledge of words and phrases that 'hang together' and his knowledge of the subject matter that allows him to make guesses and to anticipate what comes next in the text. John needs to know that the book is not setting out to make 'traps' for him. He needs to be convinced that the information or story is worth making the effort to read. He has to be given the courage to take risks so that he will make guesses and predict what is coming next in the story. Ultimately, he must be convinced that the text is meaningful and that the responsibility for correcting mistakes is his own — derived from his realization that what he has read does not make sense. It is the shift of responsibility from the teacher to the reader, from correction of 'mistakes' to getting the meaning of a passage that will eventually make for an independent, comprehending reader.

## Reading aloud: Teacher/child antics and misapprehensions

Reading is often thought of as being 'reading aloud' — some less fluent readers may feel they are not reading if they are not saying the words out loud — but reading aloud can be deceptive. The ability to read aloud has little to do with being able to understand what is read. Listening to the intonation of a reader is the way of seeing whether the reader understands what he or she is reading.

Is there a place for reading aloud at secondary school level? For the poor reader, the place is certainly not in front of the class. If round-the-class reading does take place in the classroom, exclude the poor and timid reader — it is cruelty to do otherwise. For the teacher, however, listening to a student reading and making an analysis of that reading enables him or her to have a real insight into the student's difficulties and most importantly, allows their strengths to be seen.

An excellent explanation of how to analyze reading is to be found in Helen Arnold's book, *Listening to Children Reading*. The following is a brief introduction to the method.

- **Tape record** the student reading a passage of 200–300 words
- **Record** errors on a duplicate of the passage: use a simple coding:

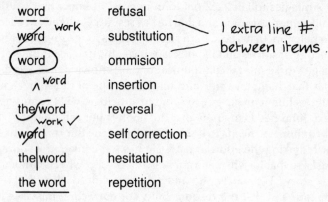

| | |
|---|---|
| word | refusal |
| word *work* | substitution |
| word (circled) | ommision |
| ∧ *word* | insertion |
| the/word | reversal |
| word *work* ✓ | self correction |
| the\|word | hesitation |
| the word | repetition |

1 extra line # between items.

## Analysis of mis-cues and ways of helping
If what the pupil does is:

1  phonically nearly correct i.e. sounding out, but not making sense — then:

> direct attention to meaning
> ask what comes next
> allow the mistake and see if it is picked up later

*Helpful activities*

Give meaningful reading activities: instructions to follow, letters, factual articles. Recipes are self-correcting reading texts — if you read it wrong it tastes awful!

Give reading that the reader *wants* to make sense of — that he or she is highly motivated to read.

Give the reader texts he or she already knows — stories already heard in class or on tape.

2  to guess wildly — what is read has no relationship to the words on the page, then:

Direct attention to the first and last parts of the word. Most words read in a meaningful context will generate only a limited number of possibilities. A phonic approach seems to work best when the reader already has a good idea of what the word might be (*Reading*, Frank Smith, CUP, 1978).

Give the word but note it. Draw attention to the internal structure of the word and other words like it after the reading session.

*Helpful activities*

Cloze comprehension with first and last letters already given. Word shapes in a sentence context.

The 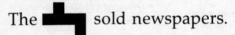 sold newspapers.

Games and puzzles where the letters in the word and their order are important.

Snap, using first two or last two letters
Rummy using word families

Kits or workshops e.g. 'Stott Programmed Reading Kit' (Holmes McDougall Publishers) have several games using first and last letter combinations

3 To ignore the grammatical constraints in the passage, then:

Check first whether all that is happening is a dialect shift rather than a meaning distortion. Does it still make sense?
Read the first part of the sentence and help the reader to guess the kind of words that might come next.

*Helpful activities*

Listening to stories on tape and familiarization of common grammatical sequences.

Cloze comprehension with deletions that are specific to the reader's difficulty: e.g. function words deleted, verbs deleted, adverbs etc.

## Listening to a student reading

For most teachers this is the kind of activity that has to be fitted in around the normal lesson commitments. It can be rewarding and interesting, however, and other interested adults — parents, sixth formers, other students can all do the listening. It has been found, though, that a structured guide to responding to a reader is beneficial.

It is the positive response of the listener — and the shift of responsibility from the listener to the reader to correct mistakes — that will bring about improvements in reading.

The following guide, based on behaviour modification with the 'reward' of praise for desired reading behaviour, has been found to work well. It is expanded on pp. 303 and 304.

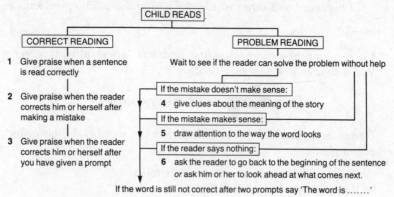

CHILD READS

CORRECT READING

1 Give praise when a sentence is read correctly

2 Give praise when the reader corrects him or herself after making a mistake

3 Give praise when the reader corrects him or herself after you have given a prompt

PROBLEM READING

Wait to see if the reader can solve the problem without help

If the mistake doesn't make sense:
4 give clues about the meaning of the story

If the mistake makes sense:
5 draw attention to the way the word looks

If the reader says nothing:
6 ask the reader to go back to the beginning of the sentence *or* ask him or her to look ahead at what comes next.

If the word is still not correct after two prompts say 'The word is ........'

## Finding texts for poor readers

'Remedial' texts, with artificially induced low reading ages, can create problems for poor readers. In order to produce such texts, short words, short sentences and stilted language are often used — at the expense of meaning and interest. In order to use a lot of short words, these texts tend to be full of pronouns. These words are easy to read but require a good deal more processing than nouns. Every pronoun must be referenced; that is, the reader must make the connection between the it, they, who etc and the word to which the pronoun refers. Without accurately processing these words, the text does not cohere, does not hang together as a piece of meaningful reading. The poor reader is often already anxious about difficulties with decoding the text, and if there is added to this initial task the complication of processing and referencing pronouns, then the book is often given up after the first page or two. Students say the book is boring — what they really mean is that they cannot get at the meaning and make it make sense.

Secondary readers with difficulties need texts which are intrinsically meaningful, and which catch their interest quickly.

**Listening to a student reading**

**1** *The reader is correct and reads a whole sentence without mistake.*
Praise the reader. Just a quiet 'well done' or 'good' which doesn't interrupt the flow is all that is needed.

**2** *The reader makes a mistake but corrects it him or herself either immediately or after going on for a little way.*
Praise the child when the correction is made.
If the mistake makes sense, and the reader doesn't notice it, allow him or her to continue, but point out the word at the end of the reading.

**3** *You have to prompt the reader, but he or she then goes back to correct the word.*
Praise the reader when the correction is made.

When the reader makes a mistake, or makes no attempt at the word, you should allow a little time for him or her to realize the mistake or to solve the problem alone.

Then give a prompt!

**4** *If the mistake doesn't make sense.*
Ask questions which give a clue about the meaning of the story.

**5** *If the mistake makes sense*
Draw attention to the way the word looks.

**6** *If the reader doesn't say anything*
Suggest looking ahead to see what comes next — this will help the reader to guess the meaning of the problem word.
*or* suggest going back to the beginning of the sentence to start again.

If the word is still not right after two prompts then say 'The word is . . .

# A case for the language experience text

However poor a reader is, it is unusual at secondary level to find that the oral language skills are hopelessly inefficient. We need to be able to harness the skills used in conversation — listening, predicting, responding, bringing one's own ideas to making sense of what is being said. We want to be able to get the reader to use these skills in reading — to read a text that is meaningful, relevant and that is in tune with his or her own linguistic knowledge.

The problem with many older poor readers is that they rarely have the experience of 'real' reading. They are given exercises ad nauseam, but rarely experience the satisfaction of reading a whole text that is meaningful and interesting and that they can read successfully. So the skills needed in reading — the ability to anticipate and predict, to confirm or reject guesses, to use prior knowledge of how words and ideas hang together, to check anticipations against the word on the page — are rarely practised. Without such successful practise we shall have problems persuading students that reading is a worthwhile activity.

## Requirements for producing a language experience text

Scribe    A sympathetic person who will interact with the student and act as the 'writer down' of the story the student wants to tell.

Text    A means of printing the written text so that it is available for the next session.

Volunteer helpers can be used as scribes to take down the stories and help in producing the printed text. Typing and photocopying is the most obvious way of producing a text — failing this, a handwritten text will still be acceptable. Illustration and binding following according to inclination and enthusiasm!

The following extracts from books written by students who could not read at all, but who learned to read through writing their own books, perhaps illustrate best the kind of lively, interesting and relevant writing generated by this method. The surprise to those who have tried out this method is the extent to which even supposedly illiterate students have internalized the grammar of stories and literary genres, and the kind of vocabulary and linguistic structures they can draw on from their language knowledge.

Part of a twenty-one chapter novel written by a 14 year old non-reader. In it he works out many of his aggressive and anti-social feelings. The following extract was written shortly after an argument with the woodwork teacher.

> Mrs Orwin came in. She was a tall, lanky woman with messy hair. She came in all worried saying that someone had broken their leg. It was a teacher. 'What do you mean? What has happened?' yelled the headmaster, 'Someone working on top of the woodwork block dropped a pole and knocked him over. Another fell on him and broke his leg.' 'Why haven't you phoned for the ambulance?' said the headmaster. 'I've phoned already' said Mrs Orwin, 'not for nothing have I got my St. John's Ambulance Certificate.' . . . In the hospital Mr Green was lying in agony. Everyone was laughing and talking about it. In the operating theatre Mr Green was on the table being stitched up. He had to have five injections!

Written by Justine, a slow learner of 11. Justine will not read most books, saying that books are boring. She dictated several chapters about her sister's wedding. Now she is writing a book about her sister's baby daughter.

**Chapter One**
Once upon a time I was bridesmaid. It was January. My sister Tracy was getting married to Nigel. They were married in Church. It was a great big church.

My grandad took a bottle of whiskey to the church and while my sister was saying all the words he was drinking it.

There were three bridesmaids. Rene and Wendy and me. Rene and Wendy were in lilac dresses on the outside and me in a pink dress in the middle. I was standing at the back of my sister who was getting married and I saw all my family and I liked it very much.

My sister had a long white dress on and she had all different coloured flowers. She had her hair permed and she had a white head-band on. Her dress was very long and I was shaking very much!

I saw my family that I had not seen for a very long time and they were very pleased to see me.

Then we were ready for the reception. There was lots of food and I was very happy. We had spotlights and disco lights and my brother-in-laws family were very nice and my sister-in-law enjoyed herself very much.

My sister went home to get changed. She wore a purple suit. It was very nice. I got changed in the changing room. My mum was very happy and she was pleased to see us.

My sister who got married was very pleased to see my mum and my brothers came down with my mum. My brother Darren said, 'Have you still got your nightdress on?' He took the micky out of us! We hit him hard and he said, 'Get lost!' He wasn't very happy because he missed football. He saw a bit of it and Spurs won and he was very happy about that.

## The initial leaflet given to adults and sixth formers to help them write their stories

### Writing a story

This is a new approach to helping children with reading difficulties. The children use their own stories to help them to read.

### Aims for readers and tutors

1 Enjoyment in writing and reading the stories
2 Enjoyment in tutor and reader working together
3 Improvement in reader's skills in reading
4 Reader becomes more independent and begins to notice his or her own mistakes
5 Reader begins to transfer his or her own skills to real books

Writing a story together

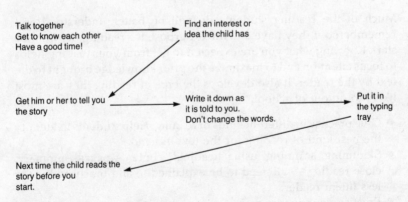

Talk together
Get to know each other
Have a good time!

Find an interest or idea the child has

Get him or her to tell you the story

Write it down as it is told to you. Don't change the words.

Put it in the typing tray

Next time the child reads the story before you start.

Don't forget to illustrate the book and decorate the cover. You can talk, look at books, visit the library to encourage the child in telling the story.

All reading practice should have as its end fast, reflective reading whether it is undertaken for learning or for pleasure. The amount we read to students and talk to them about books and communicate our own enthusiasm for reading will influence them in their attitudes towards reading.

**Checklist**
- Read good books and stories to students so that they increase their knowledge of story conventions and story language.
- Choose books for students to read on their own according to their intrinsic value and meaningfulness, not just because they are easy.
- Give very poor readers the opportunity to write their own readers.
- Make some books, stories or first chapters of books available on tape. Some are available commercially or you can make your own recordings.
- To find out quickly if a book is too difficult, stand behind the reader, ask him or her to read you a few sentences and count the mistakes. If the book is generating *more than one mistake in ten words* it may be too difficult and may interfere with the meaning. Remember that motivation to read a text overcomes many apparent difficulties.
- Involve students in the choice of books for the classroom. Publishers' catalogues, letters, visits to bookshops can be valuable ways of changing attitudes towards books and reading.

## Ways of developing reading purposes

Much of the reading students do will be better understood and remembered if they have a defined purpose for reading before they start. Knowing what you are expected to get from your reading helps to focus attention and to maximize the prior knowledge brought to the text by the reader. It also develops the type of reading they are most likely to do out of school.

- Give practice in different kinds of reading. Help students to identify the best kind of reading for the text in hand.
- Skimming, scanning, using headings, contents pages, summary, close reading — all need to be explained to and practised by, the less fluent reader.
- Practise identifying main points, developments of arguments etc.
- Give a verbal or written summary of what is about to be read before starting.
- If questions are to be answered after reading, then encourage students to read the question *before* reading the passage.

- Give plenty of reading practice which has a built-in purpose, e.g. brochures, giving information which is comparative and requires decisions; instructions which have to be followed carefully.
- Talking about what you have read, sharing perceptions and ideas is what makes reading into a purposeful and meaningful activity.

## Comprehension exercises for the slow learner

The task of finding out whether students have understood what they have read or been taught is often seen to be a case for presenting a list of questions to answer. Factual recall questions can be answered without reading or understanding the text properly and good comprehension exercises ensure that the students have understood the material, and that they are able to see beyond what is written in the text, to make inferences and generalizations and to relate what is relevant to their own experience and knowledge.

- Oral story recall — simply asking students to retell a story in their own words. Even poor readers can sometimes be surprisingly good at this exercise. You could use a tape recorder.
- Drawing a diagram or model based on close reading of a text will often ensure that students are reading for meaning and accuracy. Many texts used as a class reader can be used in this way and can give the student a clear chapter layout for later reference.
- Making sets or models of characters — their attributes or their relationships. This helps students to define characters in stories more clearly.
- Making maps, drawings, diagrams, graphs based on information generated by a story. Try these out yourself first to make sure there is enough information given in the text to make the task feasible. For example, a mixed-ability class was reading *The Rats of Nimh* as a class reader. Among the comprehension activities were
  — Drawing Mr Age's house from a close description given in the story
  — Making a map of Mrs Frisby's journey
  — Drawing a diagram of the toymaker's van showing all the things it contained
- Story retelling, or retelling factual information does not always have to be written. Plays on tape or written down, comic strips or acting can all show that the original text has been understood.
- Finding the main points in a text, putting facts in order of importance can be done with a duplicate text or newspaper article.

Use coloured underlining to point out main and subsidiary facts. Follow with discussion.

- Read a story in parts and ask for predictions of the outcome based on the story so far. Do they match up when the story is read on?
- Read a story and leave it unfinished. How much understanding of the story is shown in the conclusion given by the students?
- Give an excerpt without naming the characters. Ask students to name who is speaking based on their reading of the story or play.
- Take an excerpt from the book. Duplicate it and cut it into parts. Mix up the parts and ask the students to sequence it into the right order. Choose something with clearly defined order of events or ideas.
- Give a cloze comprehension based on the story or information (see below).

Almost all the above exercises benefit by being done in a situation where discussion and sharing of ideas is encouraged. In this way, learning is consolidated and the text is reflected on and questioned on the student's initiative rather than being used as a means to answer teacher's questions which have only one 'right' answer.

**Cloze comprehension**

One form of group comprehension particularly helpful to poor readers is the cloze comprehension exercise. Words are deleted in the passage, then the reader must put in the word that makes the passage make sense. This exercise ensures close, accurate reading, encouraging readers to use their linguistic knowledge in the service of their reading, and making them think about their reading as they go along. It also cuts down on the amount of writing the student is required to do without the 'guess' hazard of the multiple choice question. When the text is factual information or notes, it ensures that the student has accurate, clear notes in a form they can read, whilst demanding real reading and understanding in order to fill in the gaps.

**How to prepare a cloze comprehension**

**Prepare a text** from a newspaper, magazine, old text or reading book. Photocopy or type specially prepared passages.

Deletion in the text can be made with whitener, labels or inking out. Photocopies can then be made.

**Open ended answers** allow any word to be put in that makes sense. Retyping a passage and leaving a regular gap for each deletion helps to achieve this.

**Closed answers** in which there is only one answer possible can be achieved by inking out the word but leaving the shape or leaving the first and/or last letter of the word.

**Different kinds of deletions**:

1 The simplest type is the deletion of every tenth word in the passage (avoiding proper names).
2 Function words can be deleted: words like *for, to, after*; but not more than one word in ten should be deleted.
3 Descriptive words, verbs etc.
4 Words carrying information, names, new vocabulary etc from the lesson or passage.
5 Pronouns are difficult deletions but can help student's reading and referencing skills if they are taught and discussed at the same time as the cloze comprehension is undertaken. Leave the first two or three sentences whole.

It is important to remember that close exercises are *group* exercises and that the inter-active talk and reflection on the text is the main purpose of the exercise and not guessing a 'right' answer.

# Preparing worksheets

The difficulties found in remedial texts can also occur in teacher-prepared worksheets. Worksheets are often too dense, trying to encapsulate a chapter in a paragraph. They tend not to substantiate information but merely put it in another form or say it in another way. Attempts at simplification too often result in a lot of short words which create a heavy processing load for the student.

## Setting out a worksheet
- Leave plenty of white space.
- Set out clearly — define by underlining, boxing etc.
- Make instructions clear. Poor readers often could do worksheets or tests if they were able to understand what they had to do. English course books also often have difficult or ambiguous instructions — even when work is supposedly easy.
- Make clear what the student has to do.

## Worksheet content
- Information should be put in more than one way:
  — by giving a clear example

— by repeating information in a personified, story form
— by support from models or diagrams; simple flow charts can often show information clearly

- Worksheets should contain a limited amount of new information or concepts. Where possible, new concepts should be illustrated by known examples and linked to concepts or ideas already known to the student.

- Simple definitions of new vocabulary could be added for the less able.

- Worksheets should practise and extend the student's reading. Many worksheets contain too little reading with too dense an amount of information.

- If the student is required to write, a writing vocabulary of words which may be needed is useful. Examples of starting sentences or phrases can also help some students to get started.

- Written information in worksheets needs to be supported for the less able reader. It should be read through by a good reader, talked through in small groups and followed up by meaningful work which requires reflection and mediation of the material read, not just factual recall answers.

## Final word on reading

Reading should be fun, it should be enjoyable. We should all do it because we think that it is important and because it generates an enthusiasm and excitement in us that we want to share with children. There is no substitute for the kind of learning that occurs when a keen, enthusiastic teacher shares a story with a group of children. How else will poor readers learn the patterns of book language? How else will they be convinced that reading has something to offer them that will make the effort of learning to read worthwhile? Using students' own stories and helping them to read using these texts will teach teachers about reading and readers about how texts work successfully.

Students who cannot read for themselves must have access to literature through the stories that are read to them, or that they listen to themselves, otherwise they are being denied an important aspect of development. The teacher's aim when helping students with their reading should be to make them independent of the teacher, to enable them to be makers of meaning and correcters of their own mistakes and, above all, successful and happy in their reading.

# Talking and listening

Students with learning difficulties need to be encouraged to use the skills of talking and listening. They need to be given the opportunity to talk when there is not just a 'right' answer to be found, but also when talk becomes the environment for exchange and sharing of ideas.

- The way in which some students express themselves is not necessarily the way teachers anticipate. They may need much more time to reshape ideas, to get clear what they want to say.
- It may take some time before some students understand the different kinds of register appropriate to a situation.
- Lengthy stories out of their own experience may seem to be missing the point, but the importance of fitting new ideas into their previous knowledge may need this rambling approach.
- Waiting some time for a right answer and stopping others butting in may enable a slow learner to reach the right answer or conclusion for him or herself. Observation of students in class seems to show that they often do reach the right answer — but the teacher has not waited long enough for them.
- It is easier and less threatening to talk in a small group than in front of a whole class. Two or three students talking into a tape recorder will often gain far more from discussion and go deeper into issues than if they were talking to the whole class.

## How to control and encourage talk in the classroom

- Have set routines for use during class or group discussion. Who speaks and when? Raised hands, catching the teacher's eye — whatever the routine ensure that pupils stick by it. In this way, shy or slow students are not overwhelmed or intimidated by noisy dominant pupils. Encourage students to listen to each other and to follow on points rather than just be determined to state their own point of view.
- Encourage group discussion around a task. Open ended discussion is not easy for the less able to handle. They need to know what is expected of them — a set decision to come to or question to answer will produce more thoughtful and valuable talk than the instruction 'Go away and have a discussion about vandalism'.
- Appoint a spokesperson for a group to feed back ideas. In this way, some students who would be afraid to speak in front of everybody will be prepared to contribute ideas.

- Circulate when group discussion is going on. Be ready to support and encourage or to mediate if necessary for the less able in the group.
- Utilize outside visitors — workmen, caretakers, police officers, primary school teachers, students on visits. Encourage students to talk and ask questions in real situations. In this way, students unused to much conversation with adults develop their verbal skills.
- Use trips, outings or unusual school activities as situations for developing language skills.
- Social negotiations generated by playing games, sorting out instructions, using a computer program, etc can be very valuable to students who find social relationships difficult. Learning to negotiate in this way in the classroom can be a useful skill.
- Using verbal skills in drama can give a lot of satisfaction and confidence to less able students.

## Encouraging listening skills

Many less able students have poor concentration. A common complaint is that they do not listen to what they are told. Clearly defined limits and routines built into the lesson from the beginning are helpful to students with learning difficulties. Starting a lesson from quiet — with specific activities such as fetching books, putting in margin, date, checking spelling lists, writing down new vocabulary — allows the teacher to take control of the lesson from the start. Less able students do not thrive in a noisy or chaotic environment and training in this kind of self-discipline is a valuable activity.

Insistence on silence when others are speaking, and during the first part of writing sessions, allows concentration to develop and gives a threshold for listening skills to be practised. Listening and concentration skills develop as they are needed, but the teacher can set up situations in the classroom which encourage this development.

## Ways to develop listening skills

1 Give students something really worthwhile to listen to. If all the stories are good and exciting no one will want to miss any of them.
2 When giving instructions *lower* the voice rather than shouting. Go slowly and say everything twice, if possible in slightly different ways.

3 Have available a listening corner with tapes and earphones.

4 Have a low stimulus area away from the others for the student with really poor concentration. Do not use it punitively — offer it when writing is started to give everyone a chance to get settled.

5 Do work on interviewing. Get students to conduct interviews in and out of school. Teach them to listen and then pick up on points.

6 Have cards with ideas or tapes with sound effects. Get students to make up stories and record them using these. Making tapes with sound effects allows a new dimension into story-making.

7 Use the tape recorder in discussions or when making up plays or stories. This acts as a 'monitor' and encourages more discipline and less noise in the activity!

8 Watching TV programmes and discussing them — either during the programme at necessary points if they are on a video, or afterwards. Make sure you have seen the programme first, that it really is worth watching and is going to generate worthwhile discussion.

9 There are games which promote careful listening:
Some such games are
**Round Robin stories**: One person starts a story, the next person must carry on from where he or she stops and so on. Tape record it so you can listen to yourselves afterwards!
**My aunt went to market**: Again, sitting in a circle, one person starts, 'My aunt went to market and she bought a cabbage.' The next person must say the whole sentence and add another item and so on round the circle. If anything is left out, that person has to drop out. The teacher needs a good memory for this!
**Sound puzzles**: Identifying objects from the sound they make on a recording, e.g. pouring out tea, table tennis, money rattling etc. Available on record but easy to make your own recording. Students can make up tapes for each other as well.
**Paired drawings**: Pairs sit back to back. One person has a card with a simple drawing. He or she describes the drawing to the other person without saying what it is. The other person has to draw what he or she hears described. Some very odd results follow!

# Writing

Perhaps the first thing one should ask about slow learners writing is 'Why write at all?' The most common ailment of students with difficulties is 'arm ache', and when one considers the amount of meaningless unmotivated writing and copying that pupils have to undertake in school it isn't very surprising!

Practising the discrete skills within writing is only valuable when you can already write. One must think of the immature writer, whatever his or her age, as a beginning writer. Infants write for fun, to make their mark with pleasure and pride. If many of our students have not progressed much beyond this developmental point how are we going to help them to *enjoy* writing, to find a purpose for writing? The tangibility, permanence and private possibilities of writing convince skilled writers of its value. How can we help students to write competently without spoiling the creative sense of originality and enjoyment?

One approach is to divide the act of writing into two parts — the *author part* and the *secretary part*.

If two people cooperate on these tasks then it can work, whereas one person undertaking both tasks can find one activity interfering with the other. Separating these two tasks and dealing with them one at a time — allowing time for rethinking, redrafting and the performance of the secretarial function in isolation from the creative function — makes writing a possible task for the slow learner.

The division might look like this:

| **Composition** (author) | **Transcription** (secretary) |
|---|---|
| getting ideas | physical effort of writing |
| selecting words | spelling |
| getting it down (grammar) | capitalization |
| | punctuation |
| | paragraphs |
| | legibility |

This offers itself as one possible workable division; and this part of the chapter conforms to that division tackling first the author function, and then the secretarial or technical functions of writing.

## 1 Being an author

In looking at how pupils shape and reshape language and ideas the following points will be particularly helpful to the teacher dealing with less able writers:

(a)  Giving the students a model of *how* writing is done — something they rarely have access to. The teacher composes a story on the overhead projector or the blackboard — thinking aloud, changing things, asking for ideas about how to carry on — allows students to have a window onto the writing process. They see that it is a complex activity, involving re-thinking and re-shaping. Even the teacher cannot get it all right first time.

(b) Conferencing — reading aloud the story so far and then talking it through with someone else, either student or teacher. This helps students to see where they are going in their writing. It becomes obvious when their ideas are not getting across clearly. Seeing a piece of writing as an on-going, changing piece of work allows slower writers to spend time over what they are doing and to share and respect each other's work in a way that one-off writing for the teacher alone rarely achieves.

(c) Separation of spelling and handwriting from content through the reading aloud process and the re-drafting process, allows students to find confidence in what they want to say.

Emphasis on writing which is 'in process', which is not going to be finished and marked once allows a crucial process to take place. The emphasis moves from the teacher as 'corrector' to the student as self-corrector. The student begins to take responsibility for seeing where changes need to be made and decides what corrections to make.

## A method of using re-drafting techniques in the classroom

1 Exercise books or files become working places.
2 Students have a proofreading code for correcting their own mistakes.
3 The left hand side of the book or paper is used for initial ideas, and re-drafting takes place on the page opposite. More pages can be stapled alongside if necessary.
4 Class self-correction takes place using the overhead projector. The work is read out and together the class work out changes and corrections that need to be made.
5 The reading aloud of the piece allows students to see where the meaning of what they want to say is not clear. Questions from the teacher about the meaning of the piece can draw attention to a lack of clarity.
6 Students work at their own pace and re-draft only what they want to do. Sometimes one piece of writing in three would be sufficient to work on at length.

## An example:

*First draft*

> Day 1
>
> we set of to the ore port to sea
> ~~aeroplane~~ a new ~~areaplan~~ and we are
> goving to. have a (rihd)on it. and
> we are (just) cowing (a grst) The
> sea and we hren a googeing
> noise from lacn of the engine and
> and in a minit we herd the arver engir
> go and we are handing for
> the sea and we are or rit
> started and ver (sit bin) to swim for
> a mit of roke and we sow

*Margin notes (first draft):* aeroplane • ride • just • across • chugging • minute • in a • 10

*Second draft*

> Day 1
>
> We set of to the airorport to
> see a new aeroplane and we are goving to
> have a ride in it. and we are dust
> cowing across the sea Then we hren a
> chugging noise from one of the enging.
> and in a minute we herd the aver enging
> go and we are handing far the sea.
> and we are or rit and we started
> to swim for a mit of roke and we saw
> a island in frot of us. and we swem
> for it.

(A final draft was done for a wall display. Only errors found by the student were corrected and no writing on the draft was done by the teacher. Correct spellings were given where errors had been identified.)

## Using drafting and re-drafting with students

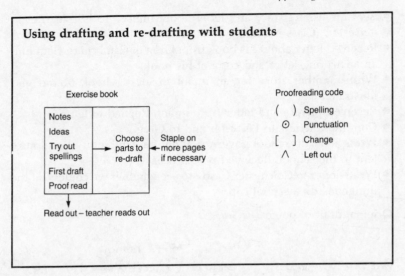

Using this approach to re-drafting, the emphasis is on clarity of communication: getting down what you really want to say. Dealing with technical skills in a defined way gives students confidence and control over their writing and allows even the weakest writers to develop a sense of pride and achievement in their writing.

All writers need a sense of purposefulness and an audience for their writing. Improvement in the less able writer's work seems to hinge on renewing a sense of purpose in what he or she is writing. For this reason, functional writing — letters, messages, stories written for others (elderly people, primary pupils), instructions — all seem to work well because there is a built-in reason for re-writing and taking care. Work displayed on the wall or in a magazine also motivates such students. Typing out work for the wall rather than allowing it to appear in poor handwriting can also help the writer's confidence.

### Spring term's writing output for Matthew aged 11

His work has been centred around purposeful activities, using his reading book as a point of communication with other students. He was a very reluctant writer and all his spelling and handwriting needs were dealt with in the context of his writing.

- Story about fishing holiday. (2 drafts about one page). Put on wall as part of holiday competition.
- Dictated fishing story to student teacher. (Reading book of 10 pages).

- Sent his fishing story and letter about himself to ESL learner in Leicester. (Class exchange of letters and stories).
- Received letter about his book from Greg in Cambridge. Sent him an answering letter and copy of his book.
- Wrote another story for an infant in local school. Bound and illustrated story.
- Received picture and letter from infant. Replied to letter.
- Continued letters to Leicester and to Greg.
- Wrote letter to school governor about an exhibition of sculpture lent to the school. Received postcard back.
- Wrote letter to Colchester Castle to see whether we could visit the dungeons on a school trip.

Original draft of poem *The Sea*.

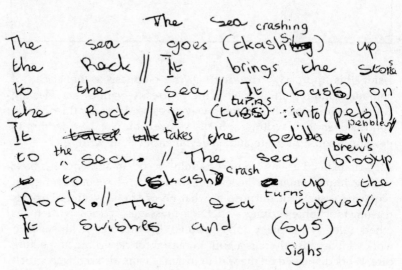

How the poem looked when typed out for the wall:

*The Sea*
*by Andrew Walker*

The sea goes crashing up the rock.
It brings the stones to the sea.
It bursts on the rock.
It turns into pebbles.
It takes the pebbles into the sea.
The sea brews up to crash up the rock.
The sea turns over.
It crashes and sighs.

(It is worth mentioning that the use of a word processor and printer achieves all the re-drafting and correction, and allows for a perfect print-out at the end. Its potential as a tool in the English classroon is considerable.)

Although poor writers' work often seems banal and uninspiring, given the right kind of help and stimulus, they can produce work which will give them and their teacher a sense of pride and satisfaction.

## Checklist

A beginning writer needs:

**Stimulus**
> Film, story, activity, pictures etc.

**Purpose**
> Knowing who is the audience
> Knowing the kind of register required
>> Letters — inter-school, penfriend, for information
>> Diaries
>> Stories — for magazine, wall, reading books
>> Books for infants

**A few purposeful ideas**
> Instructions — treasure hunts, making things, making maps
> Poems, plays
> Message board for class
> Complaints box and answers

**Story knowledge**
> How to make it hang together
> Listening to stories
> Sharing others' writing

**Help with technical skills**
> Clear guidelines of how to set out work
> Knowing first draft is not the last word
> Spelling strategies
> Handwriting skill
> Someone to read out to in order to sort out punctuation

## 2 The secretarial skills

A sense of perspective is needed if we are going to deal with children's difficulty in spelling and handwriting. These two aspects of written work are often the criteria by which the work is marked and one of the means by which teachers identify children in need of extra help. In reality, though, these are technical skills, stabilized and conventionalized by the need for uniformity when printed materials on a large scale began to be produced. Shakespeare/Shaksper/Shakesspear had no such problem!

The feeling of being a 'bad speller' is often an anxiety which becomes part of a child's self-concept; it is changing the child's perception of him or herself as a speller which is often the most difficult part of helping children to become better spellers. Changing the *teacher's* perception of spellings, from being something to be 'marked' right or wrong to being a skill in which there is a continuum of progress towards correctness, is also an essential part of this change. Spelling and handwriting are technical skills open to improvement where teachers can take positive action to help their pupils; pupils need to be warned, however, that many people do make judgements about content based on the appearance of written work and the way in which words are written and spelled, because the inaccuracies interfere with the reader's perception of the written work. This separation of spelling and handwriting from story-content can act as a spur to improving spelling and handwriting because children see it as something discrete, which they can tackle if they are given the means to do so by their teachers.

As a pupil once succinctly observed: 'He don't mark History he marks spellings and that ain't fair!'

### Helping pupils to become better handwriters

Handwriting is a learned automatic motor skill and as such is not easily susceptible to change. Getting children to change and improve their handwriting has to be a mixed approach of altering psychological attitudes and re-programming motor skills.

First, children have to be helped to see that it is important to change their handwriting. An open approach by the teacher in which reasons for better handwriting are honestly shared can be a help. Referring to a piece of small-scale research in which the same essay, in different handwriting, was variously marked from 2/10 to 9/10, can bring home to children the problem they have to deal with in their teachers! Even more pertinent can be the proven importance of good joined-up handwriting to spelling success. Children will understand this in terms of learning groups of letters that 'go together' and how the flow of joined handwriting will facilitate the learning and remembering of these letters. Spelling accuracy is in the fingers and the motor movements of the hands to some extent. Explaining and demonstrating this can be a good lead into concentrated work in a handwriting workshop.

The attitude to handwriting in a whole school can be changed by making it an important skill, reinforced across subject areas and rewarded by recognition and display. A term early on in school life, when handwriting assumes importance and is displayed and reinforced positively by all teachers, can give the motivation to even the most recalcitrant writers to make an improvement in their writing. There is no doubt that teachers get the handwriting, and to some extent the spelling, which they are prepared to accept. An across-school policy in this area can achieve remarkable results.

Support for such a policy needs to come from 'the top' in the school and to be an across the curriculum language project. As suggested on page 294 a booklet for the support of slow learners can get important language concepts across to all departments.

To children with very poor skills generally, teaching this kind of automatic motor skill can be very valuable. It can allow them to produce work which they are not ashamed of and to free them from anxiety on the level of presentation, thus allowing them to concentrate on the improvement of content.

**Stages for setting up a writing workshop**
1  Careful observation of children at work
   It is no good setting a piece of writing for children to do and then collecting it in to mark. The product will tell us little about how the child writes and the kinds of difficulties that he or she has; it is observation of the *process* of writing which will give us the necessary information.

   ● Set a piece of writing.
   ● Walk around the class observing each child writing.
   ● Mark down those who are not forming their letters correctly — these will mainly be the formation of a, d, c, b and related letters, and children writing upstrokes from the bottom to the top.
   ● Note other aberrations — poor posture, bad pens, copying a letter at a time.

2  Organizing a workshop
   Work, if possible, across a year group and put the students into homogenous groups. Good writers can work together on aspects of calligraphy, make anthologies, etc. whilst the writers in the poorest groups can start writing from the beginning. A minimum time for

these groups would seem to be about six sessions of up to an hour. They could be done in one week at the expense of disrupting the timetable or, if the English provision is block timetabled, then they could take place in two weeks' English lessons.

The following stages need to be covered in the workshop for poor writers:

## Posture

- Varying position of body for right and left handers.
- Supporting weight on non-writing arm — not holding the head in the hand

## Pens and Pencils

- Need for a pen you can control — biros bad for this.
- Have roller-writer handwriting pens available if possible; sell them if feasible.
- Use pencil or felt tips if no pens available.

## Musical accompaniment

- The use of pop music as a facilitator for handwriting is not merely a sugaring of the pill. It does provide a good motivation to the class (if not to your next door neighbour), but its main virtue is that writing to the rhythm of the music overcomes the stranglehold on the pen or pencil that most poor writers assume when attention is drawn to the activity of writing. Writing in time to music makes the hand relax and also moves the writer on in some kind of rhythmic way. It can be very helpful to the slow, cramped writer. Insistence on joined-up writing is easier when there is a natural flowing sound to write in time to.

## Exercises

There are a number of commercial writing courses available on the market. Choose one which reinforces the importance of spelling and handwriting going together and that stresses joined-up writing. If you choose to devise your own course the following points may be helpful. (Demonstrate on OHP if possible so they can see the process.)

*Exercises for practising letter formations and patterns*

These can be used as decoration or design

*Exercises for practising the difficult 'a' formation*

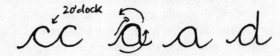

Spirals get the direction right.

Think of a clock.
Go up to 2 o'clock then back round again.
Practise these in all sizes, even with a paint brush on newspaper for very resistant students.

*Exercises for practising groups of letters*

Always choose letters that go together in words. Reinforce spelling sequences as you practise.

*acc add out ous ord*
*aul oil ain tion*

*Short pieces of writing to copy*

Jokes, riddles, short poems. Emphasize looking at the whole word and writing it down at one go, then checking.

Clarity of communication through handwriting can be re-inforced continually with even the worst writers. Once a student sees that he or she can write clearly and communicate effectively that effort will continue whenever the purpose for writing is clearly demonstrated.

## Spelling

Good spelling is largely the ability to generalize from known words to unknown words and to have internalized the way in which sequences of letters or 'letter strings' go together in the English language.

We learn to spell by generalizing from words we have seen and are familiar with. The visual patterning of words, the way they hang together, is the key to generalization. If someone asks us to spell a word and we are not sure about it we tend to write it down and see if it looks right. It is this emphasis on the *look* of the word that informs current spelling theory. Referring to how a word sounds is open to confusion. Just thinking of *ough* and its sound in *brought, tough, bough, though, through*, etc. should be enough to convince! How a word looks, attending to similarities, internal construction, known words within words, all draw attention to the letter strings which consistently hang together and allow us to generalize confidently. Feeling that there is only a limited number of ways in which words can be made up, makes us into confident spellers. It is this confidence and knowledge that we need to pass on to our students.

### Capitalizing on the visual approach — defining a strategy
This approach can ensure a word is learned when it is asked for — and also that generalization from the new word to others is effected. For example:

- A student wants the word *storm*.
- Teacher writes down *storm* — in book, on card, OHP or blackboard.
- Attention is drawn to the *or* — *worm, word, stork, work* are also written down.
- *Storm* is covered over.
- Student writes down *storm* from memory.
- Student checks with teacher's version.
- Rewrite if incorrect.

This is the strategy defined as LOOK, COVER, WRITE, CHECK. It is the most efficient and effective way to teach and correct spelling. All departments can use it and it takes away the responsibility for correct spelling from the English department alone and lays it on all teachers in the school.

Although this takes marginally longer than saying the letters of the word — often misheard or written down incorrectly — it is effective because the word is learned, because it is contextualized in other words that LOOK LIKE IT, and because the student takes the ultimate responsibility for checking that it is correct. A very poor speller can also be helped by using the finger tip to trace the letters of the word whilst saying the word — in this way, a kinaesthetic input can also be made reinforcing the visual input.

### Reversing a poor self-image
In order to reverse the poor self-image of a student perceiving him or herself as a 'dreadful speller' the approach to learning to spell and to correcting spellings must be very positive. Counting how many words you get right rather than wrong can subtly change the attitude of even

the worst spellers and give them a base to build on. In the same way writing down the *correct* words in a piece of dreadfully mis-spelled writing can draw attention to what is right, gives the teacher positive ground to work on, and encourages the student to build on words he or she already knows. Similarly, identifying the part of an incorrect word that is right or pointing out that a word is phonically possible even if incorrect — such as *detale* instead of *detail* — allows students to feel that they are on the way to becoming good spellers.

**What the student needs to know and do**
Poor spellers, as in other aspects of English, manifest the condition of 'learned helplessness'. It is the effort of getting students to take responsibility for their own spelling that is crucial to the success of the undertaking. Students need clear strategies, guidelines and instructions. It is important that we share with students our reasons for doing things this way and our belief that, by doing it in this way, we shall be successful.

**Checklist**

Students need to:
- Learn the LOOK, COVER, WRITE, CHECK strategy.
- Insist that teachers *write down* words for them.
- Start a card index box or a vocabulary book of words needed and known — spare cards in an envelope can be carried to lessons.
- Learn the words they have needed to spell — testing can be done in pairs; by writing out twenty new words learned in the week; by a class spelling list derived from common needs over a week's writing.
- Write using pen and pencil. Putting in words in pencil they are not sure about and checking afterwards.
- Identify possible errors in their own work by underlining, etc.
- Learn to look closely at words and see what other words are like them.
- Talk about words and their meanings.
- Put words together with other words that look like them in a card index or word list.
- Look at a word, close their eyes and try to visualize the word on the inside of the eyelid.
- Remember *never to copy* a word from the board or a book.
- Play lots of games with words, puzzles, computer word games. Learn to enjoy words and to use them adventurously.
- Use the letter strings in name and address to start students off with letter string work.

e.g. Martin Stephenson
    art       step
      tin

               hen
  Mars
                 son
     in

- Take a letter string from a word that has been mis-spelled e.g. uit
  — write it down
  — let student look at it
  — cover it up
  — repeat until written down four or five times
  — add beginnings and endings to show other words general-ized from the letter string
  — repeat, cover and write until all these words are known as well

uit add fr*uit*
uit    g*uit*ar
uit    recr*uit*
uit    s*uit*
uit    bis c*uit*

Enjoying words, talking about them, making them accessible to students is the key to their becoming discriminating spellers. Very bright students with spelling difficulties are often susceptible to the intellectual approach —looking at derivations or seeing how prefixes and suffixes are limited forms that carry a meaning. Seeing how words relate to language generally and to historical contexts can bring spelling and words to life, and enable students to make a new approach which is not related to their 'poor speller' image, but is capitalizing on their intelligence. This, applied with continual practice of letter strings, relating known letter strings and generalizing from them can help them to come to grips with a disabling weakness. Separate workshops for such students can be very effective as well as entertaining and enjoyable to teach.

# Endpiece

All work with spelling should be as light-hearted and economical as possible. A swift, clear drawing of attention to a correct spelling given when it is needed takes seconds rather than minutes, and the incremental effect of recording correctly words as they are needed in writing is far more valuable than copying out corections or learning irrelevant spelling lists.

Working with slow learners can be rewarding and worthwhile, but many teachers feel threatened by their presence in a class and unsure about how to help them. Understanding yourself how reading and spelling work, and the constraints on writing will help you to be a confident and effective teacher. It is the task of helping such students to become self-correcting and more effective in their communications that matters.

- Putting the responsibility for correction onto the pupil means it is no longer necessary to cover students' work with red marks which never seem to be heeded and defeat the student.
- Allowing students to decide which bits of their writing they want to work on and re-draft takes away the coercive element in writing.
- Giving writing which is purposeful and has an audience in mind makes the whole process meaningful.

Once improvement is shown, many students will put enormous effort into their work and take great pride in what they achieve. Helping such students to enjoy writing and reading, and introducing them to the pleasures of stories and poetry has given many teachers new insights into their teaching and into the magical effect that raised expectations and confidence can have upon a student.

# Recommended reading

### Books about spelling and handwriting
*Catchwords — a teacher's manual*, C Cripps and M Peters, Harcourt 1980
*Spelling: Caught or Taught?*, M Peters, Routledge & Kegan Paul, 1985
*Handwriting*, C Jarman, Blackwell, 1979

### Books about reading
*Reading*, Frank Smith, CUP, 1978
*Learning to Read*, Margaret Meek, Bodley Head, 1982
*Listening to Children Reading*, H Arnold, Hodder & Stoughton, 1982
*Retarded and Reluctant Readers*, B Raban and W Body, Centre for Teaching of Reading, Reading
*Silent Conversations*, Brigid Smith, Heinemann
Journals: *Remedial Education*, quarterly, from National Association of Remedial Education
*Reading*, quarterly, from United Kingdom Reading Association

## Books about literacy

*Achieving Literacy*, Margaret Meek, Routledge & Kegan Paul, 1983

*Errors and Expectations*, M Shaughnessey, OUP, 1977

*From Speech to Writing*, R. Binns, Scottish Curriculum Development Service, 1978

*Writing: Teachers and Children at Work*, Donald Graves, Heinemann, 1983

*Yes, they can! A Practical Guide for teaching the adolescent slow learner*, K Weber, OUP, 1978

## Books for poor readers

*Edward Arnold*: Databank, Ed., David Crystal & John Foster (Factual, well illustrated, good series)

*Cassell*:Patchwork Paperbacks (Stories set in Australia)
Onward Paperbacks
Red Lion Books ⎱ short complete stories
Banjo Books ⎰
Discovery Books, Ed Wendy Body (Factual, illustrated)

*Harrap*: Spinechillers (Ghosts etc. —factual but exciting)
Reporter series (Factual, illustrated, interesting)

*Heinemann Educational*: Booster Books: W C H Chalk (Stories — series)

*Hutchinson*: Spirals, Ed Anita Jackson (Ghosts etc., Excellent stories)

*Longman*: Knockouts (Several levels plus some tapes)
Tempo: Groves and Stratta (Structured phonic series 1–14)
Tempo plays
Inner Ring Hipsters (Stories — short but like a paperback)

*Macmillan Education*: All Rounders, Ed John Denton
Rockets (Paperbacks) Ed Aidan Chambers

*Nelson*: Help: James Webster (Three levels plus worksheets for story writing)
Getaway Series (Suitable for reluctant readers. Paperback format)

*Rupert Hart-Davies*: Adventures in Space: Shelagh McCullagh (series)

*Schofield and Sims*: Relay Readers: Barry Johnson (Graded, very short)

*Scholastic Publications*: Sprint Starter Library (American)

*Transworld Publishers*: Tracker Books (Choose your own story)

These lists are not definitive, and teachers are recommended to the *A–Z of Reading*, published by the National Association of Remedial Education. This lists all remedial readers published, and indicates reading age and interest age.

For addresses of publishers see page 365.

# 14 English by micro

Jim Payne

## The coming of the micro

Until quite recently, the school computer was a large, grey, dusty machine locked away in a Maths department store cupboard, which was dragged out four or five times a week for the Computer Studies classes. The rest of the school regarded it as an overblown calculator; something safely left in the hands of the scientists and mathematicians. It was the coming of micro-computers which began to change things.

Well then — what's so different about micro-computers? In a nutshell, they are smaller, cheaper and faster. One of their most attractive features is that they use a TV screen to beam information back to the user instead of painstakingly typing out every single message.

Five years ago, schools did their computing by telephone. Each school would have a telephone link to their local authority's huge and very expensive 'mainframe' computer which itself was housed in specially-built cellars in the local polytechnic or even the town hall! This meant that the school's computer terminal could not be moved around at will — it had to be near a telephone. It also meant that schools sometimes had to wait in a queue to use the computer and when the computer was shut down for routine maintenance then no school in the authority could do any live computing.

With the advent of cheap and portable micro-computers every school could control its own facilities, and these facilities were actually more powerful than those previously available in the telephone-link days.

About this time it slowly began to dawn on non-scientists that these machines could manipulate words with some of the flexibility they showed towards numbers, and one by one we began playing with the new toys. As we played we began to realize that here was a piece of equipment which English teachers could use to great effect in the classroom – if only we could master its intricacies. One thing we knew was that it was intrinsically different from any other audio-visual aid we had ever encountered. In fact it was more than an audio-visual aid, it was a medium in its own right, comparable with print and video in its potential.

The reason for this judgement was the amazing versatility of the creatures — they could be word-processors one minute and the next they could be processing statistics at alarming speed, and then they could be testing your irregular German verbs with a swift change of the program! They could also do complex things so rapidly — coloured diagrams drawn in a twinkling, poems printed out at the blink of an eye, a search of a long document for occurrences of a particular phrase done in half a second.

The imagination groaned with the effort of remembering that it was dealing with a machine which performed 4 million instructions every second.

And finally, with a well-written program they were also inter-active. They could respond in quite different ways depending on what the pupil had typed at the keyboard. It was this final quality which made them so distinctive and potentially such a powerful aid to learning.

So let's have a look at some of the main features of the way in which educational computing is evolving. I shall make a few obvious points about hardware first and then try to give some pointers to the software which is now becoming available.

# Hardware

This is the collective name given to the pieces of equipment which make up any computer system. A micro-computer system consists of the computer itself, a keyboard (often built-in to the computer), a monitor or TV set and either a cassette recorder or a floppy disc drive to store the programs. These are linked by cables and it takes about four or five minutes to set everything up and make sure it is working.

Once you have been shown how to connect up your own system, it is surprisingly easy to repeat the operation, so do not be intimidated by your first glance at the snaking cables! In a well-organized school, the system will be all set up for you in advance and all you will have to do is load up your program.

## Some reminders about the hardware

It may seem obvious, but in order to bring colour into your computing, you must have a computer which sends out signals in colour. (The BBC micro and the Sinclair Spectrum both do this but many older computers give only black and white). You also need a colour monitor or TV set which can display the colour signals being sent out by the computer.

Another important thing to remember is that programs written for a BBC micro will not run on a Sinclair or a Research Machines micro and vice versa. You must make sure that the programs you buy have been written for the machines in your school. Otherwise you have wasted your money. Many programs are now written in different versions to suit each of the major machines, but not all. If in doubt, get advice before buying.

Finally a word about program storage. You can store programs either on floppy discs or on audio cassette tapes. You must find out from your Computer Studies staff which of the two storage systems your school uses. The floppy disc is more expensive but much faster. If you are condemned to use a cassette recorder, you must take into account the length of time required to load up a long program. Some of the long adventure programs can take up to ten minutes to load from a cassette recorder, and unless you plan for this, you could have a very restless class by the time the program is ready.

## Which computer?

It is unlikely that you, as a mere English teacher, will have a voice in deciding which micro-computer the school should purchase. In fact, this decision is often at local authority level, and a standard machine is specified which schools are virtually obliged to purchase. The advantages of a co-ordinated local authority computing policy is that maintenance and software support can be organized economically and effectively. It also means that programs produced in one school can be instantly tried out in any other school in the area, without the lengthy process of re-writing them for other machines.

The three machines at present most frequently found in British schools are the BBC micro, made by Acorn Ltd., the 380z and the 480z, both made by Research Machines Ltd. and the Spectrum made by Sinclair Research Ltd. These machines will be found in about ninety per cent of British schools. And it is for these machines that most educational programs are being written.

## Organizing the equipment

Many schools have rapidly built up their computing facilities so that they have a dozen or more micro-computers installed in one area, supervised by a member of staff with specific responsibility for Educational Computing. This installation can then be booked for use when it is not required for Computer Studies classes.

Often the computers are linked to each other in what is called a 'network'. If this is the case then it usually means that any of the micros in the network can share the use of the network printer and the network disc-drive. If the school has organized its computing facilities in this way then it has implications for the style of teaching which is possible and the type of program you can use. In this sort of 'computer laboratory' set-up, the typical learning group is the small group (two or three at most) who can sit around and share one of the computer keyboards.

Some software is designed for the whole class to watch together and casts the teacher in the traditional role at the front of the class, pointing out things on the screen and operating the keyboard in response to decisions arrived at by the class after discussion. The computer here is being used as a device to stimulate interactions between teacher and class. This type of software is less easy to use in a computer laboratory, where the layout of the room is designed for small sub-groups of the class. However, if you have a good program which you want to use in this way then think about booking the room that is used for viewing video-tapes. This will have everything you need for your session, except the computer itself, and this can quickly be connected up before the lesson.

## 'Hands-on' experience

You must familiarize yourself with the equipment so that, eventually, you do not have to keep shouting down the corridor for help from the Computer Studies staff. The best way of doing this is by getting as much 'hands-on' experience as possible. Ask to borrow a school machine at weekends or in the holidays. (It will work plugged into your own TV at home.) Before you do, check that your household insurance and car insurance will cover you in case of theft or accident. After all, most computers with all the extras cost over £1000.

# Software

Software is the collective name given to computer programs. The most common types of software found in schools are:

1 Languages (Basic, Pilot, Prolog, Logo, etc.)
2 Word Processing packages (Wordstar, Texed etc.)
3 Administration packages (Timetabling, Pupil Records etc.)
4 Readability programs
5 Adventure Games (The Hobbit etc.)
6 Computer-Assisted Learning programs
7 Simulations
8 Data bases and query languages

## 1 Languages

The prime use of languages is to enable you to write your own programs for any of the uses to which you want to put the micro-computer. There are many different languages which computer programmers can use when writing programs. Each language has its strengths and weaknesses. These characteristics are inherited from the context in which the language was developed. For instance, FORTRAN is a language which was developed in the scientific world and so is very good at manipulating numerical information and complex mathematical formulae. No one would choose it to write a CAL (computer-assisted learning) program, especially a CAL program in the language area.

The general purpose language which has dominated the micro-computer generation so far is BASIC. Most people coming to computing for the first time learn to use BASIC. You will most certainly have it available in your school. There are now lots of books and videos on the market aiming to teach the reader/viewer how to use this language. When you choose your book, make sure that it is teaching the same BASIC that is being used on your school computer. BASIC exists in several different dialects and it is decidely inefficient to learn the Sinclair BASIC if your machines are BBC micros. Also, when you are learning, keep a copy of the computer manual by your side for reference.

Another language which you may find useful and which is fairly easy to use is PILOT. This is what is called an 'author' language and has been created to allow teachers to write instructional computer programs without knowing too much about computing. It is worth looking at some of the sample programs written in this language because they tend to adopt a conversational style of presentation which can be quite entertaining if the conversation is cleverly constructed and the dialogue sufficiently witty or outrageous.

One of the best features of this language is the 'MATCH' command. This is a command which tells the computer to accept a whole range of words as possible answers so as to permit the pupil to answer questions in a number of ways —
For example:

'Did you have a good Christmas this year?'

MATCH 1: yes, yeah, yep, great, marvellous, sure did, super, of course

MATCH 2: no, nope, lousy, rotten, hell, awful, boring

When the pupil types in his or her reply to the question, then MATCH1 and MATCH2 are used to check the reply.

If MATCH1 is successful then the program will jump to print out:

'So did I! We really had fun, but I probably ate too much, as usual!'

If MATCH2 is successful then the program will print out:

'Oh, I'm sorry to hear that. Never mind perhaps next year will be better. Who knows, it might snow next year!'

If neither is successful the program could continue in a non-committal way:

'Well I suppose it only comes once a year, so we have to make the best of it!'

Naturally this conversational approach can be applied to instructional material also and can incorporate graphics as well as words.

## 2  Word processing

Word processors allow the operator at the keyboard to type in text, make any kind of alteration in the text from simple spelling corrections to moving whole paragraphs around and then to print out the text in any format and in a range of typefaces. The edited text can then be stored on computer disk and called up to be re-edited or printed out as required.

Your school micro will be able to perform as a word processor if your school has bought one of the many word-processing programs which are available. Naturally it depends on the quality of your printer whether your system will be useful for producing teaching materials and departmental documents. Some printers give a very low quality printed image and are not designed to produce letter-quality typing. And of course it is no good being able to edit text through fifteen drafts, if the final print-out is worse quality than the printing on your till-slip from Sainsburys.

At the moment, the daisy-wheel printers are the most versatile and give the crisp, black image which is easy to photocopy or make stencils from. (They are called 'daisy-wheel' printers because the letters are on the tips of a 'daisy-wheel' which spins around to select the correct letter. Then the hammer strikes the 'petal' and so types the letter onto the paper.) The 'daisy-wheels' themselves can be changed so that different typefaces can be utilized.

**Advantages of using a word-processing package**
The advantages of using a system like this in producing classroon materials are substantial.

1  **Quality of typing**
   The quality of your initial typing can be less professional because you can scan through the text afterwards on the TV screen to correct electronically any spelling, punctuation or typing mistakes.
2  **Ease of storage**
   You can store the text on computer disk and type out new stencils when you need to run off copies. (Anyone who has tried any of the methods of storing ink-duplicator stencils will appreciate this advantage!)
3  **Ease of editing and reprinting**
   No teaching materials are perfect the very first time you use them. Inevitably some things work well and other things could be improved by a better layout or a re-phrasing of the task or an improvement of the quality of the questions etc. If you have your materials on disk it is very easy to effect these improvements on the screen and then reprint your materials in the improved version.
4  **Design and layout**
   You can control the layout and paging of your text so that you can

improve the appearance and effectiveness of your documents. Things like column-width, typeface, justification, proportional spacing, indentation and so on, are options you can set and reset to different values during print-out. This means that you can try out several layouts of your page until you find the one best suited to your needs. (Some micros allow you to format pages and see the full page on the screen so that you only need to print out those variations which interest you most.)

### Case History

Once I was in charge of drafting a Mode 3 syllabus for a committee formed from seven schools in South London. The syllabus went through about five drafts before we submitted it to the examinations board, and then went through another two or three drafts after the board's subject panel had made their recommendations. The document was about eleven A4 pages of typing.

Because I had decided to put the syllabus on to disk right from the first draft I was able to incorporate any amendments into subsequent drafts with a minimum of trouble — perhaps 15 minutes editing it on the screen and then five minutes printing out the up-dated version. It would have taken a good typist about two to three hours to have typed this length of document. And, in my school, I would have expected tc have waited between seven and ten days for a job of this size to be completed. As it was, I could often have the up-dated version ready the next day for distribution to my colleagues.

### Learning to use a word-processing program

Some word-processing programs are quite complex and take some effort to learn how to use them. Usually there are far more facilities in these programs than the average user will ever need and this tends to make the array of possible commands a little bewildering when you first begin reading the manual. The trick is to try to learn no more than a small sub-set of the commands to begin with.

### Checklist

(a) learn how to start a new file (file is computerese for a passage of text) and how to store it away on disc.
(b) learn how to call up a file that you have previously stored away on disk.
(c) learn how to do simple editing on the screen and how to type in new text.
(d) learn how to do simple formatting and how to print out your text on the printer.

Every word-processing program is different, but your educational computing adviser will most certainly be able to recommend a suitable well-designed program for the machine being used in your school. Ask for a manual and read the beginner's section before you sit down at the keyboard for your first session. If you can get yourself a place on an in-service course then take it. However, if you do go on a course, make sure that the computers and the word-processing programs being used on the course are identical to those being used in the school.

## 3 Administration packages

Computers are undoubtedly very useful in administration. They are experts in keeping records neatly and accurately. There are a host of accounting programs, stock control programs and visi-calc programs all of which would have applications in managing an English department with greater efficiency.

Unfortunately it is essential to have full control over your own admin micro, if you want to computerize the management of the department, and this is not likely to be possible in most schools today. Usually we have to share the machines with many other people and book time on them when they are available. However, occasionally, you can identify an admin task which takes a clearly-defined length of time for its completion and, if it is possible to book a micro for that period, then, provided there is a suitable program to do the job, you ought to take advantage of the speed of the computer to free you to do things more demanding of your professional skills.

### Case History
For example, my own school is part of a consortium which runs a Mode 3 exam in English. It is a one hundred per cent coursework syllabus and therefore the annual grading and standardization of coursework folders is very important. Each school in the consortium must first perform an internal standardization amongst those teachers entering exam candidates. Then the schools in the consortium meet together in groups of five or six to standardize the marking across the group. Finally the scheme's moderator will adjust each group's grades, if necessary, to correspond with Mode 1 standards.

I have written a suite of programs which handles all the purely mechanical aspects of a standardizing meeting — the production of an order of merit, the identification of middle-of-the-grade candidates, the scaling of marks from the top to the bottom of the mark ranges and which will then print out the entire set of standardized marks and give a bar chart of the total percentage obtaining each grade for each of the schools. It gives us far more time to concentrate on making those professional judgements concerning the comparative quality of coursework in candidates' folders, which is the really crucial aspect of any standardizing operation.

I can remember those necessarily protracted standardizing meetings where the whole day was spent reading folders and arguing about their relative merits until eventually we were interrupted by the caretaker putting his head round the door to tell us he was shutting up the school in ten minutes! The inevitable result was that the HOD would end up with two or three hours of tedious paperwork to complete over the weekend! If the computer can release us from that sort of work then let's use it.

# 4 Readability using the micro

Almost all the measures of readability are boring and mechanical to calculate. Counting syllables, words and sentences in a prose sample is so mind-numbing that most people try it once and avoid it forever more. If there is a use for readability measures in secondary schools, then the whole process ought to be consigned to those tirelessly servile creatures, the micro-computers. This, I am glad to say, has now happened and there are programs which will calculate the readability of any prose sample typed into the computer.

A part of my 'Readamatics' package (*see* Recommended software p. 348) is just such a readability program. This allows you to calculate the level of difficulty of a piece of prose using either the Flesch Index or the Fog Index. I use it regularly in school to prompt discussion about the reading demands being made on our pupils, particularly in the first and second year classes. I obtain photocopies of suitable text extracts from different departments' course books and carry out a readability survey using the program. Next I call a meeting of interested parties and circulate first the photocopied pages and then the readability scores for them. I also make sure that we all have the necessary information concerning the range of reading ages in the first two years. The discussions which follow always help to sharpen our awareness of mismatches between text and reader which are obstructing the learning process in our classes.

# 5 Adventure games

The majority of video games fall into the 'blob-chasing', 'alien-zappin' category where fast reactions and a nimble thumb save the planet for mankind yet again! (It is interesting to note the relative indifference that girls display to this sort of video game. Is there some in-built 'macho' element in alien-bashing?)

However, there is another type of game which is not so frenetic, depends much more upon the reading of text and requires some wit and ingenuity to succeed — the adventure game. Structurally most of these games follow a similar pattern, though the trappings could be borrowed from sources as diverse as Tolkien, Egyptian mythology or Marco Polo.

The pattern is that you, the player, are Bilbo Baggins or somebody similar and you are setting out on a quest. Your epic journey takes you from page to page of video text and computer graphics, fighting magical dwarves or being asked intricate Chinese riddles and you can vary your route through the silicon landscape by entering a compass-bearing at the end of each page's mini-adventure. Sometimes, if you have forgotten to pick up the silver key after your fight with the Trolls, then you cannot unlock the enormous oak door at the entrance to the Castle of Desolation. Which means, of course, that you have to backtrack to Troll-ville to get it. (Are you starting to get the idea?)

When you first began to play this type of game you are very quickly boiled in oil or drowned in a swamp but gradually players learn to stay alive for longer and longer. In fact, there is a rumour that a young man in Hertfordshire once actually solved one of these games. It was about 4 a.m. on a Tuesday morning last January but unfortunately he forgot how he's done it and has never succeeded since!

The games are becoming more and more sophisticated and, in some of the latest, the players can 'talk' to the characters they meet and enter their instructions in simple English sentences. However, at present, this aspect of the games is still far from satisfactory and you should not expect too much of them in this respect.

There is probably more of interest to English teachers in the possibility of adventure-game survivors being persuaded to sit down together in a group to devise their own adventure game, adapting some of the viewdata software which is available for most types of computer. In fact, it is likely that an 'Adventure game generator' program will appear on the market soon so that pupils will simply have to write the separate 'pages' of the adventure and this program will look after all the computing aspects. And then the possibilities are distinctly interesting. Instead of dungeons and dragons, one could develop the genre into a decidedly literary direction. What about a 'Lord of the

Flies' adventure game where the player is Simon or Piggy? Or a 'Treasure Island' game with Jim Hawkins making the journey? One could build in references back to the text of the book so that sections had to be re-read in order to make progress.

However, the one thing to bear in mind about these games is that they are always comparatively trivial and superficial when compared with the narrative from which they are derived. Adventure games are really a type of maze-like intellectual exercise which, like most good puzzles, can hold some of us in rapt concentration for long periods, but which will never arouse deep feelings or a profoundly imaginative response in the way that a powerfully-written book can. But, that having been said, adventure games can turn reading into a fun social experience in the way that at its best play-reading in groups can do. Their real use is probably in the area of reading development using group dynamics as a motivating force. After all, if you are sitting with your friends playing one of these games you cannot take part in the group's dicsussion if you have not read the page of text on the TV screen, can you? Adventure games are worth experimenting with, as long as you do not expect miracles of them.

# 6 Computer-assisted learning (CAL) programs

There is usually a time-lag between the educational system being sold a new type of equipment and the time when good teaching materials become available for use with this new equipment. We seem to have successfully waited out this time of software shortage and there is now a number of CAL programs arriving on the market. Obviously, much of the new software is in the Science and Maths area, but in our subject, too there is a great deal of software development going on up and down the country and some of it is now bearing fruit.

You will most certainly be able to find programs which offer various types of word games — Scrabble, Hangman, Word Squares and so on. And, of course, there are programs which adopt a multiple-choice format or offer you quizzes on English literature. I predict that this type of program will proliferate because it is relatively easy to write and the same basic structure can be dressed up in a large variety of clothing. We will soom have quizzes on Shakespeare, quizzes on Dickens, quizzes on Chaucer and so on. In fact, there is now a program called 'Questionmaster' which allows teachers to devise their own quizzes on any subejct. (For details see Recommended software p. 348.)

There are also programs which offer practice in punctuating sentences — these are far more attractive than the same type of exercise in print.

They have changing colours, flashing words, animated figures which suddenly pop out to help the pupil. These are gimmicks, true, but if they help to hold the pupils' attention then they work. But what is more important in programs of this kind is that the computer tirelessly checks and, if necessary, corrects every single mistake almost at the same instant it has been perpetrated! This close-response feedback is the sort of remedial input that we can only give a child in one-to-one teaching — a rare situation in schools. It also means that the pupil makes his or her mistakes in private. Even a totally sympathetic adult can be seen as a vaguely hostile presence by a child who has had the experience of failure too frequently. A computer has the advantage that it is non-human.

At a more complicated level, there is a number of programs which adopt a cloze passage approach and fall into the category of reading development programs.

One such program is 'Developing Tray' written by Bob Moy and now widely used in the London area. The program begins with a screenful of punctuation marks and nothing else. The class is told to choose a letter to have inserted on the screen and they are told that they have to 'pay' for each guess unless they can predict correctly at least one place on the screen where their chosen letter will appear when typed into the computer. The game may begin on the level of 'Hangman' but as the screen fills up, children are having to deploy their knowledge of spelling patterns, syntactic forms and sentence structure to predict correctly where certain letters will appear. It is possible for a pupil to run the game for a small group of classmates, but it is probably more effective where the teacher can be 'referee' and pick up teaching opportunities from the screen. They can also 'manage' the dialogue between members of the class as they reach their joint decision as to which letter to choose next.

A different cloze passage approach is seen in my own 'Readamatics' package. There are three programs in this package. The first allows the teacher to type in any passage he or she wants to use. This means that teachers can use extracts from books already familiar to their pupils. The second program allows teachers to drive a little arrow along the lines of the passage and by pressing a key, they can remove the word pointed to by the arrow and leave a **** in its place. They can then type into the memory of the computer up to four synonyms for the missing word and these will be held as reserves during the cloze passage program so that the exercise does not become too convergent, and the pupils have a range of suitable words which will be accepted as correct and not rejected as wrong. Teachers can continue this process of word-removal until they are happy with the resulting cloze passage. So teachers have under their control, the type of passage and words to be removed from the passage. What is more, the same passages can be used again, with different words removed, without having to be typed into the computer a second time.

When the pupils begin the third program, they are confronted by a cloze passage which could be three or four screens long. This will have been made up by their English teacher. At each of the blanks the computer has in reserve up to five words which it will accept as correct and insert in place of the blank. If the pupils get the exact word chosen by the author then the screen flashes on and off to congratulate them. If they type one of the five words but it is spelled wrongly then a 'window' clears in the middle of the screen and the pupil is shown the correct spelling in blocked-in outline. If the word in question is 'believed' then the window looks like this:

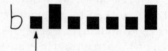

The pupils are given the first letter and the shape of the word. They have to do the spelling again. If they make a mistake then the letter is not inserted but appears over the top of the block as below:

Everything the pupils type into the computer is recorded and can be played back for a 'post mortem' by the teacher and pupils together. This can sometimes be great fun when the pupils prove that they thought of a word which would have fitted correctly into the blanks but which had not been thought of by Sir or Miss. Even the spellings can be seen again in an 'action-replay' presentation of the attempts the pupils made to correct their spelling mistakes. This can often be useful in a diagnostic way for those pupils who have persistent spelling difficulties.

### Selecting software

Almost every month new software is appearing and it is difficult to try out everything that is on the market. However, I would like to pass on some advice about selecting CAL software.

Obviously, most important, you must evaluate the educational approach which underlies the program you are interested in. But even if that is reasonably satisfactory there are other things to look for. In particular, look at how the program copes with the unexpected — wrong answers, capital letters, spelling mistakes, numbers typed in when words are expected and so on. If the program 'crashes' easily with you, then if will cause you innumerable problems in the classroom.

All programs should be 'test-driven' by at least a dozen hyperactive, ham-fisted, space-invaders addicts before they are judged robust enough to be released to the rest of us. A good program must know how to stand on its own feet in the wicked world!

# 7 Simulations

English and drama teachers have long used both simulations and role-play in their teaching schemes. Computers, with their ability to store information and release it according to a pre-determined game-plan, are very useful as a type of sophisticated 'in-tray' technique. You can use the micro to inject the randomly-spaced spurts of input into the role-play exercise so as to keep events bubbling along nicely.

For example — it would be easy to write a newsroom simulation where the computer suddenly bursts into life every few minutes, printing out fresh developments in a handful of choice news stories. These could be unfolding near home, in the local shopping centre, in Whitehall or even in Moscow. The stories would arrive on the printer in episodes, supposedly as they are reported by the Press Association over the telex (computer printer). The pupils would have to organize themselves, each taking on one or two of the stories and composing an item for the front page, progressively amending it as the story twists and turns. The second week's work could be typing the stories into a word-processor. They could be checked for accuracy and then printed out in columns of the right width for the newspaper's front page. The final stage would be to do the layout of the front page incorporating Letraset headlines and sticking down photographs adapted from last week's newspapers.

A program for this type of simulation is very straightforward to write. What is much trickier is the writing of suitable news stories, in episodes, so that they can unfold as the lesson progresses.

## 8 Databases

Information is now big business. In the future, those who organize and control information will have greater power than ever over those who suffer from information poverty. Already in this country about forty per cent of those who are eligible for various types of welfare benefit never claim these benefits because they never find out that they are eligible! As a response to this problem, there is now in existence a program which will allow a claimant to type in details of his or her financial situation and the computer will provide the information as to which welfare benefits that person can claim.

In the future, using databases of information will be as important and powerful a skill as using a directory or encyclopedia is today. It is a skill in information retrieval which falls partly into the English curriculum area. Naturally there will be considerable overlap with the Humanities and with Science, but as English has traditionally taken the lead in helping pupils use books and libraries efficiently, it seems logical to extend this arm of the English curriculum into this new and powerful method of organizing information.

Your school librarian will be familiar with the British Library's BLAISE system even though he or she may never have actually used it. It is something like *Books in Print* put on a computer. It is a vast database of print and non-print materials currently available and besides giving details of author, publisher, price and so on, it also has an entry summarizing the major aspects of the concept of the artefact. This allows you to do a KWIC search. KWIC stands for Key Words In Context and it means that you could ask the database to give you a list of books which mentioned the words 'computer', 'English' and 'school' in the summary of their contents. The resulting list would be quite small and might well contain things you did not want (or expect) such as: *Computers in English Schools* ACE report 1954 (which would not have a word in it about English teaching) — but it would certainly turn up any books in that area whose details were recorded.

A database which is becoming widely-available in schools is PRESTEL and there is now software which will allow microcomputers to communicate directly with PRESTEL through a telephone link and to display any of the 318 000 pages of information on their own screens.

The problem with using PRESTEL in schools is the cost of the telephone call and the cost of accessing each page of information (some pages are free but these are mainly advertising and public information). Unless pupils are closely supervised they use PRESTEL very much in the way they would browse through a copy of the Daily Mirror — they drift from page to page reading what interests them and moving on if a page seems dull. Unfortunately, ten minutes browsing could clock up about £1.00's worth of charges and librarians tend not to be too enthusiastic about this level of charging, especially if they are paying the bill out of the library budget. It seems essential that if PRESTEL is to be used, it should be used as part of an information skills program, where the teaching materials set up specific information retrieval exercises to be practised. Not only is this educationally more desirable, it is also good economics!

Very soon, publishers will find a way in which they can make use of the fact that, if they use computer type-setting, they will have a range of classic texts somewhere in computer memory, and once they find a way of packaging these for the education market, watch out. We already have the Bible available on eight floppy disks for silicon-age vicars, why not Shakespeare or Chaucer or Tennyson? I don't think I'm looking forward to that development. I have a deep, romantic attachment to the idea of thrusting a slim volume of poetry into my trench coat pocket before going for a long walk on the moors. A floppy disk wouldn't be the same somehow . . . .

# Endpiece

It is impossible to say anything really definitive about micro-computers in education. The whole field is still evolving so rapidly. As usual, the market-place is dominated by constant improvement in the hardware available. For example, two years ago it was normal to expect about 8K of memory in a personal computer. This is enough to store about 8000 characters in memory. Now, for the same price you can obtain a machine with 128K of memory.

The pace of software development is much slower and, though the Microelectronics in Education Project (MEP) worked hard in setting up models of good practice for designing, writing, piloting and distributing educational software, there is much which still needs to be done.

But, for now, the educational computing bandwagon is rumbling busily on its way. What is more, pupils seem to respond well to almost anything you flash onto a TV screen. Of course, the hexadecimal honeymoon will fade to a fond memory within the next few years and the programs that survive will have to be both entertaining and instructive. I look forward to the time when we begin to hear the kids in our classrooms complaining 'Do we have to work with computers again today? Why can't we all just sit around and have a good talk about something *really* interesting?'

# Recommended software

(title and supplier given)

*Wordsquare* Software Production Associates, PO Box 59, Leamington Spa, Warwickshire

*Similies Countdown* MUSE, PO Box 43, Hull

*Clues* Longman Group Ltd, Harlow, Essex

*Readamatics* Longman Group Ltd, Harlow Essex (Devised by Jim Payne)

*Punctuation* Bryants Educational Software, 1 The Hollies, Chalcroft Lane, Bognor Regis, West Sussex

*Cloze Procedure* Bryants Educational Software

*English Literature* Griffin Software, Ealing Road, Wembley, Middlesex

*Summary & Comprehension Guidelines* Sussex Software, Sussex Publications, Freepost, Devizes, Wiltshire

*Hobbit* Melbourne House, Church Yard, Tring, Herts

*Text Grader* Hutchinson Software, 62–65 Chandos Place, London WC2N 4NW

*Questionmaster* Hutchinson Software, 62–65 Chandos Place, London WC2 4NW

# 15  Staying on — another year post 16

Patrick Scott

The number of students staying in full time education for one year post 16 has grown steadily over the past ten years. The problem that lecturers, teachers and trainers face, however, only starts with the recognition that these students exist and that there are a lot of them. In making choices between, for example, GCSE re-takes or CPVE, teachers and lecturers concerned with their students' use of language face a dilemma about vocational or academic curricula, experienced as a choice between Communication and English. Communication, English teachers may claim, simply ignores all of the many and varied uses of language that it would be inconvenient to include and concentrates remorselessly on the utilitarian without acknowledging that you can't teach students by disentangling one type of language in this crude and misleading way.

F E lecturers, on the other hand, often have equally strong views about whether it makes any sense to offer 17 year olds more of the same. The last thing their students need, they would probably argue, is further exposure to models of language which place a premium on highly abstract forms of academic discourse. The pre-occupation with literature they would see as a self-indulgence, irrelevant to students who would be unemployed if they hadn't stayed on in full time education.

But the CPVE does not conform to either stereotype of 'Communication' or 'English'. Its 'main aim' is put like this:

'To develop communication skills as a way of structuring relationships between people in a changing and multicultural society.'

There's an important recognition here that Communication is about more than the acquisition of skills. The subsidiary aims are organized under sub-headings that will be familiar to English teachers — Listening, Speaking, Reading, Writing, Communication and Interpretation — and the language in which they are couched is instantly recognizable:

Aim 4: Writing
To write effectively, organizing content and observing the formal conventions of writing by
4.1. formulating and conveying written information in a variety of styles and for a range of purposes
4.2. observing the conventions of legibility, spelling, punctuation and grammar in order to maintain the confidence of the intended audience.

Compare that with this extract from the aims for the National Criteria for the GCSE:

'The course should seek to develop the ability of students to:
1.1.1. communicate accurately, appropriately and effectively in speech and writing.

## Practice

It follows that any course based on criteria such as these will take its shape from a perception *negotiated* between teacher and student, of the part that language plays in smoothing the rites of passage into adulthood. It is useful then to start this section by trying to identify what these 'rites of passage' might be. In the past, they were predominantly about the experience of starting work, about joining a world that was not unlike school — hierarchical, organized around strict routines, and stable. No longer. Unemployment has effected a fairly profound change in the way in which 17 year olds view work, for even those who get 'proper' jobs do not necessarily expect to stay in them for long, and those who have been in YTS know that the jobs they are doing will come to an end in a year. The thread of continuity is provided not by the adults with whom they will be working for the next ten or twenty years, but by the friends with whom they will be sharing the experience of intermittent periods of work and unemployment.

This, of course, has wider implications. It affects, for example, relationships, both emotional and financial, with parents and disrupts the normal patterns and assumptions that underlie the second most formative experience through which young adults go, the experience of leaving home. Finally, of course, it changes the way in which society is viewed. The apathy that is associated with unemployment derives not from a lack of imagination but from a sense of being 'locked out', of being an observer not a participant. To say that this breeds hostility or resentment would be to overstate the case, but it does give this generation of school-leavers a set of attitudes that are different from those of their predecessors.

I have spent time considering the influence of unemployment not because I think that all the students under consideration will be unemployed but because it is a way of drawing more detailed attention to the nature of the 'hostile terrain' with which they will have to cope, and the three areas of *work, home* and *society* that English teachers need to focus on. I also want to show that it is no longer a world that is clearly signposted, but one which poses problems which individuals have to solve from their own resources.

The ways in which teachers handle this will be many and varied, and the description of any particular approach will necessarily attract criticism. Here, however, are some ways of tackling it:

1 A curriculum that draws its authority from the way language is used in the 'real' world will inevitably place a far greater emphasis on *oral* work, since by far the bulk of most language work is spoken rather than written.
2 It will make extensive use of role play and simulation as a way of bringing into the classroom, under controlled conditions, the kind of experience that is likely to be met outside.
3 It will actually take students outside in order to encounter situations that they would normally miss or avoid.
4 It will be *practical*. It will ask students to produce solutions to problems making the teacher a manager and adviser rather than a pedagogue.
5 It will ask students to reflect upon the assumptions and attitudes that they bring to their work.

It could be argued that a programme of this kind is over-ambitious or that it makes unrealistic demands on teachers, and there is some justification for this feeling. It would be a shame, however, if this were the only response and there was no accompanying recognition that it might be worth trying out.

A majority of teachers would probably agree that purposeful classroom talk should be high on any list of priorities and that children should be encouraged to take more initiatives in their writing. But the

351

problems of translating that into practice with fourth and fifth years are so great that, with the exception of a few gifted individuals, most of us resort to the kind of teaching that HMIs grumble about in their reports — where worksheets are used as a form of classroom control and literature is reduced to a set of dictated notes.

Post 16, however, it is different. The opportunities are there, and they are available to any teacher willing to take the risk of creating a more open classroom. Success seems to depend less upon some kind of instinctive pedagogic authority, and more on the inherent value of the work being undertaken. I make no apologies, then, for focusing in the rest of this chapter on a programme of work that might appear to be unfamiliar or innovatory. It is less daunting than it seems to be!

## Role play

Successful role play is exploratory. In other words, it should not demand that students re-enact a pre-determined set of events leading to a known conclusion. Whilst the teacher may provide the starting point, the outcome should be left in the hands of the participants. A student, arriving in a lesson late and tired and announcing to the whole group that she was thrown out of home the previous night because of a row with her mother about the punk she is going out with, does not want to re-run the argument. Role play can be valuable, however, if she is put in the position of her mother and asked to discover how she would handle a similar situation. The complex web of social attitudes that determine her mother's feelings towards her daughter and towards punks can then be opened up for discussion, as can the whole issue of parental rights and the language that such a situation demands. That example is taken from something that occurred spontaneously at the beginning, or fairly near the beginning of a lesson. It was an opportunity worth seizing partly because that kind of frank revelation does not happen very often and should be valued when it does. Most of the time, of course, the stimulus has to be given by the teacher.

Nonetheless students can still play an important part in the devising of 'starting points' if they are asked to provide the specific detail. If the teacher were to suggest, for example, that time should be spent examining hierarchies at work, the students might draw from their own experience in offering concrete situations — the manager who consistently expects stackers in a warehouse to stay behind to clear up for anything up to half an hour after the time they should have finished; the restaurant owner who, whatever the merits of the case, discriminates in favour of the full-timer rather than the casual employee in the allocation of work.

In addition to this responsibility for initiating role play, the teacher needs to be aware of the ease with which work of this kind can lapse into the banal. The clichés of soap opera become wonderfully attractive when a role play has lost direction or purpose. If this happens, it is important to be able to provide new challenges by suggesting unforeseen, and sometimes, it should be admitted, slightly artificial constraints. Fairly conventional work on mock interviews, for example, can be given a more far-reaching significance if the interview is between the owner of a garage where all the mechanics are men and a women who has applied for a job there. Equally, a role play in a housing-action area office where the student is being expected to provide information about housing grants either over the phone or in person, can be used to present a range of unexpected difficulties, from the enquirer who cannot speak English to the man with a chip on his shoulder who will not take 'no' for an answer. What is important is that there should be choices about how to approach the problem and alternative ways of solving it. There is little point in training students in formal routines none of which will match the circumstances under which they are likely eventually to be working.

The following kinds of situations can be mined for work of this kind:

**1 Work**
(a) Hierarchies and status
   The most influential models for relationships with adults pre 16 are those with parents and with teachers. Work makes a quite different set of demands; a new language needs to be learned in order to deal with foremen, with older colleagues, with managers and with elected representatives like shop stewards.
(b) Negotiations
   The idea that, despite hierarchies, an employee's position at work, both financially and otherwise is, in part, a matter for negotiation is not one that the organization of schools prepares 17 year olds for.
(c) Customer relations
   To some extent this area speaks for itself, but no one should underestimate the difficulties faced by a young employee dealing with a complaint about, say, bad service rather than faulty goods.

**(d)** Collective working

Although many decisions, both about work itself and about conditions of employment are unalterable, some are not, and a great many companies do now devolve some decisions to the workforce. Relatively inexperienced employees might find themselves involved in a discussion about, say, arrangements for organizing flexi-time. Once again school rarely offers this kind of automony, nor does it place as much emphasis on group cooperation as it does on individual achievement.

**(e)** Breaking the rules

Perhaps this is one of the few areas in which school does give students experience of how to handle the situation! The context, at work, however, is different and the consequence perhaps more serious.

**(f)** Persuasion

A lot of jobs, particularly in the growing area of service industries, expect employees to control, modify and direct other people's behaviour, and to do so wholly through persuading, cajoling, coaxing and so on. Jobs of this kind range from, say, a medical receptionist to a social worker. It is a wholly new and potentially very difficult kind of relationship for a school-leaver.

## 2 Home

**(a)** Living together

The negotiation between parents and children about degrees of independence is a tricky one, particularly where the traditional markers, such as financial self-sufficiency are no longer available.

**(b)** Leaving home

This covers both the family row and the more measured changing of circumstances. It also anticipates the new role that students will shortly have to adopt as managers of their own lives.

## 3 Society

**(a)** Authority

Authority within this society is not vested solely in the police, of course; others are given power by virtue of the laws that regulate our lives. As adults, students need to come to terms with this legal framework.

**(b)** The Welfare State

The relationship between individual citizens and the institutions of the Welfare State is a curious one — it is not quite that of customer and provider, nor is it quite that of miscreant and authority. If the relationship is misinterpreted, the individual can easily become frustrated or be exploited.

(c) Campaigning

Students should be left free to make informed decisions about whether to accept or resist pressures exerted on them through language, and be encouraged to develop the confidence to implement change, if necessary, in their immediate environment.

It should be emphasized that this is not intended as a programme for Liberal Studies or an introduction to Sociology. The information about, say, consumer law or rent rebates that might be used in situations of this kind is incidental. What matters, is whether students can handle the relationships between people that shape and are shaped by bureaucratic procedures. The job for the teacher of English or Communication is to look at the *language* in which these kind of transactions take place, and to improve the way in which students use and respond to it.

## The case study

An emphasis on oral work should not be seen as an alternative to writing, but as an accompaniment to it. A number of the activities already described might easily be designed in order to incorporate comprehension and writing skills. A discussion, for example, about how to organize flexi-time could naturally grow out of a memo describing company policy, and a copy of the job descriptions of the people involved. If it resulted in the drawing up of a rota and the compiling of a report detailing the decisions taken, that would be a sensible outcome. Out of such an extension of role play onto paper has grown the idea of the 'Case Study'. As a way of working, it originated in more specifically vocational courses than English teachers are used to dealing with, and this should not really come as much of a surprise. Anybody training for a particular job might reasonably expect that part of the course will take them through the appropriate written procedures. This, for example, is behind the use of Case Studies in BEC exams. An exam paper in 'People and Communications' at BEC general level, for example, offers information about a firm — Jones Artwork Ltd. — for which candidates are expected to imagine they are working. Details are provided about an exhibition of paintings by Mrs Glynis Jones, joint owner of the firm. The first task requires candidates to fill in a booking form for the 'Chelton Civic Centre', where the exhibition is going to be held. Candidates are then asked to produce an invitation card, confirm catering arrangements and, using an 'outline catalogue' which includes prices, make notes for a telephone call to arrange insurance. Finally, working from the transcript of a telephone conversation, candidates have to write a memo outlining all the day's arrangements and explaining about an appointment with a reporter from the local radio station.

Even such a sketchy description as this should demonstrate the effectiveness of the technique as a way of teaching particular business skills. If the case for more widespread use were to be based on this example alone, however, it would be a fairly unconvincing one. The skills being assessed fall into a very narrow range and a number of them seem to have little general application. Candidates are not given much choice about how to approach the task and even where, as in the telephone call to the local radio station, it is accepted that the role (General Clerical Assistant) might allow the employee some autonomy, the exam paper assumes that the conversation has already taken place and provides a transcript. Finally, and perhaps most importantly, the situation does not raise any broader issues of principle. Indeed, there is no suggestion that students ought to be doing anything other than fulfilling the functions that they have been given to do.

For all these reasons, the work coming out of this case study would look out of place in, say, a conventional coursework folder of the kind that many English teachers are now familiar with. If, however, the general approach could be hi-jacked and made to serve a different purpose, a purpose that meets these criticisms, then it could become a valuable tool in a variety of courses at 17+. An example here might help to show what this would look like in practice. It is published in 'Case Study Comprehension' (Nelson 1983).

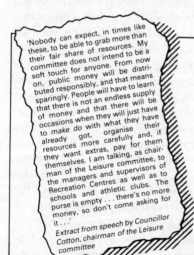

'Nobody can expect, in times like these, to be able to grab more than their fair share of resources. My committee does not intend to be a soft touch for anyone. From now on, public money will be distributed responsibly, and that means sparingly. People will have to learn that there is not an endless supply of money and that there will be occasions when they will just have to make do with what they have already got, organise their resources more carefully and, if they want extras, pay for them themselves. I am talking, as chairman of the Leisure committee, to the managers and supervisors of Recreation Centres as well as to schools and athletic clubs. The purse is empty ... there's no more money, so don't come asking for it ...'

*Extract from speech by Councillor Cotton, chairman of the Leisure committee*

## Lack of funds

You belong to the Woodington Recreational Club and frequently use their sports and games facilities.

The manager of the club was hoping to receive a council grant of at least £1,500 to help pay for repairs to the building and to replace broken sports equipment. Councillor Cotton's speech seems to have dashed these hopes.

The club's committee has gathered together to discuss how to raise the much-needed money. Someone has suggested the idea of a sponsored five-a-side football competition which, it is estimated, would raise about £600. This falls a long way short of the £1,500 needed for repairs and new equipment so the committee has to decide how best to spend the limited funds it will have available.

Several alternative schemes for spending the money are proposed and the chairman decides to inform the club's members and then put it to the vote. On the next few pages is information about the alternatives.

## Improved Facilities?

**Leisure Services Department**
Marfield Borough Council
Municipal Buildings
PO Box 236
Red Lion Place   MA5 8TW

To:
The Manager,
Woodington Recreation Centre.

Dear Mr Ross,

Enough Recreation Centres in the city now support Volleyball teams to make it worth organising a knock-out competition. It has been suggested that the event should take place on a weekday evening and that each of the six teams in the city should be invited to participate. I am writing to enquire whether you would be able to accommodate the event. The main requirement would be for adequate spectator facilities, since such an occasion could attract a crowd of as many as 40 - 50 people.

I look forward to hearing from you.
*Margaret Dain*
Mrs Dain.
Leisure Services Officer.

At present, the centre has standing room for about 20 people in a small gallery. For certain sports that do not require the entire floor, space can be found and chairs in this area would make it possible to invite audiences. The committee would then be free to organise matches and gymnastic displays that could increase the number of people using the centre.

**Cost of 40 chairs at £15 each—£600**

## A New Sport?

The following article recently appeared in the local weekly newspaper.

# ANYONE FOR TENNIS?

At this time of year Sports administrators up and down the country have to ask themselves why so few men and women are representing Great Britain at Wimbledon and why the likelihood of a British champion looks further away than ever. Nobody disputes that British tennis is in a critical state but nothing is being done to put off the day when Wimbledon becomes a showpiece for the rest of the world and, in this country, tennis is something that happens on television once a year.

What is the problem? First of all, it's not a lack of interest. In schools all round the city aspiring Austins and mini McEnroes are thumping the ball back and forth across the courts all summer. And that's just it. Come September, the cold weather sets in, the courts shut down and the rackets are stored away for another year. No Californian sun to bring *our* budding players to maturity.

Our special correspondent toured the city. On every public park in each school playing ground the story was the same—'There's nowhere we can practise during the winter.' Certainly there are *some* covered courts available, but not enough of them. And if there aren't enough courts now, there won't be any British champions in the future.

The administrators admit it; the biggest unmet demand for Sports facilities is for more tennis courts. As Wimbledon has become steadily more popular year by year, more and more people have switched off the television and picked up a racket, but just try and book a court this summer . . . and as for getting a game in December, the closest you'll get to any action, is an action replay.

The committee are keen on the idea as many of the young people who use the centre have complained that public courts are always crowded and they have no real opportunity to practise. The alternative for them is to join tennis clubs but the membership fees are often high and some clubs do not welcome youngsters.

The cost of marking out and revarnishing the floor of the sports hall and providing fixtures for the nets would come to £350. Purchase of the nets themselves would add another £200.

357

## Running Repairs?

The Manager has also received a note about the flourishing
trampolining group at the Centre.

```
Internal Memo:   From:   M.F.
                 To:     D.R.

Dave, the two trampolines are becoming very worn. We can still use them
for a bit longer, but they are not going to last out the year. I'm
worried about the safety regulations - particularly if somebody came to
inspect.
```

Cost of re-bedding 2 trampolines
at £260 each—£520

*Extract from constitution of Woodington Recreation Centre*
In the administration of the centre, the following principles should be
borne in mind:

(a) That sport contributes towards physical well-being, just as education
contributes towards mental well-being.

(b) That sporting facilities should be available to all members of the
community.

(c) That these facilities should be provided free of charge so that no
section of the community is discriminated against.

(d) That the cost of staffing and facilities at a level agreed by the Leisure
Committee should be borne by the community as a whole and paid
for from the rates.

(e) That the Leisure Committee should maintain the Recreation Centre
and the facilities contained within it in good condition and in
accordance with the appropriate health and safety regulations.

## Questions

1. As a journalist who has nothing to do with the Recreation Centre, write a brief newspaper article outlining the problems faced by the Centre.

2. About 50 people are likely to attend the general meeting and will have to be persuaded to agree about what should be done. Unfortunately, you have to go somewhere else that day, but you want to have your say nonetheless. Write out a statement that you can give to a friend to read out on your behalf. Take into account all the evidence, indicate how you would wish everybody to vote and, above all, explain your reasons fully.

3. Write a leaflet to distribute to people visiting the Centre encouraging them *either* to take part in the sponsored five-a-side football competition *or* to sponsor one of the players.

**Rôle Play**

4. Arrange a meeting between Councillor Cotton and the manager of the Centre in order to discuss sources of funding.

5. See what happens at the meeting to decide how the £600 should be spent.

6. Try to persuade a potential sponsor to sign on the dotted line.

**Discussion Points**

7. Who should pay for facilities of this kind?

8. What sort of negotiating skills might enable the manager to obtain more money from the Council?

I have deliberately chosen a context that is not associated with work in
order to show how the approach can be adapted. In this case study,
students are expected to take decisions about which of the options
they will choose, none of which is intrinsically any more 'correct' than
the others. They are given an active role to play. The material also
suggests wider issues which 17 year olds can reasonably be expected
to grapple with. The statement by Councillor Cotton and the extract
from the Leisure Centre's constitution raise the thorny issue of how
community facilities should be funded, and the respective merits of

public expenditure and private sponsorship. Indeed, in working on this, some students argued that the constitution amounted to a promise of continued funding, and were flatly hostile to the whole idea of raising money by other means.

Although the tasks here are rooted in a particular set of circumstances, they do not seem to me to be limiting. Often, indeed, they can be a way of raising the argument to a more sophisticated level. Another example illustrates this point. Interest, within my group of one year students, in a television programme about animal rights — *Rabbits Don't Cry* — was strong, but the reaction to it was predominantly sentimental. A Case Study built around a fictitious Animal Research Station called Dornham Court resulted in a television style debate between members of the group supporting the work of the centre and an audience of 'protestors'. The students followed this up by writing letters, pamphlets and newspaper articles putting their point of view. When, unprompted, a couple of students brought in some propaganda leaflets which they had picked up at a stall on the market in Manchester, it was possible to compare the homegrown efforts with the real thing. In discussion, reference was made to such things as design, layout and readability and an attempt was made to evaluate how successful they would be.

There are some constraints on work of this kind. First, it should, as far as possible, be life-like. Secondly, the context should not be merely decoration but should provide students with information that is essential. Thirdly, the audience for any written tasks should be clearly identified. Finally, the roles for writing that students are asked to adopt should not be unreasonable ones. It is also useful to have a checklist of the possible written forms that students might be expected to use. It should be stressed that the list that follows is by no means comprehensive and I have avoided sorting all the suggestions into different categories because it is the particular use to which they are put that will determine what kind of writing is produced:

- Reports (of all kinds)
- Minutes
- Newspaper articles
- Leaflets
- Handouts
- Manifestos
- Brochures
- Guides
- Instruction manuals

- Newspaper editorials
- Letters to newspapers
- Business letters (of various kinds)
- Notes
- Application Forms (not just for jobs)
- Advert

If properly framed, work of this kind can take place under a variety of banners. Its value for students post 16 is that it provides a way of allowing them to come to terms with a public world that expects considerable fluency in responding to a daunting flow of written information, some of which is of vital importance, and most of which is written in a style that invites immediate rejection.

# Experiential learning

The argument that I have been developing so far places a heavy stress on simulation of one kind or another. I have taken this line in an attempt to be practical. It has allowed me to offer examples of classroom material, description of work in progress, and suggestions that might be developed further. However, as with all teaching styles, simulation has its drawbacks. It demands a level of commitment, a readiness to enter and accept an imaginary world that not all students are willing to provide. The ideal way of overcoming this problem is to use simulation in harness with real experience so that each enhances the other. I say 'the ideal way' because I am well aware of the problems that accompany any decision to take students out of school or college on a regular basis — transport, cost, timetabling and administrative arrangements often seem insuperable obstacles. The benefits, however, can make it worthwhile.

An excellent account of work of this kind is contained in a booklet produced by the Schools Council English 16–19 project called 'New Directions in General and Communications Studies'. The booklet describes the work of a lecturer at the South East Derbyshire College who was teaching a group of fifteen mining technicians. As part of the 'Communications' element of the course, she decided to ask the students to research the problems associated with the discovery, by the National Coal Board, of a new find of coal reserves in the Belvoir Valley. Together, they identified four areas of research and using libraries, newspaper cuttings, local contacts and the NCB they set about producing a report on 'The Vale of Belvoir Project'.

The students decided whom to contact for information and in the process discovered how, for example, to write letters and use the telephone. Inevitably, the need arose for a visit to the site, where the students met and talked to miners, local farmers, protestors and so on. Speakers were later invited in, and a trip organized to the House of Commons to see two MPs who had been involved in the arguments for and against the development of the Vale of Belvoir Coal field. The lecturer is in no doubt about the value, as an exercise in Communications, of all aspects of the work, including the discovery that it is not easy to make much headway with an MP. The quality of the written work that was produced confirms this view, as does the judgement, by one student, that it was 'the best thing I've ever done'.

It was an ambitious project, made possible perhaps by the specific vocational bias of the students and the course. This, however, was not a necessary prerequisite of success. Plenty of similar opportunities exist for students not on courses of this closely defined nature. The Education Department of 'Help the Aged', for example, produce what they term 'Recall' material. The package consists of a tape/slide sequence of life in the twenties, thirties and during the war. The idea is that it should be used with old people to spark off memories of the past, and whilst it can be fairly daunting for a group of 17 year olds to be asked to visit a day centre on a project of this kind, it is astonishing how memorable the experience can be and how quickly they adjust to the demands of the situation. Local primary schools also offer opportunities to discover what kind of stories young children enjoy reading and how to write them.

## A packaged curriculum

These examples all suggest activities that could be mounted by a teacher working in isolation in a timetable organized around single subjects chosen on an 'à la carte basis. In the CPVE, however, English or Communication is part of an integrated curriculum, which includes an element of work experience. The dangers of work experience should, by now, be self evident. Students can sometimes be used as cheap, or even unpaid, labour, and given very little insight into the organization that is 'employing' them. Real value can be derived from work experience, however, when it is carefully planned and monitored. Although direct responsibility for this may lie elsewhere, teachers concerned with Communication or Language work have an important part to play.

As long ago as 1976, Coventry Local Education Authority reported on the communication skills needed in employment. This extract is taken from the summary of their findings:

*Communication Skills Needed in Employment*
'Schools should put high on their priorities for all pupils the following general skills, and should do so in all subjects across the curriculum.

- Reading complex technical literature in order to act upon it. Opportunities for this may occur most in subjects such as Sciences, Craft, Home Economics, Physical Education.
- Writing for many different purposes, and for different audiences; e.g. technical reports, instructions, memoranda, minutes of meetings, letters. In real life, tasks like these demand an attention to detail and a concern for the effectiveness of the writing which generate the need for considerable care. This is perhaps the implication behind the 'pride in perfection' mentioned by employers as something they would like to see in their employees.
- Reference Skills: indexing, cataloguing, using storage and retrieval systems and directories. The growing use of microtechnology does not remove the need for these abilities.
- Participation in situations involving oral skills, e.g. listening in order to carry out tasks successfully, interviews, developing an argument in committee, committee work in general, discussing and solving problems cooperatively.
- It is important to recognize that all oral communication takes place in a social context, and that pupils need at least as much help in learning to understand the social situation so that they recognize what behaviour is desirable, as in acquiring the oral skills as such.'

The importance of actual experience in the work place is that it allows students to observe the context within which all this takes place and begin to construct such a list of their own. The classroom can then become a refuge rather than a prison, a place more evidently devoted to the provision of opportunities to acquire vital expertise.

This kind of involvement with the local community does not have to be one sided. There have been a lot of recent initiatives in which schools and colleges, using their own facilities and resources, have provided a service to the local community. If, for example, the Technology department is involved in constructing aids for the handicapped, it also makes sense for the preliminary research — contacting local agencies, talking to the people for whom the aids are intended, and so on — to be undertaken by the students. Equally, the follow-up work — the writing of sets of instructions, reporting on the venture, mounting an exhibition, publicizing the service — can provide a number of real rather than simulated problems to solve. Other examples of this sort of cooperation between school and community taking place include a school which was invited by a local firm to design and write their sales brochure, and another school which was invited by the local council to produce a book of local walks.

Sooner or later, when working in this way, the teacher has to face the problem that real audiences demand professional standards and that, with the best will in the world, students will often fall short of this. Do you correct spelling, punctuation and grammar, for example, before 'going public' or not? Can you afford to allow letters to be sent out from the institution that do not conform to the proper conventions? Just posing the question is a way of showing how much easier it is to demonstrate the importance of such things when success or failure depends upon them. The difficulty is this: if students are excessively protected from the consequences of what they write, they will quickly sense that there is little need to develop their own expertise. Leaving them to work out their own salvation, however, may be a recipe for frustration and disappointment. The way in which the teacher intervenes is clearly important, and the dilemma is often solved by using other members of the group to monitor work before it is seen by outsiders.

I do not want to give the impression that it is only 17 year olds who will learn best through direct experience. Nonetheless, the increased maturity and breadth of experience of older students, whatever their ability, makes it easier for this kind of work to meet with success.

# Endpiece

The great problem, for the teacher of 17 year olds, is that almost by definition the students are likely to start with the sense that they are repeating some of the work done in the fifth year. More than cosmetic changes are needed if this feeling is to be dispelled. In reviewing some of the options, I have been very selective about the three areas that I have chosen for special attention. Even considered jointly, they do not add up to a syllabus and should not be judged as such. Nonetheless, they are intended to suggest ways in which a different, and more adult, slant can be given to work in English with students who have decided that they will be staying on for an extra year after sixteen.

# Recommended reading

*Education 16–19: The Role of English and Communication*, John Dixon, Macmillan, 1979

*English, Communications Skills and the Needs of People in Industry*, CRAC (Careers Research and Advisory Centre) Hobsons Press, 1982

*Engineering Your Own Communications*, Engineering Industry Training Board

*New Directions in General and Communications Studies*, Schools Council English 16–19 Project, 1976

*The Certificate of Pre-Vocational Education*, document from CPVE Joint Board Unit, January 1985

*Sixth Sense: Alternatives in Education at 16–19*, Anthony Adams and Ted Hopkin, Blackie, 1981

'The State of 16–19' by Jane Leggett & Mike Raleigh in *The English Magazine*, Summer 1984 ILEA English Centre

*The Sixth Form College in Practice*, Peter Watkins, Edward Arnold, 1982

### For the classroom

1 'The Tenement Game' — a simulation in which participants have to solve a variety of housing problems. Produced (cheaply) by Shelter.

2 'Greenham District Council' — a simulation of a council meeting of an imaginary town in which budget priorities have to be decided. Available from Community Service Volunteers, 237 Pentonville Road, N1 9NJ

3 'Understanding Trade Unions': Published by TUC. Excellent resource book of ideas for discussion and role play.

4 'People in Touch' by Pearce, Cooper, Leggot and Sprenger (pub. Arnold). Subtitled 'Assignments in Communications and Human Relations', it offers some useful Business Case Studies.

5 'Case Study Comprehension' by Patrick Scott (Nelson). A collection of case studies designed along the lines indicated in this chapter.

6 'Recall' from Help the Aged Education Dept, 218 Upper St, London N1 A tape/slide sequence and handbook of 'Reminiscence Aids'.

7 'The Old in the Community', also from Help the Aged, which includes good role play material and supporting information.

8 'Understanding British Industry' published by the CBI. This book has a lot of useful information about how industry works, and some imaginative follow-up material for use in schools and colleges.

# 16 Resources

Roy Blatchford

## Publishers

It is useful to have in the department up-to-date catalogues from publishers. Indeed, it is best if this is part of someone's responsibilities. Most publishers will willingly include Heads of Department on their mailing lists, and most offer an efficient inspection copy service.

Bell & Hyman, Denmark House, 37/39 Queen Elizabeth Street, London SE1 2QB

Benn, 25 New St. Square, London EC4A 3JA

Blackie & Son Ltd, Bishopbriggs, Glasgow, G64 2NZ

Blackwell (Basil), 108 Cowley Road, Oxford OX4 1JF

Bodley Head Ltd, 9 Bow Street, London WC2

Cambridge University Press, The Pitt Building, Trumpington Street, Cambridge CB2

Cape (Jonathan) Ltd, 30 Bedford Square, London WC1

Cassell & Co Ltd, 35 Red Lion Square, London WC1

Chatto and Windus Ltd, 40–42 William IV Street, London WC2

Collins & Co Ltd, 14 St James's Place, London SW1

Dent & Sons Ltd, 26 Albermarle Street, London W1

Deutsch, Andre, Ltd, 105 Great Russell Street, London WC1

Educational Productions Ltd, East Ardsley, Wakefield, Yorkshire

Edward Arnold Ltd, 41 Bedford Square, London WC1

Faber & Faber Ltd, 3 Queen Square, London WC1

Gollancz (Victor), 14 Henrietta Street, London WC2

Hamish Hamilton, Garden House, 57–59 Long Acre, London WC2E 9JZ

Harrap & Co Ltd, 182–4 High Holborn, London WC1

Hart-Davis, Frogmore, St Albans, Herts

Heinemann Educational, 22 Bedford Square, London WC1

Her Majesty's Stationery Office (HMSO), 49 High Holborn, London
   WC1V 6HB
Holmes McDougall, Allander House, Leith Walk, Edinburgh EH6 8NS
Hutchinson Education, 62–65 Chandos Place, London WC2N 4NW
Longman Group, Longman House, Burnt Mill, Harlow, Essex
Macmillan Publishers, Houndmills, Basingstoke, Hants
Methuen & Co Ltd, 11 New Fetter Lane, London EC4
Murray (John) Ltd, 50 Albermarle Street, London W1
Nelson (Thomas) Ltd, Nelson House, Mayfield Road, Walton-on-
   Thames, Surrey KT12 5PL
NFER, Darville House, Oxford Road East, Windsor, Berks
Open University Press, Walton Hall, Milton Keynes
Oxford University Press, Walton Street, Oxford OX2 6DP
Penguin Books, Harmondsworth, Middlesex
Pergamon Press, Headington Hill Hall, Oxford OX3 0BW
Routledge & Kegan Paul, 14 Leicester Square, London WC2H 7PH
Schofield & Sims, 35 St John's Road, Huddersfield HD1 5DT
Transworld Publishers, Century House, Uxbridge Rd, Ealing
University of London Press, St Paul's House, Warwick Lane, London
   EC4
Virago Press, 41 William IV Street, London WC2
Ward Lock Educational, 116 Baker Street, London W1
Wheaton, Hennock Road, Exeter EX2
Women's Press, 124 Shoreditch High Street, London E1

# Paperbacks for children

As Gervase Phinn indicates in his chapter 'Fiction in the Classroom' it
is clearly vital that every English department keeps abreast of the latest
children's fiction. Put yourself on the mailing lists of the following to
keep in touch.

| | |
|---|---|
| **Armada/Lions** | Collins, 14 St James' Place, London SW1 |
| **Beaver** | Hutchinson, 62–65 Chandos Place, London WC2N 4NW |
| **Carousel** | Transworld Publishers, Century House, 61–63 Uxbridge Road, Ealing, London W5 |
| **Dragon** | Granada Publishing, 29 Frogmore, St Albans, Herts |
| **Fanfares** | Faber & Faber, 3 Queens Square, London WC1 |
| **Getaway** | Thomas Nelson, Nelson House, Mayfield Road, Walton-on-Thames, Surrey KT12 5PL |
| **Hippo** | Scholastic Publications, 10 Earlham Street, London WC2 |

| Knight | Hodder & Stoughton, 47 Bedford Square, London WC1 |
| OUP | Oxford University Press, Walton Street, Oxford OX2 6DP |
| Piccolo | Pan Books, Cavaye Place, London SW10 |
| Puffin | Penguin, Harmondsworth, Middlesex |
| Sparrow | Arrow Publications, 62–65 Chandos Place, London WC2N 4NW |
| Target | Wyndham Publishers, 44 Hill Street, London W1 |
| Topliners | Macmillan, Houndmills, Basingstoke, Hants |

# Journals

The following journals feature articles about English and English teaching and/or provide useful reviews of children's literature.

**British Book News** The British Council, 65 Davies Street, London W1

**Children's Book Bulletin** Children's Rights Workshop, 4 Aldebert Terrace, London SW8

**English Magazine (The)** ILEA English Centre, Sutherland Street, London SW1

**English in Education** (journal of NATE) 49 Broomgrove Road, Sheffield S10

**English Today** Cambridge University Press, The Edinburgh Building, Shaftesbury Road, Cambridge CB2 2RU

**Multiracial Education** NAME, 86 Station Road, Mickleover, Derby

**Reading** (journal of United Kingdom Reading Association) Basil Blackwell Ltd, General Subscriptions Department, 108 Cowley Road, Oxford, OX4 1JF

**Remedial Education** (journal of National Association for Remedial Education) Longman Group Ltd, Journals Division, Burnt Mill, Harlow, Essex

**School Librarian** (journal of the School Library Association), Victoria House, George Street, Oxford

**Signal** The Thimble Press, Lockwood, Station Road, South Woodchester, Stroud, Gloucestershire GL5 5EQ

**Teaching English** (journal published by the Scottish Curriculum Development Service) Moray House College of Education, Holyrood Road, Edinburgh

**The Times Educational Supplement** Priory House, St John's Lane, London EC1M 4BX

**Use of English (The)** Scottish Academic Press Ltd, 33 Montgomery
Street, Edinburgh EH7 5JX

# Other useful addresses

**All Faiths For One Race** (AFFOR)
1 Finch Road, Lozells, Birmingham B19 1HS
Has produced some excellent classroom materials for teaching about
race and race relations.

**Black Ink**
258, Coldharbour Lane, London SW9
Wide range of poetry anthologies and other writings by black people.
Recommended source of good classroom reading material.

**Booksellers Association**
154 Buckingham Palace Road, London SW1
Offers advice on aspects of bookselling and if you happen to be in
search of a good local bookseller.

**Centre for Contemporary Cultural Studies**
Faculty of Arts, University of Birmingham, Birmingham B15 2TT
Has published interesting papers in the area of culture, media and
language study.

**Commission for Racial Equality**
Elliott House, 10/12 Allington Street, London SW1
A wide range of useful publications available, many of them free. Also
produces several journals.

**Equal Opportunities Commission**
Overseas House, Quay Street, Manchester M3 3HN
Publishes a wealth of information suitable for English teachers looking
at issues of gender, equal opportunities and anti-sexism.

**Inner London Education Authority's English Centre**
Sutherland Street, London SW1
The source of some of the best material produced by teachers for the
English classroom during the past ten years. All publications are
available from the centre upon request. Non-ILEA schools are charged
a slightly higher price for publications, but still very good value.

**Institute of Race Relations (IRR)**
247 Pentonville Road, London N1
Offers a large library of books and journals on race and ethnic
relations

**International Board on Books for Young People (IBBY)**
c/o National Book League, Book House, 45 East Hill London SW18
Involved in promoting international understanding through children's books. A valuable resource if you would like to 'twin' your pupils or department with children or a library in the Third World.

**National Foundation for Educational Research (NFER)**
The Mere, Upton Park, Slough, Berks
The source of many (expensively priced) research papers on aspects of language teaching and pupil learning across the curriculum.

**National Association for Multiracial Education (NAME)**
86 Station Road, Mickleover, Derby DE3 22FP
Concerns itself with issues relating to language and anti-racist teaching. Publishes the journal *Multiracial Education*.

**National Book League and Centre for Children's Books**
Book House, 45 East Hill, London SW18
In a sense, this is the 'home' of children's books. Able to offer information on most queries relating to the world of children's books and children's writers. Probably the best contact point if you are running a Book Week or wanting to contact writers to vist your school. (See also your local *Arts Association*).

**National Youth Bureau**
17–23 Albion Street, Leicester LE1 6GD
List of publications available; useful resource material for the English classroom.

**The Poetry Society**
21 Earls Court Square, London SW5
Another useful contact point for tracking down poets whose work you might be reading in school and would like to invite to visit pupils.

**School Bookshop Association**
1 Effingham Road, London SE12 8NZ
Offers useful advice on the establishing of a school bookshop.

**School Library Association**
Victoria House, 29–31 George Street, Oxford OX1 2AY
If your school librarian is not a member, he or she should be! If someone within the English Department has responsibility for the library, then this organization should be consulted. Publishes the journal *School Librarian*.

**Sisterwrite Bookshop**
190 Upper Street, London N1

An excellent source for teachers wanting to order books focusing on issues of gender and anti-sexism. Good selection of women writers in print.

**Writers and Readers Bookshop**
241 Camden High Street, London NW1
'Writers and Readers' have published some interesting educational texts for teachers including: *Finding a Language* by Peter Medway, *Positive Image: Towards a multiracial curriculum* by Robert Jeffcoate, *Working with Words* by Jane Mace.

# Worker writers and community publishers

A source of much excellent material for classroom study is to be found amongst the writings and publications of the Community Publishers. The following are recommended:

**Basement Writers**, 59 Watney Street, London E1
**Black Ink**, 258 Coldharbour Lane, London SW9
**Bristol Broadsides**, 110 Cheltenham Road, Bristol BS6 5RW
**Centerprise Project**, 136 Kingsland High Street, London E8
**Commonword Workshop**, 12a Piccadilly, Manchester 1
**Erdesdun Publications**, 10 Greenhaugh Road, Whitley Bay, Tyne and Wear
**Liverpool 8 Writers' Workshop**, 52 Beaconsfield Street, Liverpool 8
**Queenspark Books**, 14 Toronto Terrace, Brighton
**Scotland Road Writers' Workshop**, 1 Wyndcote Road, Mossley Hill, Liverpool 18
**Stepney Books** 196 Cable Street, Stepney, London E1

For information on all the above, you can also contact: Federation of Worker Writers and Community Publishers, 10 Brief Street, London SE5

# Audio-visual resources

**Tape material and 'spoken word'** recordings are available from:

Argo Records, 115 Fulham Road, London SW3
Audio-Visual Productions, 15 Temple Sheen Road, London SW14
Caedmon Records, 1 Westmead, Farnborough, Hampshire
Educational Productions, Bradford Road, East Ardsley, Yorkshire

Exeter Tapes, University of Exeter, Northcote House, Queen's Drive, Exeter

EAV Ltd, Butterley Street, Leeds LS10 1AX

**Films and video-cassettes** are available from:

British Film Institute, 81 Dean Street, London W1

BBC TV Enterprises, Woodston House, Oundle Road, Peterborough

Columbia-Warner, Film House, 142 Wardour Street, London W1

Concord Films, 201 Felixstowe Road, Ipswich, Suffolk

Connoisseur Films, 167 Oxford Street, London W1

Central Film Library, Government Building, Bromyard Avenue, Acton, London W2

Contemporary Films Ltd, 55 Greek Street, London W1V 6DB

Educational and Television Films Ltd, 2 Doughty Street, London WC1

Golden Films, Stewart House, 23 Francis Road, Windsor, Berks

National Audio-Visual Aids Library, Paxton Place, Gipsy Road, London SE27

National Film Board of Canada, 1 Grosvenor Square, London W1

Rank Film Library, PO Box 20, Great West Road, Brentford, Middlesex

Scottish Central Film Library, 16–17 Woodside Terrace, Charing Cross, Glasgow

See also:

BBC, Television Centre, Wood Lane, London W12

Independent Television Companies Association, 56 Mortimer Street, London W1

**Other sources** of visual display material:

Athena International, PO Box 13, Raynham Road Estate, Bishops Stortford, Herts

Pictorial Charts Educational Trust, 27 Kirchen Road, London W13

Radio Times Hulton Picture Library, 35 Marylebone High Street, London W1

Slide Loan Service, National Art Slide Library, Victoria and Albert Museum, Cromwell Road, London SW7

Visual Publications, The Green, Northleach, Cheltenham, Glos. GL54 1BR

# Examination boards

## GCSE examining groups

### Northern Examining Association

Joint Matriculation Board, Manchester M15 6EU

Associated Lancashire Schools Examining Board, 12 Harter Street, Manchester M1 6HL

North Regional Examinations Board, Wheatfield Road, Westerhope, Newcastle upon Tyne NE5 5JZ

North West Regional Examination Board, Orbit House, Albert Street, Eccles, Manchester M30 0WL

Yorkshire & Humberside Regional Examinations Board, Scarsdale House, 136 Derbyshire Lane, Sheffield S8 8SE or 31/33 Springfield Avenue, Harrogate, North Yorkshire HG1 2HW

### Midland Examining Group

Cambridge University Local Examinations Syndicate, 1 Hills Road, Cambridge CB1 2EU

Oxford and Cambridge Schools Examination Board, Elsfield Way, Oxford OX2 8EP or Brook House, 10 Trumpington Street, Cambridge CB2 1QB

Southern Universities' Joint Board, Cotham Road, Bristol BS6 6DD

East Midland Regional Examinations Board, Robins Wood House, Robins Wood Road, Aspley, Nottingham NG8 3NR

West Midlands Examination Board, Norfolk House, Smallbrook Queensway, Birmingham B5 4NJ

### London and East Anglia

University of London, University of London School Examinations Board, Stewart House, 32 Russell Square, London WC1B 5DP

East Anglian Examinations Board, The Lindens, Lexden Road, Colchester, Essex CO3 3RL

London Regional Examining Board, Lyon House, 104 Wandsworth High Street, London SW18 4LF

### Southern Examining Group

University of Oxford Delegacy of Local Examinations, Ewert Place, Summertown, Oxford OX2 7BZ

The Associated Examining Board, Wellington House, Station Road, Aldershot, Hants GU11 1BQ

Southern Regional Examinations Board, Avondale House, 33 Carlton Crescent, Southampton SO9 4YL

South-East Regional Examinations Board, Beloe House, 2–4 Mount Ephraim Road, Royal Tunbridge Wells, Kent TN1 1EU
South-Western Examinations Board, 23–29 Marsh Street, Bristol BS1 4BP

**Welsh Joint Education Committee**
245 Western Avenue, Cardiff CF5 2YX

**Northern Ireland Schools Examinations Council**
Beechill House, 42 Beechill Road, Belfast BT8 4RS

**Other examining bodies**
City and Guilds of London Institute and
Business & Technician Education Council — Joint Board for Pre-Vocational Education, 46 Britannia Street, London WC1X 9RG
Royal Society of Arts Examination Board, 18 Adam Street, Adelphi, London WC2N 6AJ
Oxford Certificate of Educational Achievement (OCEA), Oxford Delegacy, Oxford OX2 7BZ

**Further addresses**
The following bodies have curriculum overview and offer a range of publications likely to be of interest to teachers of English.
Department of Education and Science/HM Inspectorate, Elizabeth House, York Road, London SE1 7PH
Schools Curriculum Development Committee and
Secondary Examinations Council, Newcombe House, 45 Notting Hill Gate, London W11 3JB

# Recommended fiction

The following booklists have been divided by age range in an attempt to offer guidance to departments looking for material to suit particular classes. At the same time, the lists are in no way prescriptive; clearly what may suit one group of eleven year olds in one class may well be more appropriate for a group of thirteen year olds elsewhere, and so on through the secondary age range. One further point: it is encouraging to read in the document outlining the National Criteria for examining English at 16+ the following statement:

'The opportunity may be taken by Examining Groups to extend the scope of what is traditionally regarded as the canon of English

Literature, since this itself has a cultural background which may be initially unfamiliar to many candidates.'

These lists are intended for the teaching of English in and for a multicultural society.

# Novels

**Years 11-12**

| | |
|---|---|
| Terry on the Fence | Bernard Ashley, Penguin |
| The Witch's Daughter | Nina Bawden, Puffin |
| The Secret Garden | Frances Burnett, Penguin |
| The Midnight Fox | Betsy Byars, Penguin |
| Charlie and the Chocolate Factory | Roald Dahl, Penguin |
| Danny Champion of the World | Roald Dahl, Penguin |
| A Question of Courage | Marjorie Darke, Fontana Lions |
| Bud's Luck | Peter Davidson, ILEA English Centre |
| The Tale of Troy | R Green, Penguin |
| Tales of the Greek Heroes | R Green, Penguin |
| Listen to this Story | Grace Hallworth, Magnet |
| The Shrinking of Treehorn | Florence Parry Heide, Penguin |
| Summer's End | Archie Hill, Wheaton |
| The Iron Man | Ted Hughes, Faber |
| The Ear & A Game of Life and Death | Anita Jackson, Spirals |
| Emil and the Detectives | Erich Kastner, Penguin |
| The Turbulent Term of Tyke Tyler | Gene Kemp, Penguin |
| Stig of the Dump | Clive King, Penguin |
| Grange Hill Rules O.K. (and others) | Robert Leeson, Armada |
| Third Class Genie | Robert Leeson, Armada |
| Basketball Game | Julius Lester, Penguin |
| Run for your Life | David Line, Penguin |
| The Lion, the Witch and the Wardrobe (and others) | C S Lewis, Penguin |
| Thunder and Lightnings | Jan Mark, Penguin |
| Journey To Jo'burg | Beverley Naidoo, Longman Knockout |
| Albeson and the Germans | Jan Needle, Fontana Lions |
| The Size Spies | Jan Needle, Fontana Lions |

| | |
|---|---|
| Mrs Frisby and the Rats of Nimh | Robert O'Brien, Penguin |
| Tom's Midnight Garden | Philippa Pearce, Penguin |
| Cindy and the Silver Enchantress | Margaret Rogers, Penguin |
| The Silver Sword | Ian Serraillier, Penguin |
| Gumble's Yard | John Rowe Townsend, Penguin |
| The Secret Diary of Adrian Mole | Sue Townsend, Methuen |

**Years 12–13**

| | |
|---|---|
| The Kingdom Under the Sea | Joan Aiken, Penguin |
| Trouble with Donovan Croft | Bernard Ashley, Penguin |
| Sophia Scrooby Preserved | Martha Bacon, Penguin |
| Grandad with Snails | Michael Baldwin, Hutchinson |
| Carrie's War | Nina Bawden, Penguin |
| One Day, Another Day | Petronella Breinburg, Macmillan Rockets |
| The Eighteenth Emergency | Betsy Byars, Penguin |
| Ramona the Pest | Beverley Cleary, Penguin |
| The Nipper | Catherine Cookson, Penguin |
| First of Midnight | Marjorie Darke, Penguin |
| Conrad's War | Andrew Davies, Hippo |
| The Weathermonger | Peter Dickinson, Penguin |
| Playing it Right | Tony Drake, Penguin |
| Grinny | Nicholas Fisk, Penguin |
| Harriet the Spy | Louise Fitzhugh, Fontana Lions |
| The Diary of Anne Frank | Anne Frank, Pan |
| Smith | Leon Garfield, Penguin |
| Wizard of Earthsea | Ursula le Guin, Penguin |
| The Wool Pack | Cynthia Harnett, Penguin |
| The Dragon in the Garden | Reginald Maddock, Macmillan |
| Under the Autumn Garden | Jan Mark, Penguin |
| My Mate Shofiq | Jan Needle, Fontana Lions |
| Fireweed | Jill Paton Walsh, Penguin |
| Earthquake & Hurricane | Andrew Salkey, OUP |
| A Pair of Jesus Boots | Sylvia Sherry, Penguin |
| Roll of Thunder, Hear My Cry | Mildred Taylor, Penguin |
| Let the Circle be Unbroken | Mildred Taylor, Penguin |
| The Hobbit | J R R Tolkien, Allen & Unwin |
| Cue for Treason | Geoffrey Trease, Penguin |
| Viking's Dawn | Henry Treece, Penguin |
| The Machine-Gunners | Robert Westall, Penguin |

**Years 13–14**

| | |
|---|---|
| Joby | Stan Barstow, Heinemann |
| Us Boys of Westcroft | Petronella Breinburg, Macmillan |
| Under Goliath | Peter Carter, Puffin |
| The Dark is Rising | Susan Cooper, Puffin |
| The Chocolate War | Robert Cormier, Macmillan |
| The Peacock Garden & The Village By The Sea | Anita Desai, Puffin |
| Sky Girl | Dianne Doubtfire, Macmillan |
| Half a Chance | Tony Drake, Collins |
| A Strong and Willing Girl | Dorothy Edwards, Magnet |
| On the Flip Side | Nicholas Fisk, Kestrel |
| Nobody's Family Is Going to Change | Louise Fitzhugh, Fontana Lion |
| The Slave Dancer | Paula Fox, Macmillan |
| The Snow Goose | Paul Gallico, Penguin |
| Elidor | Alan Garner, Fontana Lions |
| The Owl Service | Alan Garner, Fontana Lions |
| My Side of the Mountain | Jean George |
| There Ain't No Angels No More | Godfrey Goodwin, Fontana |
| The Bonny Pit Laddie | Frederick Grice, Puffin |
| The Friends | Rosa Guy, Puffin |
| Galactic Warlord | Douglas Hill, Piccolo |
| Mischling, Second Degree | Ilse Koehn, Puffin |
| Cider With Rosie | Laurie Lee, Penguin |
| Across the Barricades | Joan Lingard, Puffin |
| The Enmead | Jan Mark, Puffin |
| Walkabout | James Vance Marshall, Puffin |
| Parveen | Anne Mehdevi, Puffin |
| Jamaica Child | Errol O'Connor, ILEA English Centre |
| Ngunga's Adventures | Pepetela, Young World Books |
| Friedrich | Hans Peter Richter, Heinemann |
| That Crazy April | Lila Perl, Fontana |
| Flambards | K M Peyton, Puffin |
| The Exeter Blitz | David Rees, Dragon |
| The Upstairs Room | Johanna Reiss, Puffin |
| Old Mali and the Boy | D Sherman, Penguin |
| Back Home | Ranjit Sumal, Commonplace Workshop |
| The Cay | Theodore Taylor, Puffin |
| Black Boy | Richard Wright, Longman |
| The Pigman | Paul Zindel, Fontana |

**Years 14–16**

| | |
|---|---|
| Things Fall Apart | Chinua Achebe, Heinemann |
| I Know Why the Caged Bird Sings | Maya Angelou, Virago |
| Rather Panchali | Bibuti Banerji, Allied Publishers |
| Tough Annie | Annie Barnes, Stepney Books |
| A Kind of Loving | Stan Barstow, Corgi |
| 19 is Too Young To Die | Gunnel Beckman, Macmillan |
| Fahrenheit 451 | Ray Bradbury, Hart-Davis |
| The Guardians | John Christopher |
| Second Class Citizen | Buchi Emecheta, Fontana |
| A Walk in the Night | Alex La Guma |
| A Measure of Time | Rosa Guy, Virago |
| Roots | Alex Haley, Picador |
| The Go-Between | L P Hartley, Penguin |
| I'm The King of the Castle | Susan Hill, Longman Imprint |
| A Kestrel for a Knave | Barry Hines, Penguin |
| Our Lives | ILEA English Centre |
| Your Friend, Rebecca | Linda Hoy, Bodley Head |
| Violence | Festus Iyayi, Longman Drumbeat |
| A Hoxton Childhood | A S Jasper, Centerprise |
| In the Castle of My Skin | George Lamming, Longman Drumbeat |
| The African Child | Camara Laye, Fontana |
| To Kill A Mockingbird | Harper Lee, Heinemann |
| It's My Life | Robert Leeson, Fontana Lions |
| A Comprehensive Education | Roger Mills, Centerprise |
| S.W.A.L.K. | Paula Milne, Thames Methuen |
| Cry, the Beloved Country | Alan Paton, Penguin |
| In The Tent | David Rees, Heinemann |
| Waves | Davis Rees, Longman Knockout |
| The L-Shaped Room | Lynne Reid Banks, Longman Imprint |
| The Catcher in the Rye | J D Salinger, Penguin |
| A Brighter Sun | Samuel Selvon, Longman Drumbeat |
| Sumitra's Story | Rukshana Smith, Bodley Head |
| The Harder They Come | Michael Thelwell, Pluto |
| Muriel at Metropolitan | Miriam Tlali, Longman Drumbeat |
| Slaughterhouse Five | Kurt Vonnegut, Panther |
| The Colour Purple | Alice Walker |

| There is a Happy Land | Keith Waterhouse, Longman Imprint |
| An Autobiography of Malcolm X | Malcolm X, Penguin |
| My Darling, My Hamburger | Paul Zindel, Bodley Head |

## Poetry

**11–13 years**

| Junior Voices | Edited Geoffrey Summerfield, Penguin |
| Moon-bells | Ted Hughes, Chatto & Windus |
| Poems & Poems 2 | Edited Michael Harrison & Christopher Stuart-Clark, OUP |
| Poetry World I & II | Edited Geoffrey Summerfield, Bell & Hyman |
| Strictly Private | Edited Roger McGough, Penguin |
| Swings and Roundabouts | Mick Gowar, Collins |
| Thoughtshapes | Edited Barry Maybury, OUP |
| Thoughtweavers | Edited Barry Maybury, OUP |
| Wordspinners | Edited Barry Maybury, OUP |
| Touchstones, Books 1–3 | Edited M & P Benton, Hodder & Stoughton |
| Voices | Edited Geoffrey Summerfield, Penguin |
| Watchwords One & Two | Edited M & P Benton, Hodder & Stoughton |
| Ways of Talking | Edited David Jackson, Ward Lock |
| Wordscapes | Edited Barry Maybury, OUP |
| You Tell Me | Roger McGough and Michael Rosen, Penguin |

**14–16 years**

| Here and Human | Selected by F E S Finn, John Murray |
| I See A Voice | Michael Rosen, Hutchinson |
| Into Poetry | Edited Richard Andrew, Ward Lock |
| New Ships — An anthology of West Indian poems | Edited D G Wilson, OUP |

| Poetry For Today | Edited George Macbeth, Longman Study Texts |
| Poetry Workshop | Edited M & P Benton, Hodder & Stoughton |
| Remains of Elmet | Ted Hughes, Faber |
| Tunes on a Tin Whistle | Edited A Crang, Wheaton/ Pergamon |
| Touchstones, Books 4–5 | Edited M & P Benton, Hodder & Stoughton |
| Voices of Today | Selected by F E S Finn, John Murray |

## Scripted drama

| Act I, II, III | Edited David Self & Ray Speakman, Hutchinson |
| Act Now Series | Edited Andrew Bethell, OUP |
| Dramascripts | Macmillan Education |
| Harrap's Theatre Workshop Series | Edited by Robert Leach, Harrap |
| Longman Imprint Series | Various volumes of playscripts |
| The Playmakers I & II | Edited Roger Mansfield, Schofield & Sims |
| Prompt I, II, III | Edited Alan Durband, Hutchinson |
| Star Plays Series | Edited Roy Blatchford, Longman |
| Studio Scripts Series | Edited David Self, Hutchinson |
| Wordplays I, II | Edited Alan Durband, Hutchinson |
| Young Drama Series | Methuen |

## Short stories

### Series
| Bell & Hyman Series | Edited Roy Blatchford, Bell & Hyman |
| Choices Series | Edited Bryan Newton, Collins |
| Heinemann Short Stories 1–5 | Edited Rhodri Jones, Heinemann |
| John Murray Series | Edited James Gibson, John Murray |

| | |
|---|---|
| The Quickening Pulse, 1–5 | Edited D J Brindley, Hodder & Stoughton |
| The Storyteller, I & II | Edited Graham Barrett and Michael Morpurgo, Ward Lock |
| Ward Lock Series | |

## 11–13 years

| | |
|---|---|
| I'm Trying To Tell You | Bernard Ashley, Puffin |
| Save the Last Dance for Me | Jan Carew, Longman Knockout |
| Stranger Than Tomorrow | Jan Carew, Longman Knockout |
| Ghosts That Haunt You | Edited Aiden Chambers, Penguin |
| The Fight of Neither Century | Robin Chambers, Dragon |
| Short Stories from Wales | Edited David Elias, Wheaton |
| Indian Tales and Legends | Retold by J E B Gray, OUP |
| Skulker Wheat | John Griffin, Heinemann |
| How The Whale Became | Ted Hughes, Puffin |
| Bonnie, Freda and Ann | Various authors, ILEA English Centre |
| Spooky Stories | Edited Barbara Ireson, Carousel |
| Dog Days and Cat Naps | Gene Kemp, Puffin |
| The Fib and other stories | George Layton, Longman Knockout |
| Harold and Bella, Jammy and Me | Robert Leeson, Fontana Lions |
| Long Journey Home | Julius Lester, Longman Knockout |
| Nothing To Be Afraid Of | Jan Mark, Puffin |
| Hairs in the Palm of The Hand | Jan Mark, Puffin |
| First Choice | Edited M Marland, Longman |
| The Robe of Blood | Kenneth McLeish, Longman Knockout |
| The Goalkeeper's Revenge and Other Stories | Bill Naughton, New Windmill |
| Robbie | Emil Pacholek, Andre Deutsch |
| The Shadow-Cage | Philippa Pearce, Puffin |
| What the Neighbours Did | Philippa Pearce, Puffin |
| Over Our Way | Edited Jean D'Costa and Velma Pollard |
| Nasty! | Michael Rosen, Longman Knockout |
| Unearthly Beasts | Jay Williams, Macmillan Topliner |
| The Practical Princess and Other Liberating Fairy Tales | Jay Williams, Hippo |

**14–16 years**

| | |
|---|---|
| Short Stories from India, Pakistan and Bangladesh | Ranjana Ash, Harrap |
| The Early Asimov 1, 2, 3 | Isaac Asimov, Panther |
| The Poison Ladies and other stories | H E Bates, Wheaton |
| A Roald Dahl Selection | Edited Roy Blatchford, Longman Imprint |
| It's Now or Never | Edited Roy Blatchford & Jane Leggett, Bell & Hyman |
| This Way for the Gas, Ladies and Gentlemen | Tadeusz Borowski, Penguin |
| The Illustrated Man | Ray Bradbury, Granada |
| Gorilla, My Love | Toni Cade Bambara, Women's Press |
| Short Stories from Ireland | Edited Kenyon Calthrop, Wheaton |
| Come to Mecca and other stories | Farrukh Dhondy, Collins |
| Poona Company | Farrukh Dhondy, Gollancz |
| The Story Inside | Edited Stuart Evans, Hutchinson |
| In Short | Edited F E S Finn, John Murray |
| Selected Stories | Nadine Gordimer, Penguin |
| Modern Short Stories 2: 1940–1980 | Edited Giles Gordon, Dent |
| The Open Road and other stories | Jennifer Gubb, Onlywomen Press |
| A Bit of Singing and Dancing | Susan Hill, Penguin |
| Love You, Hate You, Just Don't Know | Edited Josie Karavasil, Evans |
| The Woman Warrior | Maxine Hong Kingston, Pan Books |
| Short Stories for Today | Edited M Marland, Longman Study Texts |
| Meetings and Partings | Edited M Marland, Longman Imprint |
| Stories of the Waterfront | John Morrison, Penguin |
| My Oedipus Complex | Frank O'Connor, Penguin |
| The Penguin Dorothy Parker | Dorothy Parker, Penguin |
| Debbie Go Home | Alan Paton, Penguin |
| Best West Indian Stories | Edited Kenneth Ramchand, Nelson |

| | |
|---|---|
| The Lonely Londoners | Samuel Selvon, Longman Drumbeat |
| English Short Stories of Today | Edited Roger Sharrock, OUP |
| More Modern Short Stories | Edited Peter Taylor, OUP |
| You Can't Keep A Good Woman Down | Alice Walker, Women's Press |
| Jealousy and Other Stories | Edited David Wasp, Nelson Getaway |

# English course textbooks

The contributors to this volume would not have a unanimous view on the place of course books in the teaching of English. Publishers' sales figures clearly indicate however that they remain the staple diet of many pupils' experience in an English classroom. The following are listed for reference, and not for preference. They are among the major series currently available, they were published during the past twenty years, and they reflect teaching and learning trends over that period.

| | |
|---|---|
| Excellence In English | D J Brindley, Hodder & Stoughton |
| Language And Communication | I Forsyth & K Wood, Longman |
| Steps | Groves, Griffin & Grimshaw, Longman |
| Your Language | M Healy, Macmillan |
| Aspects of English | D S Higgins, Cassell |
| Network | H Hurst and J Simes, Hodder & Stoughton |
| New English First — Fifth | Rhodri Jones, Heinemann |
| English in Practice | F Mann and A Smith, University Tutorial Press |
| Englishcraft | F Mann and A Smith, University Tutorial Press |
| The Art of English | Roger Mansfield, Scofield & Sims |
| Making Language | M Newby, OUP |
| English Workshop | C Owen & A Carter, Hodder & Stoughton |
| Venturer: Exploring English | Marie Peel, Holmes McDougall |
| Openings in English | R Ridout & J R C Yglesias, Hutchinson |
| English Through Experience | Albert Rowe, Hart-Davis |

| | |
|---|---|
| Oxford Secondary English | J Seely, OUP |
| An English Course | David Self, Ward Lock |
| Framework English | D Shiach, Nelson |
| Pictorial and Practical English | John Trevaskis and Patrick Pringle, Evans |
| Mainstream English | J Yglesias & L Snellgrove, Longman |
| Study English | J Yglesias & H Hagger, Longman |

# Index

* indicates inclusion of classroom ideas on the text or author